CLASSIC FEYNMAN

CLASSIC

FEYNMAN

ALL THE ADVENTURES OF

A CURIOUS CHARACTER

RICHARD P. FEYNMAN

With a commemorative CD

Edited by

RALPH LEIGHTON

W · W · Norton & Company

New York London

Book design by Margaret M. Wagner
Production manager: Julia Druskin

ISBN-13: 978-0-7394-8440-1

W. W. Norton & Company, Inc., 500 Fifth Avenue, New York, N.Y. 10110

W. W. Norton & Company Ltd.,
Castle House, 75/76 Wells Street, London W1T 3QT

CONTENTS

Please note: the "adventures of a curious character" from *"Surely You're Joking, Mr. Feynman!"* are not indicated by a symbol, those from *"What Do You Care What Other People Think?"* are marked with ^w, and new selections are indicated by •.

Contents

CONTENTS

Acknowledgments and Credits

The following material appears in this book by permission that is gratefully appreciated:

The foreword, by Freeman Dyson.

"The Making of a Scientist," taken from *The Pleasure of Finding Things Out*, a documentary produced in 1981 by Christopher Sykes for the BBC TV *Horizon* science series and for PBS's *NOVA*. Information on how to order video copies of the documentary (if still available) may be obtained by searching the Internet using the terms "Sykes" and "Pleasure of Finding Things Out."

"Los Alamos from Below," adapted from one of nine talks given in the First Annual Lecture Series on Science and Society at the University of California at Santa Barbara in 1975. The series was published as *Reminiscences of Los Alamos, 1943–1945*, edited by L. Badash et al., ©1980 by D. Reidel Publishing Company, Dordrecht, The Netherlands. (The CD inclided with this book was produced from a recording provided by the Department of Special Collections, Davidson Library, UCSB.)

"Appendix F: Personal observations on the reliability of the Shuttle," from the *Report of the Presidential Commission on the Space Shuttle Challenger Accident, Volume II*.

"The Value of Science," a public address given at the 1955 autumn meeting of the National Academy of Sciences.

"Cargo Cult Science," Feynman's commencement address given at Caltech in 1974.

"Finding Feynman," Alan Alda's commencement address given at Caltech in 2002.

Reproductions of Feynman's drawings and notes on pages 302, 305, 315, 316, and 380 were provided by Gweneth Feynman.

The credits for the photographs and diagrams in this book are as follows:
Pages 102, 109, 113 courtesy of Gweneth Feynman
Pages 163, 341, 375 (bottom), 376 (top), courtesy of Caltech
Page 375 (top) ©BBC, Yorkshire Television
Pages 369, 376 (bottom), 377 ©Faustin Bray
Page 378 ©Yasushi Ohunki
Pages 380, 386 (bottom), 387, 397, 398, 399, 403, 404, 405, 409, 418 ©NASA
Pages 410, 411 ©Marilynn K. Yee, NYT Pictures
Page 423 courtesy of Ralph Leighton
Pages 453, 454 ©Pete Souza, The White House

CLASSIC FEYNMAN

PROLOGUES

To the Reader

It's now 2005, the year that Richard Feynman and three other American scientists are being honored with a commemorative stamp by the U.S. Postal Service. It's amusing to note that those quirky diagrams on the Feynman stamp—squiggles no one else understood at first—have become the universal standard notation for particle interactions in physics theory today.

It is also amusing that an outlandish premonition Feynman had nearly twenty years ago is steadily coming true.

The year was 1987, a year after the *Challenger* inquiry had concluded, and less than a year before Richard Feynman's life would end. Indeed, death was not far away: A *Los Angeles Times* science writer recently had called to check the veracity of a rumor that Feyman had not survived his fourth cancer operation. I quoted the line from Mark Twain ("the rumors of my death have been greatly exaggerated") and cajoled the reporter into sending Feynman a copy of his own obituary.

A paperback edition of his bestseller *"Surely You're Joking, Mr. Feynman!"* had just come out in Spanish, and Feynman was savoring his words with a Latin flavor. In the story "Distinto juego de herramientas" ("A Different Box of Tools"), an asterisk appeared after "Waffen-stoffer," the name of a fictitious theorem Feynman made up to poke fun at how mathematicians think. The Spanish translator had added his own footnote, which I write here in English: "Play on words: war is about to break out in Europe. *Waffen* = weapons; *Stoff* = substance, or material."

"Already it's happening!" Feynman exclaimed, with shock and amusement: "They're writing commentaries in the margins of the Talmud!" Upon learning that the Talmud contains stories about heroes, and commentaries on the lessons to be learned from those stories, I thought the allusion was apt.

Feynman knew he was leaving behind a legacy, and he cared about it. For the sequel to *Surely You're Joking*, I listened to him restate the conclusion of his 1955 lecture, "The Value of Science": "It is our responsibility as scientists, knowing the great progress which comes from a satisfactory philosophy of ignorance, the great progress which is the fruit of freedom of thought, to proclaim the value of this freedom; to teach how doubt is not to be feared but welcomed and discussed; and to demand this freedom as our duty to all coming generations."

But Feynman also knew that an entertaining story is often more readily received than a well-reasoned lecture. Thus he had allowed a drummer friend to record and transcribe many of his self-described "adventures of a curious character" and assemble them into the collection titled "*Surely You're Joking, Mr. Feynman!*" The success of that book encouraged him to recount his *Challenger* investigation experience—and to tell, after much difficulty, the poignant story of Arline—for a companion best-seller titled "*What Do You Care What Other People Think?*" Paperback editions of both books are still in print today.

A few years ago I suggested, and W. W. Norton agreed, that Feynman's comic/heroic stories—told "in the tradition of Mark Twain," as one reviewer observed—should be combined into a new hardcover edition that could last for generations. Thus you will find in this omnibus volume *all* of the "adventures" from his twin best-sellers (interleaved for the most part in chronological order), complemented by a recording of Feynman, at the top of his game, recounting his Los Alamos adventures to a spellbound audience. (If you listen to the CD first, you can become familiar with Feynman's voice and speaking style, and then hear him in your head as you read the book.) And as a special treat, Feynman's own words are bookended by insightful commentaries from two illustrious wise men of our age, Freeman Dyson and Alan Alda.

Along with a multitude of postage stamps adorning envelopes, may *Classic Feynman* help ensure that the legends and philosophy of this maverick modern-day hero live on. Happy birthday, Chief!

Ralph Leighton
May 11, 2005

FOREWORD

BY FREEMAN DYSON

This is a wonderful collection of stories, all true, about Dick
Feynman's adventures. As I read them, I hear Dick's voice speaking and
see his hands gesticulating. All friends of Feynman are indebted to Ralph
Leighton for preserving the stories on tape and publishing them in
books. My favorite story is "Surely You're Joking, Mr. Feynman!" in
which Dick, at his first formal tea party in Princeton, is asked by the
hostess whether he will take cream or lemon in his tea. He answers,
"Both." This reply expresses the essential core of Dick's character: He
said yes to everything—to the cream and to the lemon, to comedy and
also to tragedy. This is why he had so many crazy adventures and such a
creative life. Feynman knew as well as anyone the bitterness of chronic
illness and early death, but he also knew, as Shakespeare knew, that in
every tragedy there are moments of comedy, moments when the tragic
hero steps aside and lets his place on the stage be taken by the clown. To
remain sane as Feynman did in the midst of tragedy, it helps to be a bit
of a clown. Even when he was most serious, struggling with the infinite
self-energy of the electron at Cornell, or digging out the causes of the
Challenger shuttle disaster in Florida, or nursing his young wife Arline
through her last weeks in Albuquerque, he was never solemn.

The main thing I would like to write about in this foreword is
Feynman's propensity for hard work. From the stories that Feynman
told and the stories that other people told about him, one has the
impression that he was most of the time playing the fool and having
amusing adventures, only occasionally interrupting his carefree existence with periods of intense concentration on science during which he
made his brilliant discoveries. This impression is not entirely wrong,
but it misses the most important part of his character. The central
theme in his life was long, slow, hard work, slogging away at a difficult
scientific problem with all his strength until it was solved. The adven-

tures and the jokes were real enough, but they were not the main theme. The stories are to some extent misleading, because there was a paradoxical mismatch between the style and the substance of Feynman's contributions to science. The style of his science was brilliant and impressionistic. He used transparent pictorial diagrams instead of opaque differential equations to describe nature, and he used dramatic gestures and sound effects to accompany his lectures instead of blackboards covered with esoteric symbols.

But the substance of his science was conservative. He reached his insights by careful and laborious sifting of old theories and experiments, not by brilliant invention. He was not a revolutionary. He discarded as little as possible of the old theories while extending them to fit new experiments. He built his new theories brick by brick on the foundations of the old. Nothing that he built was done hastily, and all of it has stood the test of time. As he often said, when some new and revolutionary idea was proposed, it is more important to be right than to be brilliant. Whatever he was doing, whether he was reconstructing the basis of physics or interpreting the results of a new experiment, he took endless trouble to get the details right. He said that the job of a scientist is to listen carefully to nature, not to tell nature how to behave.

There were two great creative periods in Feynman's life as a physicist. The first lasted ten years, from 1939 to 1949, at Princeton and Cornell with an interruption at Los Alamos. The second also lasted ten years, from 1960 to 1970 at Caltech. In the Princeton-Cornell period he was reconstructing in his own way the theory of atoms and radiation and the interactions between them. In the Caltech period he was reconstructing the theory of nuclear forces and strongly-interacting particles. In both periods, he was pulling together the results of a lot of confusing experiments and using them to build coherent pictures of the way nature works. He relied as little as possible on existing theories and as much as possible on experimental facts. He built up his own theoretical pictures piece by piece, like jigsaw puzzles made of mathematical fragments, trying out a hundred different ways of arranging the pieces before finding an arrangement that fitted. Years went by while he struggled with possible arrangements that turned out to be inconsistent or wrong.

When I was a student at Cornell, watching Feynman at work, I was reminded of a description of Isaac Newton written by the economist John Maynard Keynes, who made a hobby of collecting and studying Newton's manuscripts. "His peculiar gift," wrote Keynes, "was the power of holding continuously in his mind a purely mental problem until he had seen straight through it. I fancy his preeminence is due to his muscles of intuition being the strongest and most enduring with which a man has ever been gifted." That description of Newton applies equally well to Feynman. It describes precisely Feynman's way of working. He held in his mind for ten years the problem of calculating the interaction of atoms with radiation, in full compliance with Einstein's principle of relativity, and never gave up until he solved it. I was lucky to get to know him during the last year of his ten-year struggle with atoms and radiation, when the pieces were finally beginning to fall into place. I saw him in that last year still struggling, still wandering into mathematical swamps and physical blind alleys, more often frustrated than elated. Illumination came to him the hard way, not in a flash of genius but in a slow dawn of understanding after long nights of hard work.

During his Caltech years, Feynman struggled in a similar way with the much more complicated problem of fitting the strongly-interacting nuclear particles into a coherent picture. The problem is more complicated because there is a bewildering variety of particles and interactions. Feynman solved it only halfway. He worked out a theory in which the observed particles are built out of a smaller set of elementary constituents that he called "partons." He found rules for calculating the behavior of observed particles using the simpler behavior of their constituent partons as a guide. His rules explained the results of experiments, but left many details to be filled in later. All the time while this work was in progress, he was exchanging ideas with his younger colleagues Murray Gell-Mann and George Zweig at Caltech. Gell-Mann and Zweig independently rushed ahead with theories of their own, similar to Feynman's theory but describing the partons in greater detail. Gell-Mann called his partons "quarks" and Zweig called them "aces." Now, forty years later, only the quarks are remembered and the partons and aces are forgotten. The Gell-Mann quark model of nuclear particles became the standard model that is taught to students and accepted by everybody. Feynman always gave generous credit to Gell-Mann and Zweig for discovering the theory that eclipsed his own. In 1977 he privately recommended them both for a Nobel Prize for the discovery. That would have been a second Nobel Prize for Gell-Mann. The Nobel committee did not accept Feynman's recommendation.

In the end, Feynman's greatness as a scientist does not depend on any particular discovery. His greatness is shown by the fact that he created the language that physicists all over the world now speak. His "space-time approach" and his pictorial diagrams are now used by everybody as a matter of course to describe the way nature works. The essence of the space-time approach is to take literally the saying of the ancient Greek philosopher Heraclitus: "Everything flows." According to the space-time approach, nature flows from any initial state to any final state by moving along all possible histories simultaneously. Every possible history carries an amplitude that has a magnitude and a phase. To calculate the probability of reaching the final state, all you have to do is add up the amplitudes of all the histories leading to it and square the sum of the amplitudes. The amplitude corresponding to each history is calculated by adding contributions from a set of diagrams describing the history. This "sum-over-histories" description of nature is one of the great unifying principles in the history of science.

In addition to his ten-year campaigns to clarify the foundations of atomic and nuclear physics, Feynman also worked on a wide range of other problems. He was interested in almost everything and was not afraid to plunge into unfamiliar fields. He spent a year doing experiments with viruses in the Caltech biology department. At the end of that year, he had discovered some interesting new facts about genetic mutations in viruses, but he decided he was not cut out to be a biologist and returned with renewed enthusiasm to physics. Biology in those days was all experiments and no theory, and Feynman could not live without theorizing. After he returned to physics, he made what he considered his most beautiful discovery, a new law of nature describing how the particles known as neutrinos interact with matter.

Wherever mysteries were to be found in any branch of science, Feynman plunged in. In the 1950s one of the most tempting mysteries was in low-temperature physics. In 1938 the Russian physicist Pyotr Kapitsa had discovered that liquid helium became a superfluid at temperatures close to absolute zero. For fifteen years after Kapitsa's discovery, the understanding of superfluidity was a famous unsolved problem. Superfluidity is a weird and wonderful state of matter. A superfluid once set moving will continue to flow forever without slowing down. Feynman accepted the challenge and worked out a theory of superfluidity based on the sum-over-histories method of calculation. He showed that superfluidity was a natural consequence of the sum-over-histories picture of the liquid, if you take into account the fact that all helium atoms are identical. Because the atoms are identical, you must add together histories in which they are interchanged and permuted in all possible ways. Feynman showed in a simple way that the fluid motion would organize itself into vortices that would continue spinning forever so long as the liquid was undisturbed. This theory explained why the liquid was a superfluid. After Feynman worked out the theory, new experiments at Caltech were done to test it in detail, which confirmed it was correct.

Feynman's sum-over-histories picture of physical reality is at the same time philosophically deep and practically useful. It gives us a quick and easy way to calculate what happens, and it also gives us a deep insight into the reasons why our commonsense notions of matter and motion are misleading. Feynman understood that nature's way of behaving was, as Arthur C. Clarke has said, not only stranger than we imagine but stranger than we *can* imagine. The sum-over-histories picture gives us a direct and vivid sense of nature's strangeness. But Feynman was always a calculator first and a philosopher second. For him the most important thing was to get the details right.

Like his sum-over-histories picture of physical reality, Feynman's insight into human nature is also philosophically deep and practically useful. Some of his stories are as deep as his physics. In this foreword I have emphasized the scientific side of Feynman and said little about the human side. I wrote it this way because the book is mostly about the human side. If you want to see the human side of Feynman, the best way is to read the story of the life and death of his first wife, Arline. The story is told in Feynman's own words in the selection "What Do You Care What Other People Think?" It is the longest piece in the book, and it was the most difficult story for Feynman to tell. His spirit shines through it along with hers.

FROM
FAR ROCKAWAY
TO MIT

THE MAKING
OF A SCIENTIST

I have a friend who's an artist, and he sometimes takes a view which I don't agree with. He'll hold up a flower and say, "Look how beautiful it is," and I'll agree. But then he'll say, "I, as an artist, can see how beautiful a flower is. But you, as a scientist, take it all apart and it becomes dull." I think he's kind of nutty.

First of all, the beauty that he sees is available to other people—and to me, too, I believe. Although I might not be quite as refined aesthetically as he is, I can appreciate the beauty of a flower. But at the same time, I see much more in the flower than he sees. I can imagine the cells inside, which also have a beauty. There's beauty not just at the dimension of one centimeter; there's also beauty at a smaller dimension.

There are the complicated actions of the cells, and other processes. The fact that the colors in the flower have evolved in order to attract insects to pollinate it is interesting; that means insects can see the colors. That adds a question: does this aesthetic sense we have also exist in lower forms of life? There are all kinds of interesting questions that come from a knowledge of science, which only *adds* to the excitement and mystery and awe of a flower. It only adds. I don't understand how it subtracts.

I've always been very one-sided about science, and when I was younger I concentrated almost all my effort on it. In those days I didn't have time, and I didn't have much patience, to learn what's called the humanities. Even though there were humanities courses in the university that you had to take in order to graduate, I tried my best to avoid them. It's only afterwards, when I've gotten older and more relaxed, that I've spread out a little bit. I've learned to draw and I read a little bit, but I'm really still a very one-sided person and I don't know a great deal. I have a limited intelligence and I use it in a particular direction.

■   ■   ■

Before I was born, my father told my mother, "If it's a boy, he's going to be a scientist."* When I was just a little kid, very small in a highchair, my father brought home a lot of little bathroom tiles—seconds—of different colors. We played with them, my father setting them up vertically on my highchair like dominoes, and I would push one end so they would all go down.

Then after a while, I'd help set them up. Pretty soon, we're setting them up in a more complicated way: two white tiles and a blue tile, two white tiles and a blue tile, and so on. When my mother saw that she said, "Leave the poor child alone. If he wants to put a blue tile, let him put a blue tile!"

But my father said, "No, I want to show him what patterns are like and how interesting they are. It's a kind of elementary mathematics." So he started very early to tell me about the world and how interesting it is.

We had the *Encyclopaedia Britannica* at home. When I was a small boy he used to sit me on his lap and read to me from the *Britannica.* We would be reading, say, about dinosaurs. It would be talking about the *Tyrannosaurus rex,* and it would say something like, "This dinosaur is twenty-five feet high and its head is six feet across."

My father would stop reading and say, "Now, let's see what that means. That would mean that if he stood in our front yard, he would be tall enough to put his head through our window up here." (We were on the second floor.) "But his head would be too wide to fit in the window." Everything he read to me he would translate as best he could into some reality.

It was very exciting and very, very interesting to think there were animals of such magnitude—and that they all died out, and that nobody knew why. I wasn't frightened that there would be one coming in my window as a consequence of this. But I learned from my father to translate: Everything I read I try to figure out what it really means, what it's really saying.

We used to go to the Catskill Mountains, a place where people from New York City would go in the summer. The fathers would all return to New York to work during the week, and come back only for the weekend. On weekends, my father would take me for walks in the woods and he'd tell me about interesting things that were going on in the woods. When the other mothers saw this, they thought it was wonderful and

---

*Richard's younger sister, Joan, has a Ph.D. in physics, in spite of this preconception that only boys can be scientists. —RL

that the other fathers should take their sons for walks. They tried to work on them but they didn't get anywhere at first. They wanted my father to take all the kids, but he didn't want to because he had a special relationship with me. So it ended up that the other fathers had to take their children for walks the next weekend.

The next Monday, when the fathers were all back at work, we kids were playing in a field. One kid says to me, "See that bird? What kind of bird is that?"

I said, "I haven't the slightest idea what kind of a bird it is."

He says, "It's a brown-throated thrush. Your father doesn't teach you anything!"

But it was the opposite. He had already taught me: "See that bird?" he says. "It's a Spencer's warbler." (I knew he didn't know the real name.) "Well, in Italian, it's a *Ciutto Lapittida*. In Portuguese, it's a *Bom da Peida*. In Chinese, it's a *Chung-long-tah*, and in Japanese, it's a *Katano Tekeda*. You can know the name of that bird in all the languages of the world, but when you're finished, you'll know absolutely nothing whatever about the bird. You'll only know about humans in different places, and what they call the bird. So let's look at the bird and see what it's *doing*—that's what counts." (I learned very early the difference between knowing the name of something and knowing something.)

He said, "For example, look: the bird pecks at its feathers all the time. See it walking around, pecking at its feathers?"

"Yeah."

He says, "Why do you think birds peck at their feathers?"

I said, "Well, maybe they mess up their feathers when they fly, so they're pecking them in order to straighten them out."

"All right," he says. "If that were the case, then they would peck a lot just after they've been flying. Then, after they've been on the ground a while, they wouldn't peck so much any more—you know what I mean?"

"Yeah."

He says, "Let's look and see if they peck more just after they land."

It wasn't hard to tell: there was not much difference between the birds that had been walking around a bit and those that had just landed. So I said, "I give up. Why does a bird peck at its feathers?"

"Because there are lice bothering it," he says. "The lice eat flakes of protein that come off its feathers."

He continued, "Each louse has some waxy stuff on its legs, and little mites eat that. The mites don't digest it perfectly, so they emit from their rear ends a sugar-like material, in which bacteria grow."

Finally he says, "So you see, everywhere there's a source of food, there's *some* form of life that finds it."

Now, I knew that it may not have been exactly a louse, that it might not be exactly true that the louse's legs have mites. That story was probably incorrect in *detail*, but what he was telling me was right in *principle*.

Another time, when I was older, he picked a leaf off of a tree. This leaf had a flaw, a thing we never look at much. The leaf was sort of deteriorated; it had a little brown line in the shape of a C, starting somewhere in the middle of the leaf and going out in a curl to the edge.

"Look at this brown line," he says. "It's narrow at the beginning and it's wider as it goes to the edge. What this is, is a fly—a blue fly with yellow eyes and green wings has come and laid an egg on this leaf. Then, when the egg hatches into a maggot (a caterpillar-like thing), it spends its whole life eating this leaf—that's where it gets its food. As it eats along, it leaves behind this brown trail of eaten leaf. As the maggot grows, the trail grows wider until he's grown to full size at the end of the leaf, where he turns into a fly—a blue fly with yellow eyes and green wings—who flies away and lays an egg on another leaf."

Again, I knew that the details weren't precisely correct—it could have even been a beetle—but the idea that he was trying to explain to me was the amusing part of life: the whole thing is just reproduction. No matter how complicated the business is, the main point is to do it again!

Not having experience with many fathers, I didn't realize how remarkable he was. How did he learn the deep principles of science and the love of it, what's behind it, and why it's worth doing? I never really asked him, because I just assumed that those were things that fathers knew.

My father taught me to notice things. One day, I was playing with an "express wagon," a little wagon with a railing around it. It had a ball in it, and when I pulled the wagon, I noticed something about the way the ball moved. I went to my father and said, "Say, Pop, I noticed something. When I pull the wagon, the ball rolls to the back of the wagon. And when I'm pulling it along and I suddenly stop, the ball rolls to the front of the wagon. Why is that?"

"That, nobody knows," he said. "The general principle is that things which are moving tend to keep on moving, and things which are standing still tend to stand still, unless you push them hard. This tendency is called 'inertia,' but nobody knows why it's true." Now, that's a deep understanding. He didn't just give me the name.

He went on to say, "If you look from the side, you'll see that it's the back of the wagon that you're pulling against the ball, and the ball stands still. As a matter of fact, from the friction it starts to move forward a little bit in relation to the ground. It doesn't move back."

I ran back to the little wagon and set the ball up again and pulled the wagon. Looking sideways, I saw that indeed he was right. Relative to the sidewalk, it moved forward a little bit.

That's the way I was educated by my father, with those kinds of examples and discussions: no pressure—just lovely, interesting discussions. It has motivated me for the rest of my life, and makes me interested in *all* the sciences. (It just happens I do physics better.)

I've been caught, so to speak—like someone who was given something wonderful when he was a child, and he's always looking for it again. I'm always looking, like a child, for the wonders I know I'm going to find—maybe not every time, but every once in a while.

. . .

Around that time my cousin, who was three years older, was in high school. He was having considerable difficulty with his algebra, so a tutor would come. I was allowed to sit in a corner while the tutor would try to teach my cousin algebra. I'd hear him talking about x.

I said to my cousin, "What are you trying to do?"

"I'm trying to find out what x is, like in $2x + 7 = 15$."

I say, "You mean 4."

"Yeah, but you did it by arithmetic. You have to do it by algebra."

I learned algebra, fortunately, not by going to school, but by finding my aunt's old schoolbook in the attic, and understanding that the whole idea was to find out what x is—it doesn't make any difference how you do it. For me, there was no such thing as doing it "by arithmetic," or doing it "by algebra." "Doing it by algebra" was a set of rules which, if you followed them blindly, could produce the answer: "subtract 7 from both sides; if you have a multiplier, divide both sides by the multiplier," and so on—a series of steps by which you could get the answer if you didn't understand what you were trying to do. The rules had been invented so that the children who have to study algebra can all pass it. And that's why my cousin was never able to do algebra.

There was a series of math books in our local library which started out with *Arithmetic for the Practical Man*. Then came *Algebra for the Practical Man*, and then *Trigonometry for the Practical Man*. (I learned trigonometry from that, but I soon forgot it again, because I didn't understand it very well.) When I was about thirteen, the library was going to get *Calculus for the Practical Man*. By this time I knew, from reading the encyclopedia, that calculus was an important and interesting subject, and I ought to learn it.

When I finally saw the calculus book at the library, I was very excited. I went to the librarian to check it out, but she looked at me and said, "You're just a child. What are you taking this book out for?"

It was one of the few times in my life I was uncomfortable and I lied. I said it was for my father.

I took the book home and I began to learn calculus from it. I thought it was relatively simple and straightforward. My father started to read it, but he found it confusing and he couldn't understand it. So I tried to explain calculus to him. I didn't know he was so limited, and it bothered me a little bit. It was the first time I realized that I had learned more in some sense than he.

.   .   .

One of the things that my father taught me besides physics—whether it's correct or not—was a disrespect for certain kinds of things. For example, when I was a little boy, and he would sit me on his knee, he'd show me rotogravures in the *New York Times*—that's printed pictures which had just come out in newspapers.

One time we were looking at a picture of the pope and everybody bowing in front of him. My father said, "Now, look at those humans. Here's one human standing here, and all these others are bowing in front of him. Now, what's the difference? This one is the pope"—he hated the pope anyway. He said, "This difference is the hat he's wearing." (If it was a general, it was the epaulets. It was always the costume, the uniform, the position.) "But," he said, "this man has the same problems as everybody else: he eats dinner; he goes to the bathroom. He's a human being." (By the way, my father was in the uniform business, so he knew what the difference is in a man with the uniform off and the uniform on—it was the same man for him.)

.   .   .

He was happy with me, I believe. Once, though, when I came back from MIT (I'd been there a few years), he said to me, "Now that you've become educated about these things, there's one question I've always had that I've never understood very well."

I asked him what it was.

He said, "I understand that when an atom makes a transition from one state to another, it emits a particle of light called a photon."

"That's right," I said.

He says, "Is the photon in the atom ahead of time?"

"No, there's no photon beforehand."

"Well," he says, "where does it come from, then? How does it come out?"

I tried to explain it to him—that photon numbers aren't conserved; they're just created by the motion of the electron—but I couldn't explain it very well. I said, "It's like the sound that I'm making now: it wasn't in me before." (It's not like my little boy, who suddenly announced one day, when he was very young, that he could no longer say a certain word—the word turned out to be "cat"—because his "word bag" had run out of the word. There's no word bag that makes you use up words as they come out; in the same sense, there's no "photon bag" in an atom.)

He was not satisfied with me in that respect. I was never able to explain any of the things that he didn't understand. So he was unsuccessful: he sent me to all these universities in order to find out those things, and he never did find out.

■   ■   ■

Although my mother didn't know anything about science, she had a great influence on me as well. In particular, she had a wonderful sense of humor, and I learned from her that the highest forms of understanding we can achieve are laughter and human compassion.

HE FIXES RADIOS
BY THINKING!

When I was about eleven or twelve I set up a lab in my house, at 792 Cornaga Avenue* in Far Rockaway. It consisted of an old wooden packing box that I put shelves in. I had a heater, and I'd put in fat and cook french-fried potatoes all the time. I also had a storage battery, and a lamp bank.

To build the lamp bank I went down to the five-and-ten and got some sockets you can screw down to a wooden base, and connected them with pieces of bell wire. By making different combinations of switches—in series or parallel—I knew I could get different voltages. But what I hadn't realized was that a bulb's resistance depends on its temperature, so the results of my calculations weren't the same as the stuff that came out of the circuit. But it was all right, and when the bulbs were in series, all half-lit, they would *glooooooooooow*, very pretty—it was great!

I had a fuse in the system so if I shorted anything, the fuse would blow. Now, I had to have a fuse that was weaker than the fuse in the house, so I made my own fuses by taking tin foil and wrapping it around an old burnt-out fuse. Across my fuse I had a 5-watt bulb, so when my fuse blew, the load from the trickle charger that was always charging the storage battery would light up the bulb. The bulb was on the switchboard behind a piece of brown candy paper (it looks red when a light's behind it)—so if something went off, I'd look up to the switchboard and there would be a big red spot where the fuse went. It was *fun!*

I enjoyed radios. I started with a crystal set that I bought at the store, and I used to listen to it at night in bed while I was going to sleep, through a pair of earphones. When my mother and father went out until late at night, they would come into my room and take the earphones off—and worry about what was going into my head while I was asleep.

*Renamed "Richard Feynman Way" by the City of New York on May 11, 2005. —RL

About that time I invented a burglar alarm, which was a very simple-minded thing: it was just a big battery and a bell connected with some wire. When the door to my room opened, it pushed the wire against the battery and closed the circuit, and the bell would go off.

One night my mother and father came home from a night out and very, very quietly, so as not to disturb the child, opened the door to come into my room to take my earphones off. All of a sudden this tremendous bell went off with a helluva racket—BONG BONG BONG BONG BONG!!! I jumped out of bed yelling, "It worked! It worked!"

I had a Ford coil—a spark coil from an automobile—and I had the spark terminals at the top of my switchboard. I would put a Raytheon RH tube, which had argon gas in it, across the terminals, and the spark would make a purple glow inside the vacuum—it was just great!

One day I was playing with the Ford coil, punching holes in paper with the sparks, and the paper caught on fire. Soon I couldn't hold it any more because it was burning near my fingers, so I dropped it in a metal wastebasket which had a lot of newspapers in it. Newspapers burn fast, you know, and the flame looked pretty big inside the room. I shut the door so my mother—who was playing bridge with some friends in the living room—wouldn't find out there was a fire in my room, took a magazine that was lying nearby, and put it over the wastebasket to smother the fire.

After the fire was out I took the magazine off, but now the room began to fill up with smoke. The wastebasket was still too hot to handle, so I got a pair of pliers, carried it across the room, and held it out the window for the smoke to blow out.

But because it was breezy outside, the wind lit the fire again, and now the magazine was out of reach. So I pulled the flaming wastebasket back in through the window to get the magazine, and I noticed there were curtains in the window—it was very dangerous!

Well, I got the magazine, put the fire out again, and this time kept the magazine with me while I shook the glowing coals out of the wastepaper basket onto the street, two or three floors below. Then I went out of my room, closed the door behind me, and said to my mother, "I'm going out to play," as the smoke went out slowly through the windows.

■　■　■

I also did some things with electric motors and built an amplifier for a photo cell that I bought that could make a bell ring when I put my hand in front of the cell. I didn't get to do as much as I wanted to, because my mother kept putting me out all the time, to play. But I was often in the house, fiddling with my lab.

I bought radios at rummage sales. I didn't have any money, but it wasn't very expensive—they were old, broken radios, and I'd buy them and try to fix them. Usually they were broken in some simple-minded way—some obvious wire was hanging loose, or a coil was broken or partly unwound—so I could get some of them going. On one of these radios one night I got WACO in Waco, Texas—it was tremendously exciting.

On this same tube radio up in my lab I was able to hear a station up in Schenectady called WGN. Now, all of us kids—my two cousins, my sister, and the neighborhood kids—listened on the radio downstairs to a program called the Eno Crime Club—Eno effervescent salts—it was *the* thing. Well, I discovered that I could hear this program up in my lab on WGN one hour before it was broadcast in New York. So I'd discover what was going to happen, and then, when we were all sitting around the radio downstairs listening to the Eno Crime Club, I'd say, "You know, we haven't heard from so-and-so in a long time. I betcha he comes in now and saves the situation."

Two seconds later, *bup-bup*, there he is! So they all got excited about this, and I predicted a couple of other things. Then they realized that there must be some trick to it—that I must know, somehow. So I owned up to what it was, that I could hear it upstairs the hour before.

You know what the result was, naturally. Now they couldn't wait for the regular hour. They all had to sit upstairs in my lab with this little creaky radio for half an hour, listening to the Eno Crime Club from Schenectady.

We lived at that time in a big house; it was left by my grandfather to his children, and they didn't have much money aside from the house. It was a very large, wooden house, and I would run wires all around the outside, and had plugs in all the rooms, so I could always listen to my radios, which were upstairs in my lab. I also had a loudspeaker—not the whole speaker, but the part without the big horn on it.

One day, when I had my earphones on, I connected them to the loudspeaker, and I discovered something: when I put my finger in the speaker and scratched it, I could hear it in the earphones. So I discovered that the speaker could act like a microphone, and you didn't even need any batteries. At school we were talking about Alexander Graham Bell, so I gave a demonstration of the speaker and the earphones. I didn't know it at the time, but I think it was the type of telephone he originally used.

So now I had a microphone, and I could broadcast from upstairs to downstairs, and from downstairs to upstairs, using the amplifiers of my rummage-sale radios. At that time my sister Joan, who was nine years younger than I was, must have been about two or three, and there was a guy on the radio called Uncle Don that she liked to listen to. He'd sing little songs about "good children," and so on, and he'd read cards sent in by parents telling that "Mary So-and-so is having a birthday this Saturday at 25 Flatbush Avenue."

One day my cousin Frances and I sat Joan down and said that there was a special program she should listen to. Then we ran upstairs and we started to broadcast: "This is Uncle Don. We know a very nice little girl named Joan who lives at 71 New Broadway;* she's got a birthday coming—not today, but such-and-such. She's a cute girl." We sang a little song, and then we made music: "*Deedle leet deet, doodle doodle loot doot; deedle deedle leet, doodle loot doot doo . . .*" We went through the whole deal, and then we came downstairs: "How was it? Did you like the program?"

"It was good," she said, "but why did you make the music with your mouth?"

    ■   ■   ■

One day I got a telephone call: "Mister, are you Richard Feynman?"

"Yes."

"This is a hotel. We have a radio that doesn't work, and would like it repaired. We understand you might be able to do something about it."

"But I'm only a little boy," I said. "I don't know how—"

"Yes, we know that, but we'd like you to come over anyway."

It was a hotel that my aunt was running, but I didn't know that. I went over there with—they still tell the story—a big screwdriver in my back pocket. Well, I was small, so *any* screwdriver looked big in my back pocket.

I went up to the radio and tried to fix it. I didn't know anything about it, but there was also a handyman at the hotel, and either he noticed, or I noticed, a loose knob on the rheostat—to turn up the volume—so that it wasn't turning the shaft. He went off and filed something, and fixed it up so it worked.

The next radio I tried to fix didn't work at all. That was easy: it wasn't plugged in right. As the repair jobs got more and more complicated, I got better and better, and more elaborate. I bought myself a milliam-

---

*An earlier address for the house on Cornaga Ave. —RL

meter in New York and converted it into a voltmeter that had different scales on it by using the right lengths (which I calculated) of very fine copper wire. It wasn't very accurate, but it was good enough to tell whether things were in the right ballpark at different connections in those radio sets.

The main reason people hired me was the Depression. They didn't have any money to fix their radios, and they'd hear about this kid who would do it for less. So I'd climb on roofs to fix antennas, and all kinds of stuff. I got a series of lessons of ever-increasing difficulty. Ultimately I got some job like converting a DC set into an AC set, and it was very hard to keep the hum from going through the system, and I didn't build it quite right. I shouldn't have bitten that one off, but I didn't know.

One job was really sensational. I was working at the time for a printer, and a man who knew that printer knew I was trying to get jobs fixing radios, so he sent a fellow around to the print shop to pick me up. The guy is obviously poor—his car is a complete wreck—and we go to his house which is in a cheap part of town. On the way, I say, "What's the trouble with the radio?"

He says, "When I turn it on it makes a noise, and after a while the noise stops and everything's all right, but I don't like the noise at the beginning."

I think to myself: "What the hell—if he hasn't got any money, you'd think he could stand a little noise for a while!"

And all the time, on the way to his house, he's saying things like, "Do you know anything about radios? How do you know about radios—you're just a little boy!"

He's putting me down the whole way, and I'm thinking, "So what's the matter with him? So it makes a little noise."

When we got there I went over to the radio and turned it on. Little noise? *My god!* No wonder the poor guy couldn't stand it. The thing began to roar and wobble—WUH BUH BUH BUH BUH—a *tremendous* amount of noise! Then it quieted down and played correctly. So I started to think: "How can that happen?"

I start walking back and forth, thinking, and I realize that one way it can happen is that the tubes are heating up in the wrong order—that is, the amplifier's all hot, the tubes are ready to go, and there's nothing feeding in, or there's some back circuit feeding in, or something wrong in the beginning part—the RF part—and therefore it's making a lot of noise picking up something. And when the RF circuit's finally going and the grid voltages are adjusted, everything's all right.

So the guy says, "What are you doing? You come to fix the radio, but you're only walking back and forth!"

I say, "I'm thinking!" Then I said to myself, "All right, take the tubes out, and reverse the order completely in the set." (Many radio sets in those days used the same tubes in different places—212's, I think they were, or 212-A's.) So I changed the tubes around, stepped to the front of the radio, turned the thing on, and it's as quiet as a lamb: it waits until it heats up, and then plays perfectly—no noise.

When a person has been negative to you, and then you do something like that, they're usually a hundred percent the other way, kind of to compensate. He got me other jobs, and kept telling everybody what a tremendous genius I was, saying, "He fixes radios by *thinking!*" The whole idea of thinking, to fix a radio—a little boy stops and thinks, and figures out how to do it—he never thought that was possible.

Radio circuits were much easier to understand in those days because everything was out in the open. After you took the set apart, you could see this was a resistor, that's a condenser, here's a this, there's a that; they were all labeled. And if wax had been dripping from the condenser, it was too hot and you could tell that the condenser was burned out. If there was charcoal on one of the resistors, you knew where the trouble was. Or, if you couldn't tell what was the matter by looking at it, you'd test it with your voltmeter and see whether voltage was coming through. The sets were simple, the circuits were not complicated. The voltage on the grids was always about one and a half or two volts, and the voltages on the plates were one hundred or two hundred, DC. So it wasn't hard for me to fix a radio by understanding what was going on inside, noticing that something wasn't working right, and fixing it.

Sometimes it took quite a while. I remember one particular time when it took the whole afternoon to find a burned-out resistor that was not apparent. That particular time it happened to be a friend of my mother, so I had time—there was nobody on my back saying, "What are you doing?" Instead, they were saying, "Would you like a little milk, or some cake?" I finally fixed it because I had, and still have, persistence. Once I get on a puzzle, I can't get off. If my mother's friend had said, "Never mind, it's too much work," I'd have blown my top, because I want to beat this damn thing as long as I've gone this far. I can't just leave it after I've found out so much about it. I have to keep going to find out ultimately what is the matter with it in the end.

■   ■   ■

That's a puzzle drive. It's what accounts for my wanting to decipher Mayan hieroglyphics, for trying to open safes. I remember in high school, during first period a guy would come to me with a puzzle in geometry, or something which had been assigned in his advanced math class. I wouldn't stop until I figured the damn thing out—it would take me fifteen or twenty minutes. But during the day, other guys would come to me with the same problem, and I'd do it for them in a flash. So for one guy, to do it took me twenty minutes, while there were five guys who thought I was a super-genius.

So I got a fancy reputation. During high school every puzzle that was known to man must have come to me. Every damn, crazy conundrum that people had invented, I knew. So when I got to MIT there was a dance, and one of the seniors had his girlfriend there; she knew a lot of puzzles, and he was telling her that I was pretty good at them. So during the dance she came over to me and said, "They say you're a smart guy, so here's one for you: A man has eight cords of wood to chop . . ."

I said, "He starts by chopping every other one in three parts," because I had heard that one.

Then she'd go away and come back with another one, and I'd always know it.

This went on for quite a while. Finally, near the end of the dance, she came over, looking as if she was going to get me for sure this time. She said, "A mother and daughter are traveling to Europe . . ."

"The daughter got the bubonic plague."

She collapsed. That was hardly enough clues to get the answer to that one: It was the long story about how a mother and daughter stop at a hotel and stay in separate rooms, and the next day the mother goes to the daughter's room and there's nobody there, or somebody else is there, and she says, "Where's my daughter?" and the hotel keeper says, "What daughter?" and the register's got only the mother's name, and so on, and there's a big mystery as to what happened. The answer is, the daughter got bubonic plague—and the hotel, not wanting to have to close up, spirits the daughter away, cleans up the room, and erases all evidence of her having been there. It was a long tale, but I had heard it, so when the girl started out with, "A mother and daughter are traveling to Europe," I knew one puzzle that started that way, so I took a flying guess, and got it.

■ ■ ■

We had a thing at high school called the algebra team, which consisted of five kids, and we would travel to different schools as a team and have competitions. We would sit in one row of seats and the other team would sit in another row. A teacher, who was running the contest, would take out an envelope, and on the envelope it says "45 seconds." She opens it up, writes the problem on the blackboard, and says, "Go!"—so you really have more than 45 seconds because while she's writing you can think. Now the game was this: You have a piece of paper, and on it you can write anything, you can *do* anything. The only thing that counted was the answer. If the answer was "six books," you'd have to write "6," and put a big circle around it. If what was in the circle was right, you won; if it wasn't, you lost.

One thing was for sure: It was practically impossible to do the problem in any conventional, straightforward way, like putting "A is the number of red books, B is the number of blue books," grind, grind, grind, until you get "six books." That would take you 50 seconds, because the people who set up the timings on these problems had made them all a trifle short. So you had to think, "Is there a way to *see* it?" Sometimes you could see it in a flash, and sometimes you'd have to invent another way to do it and then do the algebra as fast as you could. It was wonderful practice, and I got better and better, and I eventually got to be the head of the team. So I learned to do algebra very quickly, and it came in handy in college. When we had a problem in calculus, I was very quick to see where it was going and to do the algebra—fast.

Another thing I did in high school was to invent problems and theorems. I mean, if I were doing any mathematical thing at all, I would find some practical example for which it would be useful. I invented a set of right-triangle problems. But instead of giving the lengths of two of the sides to find the third, I gave the difference of the two sides. A typical example was: There's a flagpole, and there's a rope that comes down from the top. When you hold the rope straight down, it's three feet longer than the pole, and when you pull the rope out tight, it's five feet from the base of the pole. How high is the pole?

I developed some equations for solving problems like that, and as a result I noticed some connection—perhaps it was $\sin^2 + \cos^2 = 1$—that reminded me of trigonometry. Now, a few years earlier, perhaps when I was eleven or twelve, I had read a book on trigonometry that I had checked out from the library, but the book was by now long gone. I remembered only that trigonometry had something to so with relations between sines and cosines. So I began to work out all the relations by drawing triangles, and each one I proved by myself. I also calculated the sine, cosine, and tangent of every five degrees, starting with the sine of five degrees as given, by addition and half-angle formulas that I had worked out.

A few years later, when we studied trigonometry in school, I still had my notes and I saw that my demonstrations were often different from those in the book. Sometimes, for a thing where I didn't notice a simple way to do it, I went all over the place till I got it. Other times, my way was most clever—the standard demonstration in the book was much more complicated. So sometimes I had 'em beat, and sometimes it was the other way around.

While I was doing all this trigonometry, I didn't like the symbols for sine, cosine, tangent, and so on. To me, "sin f" looked like s times i times n times f! So I invented another symbol, like a square root sign, that was a sigma with a long arm sticking out of it, and I put the f underneath. For the tangent it was a tau with the top of the tau extended, and for the cosine I made a kind of gamma, but it looked a little bit like the square root sign.

Now the inverse sine was the same sigma, but left-to-right reflected so that it started with the horizontal line with the value underneath, and then the sigma. *That* was the inverse sine, *not* $\sin^{-1}$ f—that was crazy! They had that in books! To me, $\sin^{-1}$ meant 1/sine, the reciprocal. So my symbols were better.

I didn't like $f(x)$—that looked to me like f times x. I also didn't like dy/dx—you have a tendency to cancel the d's—so I made a different sign, something like an & sign. For logarithms it was a big L extended to the right, with the thing you take the log of inside, and so on.

I thought my symbols were just as good, if not better, than the regular symbols—it doesn't make any difference *what* symbols you use—but I discovered later that it *does* make a difference. Once when I was explaining something to another kid in high school, without thinking I started to make these symbols, and he said, "What the hell are those?" I realized then that if I'm going to talk to anybody else, I'll have to use the standard symbols, so I eventually gave up my own symbols.

I had also invented a set of symbols for the typewriter, like FORTRAN has to do, so I could type equations. I also fixed typewriters, with paper clips and rubber bands (the rubber bands didn't break down like they do here in Los Angeles), but I wasn't a professional repairman; I'd just fix them so they would work. But the whole problem of discovering what was the matter, and figuring out what you have to do to fix it—that was interesting to me, like a puzzle.

STRING BEANS

I must have been seventeen or eighteen when I worked one summer in a hotel run by my aunt. I don't know how much I got—twenty-two dollars a month, I think—and I alternated eleven hours one day and thirteen the next as a desk clerk or as a busboy in the restaurant. And during the afternoon, when you were desk clerk, you had to bring milk up to Mrs. D——, an invalid woman who never gave us a tip. That's the way the world was: You worked long hours and got nothing for it, every day.

This was a resort hotel, by the beach, on the outskirts of New York City. The husbands would go to work in the city and leave the wives behind to play cards, so you would always have to get the bridge tables out. Then at night the guys would play poker, so you'd get the tables ready for them—clean out the ashtrays and so on. I was always up until late at night, like two o'clock, so it really *was* thirteen and eleven hours a day.

There were certain things I didn't like, such as tipping. I thought we should be paid more, and not have to have any tips. But when I proposed that to the boss, I got nothing but laughter. She told everybody, "Richard doesn't want his tips, hee, hee, hee; he doesn't want his tips, ha, ha, ha!" The world is full of this kind of dumb smart-alec who doesn't understand anything.

Anyway, at one stage there was a group of men who, when they'd come back from working in the city, would right away want ice for their drinks. Now the other guy working with me had really been a desk clerk. He was older than I was, and a lot more professional. One time he said to me, "Listen, we're always bringing ice up to that guy Ungar and he never gives us a tip—not even ten cents. Next time, when he asks for ice, just don't do a damn thing. Then he'll call you back, and when he calls you back, you say, 'Oh, I'm sorry. I forgot. We're all forgetful sometimes.' "

So I did it, and Ungar gave me fifteen cents! But now, when I think back on it, I realize that the other desk clerk, the professional, had *really* known what to do—tell the *other* guy to take the risk of getting into trouble. He put *me* to the job of training this fella to give tips. He never said anything; he made *me* do it!

I had to clean up tables in the dining room as a busboy. You pile all this stuff from the tables on to a tray at the side, and when it gets high enough you carry it into the kitchen. So you get a new tray, right? You *should* do it in two steps—take the old tray away, and put in a new one—but I thought, "I'm going to do it in one step." So I tried to slide the new tray under, and pull the old tray out at the same time, and it slipped—BANG! All the stuff went on the floor. And then, naturally, the question was, "What were you doing? How did it fall?" Well, how could I explain that I was trying to invent a new way to handle trays?

Among the desserts there was some kind of coffee cake that came out very pretty on a doily, on a little plate. But if you would go in the back you'd see a man called the pantry man. His problem was to get the stuff ready for desserts. Now this man must have been a miner, or something—heavy-built, with very stubby, rounded, thick fingers. He'd take this stack of doilies, which are manufactured by some sort of stamping process, all stuck together, and he'd take these stubby fingers and try to separate the doilies to put them on the plates. I always heard him say, "Damn deez doilies!" while he was doing this, and I remember thinking, "What a contrast—the person sitting at the table gets this nice cake on a doilied plate, while the pantry man back there with the stubby thumbs is saying, 'Damn deez doilies!' " So that was the difference between the real world and what it looked like.

My first day on the job the pantry lady explained that she usually made a ham sandwich, or something, for the guy who was on the late shift. I said that I liked desserts, so if there was a dessert left over from supper, I'd like that. The next night I was on the late shift till 2:00 A.M. with these guys playing poker. I was sitting around with nothing to do, getting bored, when suddenly I remembered there was a dessert to eat. I went over to the icebox and opened it up, and there she'd left *six* desserts! There was a chocolate pudding, a piece of cake, some peach slices, some rice pudding, some Jell-O—there was everything! So I sat there and ate the six desserts—it was sensational!

The next day she said to me, "I left a dessert for you . . ."

"It was wonderful," I said, "absolutely wonderful!"

"But I left you six desserts because I didn't know which one you liked the best."

So from that time on she left six desserts. Every evening I had six desserts. They weren't always different, but there were always six desserts.

■   ■   ■

One time when I was desk clerk a girl left a book by the telephone at the desk while she went to eat dinner, so I looked at it. It was *The Life of Leonardo*, and I couldn't resist: The girl let me borrow it and I read the whole thing.

I slept in a little room in the back of the hotel, and there was some stew about turning out the lights when you leave your room, which I couldn't ever remember to do. Inspired by the Leonardo book, I made a gadget which consisted of a system of strings and weights—Coke bottles full of water—that would operate when I'd open the door, lighting the pull-chain light inside. You open the door, and things would go, and light the light; then you close the door behind you, and the light would go out. But my *real* accomplishment came later.

I used to cut vegetables in the kitchen. String beans had to be cut into one-inch pieces. The way you were supposed to do it was: You hold two beans in one hand, the knife in the other, and you press the knife against the beans and your thumb, almost cutting yourself. It was a slow process. So I put my mind to it, and I got a pretty good idea. I sat down at the wooden table outside the kitchen, put a bowl in my lap, and stuck a very sharp knife into the table at a forty-five-degree angle away from me. Then I put a pile of the string beans on each side, and I'd pick out a bean, one in each hand, and bring it towards me with enough speed that it would slice, and the pieces would slide into the bowl that was in my lap.

So I'm slicing beans one after the other—*chig, chig, chig, chig, chig*—and everybody's giving me the beans, and I'm going like sixty when the boss comes by and says, "What are you *doing?*"

I say, "Look at the way I have of cutting beans!"—and just at that moment I put a finger through instead of a bean. Blood came out and went on the beans, and there was a big excitement: "Look at how many beans you spoiled! What a stupid way to do things!" and so on. So I was never able to make any improvement, which would have been easy—with a guard, or something—but no, there was no chance for improvement.

I had another invention, which had a similar difficulty. We had to slice potatoes after they'd been cooked, for some kind of potato salad. They were sticky and wet, and difficult to handle. I thought of a whole lot of knives, parallel in a rack, coming down and slicing the whole thing. I thought about this a long time, and finally I got the idea of wires in a rack.

So I went to the five-and-ten to buy some knives or wires, and saw exactly the gadget I wanted—it was for slicing eggs. The next time the potatoes came out I got my little egg slicer out and sliced all the potatoes in no time, and sent them back to the chef. The chef was a German, a great big guy who was King of the Kitchen, and he comes storming out, blood vessels sticking out of his neck, livid red. "What's the matter with the potatoes?" he says. "They're not sliced!"

I had them sliced, but they were all stuck together. He says, "How can I separate them?"

"Stick 'em in water," I suggest.

"IN WATER? EAGHHHHHHHHHHHH!!!"

Another time I had a *really* good idea. When I was desk clerk I had to answer the telephone. When a call came in, something buzzed, and a flap came down on the switchboard so you could tell which line it was. Sometimes, when I was helping the women with the bridge tables or sitting on the front porch in the middle of the afternoon (when there were very few calls), I'd be some distance from the switchboard when suddenly it would go. I'd come running to catch it, but the way the desk was made, in order to get to the switchboard you had to go quite a distance further down, then around, in behind, and then back up to see where the call was coming from—it took extra time.

So I got a good idea. I tied threads to the flaps on the switchboard, and strung them over the top of the desk and then down, and at the end of each thread I tied a little piece of paper. Then I put the telephone talking piece up on top of the desk, so I could reach it from the front. Now when a call came, I could tell which flap was down by which piece of paper was up, so I could answer the phone appropriately, from the front, to save time. Of course I still had to go around back to switch it in, but at least I was answering it. I'd say, "Just a moment," and then go around to switch it in.

I thought that was perfect, but the boss came by one day, and *she* wanted to answer the phone, and she couldn't figure it out—too complicated. "What are all these papers doing? Why is the telephone on this side? Why don't you . . . *raaaaaaaa!*"

I tried to explain—it was my own aunt—that there was no reason *not* to do that, but you can't say that to anybody who's *smart*, who *runs a hotel!* I learned there that innovation is a very difficult thing in the real world.

WHO STOLE
THE DOOR?

At MIT the different fraternities all had "smokers" where they tried to get the new freshmen to be their pledges, and the summer before I went to MIT I was invited to a meeting in New York of Phi Beta Delta, a Jewish fraternity. In those days, if you were Jewish or brought up in a Jewish family, you didn't have a chance in any other fraternity—nobody else would look at you. I wasn't particularly looking to be with other Jews, and the guys from the Phi Beta Delta fraternity didn't care how Jewish I was—in fact, I didn't believe anything about that stuff, and was certainly not in any way religious. Anyway, some guys from the fraternity asked me some questions and gave me a little bit of advice—that I ought to take the first-year calculus exam so I wouldn't have to take the course—which turned out to be good advice. I liked the fellas who came down to New York from the fraternity, and the two guys who talked me into it, I later became their roommate.

There was another Jewish fraternity at MIT, called "SAM," and their idea was to give me a ride up to Boston and I could stay with them. I accepted the ride, and stayed upstairs in one of the rooms that first night.

The next morning I looked out the window and saw the two guys from the other fraternity (that I met in New York) walking up the steps. Some guys from the Sigma Alpha Mu ran out to talk to them and there was a big discussion.

I yelled out the window, "Hey, I'm supposed to be with *those* guys!" and I rushed out of the fraternity without realizing that they were all operating, competing for my pledge. I didn't have any feelings of gratitude for the ride, or anything.

The Phi Beta Delta fraternity had almost collapsed the year before, because there were two different cliques: There was a group of socialite characters, who liked to have dances and fool around in their cars afterwards, and so on, and there was a group of guys who did nothing but study, and never went to the dances.

Just before I came to the fraternity they had had a big meeting and had made an important compromise. They were going to get together and help each other out. Everyone had to have a grade level of at least such-and-such. If they were sliding behind, the guys who studied all the time would teach them and help them do their work. On the other side, everybody had to go to every dance. If a guy didn't know how to get a date, the other guys would *get* him a date. If the guy didn't know how to dance, they'd *teach* him to dance. One group was teaching the other how to think, while the other guys were teaching them how to be social.

That was just right for me, because I was *not* very good socially. I was so timid that when I had to take the mail out and walk past some seniors sitting on the steps with some girls, I was petrified: I didn't know how to walk past them. And it didn't help any when a girl would say, "Oh, he's cute!"

It was only a little while after that the sophomores brought their girlfriends and their girlfriends' friends over to teach us to dance. Much later, one of the guys taught me how to drive his car. They worked very hard to get us intellectual characters to socialize and be more relaxed, and vice versa. It was a good balancing out.

I had some difficulty understanding what exactly it meant to be social. Soon after these "social" guys had taught me how to meet girls, I saw a nice waitress in a restaurant where I was eating by myself one day. With great effort I finally got up enough nerve to ask her to be my date at the next fraternity dance, and she said yes.

Back at the fraternity, when we were talking about the dates for the next dance, I told the guys I didn't need a date this time—I had found one on my own. I was very proud of myself.

When the upperclassmen found out my date was a waitress, they were horrified. They told me *that* was not possible; they would get me a "proper" date. They made me feel as though I had strayed, that I was amiss. They decided to take over the situation. They went to the restaurant, found the waitress, talked her out of it, and got me another girl. They were trying to educate their "wayward son," so to speak, but they were wrong, I think. I was only a freshman then, and I didn't have enough confidence yet to stop them from breaking my date.

When I became a pledge they had various ways of hazing. One of the things they did was to take us, blindfolded, far out into the country-side in the dead of winter and leave us by a frozen lake about a hundred feet apart. We were in the middle of absolutely *nowhere*—no houses, no nothing—and we were supposed to find our way back to the fraternity. We were a little bit scared, because we were young, and we didn't say much—except for one guy, whose name was Maurice Meyer: You couldn't stop him from joking around, making dumb puns, and having this happy-go-lucky attitude of "Ha, ha, there's nothing to worry about. Isn't this fun!"

We were getting mad at Maurice. He was always walking a little bit behind and laughing at the whole situation, while the rest of us didn't know how we were ever going to get out of this.

We came to an intersection not far from the lake—there were still no houses or anything—and the rest of us were discussing whether we should go this way or that way, when Maurice caught up to us and said, "Go *this* way."

"What the hell do *you* know, Maurice?" we said, frustrated. "You're always making these jokes. Why should we go *this* way?"

"Simple—look at the telephone lines: where there's more wires, it's going toward the central station."

This guy, who looked like he wasn't paying attention to anything, had come up with a terrific idea! We walked straight into town without making an error.

On the following day there was going to be a schoolwide freshman versus sophomore mudeo (various forms of wrestling and tug of wars that take place in the mud). Late in the evening, into our fraternity comes a whole bunch of sophomores—some from our fraternity and some from outside—and they kidnap us: they want us to be tired the next day so they can win.

The sophomores tied up all the freshmen relatively easily—except me: I didn't want the guys in the fraternity to find out that I was a sissy. (I was never any good in sports; I was always terrified if a tennis ball would come over the fence and land near me, because I never could get it back over the fence.) I figured this was a new situation, a new world, and I could make a new reputation. So in order that I wouldn't look like I didn't know how to fight, I fought like a son of a gun as best I could (not knowing what I was doing), and it took three or four guys many tries before they were finally able to tie me up. The sophomores took us to a house, far away in the woods, and tied us all down to a wooden floor with big U tacks.

I tried all sorts of ways to escape, but there were sophomores guarding us, and none of my tricks worked. I remember distinctly one young man they were afraid to tie down because he was so terrified: his face was pale yellow-green and he was shaking. I found out later he was from Europe—this was in the early 1930s—and he didn't realize that these guys all tied down to the floor was some kind of a joke; he knew what kinds of things were going on in Europe. The guy was frightening to look at, he was so scared.

By the time the night was over, there were only three sophomores guarding twenty of us freshmen, but we didn't know that. The sophomores had driven their cars in and out a few times to make it sound as if there was a lot of activity, and we didn't notice it was always the same cars and the same people. So we didn't win that one.

My father and mother happened to come up that morning to see how their son was doing in Boston, and the fraternity kept putting them off until we came back from being kidnapped. I was so bedraggled and dirty from struggling so hard to escape and from lack of sleep that they were really horrified to discover what their son looked like at MIT!

I had also gotten a stiff neck, and I remember standing in line for inspection that afternoon at ROTC, not being able to look straight forward. The commander grabbed my head and turned it, shouting, "Straighten up!"

I winced, as my shoulders went at an angle: "I can't help it, sir!"

"Oh, excuse *me!*" he said, apologetically.

Anyway, the fact that I fought so long and hard not to be tied up gave me a terrific reputation, and I never had to worry about that "sissy" business again—a tremendous relief.

■ ■ ■

I often listened to my roommates—they were both seniors—studying for their theoretical physics course. One day they were working pretty hard on something that seemed pretty clear to me, so I said, "Why don't you use the Baronallai's equation?"

"What's that?" they exclaimed. "What are you talking about?"

I explained to them what I meant and how it worked in this case, and it solved the problem. It turned out it was Bernoulli's equation that I meant, but I had read all this stuff in the encyclopedia without talking to anybody about it, so I didn't know how to pronounce anything.

But my roommates were very excited, and from then on they discussed their physics problems with me—even though I wasn't so lucky with many of them—and the next year, when I took the course, I advanced rapidly. That was a very good way to get educated, working on the senior problems and learning how to pronounce things.

I liked to go to a place called the Raymor and Playmore Ballroom—two ballrooms that were connected together—on Tuesday nights. My fraternity brothers didn't go to these "open" dances; they preferred their own dances, where the girls they brought were upper crust ones they had met "properly." I didn't care, when I met somebody, where they were from, or what their background was, so I would go to these dances—even though my fraternity brothers disapproved (I was a junior by this time, and they couldn't stop me)—and I had a very good time.

One time I danced with a certain girl a few times, and didn't say much. Finally, she said to me, "Who hants vewwy nice-ee."

I couldn't quite make it out—she had some difficulty in speech—but I thought she said, "You dance very nicely."

"Thank you," I said. "It's been an honor."

We went over to a table where a friend of hers had found a boy she was dancing with and we sat, the four of us, together. One girl was very hard of hearing, and the other girl was nearly deaf.

When the two girls conversed they would do a large amount of signaling very rapidly back and forth, and grunt a little bit. It didn't bother me; the girl danced well, and she was a nice person.

After a few more dances, we're sitting at the table again, and there's a large amount of signaling back and forth, back and forth, back and forth, until finally she says something to me which I gathered means, she'd like us to take them to some hotel.

I ask the other guy if he wants to go.

"What do they want us to go to this hotel *for?*" he asks.

"Hell, I don't know—we didn't talk well enough!" But I don't *have* to know. It's just fun, seeing what's going to happen; it's an adventure!

The other guy's afraid, so he says no. So I take the two girls in a taxi to the hotel, and discover that there's a dance organized by the deaf and dumb, believe it or not—they all belonged to a club. It turns out many of them can feel the rhythm enough to dance to the music and applaud the band at the end of each number.

It was very, very interesting! I felt as if I was in a foreign country and couldn't speak the language: I could speak, but nobody could hear me. Everybody was talking with signs to everybody else, and I couldn't understand anything! I asked my girl to teach me some signs and I learned a few, like you learn a foreign language, just for fun.

Everyone was so happy and relaxed with each other, making jokes and smiling all the time; they didn't seem to have any real difficulty of any kind communicating with each other. It was the same as with any other language, except for one thing: as they're making signs to each other, their heads were always turning from one side to the other. I realized what that was: when someone wants to make a side remark or interrupt you, he can't yell, "Hey, Jack!"; he can only make a signal, which you won't catch unless you're in the habit of looking around all the time.

They were completely comfortable with each other. It was *my* problem to be comfortable. It was a wonderful experience.

The dance went on for a long time, and when it closed down we went to a cafeteria. They were all ordering things by pointing to them. I remember somebody asking in signs, "Where-are-you-from?" and my girl spelling out "N-e-w Y-o-r-k." I still remember a guy signing to me "Good sport!"—he holds his thumb up, and then touches an imaginary lapel, for "sport." It's a nice system.

Everybody was sitting around, making jokes, and getting me into their world very nicely. I wanted to buy a bottle of milk, so I went up to the guy at the counter and mouthed the world "milk" without saying anything.

The guy didn't understand.

I made the symbol for "milk," which is two fists moving as if you're milking a cow, and he didn't catch that either.

I tried to point to the sign that showed the price of milk, but he still didn't catch on.

Finally, some stranger nearby ordered milk, and I pointed to it.

"Oh! Milk!" he said, as I nodded my head yes.

He handed me the bottle, and I said, "Thank you very much!"

"You *son* of a *gun*!" he said, smiling.

■　　■　　■

I often liked to play tricks on people when I was at MIT. One time, in mechanical drawing class, some joker picked up a French curve (a piece of plastic for drawing smooth curves—a curly, funny-looking thing) and said, "I wonder if the curves on this thing have some special formula."

I thought for a moment and said, "Sure they do. The curves are very special curves. Lemme show ya," and I picked up my French curve and began to turn it slowly. "The French curve is made so that at the lowest point on each curve, no matter how you turn it, the tangent is horizontal."

All the guys in the class were holding their French curve up at different angles, holding their pencil up to it at the lowest point and laying it along, and discovering that, sure enough, the tangent is horizontal. They were all excited by this "discovery"—even though they had already gone through a certain amount of calculus and had already "learned" that the derivative (tangent) of the minimum (lowest point) of *any* curve is zero (horizontal). They didn't put two and two together. They didn't even know what they "knew."

I don't know what's the matter with people: they don't learn by understanding; they learn by some other way—by rote, or something. Their knowledge is so fragile.

I did the same kind of trick four years later at Princeton when I was talking with an experienced character, an assistant of Einstein, who was surely working with gravity all the time. I gave him a problem: You blast off in a rocket which has a clock on board, and there's a clock on the ground. The idea is that you have to be back when the clock on the ground says one hour has passed. Now you want it so that when you come back, your clock is as far ahead as possible. According to Einstein, if you go very high, your clock will go faster, because the higher something is in a gravitational field, the faster its clock goes. But if you try to go too high, since you've only got an hour, you have to go so fast to get there that the speed slows your clock down. So you can't go *too* high. The question is, exactly what program of speed and height should you make so that you get the maximum time on your clock?

This assistant of Einstein worked on it for quite a bit before he realized that the answer is the real motion of matter. If you shoot something up in a normal way, so that the time it takes to go up and come down is an hour, that's the correct motion. It's the fundamental principle of Einstein's gravity—that is, what's called the "proper time" is at a maximum for the actual curve. But when I put it to him, about a rocket with a clock, he didn't recognize it. It was just like the guys in mechanical drawing class, but this time it wasn't dumb freshmen. So this kind of fragility is, in fact, fairly common, even with more learned people.

*   *   *

When I was a junior or senior I used to eat at a certain restaurant in Boston. I went there by myself, often on successive evenings. People got to know me, and I had the same waitress all the time.

I noticed that they were always in a hurry, rushing around, so one day, just for fun, I left my tip, which was usually ten cents (normal for those days), in two nickels, under two glasses: I filled each glass to the very top, dropped a nickel in, and with a card over it, turned it over so it was upside down on the table. Then I slipped out the card (no water leaks out because no air can come in—the rim is too close to the table for that).

I put the tip under two glasses because I knew they were always in a hurry. If the tip was a dime in one glass, the waitress, in her haste to get the table ready for the next customer, would pick up the glass, the water would spill out, and that would be the end of it. But after she does that with the first glass, what the hell is she going to do with the second one? She can't just have the nerve to lift it up now!

On the way out I said to my waitress, "Be careful, Sue. There's something funny about the glasses you gave me—they're filled in on the top, and there's a hole on the bottom!"

The next day I came back, and I had a new waitress. My regular waitress wouldn't have anything to do with me. "Sue's very angry at you," my new waitress said. "After she picked up the first glass and water went all over the place, she called the boss out. They studied it a little bit, but they couldn't spend all day figuring out what to do, so they finally picked up the other one, and water went out *again*, all over the floor. It was a terrible mess."

I laughed.

She said, "It's not funny! How would *you* like it if someone did that to you—what would *you* do?"

"I'd get a soup plate and then slide the glass very carefully over to the edge of the table, and let the water run into the soup plate—it doesn't have to run onto the floor. Then I'd take the nickel out."

That evening I left my tip under a coffee cup, which I left upside down on the table.

The next night I came and I had the same new waitress.

"What's the idea of leaving the cup upside down last time?"

"Well, I thought that even though you were in a hurry, you'd have to go back into the kitchen and get a soup plate; then you'd have to sloooowly and carefully slide the cup over to the edge of the table . . ."

"I *did* that," she complained, "but there was no *water* in it!"

．　．　．

My masterpiece of mischief happened at the fraternity. One morning I woke up very early, about five o'clock, and couldn't go back to sleep, so I went downstairs from the sleeping rooms and discovered some signs hanging on strings which said things like "DOOR! DOOR! WHO STOLE THE DOOR?" I saw that someone had taken a door off its hinges, and in its place they hung a sign that said, "PLEASE CLOSE THE DOOR!"—the sign that used to be on the door that was missing.

I immediately figured out what the idea was. In that room a guy named Pete Bernays and a couple of other guys liked to work very hard, and always wanted it quiet. If you wandered into their room looking for something, or to ask them how they did problem such and such, when you would leave you would always hear these guys scream, "Please close the door!"

Somebody had gotten tired of this, no doubt, and had taken the door off. Now this room, it so happened, had two doors, the way it was built, so I got an idea: I took the other door off its hinges, carried it downstairs, and hid it in the basement behind the oil tank. Then I quietly went back upstairs and went to bed.

Later that morning I made believe I woke up and came downstairs a little late. The other guys were milling around, and Pete and his friends were all upset: The doors to their room were missing, and they had to study, blah, blah, blah, blah. I was coming down the stairs and they said, "Feynman! Did you take the doors?"

"Oh, yeah!" I said. "*I* took the door. You can see the scratches on my knuckles here, that I got when my hands scraped against the wall as I was carrying it down into the basement."

They weren't satisfied with my answer; in fact, they didn't believe me.

The guys who took the first door had left so many clues—the handwriting on the signs, for instance—that they were soon found out. My idea was that when it was found out who stole the first door, everybody would think they also stole the other door. It worked perfectly: The guys who took the first door were pummeled and tortured and worked on by everybody, until finally, with much pain and difficulty, they convinced their tormentors that they had only taken one door, unbelievable as it might be.

I listened to all this, and I was happy.

The other door stayed missing for a whole week, and it became more and more important to the guys who were trying to study in that room that the other door be found.

Finally, in order to solve the problem, the president of the fraternity says at the dinner table, "We have to solve this problem of the other door. I haven't been able to solve the problem myself, so I would like suggestions from the rest of you as to how to straighten this out, because Pete and the others are trying to study."

Somebody makes a suggestion, then someone else.

After a little while, I get up and make a suggestion. "All right," I say in a sarcastic voice, "whoever you are who stole the door, we know you're wonderful. You're so *clever!* We can't figure out *who* you are, so you must be some sort of super-genius. You don't have to tell us who you are; all we want to know is where the door is. So if you will leave a note somewhere, telling us where the door is, we will honor you and admit *forever* that you are a super-marvel, that you are so *smart* that you could take the other door without us being able to figure out who you are. But for god's sake, just leave the note somewhere, and we will be forever grateful to you for it."

The next guy makes his suggestion: "I have another idea," he says. "I think that you, as president, should ask each man on his word of honor towards the fraternity to say whether he took the door or not."

The president says, "That's a *very* good idea. On the fraternity word of honor!" So he goes around the table, and asks each guy, one by one: "Jack, did *you* take the door?"

"No, sir, I did not take the door."

"Tim: Did *you* take the door?"

"No, sir! I did not take the door!"

"Maurice. Did *you* take the door?"

"No, I did not take the door, sir."

"Feynman, did *you* take the door?"

"Yeah, I took the door."

"Cut it out, Feynman; this is *serious!* Sam! Did *you* take the door . . ."—it went all the way around. Everyone was *shocked.* There must be some real *rat* in the fraternity who didn't respect the fraternity word of honor!

That night I left a note with a little picture of the oil tank and the door next to it, and the next day they found the door and put it back.

Sometime later I finally admitted to taking the other door, and I was accused by everybody of lying. They couldn't remember what I had said. All they could remember was their conclusion after the president of the fraternity had gone around the table and asked everybody, that nobody admitted taking the door. The idea they remembered, but not the words.

People often think I'm a faker, but I'm usually honest, in a certain way—in such a way that often nobody believes me!

Always Trying
to Escape

When I was a student at MIT I was interested only in science; I was no good at anything else. But at MIT there was a rule: You have to take some humanities courses to get more "culture." Besides the English classes required were two electives, so I looked through the list, and right away I found astronomy—as a *humanities* course! So that year I escaped with astronomy. Then next year I looked further down the list, past French literature and courses like that, and found philosophy. It was the closest thing to science I could find.

Before I tell you what happened in philosophy, let me tell you about the English class. We had to write a number of themes. For instance, Mill had written something on liberty, and we had to criticize it. But instead of addressing myself to *political* liberty, as Mill did, I wrote about liberty in social occasions—the problem of having to fake and lie in order to be polite, and whether this perpetual game of faking in social situations leads to the "destruction of the moral fiber of society." An interesting question, but *not* the one we were supposed to discuss.

Another essay we had to criticize was by Huxley, "On a Piece of Chalk," in which he describes how an ordinary piece of chalk he is holding is the remains from animal bones, and the forces inside the earth lifted it up so that it became part of the White Cliffs, and then it was quarried and is now used to convey ideas through writing on the blackboard.

But again, instead of criticizing the essay assigned to us, I wrote a parody called, "On a Piece of Dust," about how dust makes the colors of the sunset and precipitates the rain, and so on. I was always a faker, always trying to escape.

But when we had to write a theme on Goethe's *Faust*, it was hopeless: The work was too long to make a parody of it or to invent something else. I was storming back and forth in the fraternity saying, "I can't do it. I'm just *not* gonna do it!"

One of my fraternity brothers said, "OK, Feynman, you're not gonna do it. But the professor will think you didn't do it because you don't want to do the work. You oughta write a theme on *something*—same number of words—and hand it in with a note saying that you just couldn't understand the *Faust*, you haven't got the heart for it, and that it's impossible for you to write a theme on it."

So I did that. I wrote a long theme, "On the Limitations of Reason." I had thought about scientific techniques for solving problems, and how there are certain limitations—moral values cannot be decided by scientific methods, yak, yak, yak, and so on.

Then another fraternity brother offered some more advice. "Feynman," he said, "it ain't gonna work, handing in a theme that's got nothing to do with *Faust*. What you oughta do is work that thing you wrote *into* the *Faust*."

"Ridiculous!" I said.

But the other fraternity guys think it's a good idea.

"All right, all right," I say, protesting. "I'll try."

So I added half a page to what I had already written, and said that Mephistopheles represents reason, and Faust represents the spirit, and Goethe is trying to show the limitations of reason. I stirred it up, cranked it all in, and handed in my theme.

The professor had us each come in individually to discuss our theme. I went in expecting the worst.

He said, "The introductory material is fine, but the *Faust* material is a bit too brief. Otherwise, it's very good—B+." I escaped again!

．　．　．

Now to the philosophy class. The course was taught by an old bearded professor named Robinson, who always mumbled. I would go to the class, and he would mumble along, and I couldn't understand a *thing*. The other people in the class seemed to understand him better, but they didn't seem to pay any attention. I happened to have a small drill, about one-sixteenth-inch, and to pass the time in that class, I would twist it between my fingers and drill holes in the sole of my shoe, week after week.

Finally one day at the end of the class, Professor Robinson went "wugga mugga mugga wugga wugga . . ." and everybody got excited! They were all talking to each other and discussing, so I figured he'd said something interesting, thank god! I wondered what it was.

I asked somebody, and they said, "We have to write a theme, and hand it in in four weeks."

"A theme on what?"

"On what he's been talking about all year."

I was stuck. The only thing that I had heard during that entire term that I could remember was a moment when there came this upwelling, "muggawuggastreamofconsciousnessmuggawugga," and *phoom*—it sank back into chaos.

This "stream of consciousness" reminded me of a problem my father had given to me many years before. He said, "Suppose some Martians were to come down to Earth, and that they never sleep, but instead are perpetually active. Suppose they didn't have this crazy phenomenon that we have, called sleep. So they ask you the question: 'How does it *feel* to go to sleep? What *happens* when you go to sleep? Do your thoughts suddenly stop, or do they move less aanndd lleeessss rraaaaapppppiiddddddlllllllllyyyyyyyyyyyyyyy? How does the mind actually turn off?' "

I got interested. Now I had a question to answer: How does the stream of consciousness *end*, when you go to sleep?

So every afternoon for the next four weeks I would work on my theme. I would pull down the shades in my room, turn off the lights, and go to sleep. And I'd watch what *happened*, when I went to sleep.

Then at night I'd go to sleep again, so I had two times each day when I could make observations—it was very good!

At first I noticed a lot of subsidiary things that had little to do with falling asleep. I noticed, for instance, that I did a lot of thinking by speaking to myself internally. I could also imagine things visually.

Then, when I was getting tired, I noticed that I could think of two things at once. I discovered this when I was talking internally to myself about something, and *while* I was doing this, I was idly imagining two ropes connected to the end of my bed, going through some pulleys, and winding around a turning cylinder, slowly lifting the bed. I wasn't *aware* that I was imagining these ropes until I began to worry that one rope would catch on the other rope, and they wouldn't wind up smoothly. But I said, internally, "Oh, the tension will take care of that," and this interrupted the first thought I was having, and made me aware that I was thinking of two things at once.

I also noticed that as you go to sleep the ideas continue, but they become less and less logically interconnected. You don't *notice* that they're not logically connected until you ask yourself, "What made me think of that?"—and you try to work your way back, and often you can't remember what the hell *did* make you think of that!

So you get every *illusion* of logical connection, but the actual fact is that the thoughts become more and more cockeyed until they're completely disjointed—and beyond that, you fall asleep.

After four weeks of sleeping all the time, I wrote my theme, and explained the observations I had made. At the end of the theme I pointed out that all of these observations were made while I was *watching* myself fall asleep, and I don't really know what it's like to fall asleep when I'm *not* watching myself. I concluded the theme with a little verse I made up, which pointed out this problem of introspection:

> I wonder why. I wonder why.
> I wonder why I wonder.
> I wonder *why* I wonder why
> I wonder why I wonder!

We hand in our themes, and the next time our class meets, the professor reads one of them: "Mum bum wugga mum bum . . ." I can't tell what the guy wrote.

He reads another theme: "Mugga wugga mum bum wugga wugga . . ." I don't know what that guy wrote either, but at the end of it, he goes:

> Uh wugga wuh. Uh wugga wuh.
> Uh wugga wugga wugga.
> Uh wugga *wuh* uh wugga wuh
> Uh wugga wugga wugga.

"Aha!" I say. "That's *my* theme!" I honestly didn't recognize it until the end.

After I had written the theme I continued to be curious, and I kept practicing this watching myself as I went to sleep. One night, while I was having a dream, I realized I was observing myself *in* the dream. I had gotten all the way down into the sleep itself!

In the first part of the dream I'm on top of a train and we're approaching a tunnel. I get scared, pull myself down, and we go into the tunnel—*whoosh!* I say to myself, "So you can get the feeling of fear, and you can hear the sound change when you go into the tunnel."

I also noticed that I could see colors. Some people had said that you dream in black and white, but no, I was dreaming in color.

By this time I was inside one of the train cars, and I can feel the train lurching about. I say to myself, "So you can get kinesthetic feelings in a dream." I walk with some difficulty down to the end of the car, and I see a big window, like a store window. Behind it there are—not mannequins, but three live girls in bathing suits, and they look pretty good!

I continue walking into the next car, hanging onto the straps overhead as I go, when I say to myself, "Hey! It would be interesting to get excited—sexually—so I think I'll go back into the other car. I discovered that I could turn around, and walk back through the train—I could control the direction of my dream. I get back to the car with the special window, and I see three old guys playing violins—but they turned back into girls! So I could modify the direction of my dream, but not perfectly.

Well, I began to get excited, intellectually as well as sexually, saying things like, "Wow! It's working!"—and I woke up.

I made some other observations while dreaming. Apart from always asking myself, "Am I *really* dreaming in color?" I wondered, "How accurately do you see something?"

The next time I had a dream, there was a girl lying in tall grass, and she had red hair. I tried to see if I could see *each* hair. You know how there's a little area of color just where the sun is reflecting—the diffraction effect, I could see *that!* I could see each hair as sharp as you want: perfect vision!

Another time I had a dream in which a thumbtack was stuck in a doorframe. I see the tack, run my fingers down the doorframe, and I feel the tack. So the "seeing department" and the "feeling department" of the brain seem to be connected. Then I say to myself, "Could it be that they *don't* have to be connected?" I look at the doorframe again, and there's no thumbtack. I run my finger down the doorframe, and I *feel* the tack!

Another time I'm dreaming and I hear "knock-knock; knock-knock." Something was happening in the dream that made this knocking fit in, but not perfectly—it seemed sort of foreign. I thought: "Absolutely guaranteed that this knocking is coming from *outside* my dream, and I've invented this part of the dream to fit with it. I've *got* to wake up and find out what the hell it is!"

The knocking is still going, I wake up, and . . . Dead silence. There was nothing. So it wasn't connected to the outside.

Other people have told me that they have incorporated external noises into their dreams, but when I had this experience, carefully "watching from below," and *sure* the noise was coming from outside the dream, it wasn't.

During the time of making observations in my dreams, the process of waking up was a rather fearful one. As you're beginning to wake up there's a moment when you feel rigid and tied down, or underneath many layers of cotton batting. It's hard to explain, but there's a moment when you get the feeling you can't get out; you're not sure you can wake up. So I would have to tell myself—after I was awake—that that's ridiculous. There's no disease I know of where a person falls asleep naturally and can't wake up. You can *always* wake up. And after talking to myself many times like that, I became less and less afraid, and in fact I found the process of waking up rather thrilling—something like a roller coaster: After a while you're not so scared, and you begin to enjoy it a little bit.

You might like to know how this process of observing my dreams stopped (which it has for the most part; it's happened just a few times since). I'm dreaming one night as usual, making observations, and I see on the wall in front of me a pennant. I answer for the twenty-fifth time, "Yes, I'm dreaming in color," and then I realize that I've been sleeping with the back of my head against a brass rod. I put my hand behind my head and I feel that the back of my head is *soft*. I think, "Aha! *That's* why I've been able to make all these observations in my dreams: the brass rod has disturbed my visual cortex. All I have to do is sleep with a brass rod under my head, and I can make these observations any time I want. So I think I'll stop making observations on this one, and go into deeper sleep."

When I woke up later, there was no brass rod, nor was the back of my head soft. Somehow I had become tired of making these observations, and my brain had invented some false reasons as to why I shouldn't do it any more.

As a result of these observations I began to get a little theory. One of the reasons that I liked to look at dreams was that I was curious as to how you can see an image—of a person, for example—when your eyes are closed, and nothing's coming in. You say it might be random, irregular nerve discharges, but you can't get the nerves to discharge in exactly the same delicate patterns when you are sleeping as when you are awake, looking at something. Well, then, how could I "see" in color, and in better detail, when I was asleep?

I decided there must be an "interpretation department." When you are actually looking at something—a man, a lamp, or a wall—you don't just see blotches of color. Something tells you what it is; it has to be interpreted. When you're dreaming, this interpretation department is still operating, but it's all slopped up. It's telling you that you're seeing a human hair in the greatest detail, when it isn't true: it's interpreting the random junk entering the brain as a clear image.

One other thing about dreams. I had a friend named Deutsch, whose wife was from a family of psychoanalysts in Vienna. One evening, during a long discussion about dreams, he told me that dreams have significance: there are symbols in dreams that can be interpreted psychoanalytically. I didn't believe most of this stuff, but that night I had an interesting dream: We're playing a game on a billiard table with three balls—a white ball, a green ball, and a gray ball—and the name of the game is "titsies." There was something about trying to get the balls into the pocket: the white ball and the green ball are easy to sink into the pocket, but the gray one, I can't get to it.

I wake up, and the dream is very easy to interpret: the name of the game gives it away, of course—them's girls! The white ball was easy to figure out, because I was going out, sneakily, with a married woman who worked at the time as a cashier in a cafeteria and wore a white uniform. The green one was also easy, because I had gone out about two nights before to a drive-in movie with a girl in a green dress. But the gray one—what the hell was the gray one? I knew it *had* to be *somebody;* I *felt* it. It's like when you're trying to remember a name, and it's on the tip of your tongue, but you can't get it.

It took me half a day before I remembered that I had said goodbye to a girl I liked very much, who had gone to Italy about two or three months before. She was a very nice girl, and I had decided that when she came back I was going to see her again. I don't know if she wore a gray suit, but it was perfectly clear, as soon as I thought of her, that she was the gray one.

I went back to my friend Deutsch, and I told him he must be right—there *is* something to analyzing dreams. But when he heard about my "interesting" dream, he said, "No, that one was too perfect—too cut and dried. Usually you have to do a bit more analysis."

THE CHIEF
RESEARCH CHEMIST
OF THE
METAPLAST CORPORATION

After I finished at MIT I wanted to get a summer job. I had applied two or three times to the Bell Labs, and had gone out a few times to visit. Bill Shockley, who knew me from the lab at MIT, would show me around each time, and I enjoyed those visits terrifically, but I never got a job there.

I had letters from some of my professors to two specific companies. One was to the Bausch and Lomb Company for tracing rays through lenses; the other was to Electrical Testing Labs in New York. At that time nobody knew what a physicist even was, and there weren't any positions in industry for physicists. Engineers, OK, but physicists—nobody knew how to use them. It's interesting that very soon, after the war, it was the exact opposite: people wanted physicists everywhere. So I wasn't getting anywhere as a physicist looking for a job late in the Depression.

About that time I met an old friend of mine by the name of Bernie Walker on the beach at our home town of Far Rockaway. We had gone to school together when we were about eleven or twelve, and were very good friends. We were both scientifically minded. He had a "laboratory," and I had a "laboratory." We often played together, and discussed things together.

We used to put on magic shows—chemistry magic—for the kids on the block. Bernie was a pretty good showman, and I kind of liked that too. We did our tricks on a little table, with Bunsen burners at each end going all the time. On the burners we had watch glass plates (flat glass discs) with iodine on them, which made a beautiful purple vapor that went up on each side of the table while the show went on. It was great! We did a lot of tricks, such as turning "wine" into water, and other chemical color changes. For our finale, we did a trick that used something which we had discovered. I would put my hands (secretly) first into a sink of water, and then into benzine. Then I would "accidentally" brush by one of the Bunsen burners, and one hand would light up. I'd clap my hands, and both hands would then be burning. (It doesn't hurt because it burns fast and the water keeps it cool.) Then I'd wave my hands, running around yelling, "FIRE! FIRE!" and everybody would get all excited. They'd run out of the room, and that was the end of the show.

Later on I told this story at college to my fraternity brothers and they said, "Nonsense! You can't *do* that."

(I often had this problem of demonstrating to these fellas something that they didn't believe—like the time we got into an argument as to whether urine just ran out of you by gravity, and I had to demonstrate that that wasn't the case by showing them that you can pee standing on your head. Or the time when somebody claimed that if you took aspirin and Coca-Cola you'd fall over in a dead faint directly. I told them I thought it was a lot of baloney, and offered to take aspirin and Coca-Cola together. Then they got into an argument whether you should have the aspirin before the Coke, just after the Coke, or mixed in the Coke. So I had six aspirin and three Cokes, one right after the other. First, I took two aspirins and then a Coke, then we dissolved two aspirins in a Coke and I took that, and then I took a Coke and two aspirins. Each time the idiots who believed it were standing around me, waiting to catch me when I fainted. But nothing happened. I do remember that I didn't sleep very well that night, so I got up and did a lot of figuring, and worked out some of the formulas for what is called the Riemann-Zeta function.)

"All right, guys," I said. "Let's go out and get some benzine."

They got the benzine ready, I stuck my hand in the water in the sink and then into the benzine and lit it . . . and it hurt like hell! You see, in the meantime I had grown *hairs* on the back of my hand, which acted like wicks and held the benzine in place while it burned, whereas when I had done it earlier I had no hairs on the back of my hand. (After I did that experiment for my fraternity brothers, I didn't have any hairs on the back of my hands either!)

Well, my pal Bernie and I met on the beach, and he told me that he had a process for metal-plating plastics. I said that was impossible, because there's no conductivity—you can't attach a wire. But he said he could metal-plate anything, and I still remember him picking up a peach pit that was in the sand, trying to impress me, and saying he could metal-plate *that*.

What was nice was that he offered me a job at his little company, which was on the top floor of a building in New York. There were only four people in the company. His father was the one who was getting the money together and was, I think, the "president." Bernie was the "vice-president," along with another fella who was a salesman. I was the "chief research chemist," and Bernie's brother, who was not very clever, was the bottle washer. We had six metal-plating baths.

Bernie had this process for metal-plating plastics, and the scheme was to first deposit silver on the object by precipitating silver from a silver nitrate bath with a reducing agent (like you make mirrors), then stick the object, with silver on it as a conductor, into an electroplating bath, and the silver gets plated.

The problem was, does the silver stick to the object?

It doesn't. It peels off easily. So there was a step in between, to make the silver stick better to the object. It depended on the material. For things like Bakelite, which was an important plastic in those days, Bernie had found that if he sandblasted it first, and then soaked it for many hours in stannous hydroxide, which got into the pores of the Bakelite, the silver would hold onto the surface very nicely.

But it worked only on a few plastics, and new kinds of plastics were coming out all the time, such as methyl methacrylate (which we now call plexiglass), that we couldn't plate directly, at first. And cellulose acetate, which was very cheap, was another one we couldn't plate at first, though we finally discovered that putting it in sodium hydroxide for a little while before using the stannous chloride made it plate very well.

I was pretty successful as a "chemist" in the company. My advantage was that my pal had done no chemistry at all: he had done no experiments; he just knew how to do something once. I set to work putting lots of different knobs in bottles, and putting all kinds of chemicals in. By trying everything and keeping track of everything I found ways of plating a wider range of plastics than he had done before.

I was also able to simplify his process. From looking in books I changed the reducing agent from glucose to formaldehyde, and was able to recover 100 percent of the silver immediately, instead of having to recover the silver left in solution at a later time.

I also got the stannous hydroxide to dissolve in water by adding a little bit of hydrochloric acid—something I remembered from a college chemistry course—so a step that used to take hours now took about five minutes.

My experiments were always being interrupted by the salesman, who would come back with some plastic from a prospective customer. I'd have all these bottles lined up, with everything marked, when all of a sudden, "You gotta stop the experiment to do a 'super job' for the sales department!" So, a lot of experiments had to be started more than once.

One time we got into one hell of a lot of trouble. There was an artist who was trying to make a picture for the cover of a magazine about automobiles. He had very carefully built a wheel out of plastic, and somehow or other this salesman had told him we could plate anything, so the artist wanted us to metal-plate the hub so it would be a shiny, silver hub. The wheel was made of a new plastic that we didn't know very well how to plate—the fact is, the salesman never knew what we *could* plate, so he was always promising things—and it didn't work the first time. So, to fix it up we had to get the old silver off, and we couldn't get it off easily. I decided to use concentrated nitric acid on it, which took the silver off all right, but also made pits and holes in the plastic. We were really in hot water *that* time! In fact, we had lots of "hot water" experiments.

The other fellas in the company decided we should run advertisements in *Modern Plastics* magazine. A few things we metal-plated were very pretty; they looked good in the advertisements. We also had a few things out in a showcase in front for prospective customers to look at, but nobody could pick up the things in the advertisements or in the showcase to see how well the plating stayed on. Perhaps some of them were, in fact, pretty good jobs. But they were made specially; they were not regular products.

Right after I left the company at the end of the summer to go to Princeton, they got a good offer from somebody who wanted to metal-plate plastic pens. Now people could have silver pens that were light, and easy, and cheap. The pens immediately sold, all over, and it was rather exciting to see people walking around everywhere with these pens—and you knew where they came from.

But the company hadn't had much experience with the material—or perhaps with the filler that was used in the plastic (most plastics aren't pure; they have a "filler," which in those days wasn't very well controlled)—and the darn things would develop a blister. When you have something in your hand that has a little blister that starts to peel, you can't help fiddling with it. So everybody was fiddling with all the peelings coming off the pens.

Now the company had this *emergency* problem to fix the pens, and

Bernie decided he needed a big microscope, and so on. He didn't know what he was going to look at, or why, and it cost his company a lot of money for this fake research. The result was, they had trouble. They never solved the problem, and the company failed, because their first big job was such a failure.

. . .

A few years later I was in Los Alamos, where there was a man named Frederic de Hoffman, who was a sort of scientist; but more, he was also very good at administrating. He liked mathematics, and worked very hard; he compensated for his lack of training by hard work. Later he became the president or vice president of General Atomics and he was a big industrial character after that. But at the time he was just a very energetic, open-eyed, enthusiastic boy, helping along with the Project as best he could.

One day we were eating at the Fuller Lodge, and he told me he had been working in England before coming to Los Alamos.

"What kind of work were you doing there?" I asked.

"I was working on a process for metal-plating plastics. I was one of the guys in the laboratory."

"How did it go?"

"It was going along pretty well, but we had our problems."

"Oh?"

"Just as we were beginning to develop our process, there was a company in New York . . ."

"*What* company in New York?"

"It was called the Metaplast Corporation. They were developed further than we were."

"How could you tell?"

"They were advertising all the time in *Modern Plastics* with full-page advertisements showing all the things they could plate, and we realized that they were further along than we were."

"Did you have any stuff from them?"

"No, but you could tell from the advertisements that they were way ahead of what we could do. Our process was pretty good, but it was no use trying to compete with an American process like that."

"How many chemists did you have working in the lab?"

"We had six chemists working."

"How many chemists do you think the Metaplast Corporation had?"

"Oh! They must have had a *real* chemistry department!"

"Would you describe for me what you think the chief research chemist at the Metaplast Corporation might look like, and how his laboratory might work?"

"I would guess they must have twenty-five or fifty chemists, and the chief research chemist has his own office—special, with glass. You know, like they have in the movies—guys coming in all the time with research projects that they're doing, getting his advice, and rushing off to do more research, people coming in and out all the time. With twenty-five or fifty chemists, how the hell could we compete with them?"

I laughed. "You'll be interested to know that you are now talking to the chief research chemist of the Metaplast Corporation—whose staff consisted of one bottle washer!"

THE
PRINCETON
YEARS

"Surely You're Joking,
Mr. Feynman!"

When I was an undergraduate at MIT I loved it. I thought it was a great place, and I wanted to go to graduate school there too, of course. But when I went to Professor Slater and told him of my intentions, he said, "We won't let you in here."

I said, "What?"

Slater asked, "Why do you think you should go to graduate school at MIT?"

"Because MIT is the best school for science in the country."

"You *think* that?"

"Yeah."

"That's why you should go to some other school. You should find out how the rest of the world is."

So I decided to go to Princeton. Now, Princeton had a certain aspect of elegance. It was an imitation of an English school, partly. So the guys in the fraternity, who knew my rather rough, informal manners, started making remarks like "Wait till they find out who they've got coming to Princeton! Wait till they see the mistake they made!" So I decided to try to be nice when I got to Princeton.

My father took me to Princeton in his car, I got my room, and he left. I hadn't been there an hour when I was met by a man: "I'm the Mahstah of Residences heah, and I should like to tell you that the Dean is having a Tea this ahftanoon, and he should like to have all of you come. Perhaps you would be so kind as to inform your roommate, Mr. Serette."

That was my introduction to the Graduate College at Princeton, where all the students lived. It was like an imitation Oxford or Cambridge—complete with accents (the master of residences was a professor of "French littrachaw"). There was a porter downstairs, everybody had nice rooms, and we ate all our meals together, wearing academic gowns, in a great hall that had stained-glass windows.

So the very afternoon I arrived in Princeton I'm going to the Dean's Tea, and I didn't even know what a "tea" was, or why. I had no social abilities whatsoever; I had no experience with this sort of thing.

So I come up to the door, and there's Dean Eisenhart, greeting the new students: "Oh, you're Mr. Feynman," he says. "We're glad to have you." So that helped a little, because he recognized me, somehow.

I go through the door, and there are some ladies, and some girls, too. It's all very formal and I'm thinking about where to sit down and should I sit next to this girl, or not, and how should I behave, when I hear a voice behind me.

"Would you like cream or lemon in your tea, Mr. Feynman?" It's Mrs. Eisenhart, pouring tea.

"I'll have both, thank you," I say, still looking for where I'm going to sit, when suddenly I hear "Heh-heh-heh-heh-heh. Surely you're *joking*, Mr. Feynman!"

Joking? Joking? What the hell did I just say? Then I realized what I had done. So that was my first experience with this tea business.

Later on, after I had been at Princeton longer, I got to understand this "Heh-heh-heh-heh-heh." In fact it was at that first tea, as I was leaving, that I realized it meant "You're making a social error." Because the *next* time I heard this same cackle, "Heh-heh-heh-heh-heh," from Mrs. Eisenhart, somebody was kissing her hand as he left.

Another time, perhaps a year later, at another tea, I was talking to Professor Wildt, an astronomer who had worked out some theory about the clouds on Venus. They were supposed to be formaldehyde (it's wonderful to know what we once worried about) and he had it all figured out, how the formaldehyde was precipitating, and so on. It was extremely interesting. We were talking about all this stuff, when a little lady came up and said, "Mr. Feynman, Mrs. Eisenhart would like to see you."

"OK, just a minute," and I kept talking to Wildt.

The little lady came back again and said, "Mr. *Feynman*, Mrs. Eisenhart would like to see you."

"OK, OK!" and I go over to Mrs. Eisenhart, who's pouring tea.

"Would you like to have some coffee or tea, Mr. Feynman?"

"Mrs. So-and-so says you wanted to talk to me."

"Heh-heh-heh-heh-heh. Would you like to have *coffee* or *tea*, Mr. Feynman?"

"Tea," I said, "thank you."

A few moments later Mrs. Eisenhart's daughter and a schoolmate came over, and we were introduced to each other. The whole idea of *this* "heh-heh-heh" was: Mrs. Eisenhart didn't want to talk to me, she wanted me over there getting tea when her daughter and friend came over, so they would have someone to talk to. That's the way it worked. By that time I knew what to do when I heard "Heh-heh-heh-heh-heh." I didn't say, "What do you mean, 'Heh-heh-heh-heh-heh'?"; I knew the "heh-heh-heh" meant "error," and I'd better get it straightened out.

Every night we wore academic gowns to dinner. The first night it scared the life out of me, because I didn't like formality. But I soon realized that the gowns were a great advantage. Guys who were out playing tennis could rush into their room, grab their academic gown, and put it on. They didn't have to take time off to change their clothes or take a shower. So underneath the gowns there were bare arms, T-shirts, everything. Furthermore, there was a rule that you never cleaned the gown, so you could tell a first-year man from a second-year man, from a third-year man, from a pig! You never cleaned the gown and you never repaired it, so the first-year men had very nice, relatively clean gowns, but by the time you got to the third year or so, it was nothing but some kind of cardboard thing on your shoulders with tatters hanging down from it.

So when I got to Princeton, I went to that tea on Sunday afternoon and had dinner that evening in an academic gown at the College. But on Monday, the first thing I wanted to do was to see the cyclotron.

■   ■   ■

MIT *had built a new cyclotron* while I was a student there, and it was just *beautiful!* The cyclotron itself was in one room, with the controls in another room. It was beautifully engineered. The wires ran from the control room to the cyclotron underneath in conduits, and there was a whole console of buttons and meters. It was what I would call a gold-plated cyclotron.

Now I had read a lot of papers on cyclotron experiments, and there weren't many from MIT. Maybe they were just starting. But there were lots of results from places like Cornell, and Berkeley, and above all, Princeton. Therefore what I really wanted to see, what I was looking forward to, was the PRINCETON CYCLOTRON. That must be *something!*

So first thing on Monday, I go into the physics building and ask, "Where is the cyclotron—which building?"

"It's downstairs, in the basement—at the end of the hall."

In the *basement?* It was an old building. There was no room in the basement for a cyclotron. I walked down to the end of the hall, went through the door, and in ten seconds I learned why Princeton was right for me—the best place for me to go to school. In this room there were wires strung *all over the place!* Switches were hanging from the wires, cooling water was dripping from the valves, the room was *full* of stuff, all out in the open. Tables piled with tools were everywhere; it was the most godawful mess you ever saw. The whole cyclotron was there in one room—it was complete, absolute chaos.

It reminded me of my lab at home. Nothing at MIT had ever reminded me of my lab at home. I suddenly realized why Princeton was getting results: They were working with the instrument. They *built* the instrument; they knew where everything was, they knew how everything worked; there was no engineer involved, except maybe he was working there too. It was much smaller than the cyclotron at MIT, and—"gold-plated?" It was the exact opposite. When they wanted to fix a vacuum, they'd drip glyptal on it, so there were drops of glyptal on the floor. It was wonderful, because they *worked* with it—they didn't have to sit in another room and push buttons. (Incidentally, they had a fire in that room, because of all the chaotic mess that they had—too many wires—and it destroyed the cyclotron. But I'd better not tell about that!)

(Years later, when I got to Cornell I went to look at the cyclotron there. This cyclotron hardly required a room: It was about a yard across—the diameter of the whole thing. It was the world's smallest cyclotron, but they had got fantastic results. They had all kinds of special techniques and tricks. If they wanted to change something in the "D's"—the D-shaped half circles that the particles go around—they'd take a screwdriver, and remove the D's by hand, fix them, and put them back. At Princeton it was a lot harder, and at MIT you had to take a crane that came rolling across the ceiling, lower the hooks, and it was a *hellllll* of a job.)

I learned a lot of different things from different schools. MIT is a *very* good place; I'm not trying to put it down. I was just in love with it. It has developed for itself a spirit, so that every member of the whole place thinks that it's the most wonderful place in the world—it's the *center*, somehow, of scientific and technological development in the United States, if not the world. It's like a New Yorker's view of New York: they forget the rest of the country. And while you don't get a good sense of proportion there, you do get an excellent sense of being *with* it and *in* it, and having motivation and desire to keep on—that you're specially chosen, and lucky to be there.

So MIT was good, but Slater was right to warn me to go to another school for my graduate work. And I often advise my students the same way. Learn what the rest of the world is like. The variety is worthwhile.

I once did an experiment in the cyclotron laboratory at Princeton that had some startling results. There was a problem in a hydrodynamics book that was being discussed by all the physics students. The problem is this: You have an S-shaped lawn sprinkler—an S-shaped pipe on a pivot—and the water squirts out at right angles to the axis and makes it spin in a certain direction. Everybody knows which way it goes around; it backs away from the outgoing water. Now the question is this: If you had a lake, or swimming pool—a big supply of water—and you put the sprinkler completely under water, and sucked the water in, instead of squirting it out, which way would it turn? Would it turn the same way as it does when you squirt water out into the air, or would it turn the other way?

The answer is perfectly clear at first sight. The trouble was, some guy would think it was perfectly clear one way, and another guy would think it was perfectly clear the other way. So everybody was discussing it. I remember at one particular seminar, or tea, somebody went up to Professor John Wheeler and said, "Which way do *you* think it goes around?"

Wheeler said, "Yesterday, Feynman convinced me that it went around backwards. Today, he's convinced me equally well that it goes around the other way. I don't know *what* he'll convince me of tomorrow!"

I'll tell you an argument that will make you think it's one way, and another argument that will make you think it's the other way, OK?

One argument is that when you're sucking water in, you're sort of pulling the water with the nozzle, so it will go forward, towards the incoming water.

But then another guy comes along and says, "Suppose we hold it still and ask what kind of a torque we need to hold it still. In the case of the water going out, we all know you have to hold it on the outside of the curve, because of the centrifugal force of the water going around the curve. Now, when the water goes around the same curve the *other* way, it still makes the same centrifugal force toward the outside of the curve. Therefore the two cases are the same, and the sprinkler will go around the same way, whether you're squirting water out or sucking it in."

After some thought, I finally made up my mind what the answer was, and in order to demonstrate it, I wanted to do an experiment.

In the Princeton cyclotron lab they had a big carboy—a monster bottle of water. I thought this was just great for the experiment. I got a piece of copper tubing and bent it into an S-shape. Then in the middle I drilled a hole, stuck in a piece of rubber hose, and led it up through a hole in a cork I had put in the top of the bottle. The cork had another hole, into which I put another piece of rubber hose, and connected it to the air pressure supply of the lab. By blowing air into the bottle, I could force water into the copper tubing exactly as if I were sucking it in. Now, the S-shaped tubing wouldn't turn around, but it would twist (because of the flexible rubber hose), and I was going to measure the speed of the water flow by measuring how far it squirted out of the top of the bottle.

I got it all set up, turned on the air supply, and it went *"Puup!"* The air pressure blew the cork out of the bottle. I wired it in very well, so it wouldn't jump out. Now the experiment was going pretty good. The water was coming out, and the hose was twisting, so I put a little more pressure on it, because with a higher speed, the measurements would be more accurate. I measured the angle very carefully, and measured the distance, and increased the pressure again. Suddenly the whole thing just blew: glass and water flew in all directions throughout the laboratory. A guy who had come to watch got all wet and had to go home and change his clothes—it's a miracle he didn't get cut by the glass—and lots of cloud chamber pictures that had been taken patiently using the cyclotron were all wet, but for some reason I was far enough away, or in some such position that I didn't get very wet. But I'll always remember how the great Professor Del Sasso, who was in charge of the cyclotron, came over to me and said sternly, "The freshman experiments should be done in the freshman laboratory!"

Mon∫ter Mind∫

While I was a graduate student at Princeton, I worked as a research assistant under John Wheeler. He gave me a problem to work on, and it got hard, and I wasn't getting anywhere. So I went back to an idea that I had had earlier, at MIT. The idea was that electrons don't act on themselves, they only act on other electrons.

There was this problem: When you shake an electron, it radiates energy, and so there's a loss. That means there must be a force on it. And there must be a different force when it's charged than when it's not charged. (If the force were exactly the same when it was charged and not charged, in one case it would lose energy, and in the other it wouldn't. You can't have two different answers to the same problem.)

The standard theory was that it was the electron acting on itself that made that force (called the force of radiation reaction), and I had only electrons acting on other electrons. So I was in some difficulty, I realized, by that time. (When I was at MIT, I got the idea without noticing the problem, but by the time I got to Princeton, I knew that problem.)

What I thought was: I'll shake this electron. It will make some nearby electron shake, and the effect back from the nearby electron would be the origin of the force of radiation reaction. So I did some calculations and took them to Wheeler.

Wheeler, right away, said, "Well, that isn't right because it varies inversely as the square of the distance of the other electrons, whereas it should not depend on any of these variables at all. It'll also depend inversely upon the mass of the other electron; it'll be proportional to the charge on the other electron."

What bothered me was, I thought he must have *done* the calculation. I only realized later that a man like Wheeler could immediately *see* all that stuff when you give him the problem. I had to calculate, but he could see.

Then he said, "And it'll be delayed—the wave returns late—so all you've described is reflected light."

"Oh! Of course," I said.

"But wait," he said. "Let's suppose it returns by advanced waves—reactions backward in time—so it comes back at the right time. We saw the effect varied inversely as the square of the distance, but suppose there are a lot of electrons, all over space: the number is proportional to the square of the distance. So maybe we can make it all compensate."

We found out we could do that. It came out very nicely, and fit very well. It was a classical theory that could be right, even though it differed from Maxwell's standard, or Lorentz's standard theory. It didn't have any trouble with the infinity of self-action, and it was ingenious. It had actions and delays, forwards and backwards in time—we called it "half-advanced and half-retarded potentials."

Wheeler and I thought the next problem was to turn to the quantum theory of electrodynamics, which had difficulties (I thought) with the self-action of the electron. We figured if we could get rid of the difficulty first in classical physics, and then make a quantum theory out of that, we could straighten out the quantum theory as well.

Now that we had got the classical theory right, Wheeler said, "Feynman, you're a young fella—you should give a seminar on this. You need experience in giving talks. Meanwhile, I'll work out the quantum theory part and give a seminar on that later."

So it was to be my first technical talk, and Wheeler made arrangements with Eugene Wigner to put it on the regular seminar schedule.

A day or two before the talk I saw Wigner in the hall. "Feynman," he said, "I think that work you're doing with Wheeler is very interesting, so I've invited Russell to the seminar." Henry Norris Russell, the famous, great astronomer of the day, was coming to my lecture!

Wigner went on. "I think Professor von Neumann would also be interested." Johnny Von Neumann was the greatest mathematician around. "And Professor Pauli is visiting from Switzerland, it so happens, so I've invited Professor Pauli to come"—Pauli was a very famous physicist—and by this time, I'm turning yellow. Finally, Wigner said, "Professor Einstein only rarely comes to our weekly seminars, but your work is so interesting that I've invited him specially, so he's coming, too."

By this time I must have turned green, because Wigner said, "No, no! Don't worry! I'll just warn you, though: If Professor Russell falls asleep—and he will undoubtedly fall asleep—it doesn't mean that your seminar is bad; he falls asleep in all the seminars. On the other hand, if Professor Pauli is nodding all the time, and seems to be in agreement as you go along, pay no attention. Professor Pauli has palsy."

I went back to Wheeler and named all the big, famous people who were coming to the talk he got me to give, and told him I was uneasy about it.

"It's all right," he said. "Don't worry. I'll answer all the questions."

So I prepared my talk, and when the day came, I went in and did something that young men who have had no experience in giving talks often do—I put too many equations up on the blackboard. You see, a young fella doesn't know how to say, "Of course that varies inversely, and this goes this way . . ." because everybody listening already knows; they can see it. But *he* doesn't know. He can only make it come out by actually doing the algebra—and therefore the reams of equations.

As I was writing these equations all over the blackboard ahead of time, Einstein came in and said pleasantly, "Hello, I'm coming to your seminar. But first, where is the tea?"

I told him (at least I answered Einstein's *first* question correctly!), and continued writing the equations.

Then the time came to give my talk, and here are these *monster minds* in front of me, waiting! My first technical talk, and I have *this* audience! I figured they would put me through the wringer. I remember very clearly seeing my hands shaking as they were pulling out my notes from a brown envelope.

But then a miracle occurred, as it has occurred again and again in my life, and it's very lucky for me: The moment I start to think about the physics and have to concentrate on what I'm explaining, nothing else occupies my mind—I'm completely immune to being nervous. So after I started to go, I just didn't know who was in the room. I was only explaining this idea, that's all.

But then the end of the seminar came, and it was time for questions. First off, Pauli, who was sitting next to Einstein, gets up and says, "I do not sink dis teory can be right, because of dis, and dis, and dis," and he turns to Einstein and says, "Don't you agree, Professor Einstein?"

Einstein says, "Nooooooooooooooo," a nice, German-sounding "No,"—very polite. "I find only that it would be very difficult to make a corresponding theory for gravitational interaction." He meant for the general theory of relativity, which was his baby. He continued: "Since we have at this time not a great deal of experimental evidence, I am not absolutely sure of the correct gravitational theory." Einstein appreciated that things might be different from what his theory stated; he was very tolerant of other ideas.

I wish I had remembered what Pauli said, because I discovered years later that the theory was not satisfactory when it came to making the quantum theory. It's possible that that great man noticed the difficulty immediately and explained it to me in the question, but I was so relieved at not having to answer the questions that I didn't really listen to them carefully. I do remember walking up the steps of Palmer Library with Pauli, who said to me, "What is Wheeler going to say about the quantum theory when he gives his talk?"

I said, "I don't know. He hasn't told me. He's working it out himself."

"Oh?" he said. "The man works and doesn't tell his assistant what he's doing on the quantum theory?" He came closer to me and said in a low, secretive voice, "Wheeler will never give that seminar."

And it's true—Wheeler didn't give the seminar. He thought it would be easy to work out the quantum part; he thought he had it, almost. But he didn't. And by the time the seminar came around, he realized he didn't know how to do it, and therefore didn't have anything to say.

I never solved it, either—a quantum theory of half-advanced, half-retarded potentials—and I worked on it for years.

A Different
Box of Tools

At the Princeton graduate school, the physics department and the math department shared a common lounge, and every day at four o'clock we would have tea. It was a way of relaxing in the afternoon, in addition to imitating an English college. People would sit around playing Go, or discussing theorems. In those days topology was the big thing.

I still remember a guy sitting on the couch, thinking very hard, and another guy standing in front of him, saying, "And therefore such-and-such is true."

"Why is that?" the guy on the couch asks.

"It's trivial! It's trivial!" the standing guy says, and he rapidly reels off a series of logical steps: "First you assume thus-and-so, then we have Kerchoff's this-and-that; then there's Waffenstoffer's Theorem, and we substitute this and construct that. Now you put the vector which goes around here and then thus-and-so . . ." The guy on the couch is struggling to understand all this stuff, which goes on at high speed for about fifteen minutes!

Finally the standing guy comes out the other end, and the guy on the couch says, "Yeah, yeah. It's trivial."

We physicists were laughing, trying to figure them out. We decided that "trivial" means "proved." So we joked with the mathematicians: "We have a new theorem—that mathematicians can prove only trivial theorems, because every theorem that's proved is trivial."

The mathematicians didn't like that theorem, and I teased them about it. I said there are never any surprises—that the mathematicians only prove things that are obvious.

Topology was not at all obvious to the mathematicians. There were all kinds of weird possibilities that were "counterintuitive." Then I got an idea. I challenged them: "I bet there isn't a single theorem that you can tell me—what the assumptions are and what the theorem is in terms I can understand—where I can't tell you right away whether it's true or false."

It often went like this: They would explain to me, "You've got an orange, OK? Now you cut the orange into a finite number of pieces, put it back together, and it's as big as the sun. True or false?"

"No holes?"

"No holes."

"Impossible! There ain't no such a thing."

"Ha! We got him! Everybody gather around! It's So-and-so's theorem of immeasurable measure!"

Just when they think they've got me, I remind them, "But you said an orange: You can't cut the orange peel any thinner than the atoms."

"But we have the condition of continuity: We can keep on cutting!"

"No, you said an orange, so I *assumed* that you meant a *real orange*."

So I always won. If I guessed it right, great. If I guessed it wrong, there was always something I could find in their simplification that they left out.

Actually, there was a certain amount of genuine quality to my guesses. I had a scheme, which I still use today when somebody is explaining something that I'm trying to understand: I keep making up examples. For instance, the mathematicians would come in with a terrific theorem, and they're all excited. As they're telling me the conditions of the theorem, I construct something which fits all the conditions. You know, you have a set (one ball)—disjoint (two balls). Then the balls turn colors, grow hairs, or whatever, in my head as they put more conditions on. Finally they state the theorem, which is some dumb thing about the ball that isn't true for my hairy green ball thing, so I say, "False!"

If it's true, they get all excited, and I let them go on for a while. Then I point out my counterexample.

"Oh. We forgot to tell you that it's Class 2 Hausdorff homomorphic."

"Well, then," I say, "It's trivial! It's trivial!" By that time I know which way it goes, even though I don't know what Hausdorff homomorphic means.

I guessed right most of the time because although the mathematicians thought their topology theorems were counterintuitive, they weren't really as difficult as they looked. You can get used to the funny properties of this ultra-fine cutting business and do a pretty good job of guessing how it will come out.

Although I gave the mathematicians a lot of trouble, they were always very kind to me. They were a happy bunch of boys who were developing things, and they were terrifically excited about it. They would discuss their "trivial" theorems, and always try to explain something to you if you asked a simple question.

Paul Olum and I shared a bathroom. We got to be good friends, and he tried to teach me mathematics. He got me up to homotopy groups, and at that point I gave up. But the things below that I understood fairly well.

One thing I never did learn was contour integration. I had learned to do integrals by various methods shown in a book that my high school physics teacher Mr. Bader had given me.

One day he told me to stay after class. "Feynman," he said, "you talk too much and you make too much noise. I know why. You're bored. So I'm going to give you a book. You go up there in the back, in the corner, and study this book, and when you know everything that's in it, you can talk again."

So every physics class, I paid no attention to what was going on with Pascal's Law, or whatever they were doing. I was up in the back with this book: *Advanced Calculus*, by Woods. Bader knew I had studied *Calculus for the Practical Man* a little bit, so he gave me the real works—it was for a junior or senior course in college. It had Fourier series, Bessel functions, determinants, elliptic functions—all kinds of wonderful stuff that I didn't know anything about.

That book also showed how to differentiate parameters under the integral sign—it's a certain operation. It turns out that it's not taught very much in the universities; they don't emphasize it. But I caught on how to use that method, and I used that one damn tool again and again. So because I was self-taught using that book, I had peculiar methods of doing integrals.

The result was, when guys at MIT or Princeton had trouble doing a certain integral, it was because they couldn't do it with the standard methods they had learned in school. If it was contour integration, they would have found it; if it was a simple series expansion, they would have found it. Then I come along and try differentiating under the integral sign, and often it worked. So I got a great reputation for doing integrals, only because my box of tools was different from everybody else's, and they had tried all their tools on it before giving the problem to me.

It's as Simple as One,
Two, Three . . .

When I was a kid growing up in Far Rockaway, I had a friend named Bernie Walker. We both had "labs" at home, and we would do various "experiments." One time, we were discussing something—we must have been eleven or twelve at the time—and I said, "Thinking is nothing but talking to yourself inside."

"Oh yeah?" Bernie said. "Do you know the crazy shape of the crankshaft in a car?"

"Yeah, what of it?"

"Good. Now, tell me: how did you describe it when you were talking to yourself?"

So I learned from Bernie that thoughts can be visual as well as verbal.

Later on, in college, I became interested in dreams. I wondered how things could look so real, just as if light were hitting the retina of the eye, while the eyes are closed: Are the nerve cells on the retina actually being stimulated in some other way—by the brain itself, perhaps—or does the brain have a "judgment department" that gets slopped up during dreaming? I never got satisfactory answers to such questions from psychology, even though I became very interested in how the brain works. Instead, there was all this business about interpreting dreams, and so on.

When I was in graduate school at Princeton a kind of dumb psychology paper came out that stirred up a lot of discussion. The author had decided that the thing controlling the "time sense" in the brain is a chemical reaction involving iron. I thought to myself, "Now, how the hell could he figure that?"

Well, the way he did it was, his wife had a chronic fever which went up and down a lot. Somehow he got the idea to test her sense of time. He had her count seconds to herself (without looking at a clock), and checked how long it took her to count up to 60. He had her counting—the poor woman—all during the day: when her fever went up, he found she counted quicker; when her fever went down, she counted slower. Therefore, he thought, the thing that governed the "time sense" in the brain must be running faster when she's got fever than when she hasn't got fever.

Being a very "scientific" guy, the psychologist knew that the rate of a chemical reaction varies with the surrounding temperature by a certain formula that depends on the energy of the reaction. He measured the differences in speed of his wife's counting, and determined how much the temperature changed the speed. Then he tried to find a chemical reaction whose rates varied with temperature in the same amounts as his wife's counting did. He found that iron reactions fit the pattern best. So he deduced that his wife's sense of time was governed by a chemical reaction in her body involving iron.

Well, it all seemed like a lot of baloney to me—there were so many things that could go wrong in his long chain of reasoning. But it *was* an interesting question: what *does* determine the "time sense"? When you're trying to count at an even rate, what does that rate depend on? And what could you do to yourself to change it?

I decided to investigate. I started by counting seconds—without looking at a clock, of course—up to 60 in a slow, steady rhythm: 1, 2, 3, 4, 5. . . . When I got to 60, only 48 seconds had gone by, but that didn't bother me: the problem was not to count for exactly one minute, but to count at a standard rate. The next time I counted to 60, 49 seconds had passed. The next time, 48. Then 47, 48, 49, 48, 48. . . . So I found I could count at a pretty standard rate.

Now, if I just sat there, without counting, and waited until I thought a minute had gone by, it was very irregular—complete variations. So I found it's very poor to estimate a minute by sheer guessing. But by counting, I could get very accurate.

Now that I knew I could count at a standard rate, the next question was: what affects the rate?

Maybe it has something to do with the heart rate. So I began to run up and down the stairs, up and down, to get my heart beating fast. Then I'd run into my room, throw myself down on the bed, and count up to 60.

I also tried running up and down the stairs and counting to myself *while* I was running up and down.

The other guys saw me running up and down the stairs, and laughed. "What are you doing?"

I couldn't answer them—which made me realize I couldn't talk while I was counting to myself—and kept right on running up and down the stairs, looking like an idiot.

(The guys at the graduate college were used to me looking like an idiot. On another occasion, for example, a guy came into my room—I had forgotten to lock the door during the "experiment"—and found me in a chair wearing my heavy sheepskin coat, leaning out of the wide-open window in the dead of winter, holding a pot in one hand and stirring with the other. "Don't bother me! Don't bother me!" I said. I was stirring Jell-O and watching it closely: I had gotten curious as to whether Jell-O would coagulate in the cold if you kept it moving all the time.)

Anyway, after trying every combination of running up and down the stairs and lying on the bed, surprise! The heart rate had no effect. And since I got very hot running up and down the stairs, I figured temperature had nothing to do with it either (although I must have known that your temperature doesn't really go up much when you exercise). In fact, I couldn't find anything that affected my rate of counting.

Running up and down stairs got pretty boring, so I started counting while I did things I had to do anyway. For instance, when I put out the laundry, I had to fill out a form saying how many shirts I had, how many pants, and so on. I found I could write down "3" in front of "pants" or "4" in front of "shirts," but I couldn't count my socks. There were too many of them: I'm already using my "counting machine"—36, 37, 38—and here are all these socks in front of me—39, 40, 41. . . . How do I count the socks?

I found I could arrange them in geometrical patterns—like a square, for example: a pair of socks in this corner, a pair in that one; a pair over here, and a pair over there—eight socks.

I continued this game of counting by patterns, and found I could count the lines in a newspaper article by grouping the lines into patterns of 3, 3, 3, and 1 to get 10; then 3 of those patterns, 3 of those patterns, 3 of those patterns, and 1 of those patterns made 100. I went right down the newspaper like that. After I had finished counting up to 60, I knew where I was in the patterns and could say, "I'm up to 60, and there are 113 lines." I found that I could even *read* the articles while I counted to 60, and it didn't affect the rate! In fact, I could do anything while counting to myself—except talk out loud, of course.

What about typing—copying words out of a book? I found that I could do that, too, but here my time was affected. I was excited: Finally, I've found something that appears to affect my counting rate! I investigated it more.

I would go along, typing the simple words rather fast, counting to myself 19, 20, 21, typing along, counting 27, 28, 29, typing along, until—What the hell is that word?—Oh, yeah—and then continue counting 30, 31, 32, and so on. When I'd get to 60, I'd be late.

After some introspection and further observation, I realized what must have happened: I would interrupt my counting when I got to a difficult word that "needed more brains," so to speak. My counting rate wasn't slowing down; rather, the counting itself was being held up temporarily from time to time. Counting to 60 had become so automatic that I didn't even notice the interruptions at first.

The next morning, over breakfast, I reported the results of all these experiments to the other guys at the table. I told them all the things I could do while counting to myself, and said the only thing I absolutely could not do while counting to myself was talk.

One of the guys, a fella named John Tukey, said, "I don't believe you can read, and I don't see why you can't talk. I'll bet you I can talk while counting to myself, and I'll bet you you can't read."

So I gave a demonstration. They gave me a book and I read it for a while, counting to myself. When I reached 60 I said, "Now!"—48 seconds, my regular time. Then I told them what I had read.

Tukey was amazed. After we checked him a few times to see what his regular time was, he started talking: "Mary had a little lamb; I can say anything I want to, it doesn't make any difference; I don't know what's bothering you"—blah, blah, blah, and finally, "Okay!" He hit his time right on the nose. I couldn't believe it!

We talked about it a while, and we discovered something. It turned out that Tukey was counting in a different way: He was visualizing a tape with numbers on it going by. He would say, "Mary had a little lamb," and he would *watch* it! Well, now it was clear: He's "looking" at his tape going by, so he can't read, and I'm "talking" to myself when I'm counting, so I can't speak!

After that discovery, I tried to figure out a way of reading out loud while counting—something neither of us could do. I figured I'd have to use a part of my brain that wouldn't interfere with the seeing or speaking departments, so I decided to use my fingers, since that involved the sense of touch.

I soon succeeded in counting with my fingers and reading out loud. But I wanted the whole process to be mental, and not rely on any physical activity. So I tried to imagine the feeling of my fingers moving while I was reading out loud.

I never succeeded. I figured that was because I hadn't practiced enough, but it might be impossible—I've never met anybody who can do it.

By that experience Tukey and I discovered that what goes on in different people's heads when they *think* they're doing the same thing—something as simple as *counting*—is different for different people. And we discovered that you can externally and objectively test how the brain works: You don't have to ask a person how he counts and rely on his own observations of himself; instead, you observe what he can and can't do while he counts. The test is absolute. There's no way to beat it; no way to fake it.

It's natural to explain an idea in terms of what you already have in your head. Concepts are piled on top of each other: This idea is taught in terms of that idea, and that idea is taught in terms of another idea, which comes from counting, which can be so different for different people!

I often think about that, especially when I'm teaching some esoteric technique such as integrating Bessel functions. When I see equations, I see the letters in colors—I don't know why. As I'm talking, I see vague pictures of Bessel functions from Jahnke and Emde's book, with light-tan j's, slightly violet-bluish n's, and dark brown x's flying around. And I wonder what the hell it must look like to the students.

MEEEEEEEEEE!

On Wednesdays at the Princeton Graduate College, various people would come in to give talks. The speakers were often interesting, and in the discussions after the talks we used to have a lot of fun. For instance, one guy in our school was very strongly anti-Catholic, so he passed out questions in advance for people to ask a religious speaker, and we gave the speaker a hard time.

Another time somebody gave a talk about poetry. He talked about the structure of the poem and the emotions that come with it; he divided everything up into certain kinds of classes. In the discussion that came afterwards, he said, "Isn't that the same as in mathematics, Dr. Eisenhart?"

Dr. Eisenhart was the dean of the graduate school and a great professor of mathematics. He was also very clever. He said, "I'd like to know what Dick Feynman thinks about it in reference to theoretical physics." He was always putting me on in this kind of situation.

I got up and said, "Yes, it's very closely related. In theoretical physics, the analog of the word is the mathematical formula, the analog of the structure of the poem is the interrelationship of the theoretical such-and-such with the so-and-so"—and I went through the whole thing, making a perfect analogy. The speaker's eyes were *beaming* with happiness.

Then I said, "It seems to me that no matter *what* you say about poetry, I could find a way of making up an analog with *any* subject, just as I did for theoretical physics. I don't consider such analogs meaningful."

In the great big dining hall with stained-glass windows, where we always ate in our steadily deteriorating academic gowns, Dean Eisenhart would begin each dinner by saying grace in Latin. After dinner he would often get up and make some announcements. One night Dr. Eisenhart got up and said, "Two weeks from now, a professor of psychology is coming to give a talk about hypnosis. Now, this professor thought it would be much better if we had a real demonstration of hypnosis instead of just talking about it. Therefore he would like some people to volunteer to be hypnotized . . ."

I get all excited: There's no question but that I've *got* to find out about hypnosis. This is going to be terrific!

Dean Eisenhart went on to say that it would be good if three or four people would volunteer so that the hypnotist could try them out first to see which ones would be able to be hypnotized, so he'd like to urge very much that we apply for this. (*He's wasting all this time*, for god's sake!)

Eisenhart was down at one end of the hall, and I was way down at the other end, in the back. There were hundreds of guys there. I knew that everybody was going to want to do this, and I was terrified that he wouldn't see me because I was so far back. I just *had* to get in on this demonstration!

Finally Eisenhart said, "And so I would like to ask if there are going to be any volunteers . . ."

I raised my hand and shot out of my seat, screaming as loud as I could, to make sure that he would hear my voice: "MEEEEEEEEEE!"

He heard me all right, because there wasn't another soul. My voice reverberated throughout the hall—it was very embarrassing. Eisenhart's immediate reaction was, "Yes, of course, I knew *you* would volunteer, Mr. Feynman, but I was wondering if there would be anybody *else*."

Finally a few other guys volunteered, and a week before the demonstration the man came to practice on us, to see if any of us would be good for hypnosis. I knew about the phenomenon, but I didn't know what it was like to be hypnotized.

He started to work on me and soon I got into a position where he said, "You can't open your eyes."

I said to myself, "I bet I could open my eyes, but I don't want to disturb the situation—let's see how much further it goes." It was an interesting situation: You're only slightly fogged out, and although you've lost a little bit, you're pretty sure you *could* open your eyes. But, of course, you're *not* opening your eyes . . .

He went through a lot of stuff and decided that I was pretty good.

When the real demonstration came he had us walk on stage, and he hypnotized us in front of the whole Princeton Graduate College. This time the effect was stronger; I guess I had learned how to become hypnotized. The hypnotist made various demonstrations, having me do things that I couldn't normally do, and at the end he said that after I came out of hypnosis, instead of returning to my seat directly, which was the natural way to go, I would walk all the way around the room and go to my seat from the back.

All through the demonstration I was vaguely aware of what was going on, and cooperating with the things the hypnotist said, but this time I decided, "Damn it, enough is enough! I'm gonna go straight to my seat."

When it was time to get up and go off the stage, I started to walk straight to my seat. But then an annoying feeling came over me: I felt so uncomfortable that I couldn't continue. I walked all the way around the hall.

I was hypnotized in another situation some time later by a woman. While I was hypnotized she said, "I'm going to light a match, blow it out, and immediately touch the back of your hand with it. You will feel no pain."

I thought, "Baloney!" She took a match, lit it, blew it out, and touched it to the back of my hand. It felt slightly warm. My eyes were closed through out all of this, but I was thinking, "That's easy. She lit one match, but touched a different match to my hand. There's nothin' to *that;* it's a fake!"

When I came out of the hypnosis and looked at the back of my hand, I got the biggest surprise: There was a burn on the back of my hand. Soon a blister grew, and it never hurt at all, even when it broke.

So I found hypnosis to be a very interesting experience. All the time you're saying to yourself, "I could do that, but I won't"—which is just another way of saying that you can't.

MIND READER∫

My father was always interested in magic and carnival tricks, and wanting to see how they worked. One of the things he knew about was mind readers. When he was a little boy, growing up in a small town called Patchogue in the middle of Long Island, it was announced on advertisements posted all over that a mind reader was coming next Wednesday. The posters said that some respected citizens—the mayor, a judge, a banker—should take a five-dollar bill and hide it somewhere, and when the mind reader came to town, he would find it.

When he came, the people gathered around to watch him do his work. He takes the hands of the banker and the judge, who had hidden the five-dollar bill, and starts to walk down the street. He gets to an intersection, turns the corner, walks down another street, then another, to the correct house. He goes with them, always holding their hands, into the house, up to the second floor, into the right room, walks up to a bureau, lets go of their hands, opens the correct drawer, and there's the five-dollar bill. Very dramatic!

In those days it was difficult to get a good education, so the mind reader was hired as a tutor for my father. Well, my father, after one of his lessons, asked the mind reader how he was able to find the money without anyone telling him where it was.

The mind reader explained that you hold onto their hands, loosely, and as you move, you jiggle a little bit. You come to an intersection, where you can go forward, to the left, or to the right. You jiggle a little bit to the left, and if it's incorrect, you feel a certain amount of resistance, because they don't expect you to move that way. But when you move in the right direction, because they think you might be able to do it, they give way more easily, and there's less resistance. So you must be always be jiggling a little bit, testing out which seems to be the easiest way.

My father told me the story and said he thought it would still take a lot of practice. He never tried it himself.

Later, when I was doing graduate work at Princeton, I decided to try it on a fellow named Bill Woodward. I suddenly announced that I was a mind reader, and could read his mind. I told him to go into the "laboratory"—a big room with rows of tables covered with equipment of various kinds, with electric circuits, tools, and junk all over the place—pick out a certain object, somewhere, and come out. I explained, "Now I'll read your mind and take you right up to the object."

He went into the lab, noted a particular object, and came out. I took his hand and started jiggling. We went down this aisle, then that one, right to the object. We tried it three times. One time I got the object right on—and it was in the middle of a whole bunch of stuff. Another time I went to the right place but missed the object by a few inches—wrong object. The third time, something went wrong. But it worked better than I thought. It was easy.

Some time after that, when I was about twenty-six or so, my father and I went to Atlantic City, where they had various carnival things going on outdoors. While my father was doing some business, I went to see a mind reader. He was seated on the stage with his back to the audience, dressed in robes and wearing a great big turban. He had an assistant, a little guy who was running around through the audience, saying things like, "Oh, Great Master, what is the color of this pocketbook?"

"Blue!" says the master.

"And oh, Illustrious Sir, what is the name of this woman?"

"Marie!"

Some guy gets up: "What's my name?"

"Henry."

I get up and say, "What's *my* name?"

He doesn't answer. The other guy was obviously a confederate, but I couldn't figure out how the mind reader did the other tricks, like telling the color of the pocketbook. Did he wear earphones underneath the turban?

When I met up with my father, I told him about it. He said, "They have a code worked out, but I don't know what it is. Let's go back and find out."

We went back to the place, and my father said to me, "Here's fifty cents. Go get your fortune read in the booth back there, and I'll see you in half an hour."

I knew what he was doing. He was going to tell the man a story, and it would go smoother if his son wasn't there going, "Ooh, ooh!" all the time. He had to get me out of the way.

When he came back he told me the whole code: "Blue is 'Oh, Great Master,' Green is 'Oh, Most Knowledgeable One,' " and so forth. He explained, "I went up to him, afterwards, and told him I used to do a show in Patchogue, and we had a code, but it couldn't do many numbers, and the range of colors was shorter. I asked him, 'How do you carry so much information?' "

The mind reader was so proud of his code that he sat down and explained the *whole works* to my father. My father was a salesman—he could set up a situation like that. I can't do stuff like that.

MIXING PAINTS

The reason why I say I'm "uncultured" or "anti-intellectual" probably goes all the way back to the time when I was in high school. I was always worried about being a sissy; I didn't want to be too delicate. To me, no *real* man ever paid any attention to poetry and such things. How poetry ever got *written*—that never struck me! So I developed a negative attitude toward the guy who studies French literature, or studies too much music or poetry—all those "fancy" things. I admired better the steelworker, the welder, or the machine shop man. I always thought the guy who worked in the machine shop and could make things, now *he* was a *real guy*. That was my attitude. To be a practical man was, to me, always a positive virtue, and to be "cultured" or "intellectual" was not. The first was right, of course, but the second was crazy.

I still had this feeling when I was doing my graduate study at Princeton, as you'll see. I used to eat often in a nice little restaurant called Papa's Place. One day, while I was eating there, a painter in his painting clothes came down from an upstairs room he'd been painting, and sat near me. Somehow we struck up a conversation and he started talking about how you've got to learn a lot to be in the painting business. "For example," he said, "in this restaurant, what colors would you use to paint the walls, if *you* had the job to do?"

I said I didn't know, and he said, "You have a dark band up to such-and-such a height, because, you see, people who sit at the tables rub their elbows against the walls, so you don't want a nice, white wall there—it gets dirty too easily. But above that, you *do* want it white to give a feeling of cleanliness to the restaurant."

The guy seemed to know what he was doing, and I was sitting there, hanging on his words, when he said, "And you also have to know about colors—how to get different colors when you mix the paint. For example, what colors would *you* mix to get yellow?"

I didn't know how to get yellow by mixing paints. If it's *light*, you mix green and red, but I knew he was talking *paints*. So I said, "I don't know how you get yellow without using yellow."

"Well," he said, "if you mix red and white, you'll get yellow."

"Are you sure you don't mean *pink?*"

"No," he said, "you'll get yellow"—and I believed that he got yellow, because he was a professional painter, and I always admired guys like that. But I still wondered how he did it.

I got an idea. "It must be some kind of *chemical* change. Were you using some special kind of pigments that make a chemical change?"

"No," he said, "any old pigments will work. You go down to the five-and-ten and get some paint—just a regular can of red paint and a regular can of white paint—and I'll mix 'em, and I'll show how you get yellow."

At this juncture I was thinking, "Something is crazy. I know enough about paints to know you won't get yellow, but *he* must know that you *do* get yellow, and therefore something interesting happens. I've got to see what it is!"

So I said, "OK, I'll get the paints."

The painter went back upstairs to finish his painting job, and the restaurant owner came over and said to me, "What's the idea of arguing with that man? The man is a painter; he's been a painter all his life, and *he* says he gets yellow. So why argue with him?"

I felt embarrassed. I didn't know what to say. Finally I said, "All my life, I've been studying light. And I think that with red and white you *can't* get yellow—you can only get pink."

So I went to the five-and-ten and got the paint, and brought it back to the restaurant. The painter came down from upstairs, and the restaurant owner was there too. I put the cans of paint on an old chair, and the painter began to mix the paint. He put a little more red, he put a little more white—it still looked pink to me—and he mixed some more. Then he mumbled something like, "I used to have a little tube of yellow here, to sharpen it up a bit—then this'll be yellow."

"Oh!" I said. "Of course! You add yellow, and you can get yellow, but you couldn't do it without the yellow."

The painter went back upstairs to paint.

The restaurant owner said, "That guy has his nerve, arguing with a guy who's studied light all his life!"

But that shows you how much I trusted these "real guys." The painter had told me so much stuff that was reasonable that I was ready to give a certain chance that there was an odd phenomenon I didn't know. I was expecting pink, but my set of thoughts were, "The only way to get yellow will be something new and interesting, and I've got to see this."

I've very often made mistakes in my physics by thinking the theory isn't as good as it really is, thinking that there are lots of complications that are going to spoil it—an attitude that anything can happen, in spite of what you're pretty sure should happen.

LATIN OR ITALIAN?

There was an Italian radio station in Brooklyn, and as a boy I used to listen to it all the time. I LOVed the ROLLing SOUNds going over me, as if I was in the ocean and the waves weren't too high. I used to sit there and have the water come over me, in this BEAUtiful iTALian. In the Italian programs there was always some kind of family situation where there were discussions and arguments between the mother and father.

High voice: "*Nio teco TIEto capeto TUtto . . .*"

Loud, low voice: "*DRO tone pala TUtto!!*" (with hand slapping).

It was great! So I learned to make all these emotions: I could cry; I could laugh; all this stuff. Italian is a lovely language.

There were a number of Italian people living near us in New York. Once while I was riding my bicycle, some Italian truck driver got upset at me, leaned out of his truck, and, gesturing, yelled something like, "*Me aRRUcha LAMpe etta TIche!*"

I felt like a crapper. What did he say to me? What should I yell back?

So I asked an Italian friend of mine at school, and he said, "Just say, '*A te! A te!*'—which means 'The same to you! The same to you!'"

I thought it was a great idea. I would say "*A te! A te!*" back—gesturing, of course. Then, as I gained confidence, I developed my abilities further. I would be riding my bicycle, and some lady would be driving in her car and get in the way, and I'd say, "*PUzzia a la maLOche!*"—and she'd shrink! Some terrible Italian boy had cursed a terrible curse at her!

It was not so easy to recognize it as fake Italian. Once, when I was at Princeton, as I was going into the parking lot at Palmer Laboratory on my bicycle, somebody got in the way. My habit was always the same: I gesture to the guy, "*oREzze caBONca MIche!*", slapping the back of one hand against the other.

And way up on the other side of a long area of grass, there's an

Italian gardener putting in some plants. He stops, waves, and shouts happily, "*REzza ma LIa!*"

I call back, "*RONte BALta!*", returning the greeting. He didn't know I didn't know, and I didn't know what he said, and he didn't know what I said. But it was OK! After all, when they hear the intonation, they recognize it immediately as Italian—maybe it's Milano instead of Romano, what the hell. But he's an iTALian! So it's just great. But you have to have absolute confidence. Keep right on going, and nothing will happen.

One time I came home from college for a vacation, and my sister was sort of unhappy, almost crying: her Girl Scouts were having a father-daughter banquet, but our father was out on the road, selling uniforms. So I said I would take her, being the brother. (I'm nine years older, so it wasn't so crazy.)

When we got there, I sat among the fathers for a while, but soon became sick of them. All these fathers bring their daughters to this nice little banquet, and all they talk about is the stock market—they don't know how to talk to their own children, much less their children's friends.

During the banquet the girls entertained us by doing little skits, reciting poetry, and so on. Then all of a sudden they bring out this funny-looking, apron-like thing, with a hole at the top to put your head through. The girls announce that the fathers are now going to entertain *them*.

So each father has to get up and stick his head through and say something—one guy recites "Mary Had a Little Lamb"; they don't know what to do. I didn't know what to do either, but by the time I got up there, I told them that I was going to recite a little poem, and I'm sorry that it's not in English, but I'm sure they will appreciate it anyway:

A TUZZO LANTO
—Poici di Pare

TANto SAca TULna TI, na PUta TUchi PUti TI la.
RUNto CAta CANto CIANta MANto CHI la TI da.
YALta CAra SULda MI la CHAta PIcha PIno TIto BRALda
Pe te CHIna nana CIUNda lala CINda lala CIUNda!
RONto piti CA le, a TANto CINto quinta LALda
O la TINta dalla LALta, IENta PUcha lalla TALta!

I do this for three or four stanzas, going through all the emotions that I heard on Italian radio, and the kids are unraveled, rolling in the aisles, laughing with happiness.

After the banquet was over, the scoutmaster and a schoolteacher came over and told me they had been discussing my poem. One of them thought it was Italian, and the other thought it was Latin. The schoolteacher asks, "Which one of us is right?"

I said, "You'll have to go ask the girls—they understood what language it was right away."

ARLENE

"What Do You Care
What Other People
Think?"

When I was a young fella, about thirteen, I had somehow gotten in with a group of guys who were a little older than I was, and more sophisticated. They knew a lot of different girls, and would go out with them—often to the beach.

One time when we were at the beach, most of the guys had gone out on some jetty with the girls. I was interested in a particular girl a little bit, and sort of thought out loud: "Gee, I think I'd like to take Barbara to the movies . . ."

That's all I had to say, and the guy next to me gets all excited. He runs out onto the rocks and finds her. He pushes her back, all the while saying in a loud voice, "Feynman has something he wants to say to you, Barbara!" It was most embarrassing.

Pretty soon the guys are all standing around me, saying, "Well, *say* it, Feynman!" So I invited her to the movies. It was my first date.

I went home and told my mother about it. She gave me all kinds of advice on how to do this and that. For example, if we take the bus, I'm supposed to get off the bus first, and offer Barbara my hand. Or if we have to walk in the street, I'm supposed to walk on the outside. She even told me what kinds of things to say. She was handing down a cultural tradition to me: The women teach their sons how to treat the next generation of women well.

After dinner, I get all slicked up and go to Barbara's house to call for her. I'm nervous. She isn't ready, of course (it was always like that), so her family has me wait for her in the dining room, where they're eating with friends—a lot of people. They say things like, "Isn't he cute!" and all kinds of other stuff. I didn't feel cute. It was absolutely terrible!

I remember everything about the date. As we walked from her house to the new, little theater in town, we talked about playing the piano. I told her how, when I was younger, they made me learn piano for a while, but after six months I was still playing "Dance of the Daisies" and couldn't stand it any more. You see, I was worried about being a sissy, and to be stuck for weeks playing "Dance of the Daisies" was too much for me, so I quit. I was so sensitive about being a sissy that it even bothered me when my mother sent me to the market to buy some snacks called Peppermint Patties and Toasted Dainties.

We saw the movie, and I walked her back to her home. I complimented her on the nice, pretty gloves she was wearing. Then I said goodnight to her on the doorstep.

Barbara says to me, "Thank you for a very lovely evening."

"You're welcome!" I answered. I felt terrific.

The next time I went out on a date—it was with a different girl—I say goodnight to her, and she says, "Thank you for a very lovely evening."

I didn't feel quite so terrific.

When I said goodnight to the third girl I took out, she's got her mouth open, ready to speak, and I say, "Thank you for a very lovely evening!"

She says, "Thank you—uh—Oh!—Yes—uh, I had a lovely evening, too, thank you!"

.   .   .

One time I was at a party with my beach crowd, and one of the older guys was in the kitchen teaching us how to kiss, using his girlfriend to demonstrate: "You have to have your lips like this, at right angles, so the noses don't collide," and so on. So I go into the living room and find a girl. I'm sitting on the couch with my arm around her, practicing this new art, when suddenly there's all kinds of excitement: "Arlene is coming! Arlene is coming!" I don't know who Arlene is.

Then someone says, "She's here! She's here!"—and everybody stops what they're doing and jumps up to see this queen. Arlene was very pretty, and I could see why she had all this admiration—it was well deserved—but I didn't believe in this undemocratic business of changing what you're doing just because the queen is coming in.

So, while everybody's going over to see Arlene, I'm still sitting there on the couch with my girl.

(Arlene told me later, after I had gotten to know her, that she remembered that party with all the nice people—except for one guy who was over in the corner on the couch smooching with a girl. What she didn't know was that two minutes before, all the others were doin' it too!)

The first time I ever said anything to Arlene was at a dance. She was very popular, and everybody was cutting in and dancing with her. I remember thinking I'd like to dance with her, too, and trying to decide when to cut in. I always had trouble with that problem: First of all, when she's over on the other side of the dance floor dancing with some guy, it's too complicated—so you wait until they come closer. Then when she's near you, you think, "Well, no, this isn't the kind of music I'm good at dancing to." So you wait for another type of music. When the music changes to something you like, you sort of step forward—at least you *think* you step forward to cut in—when some other guy cuts in just in front of you. So now you have to wait a few minutes because it's impolite to cut in too soon after someone else has. And by the time a few minutes have passed, they're over at the other side of the dance floor again, or the music has changed again, or whatever!

After a certain amount of this stalling and fooling around, I finally mutter something about wanting to dance with Arlene. One of the guys I was hanging around with overhears me and makes a big announcement to the other guys: "Hey, listen to this, guys; Feynman wants to dance with Arlene!" Soon one of them is dancing with Arlene and they dance over towards the rest of us. The others push me out onto the dance floor and I finally "cut in." You can see the condition I was in by my first words to her, which were an honest question: "How does it feel to be so popular?" We only danced a few minutes before somebody else cut in.

My friends and I had taken dancing lessons, although none of us would ever admit it. In those Depression days, a friend of my mother was trying to make a living by teaching dancing in the evening, in an upstairs dance studio. There was a back door to the place, and she arranged it so the young men could come up through the back way without being seen.

Every once in a while there would be a social dance at this lady's studio. I didn't have the nerve to test this analysis, but it seemed to me that the girls had a much harder time than the boys did. In those days, girls couldn't ask to cut in and dance with boys; it wasn't "proper." So the girls who weren't very pretty would sit for hours at the side, just sad as hell.

I thought, "The guys have it easy: they're free to cut in whenever they want." But it wasn't easy. You're "free," but you haven't got the guts, or the sense, or whatever it takes to relax and enjoy dancing.

Instead, you tie yourself in knots worrying about cutting in or inviting a girl to dance with you.

For example, if you saw a girl who was not dancing, who you thought you'd like to dance with, you might think, "Good! Now at least I've got a chance!" But it was usually very difficult: often the girl would say, "No, thank you, I'm tired. I think I'll sit this one out." So you go away somewhat defeated—but not completely, because maybe she really *is* tired—when you turn around and some other guy comes up to her, and there she is, dancing with him! Maybe this guy is her boyfriend and she knew he was coming over, or maybe she didn't like the way you look, or maybe something else. It was always so complicated for such a simple matter.

One time I decided to invite Arlene to one of these dances. It was the first time I took her out. My best friends were also at the dance; my mother had invited them, to get more customers for her friend's dance studio. These guys were contemporaries of mine, guys my own age from school. Harold Gast and David Leff were literary types, while Robert Stapler was a scientific type. We would spend a lot of time together after school, going on walks and discussing this and that.

Anyway, my best friends were at the dance, and as soon as they saw me with Arlene, they called me into the cloakroom and said, "Now listen, Feynman, we want you to understand that *we* understand that Arlene is *your* girl tonight, and we're not gonna bother you with her. She's out of bounds for us," and so on. But before long, there was cutting in and competition coming from precisely these guys! I learned the meaning of Shakespeare's phrase "[He] doth protest too much, methinks."

You must appreciate what I was like then. I was a very shy character, always feeling uncomfortable because everybody was stronger than me, and I was always afraid I would look like a sissy. Everybody else played baseball; everybody else did all kinds of athletic things. If there was a game somewhere, and a ball would come rolling across the road, I would be petrified that maybe I'd have to pick it up and throw it back—because if I threw it, it would be about a radian off the correct direction, and not anywhere near the distance—and then everybody would laugh. It was terrible, and I was very unhappy about it.

One time I was invited to a party at Arlene's house. Everybody was there because Arlene was the most popular girl around: She was number one, the nicest girl, and everybody liked her. Well, I'm sitting in a big armchair with nothing to do, when Arlene comes over and sits on the arm of the chair to talk to me. That was the beginning of the feeling,

"Oh, boy! The world is just wonderful now! Somebody I like has paid attention to me!"

. . .

In those days, in Far Rockaway, there was a youth center for Jewish kids at the temple. It was a big club that had many activities. There was a writers group that wrote stories and would read them to each other; there was a drama group that put on plays; there was a science group, and an art group. I had no interest in any subject except science, but Arlene was in the art group, so I joined it too. I struggled with the art business—learning how to make plaster casts of the face and so on (which I used much later in life, it turned out)—just so I could be in the same group with Arlene.

But Arlene had a boyfriend named Jerome in the group, so there was no chance for me. I just hovered around in the background.

One time, when I wasn't there, somebody nominated me for president of the youth center. The elders began getting nervous, because I was an avowed atheist by that time.

I had been brought up in the Jewish religion—my family went to the temple every Friday, I was sent to what we called "Sunday school," and I even studied Hebrew for a while—but at the same time, my father was telling me about the world. When I would hear the rabbi tell about some miracle such as a bush whose leaves were shaking but there wasn't any wind, I would try to fit the miracle into the real world and explain it in terms of natural phenomena.

Some miracles were harder than others to understand. The one about the leaves was easy. When I was walking to school, I heard a little noise: Although the wind was hardly noticeable, the leaves of a bush were wiggling a little bit because they were in just the right position to make a kind of resonance. And I thought, "Aha! This is a good explanation for Elijah's vision of the quaking bush."

But there were some miracles I never did figure out. For instance, there was a story in which Moses throws down his staff and it turns into a snake. I couldn't figure out what the witnesses saw that made them think his staff was a snake.

If I had thought back to when I was much younger, the Santa Claus story could have provided a clue for me. But it didn't hit me hard enough at the time to produce the possibility that I should doubt the truth of stories that don't fit with nature. When I found out that Santa Claus wasn't real, I wasn't upset; rather, I was relieved that there was a much simpler phenomenon to explain how so many children all over the world got presents on the same night. The story had been getting pretty complicated—it was getting out of hand.

Santa Claus was a particular custom we celebrated in our family, and it wasn't very serious. But the miracles I was hearing about were connected with real things: There was the temple, where people would go every week; there was the Sunday school, where rabbis taught children about miracles; it was much more of a dramatic thing. Santa Claus didn't involve big institutions like the temple, which I knew were real.

So all the time I was going to the Sunday school, I was believing everything and having trouble putting it together. But, of course, ultimately it had to come to a crisis, sooner or later.

The crisis came when I was eleven or twelve. The rabbi was telling us a story about the Spanish Inquisition, during which the Jews suffered terrible tortures. He told us about a particular individual whose name was Ruth, exactly what she was supposed to have done, what the arguments were in her favor and against her—the whole thing, as if it had all been documented by a court reporter. And I was just an innocent kid, listening to all this stuff and believing it was a true commentary, because the rabbi had never indicated otherwise.

At the end, the rabbi described how Ruth was dying in prison: "And she thought, while she was dying"—blah, blah.

That was a shock to me. After the lesson was over, I went up to him and said, "How did they know what she thought when she was dying?"

He says, "Well, of course, in order to explain more vividly how the Jews suffered, we made up the story of Ruth. It wasn't a real individual."

That was too much for me. I felt terribly deceived: I wanted the straight story—not fixed up by somebody else—so I could decide for myself what it meant. But it was difficult for me to argue with adults. All I could do was get tears in my eyes. I started to cry, I was so upset.

He said, "What's the matter?"

I tried to explain. "I've been listening to all these stories, and now I don't know, of all the things you told me, which were true, and which were not true—I don't know what to do with everything that I've learned!" I was trying to explain that I was losing everything at the moment, because I was no longer sure of the data, so to speak. Here I had been struggling to understand all these miracles, and now—well, it solved a lot of miracles, all right! But I was unhappy.

The rabbi said, "If it is so traumatic for you, why do you come to Sunday school?"

"Because my parents make me."

I never talked to my parents about it, and I never found out whether the rabbi communicated with them or not, but my parents never made me go again. And it was just before I was supposed to get confirmed as a believer.

Anyway, that crisis resolved my difficulty rather rapidly, in favor of the theory that all the miracles were stories made up to help people understand things "more vividly," even if they conflicted with natural phenomena. But I thought nature itself was so interesting that I didn't want it distorted like that. And so I gradually came to disbelieve the whole religion.

Anyway, the Jewish elders had organized this club with all its activities not just to get us kids off the street, but to get us interested in the Jewish way of life. So to have someone like me elected as president would have made them very embarrassed. To our mutual relief I wasn't elected, but the center eventually failed anyway—it was on its way out when I was nominated, and had I been elected, I surely would have been blamed for its demise.

■   ■   ■

One day Arlene told me Jerome isn't her boyfriend anymore—she's not tied up with him. That was a big excitement for me, the beginning of hope! She invited me over to her house, at 154 Westminster Avenue in nearby Cedarhurst.

When I went to her house that time, it was dark and the porch wasn't lit. I couldn't see the numbers. Not wanting to disturb anyone by asking if it was the right house, I crawled up, quietly, and felt the numbers on the door: 154.

Arlene was having trouble with her homework in philosophy class. "We're studying Descartes," she said. "He starts out with 'Cogito, ergo sum'—'I think, therefore I am'—and ends up proving the existence of God."

"Impossible!" I said, without stopping to think that I was doubting the great Descartes. (It was a reaction I learned from my father: Have no respect *whatsoever* for authority; forget who said it and instead look at what he starts with, where he ends up, and ask yourself, "Is it reasonable?") I said, "How can you deduce one from the other?"

"I don't know," she said.

"Well, let's look it over," I said. "What's the argument?"

So we look it over, and we see that Descartes' statement "Cogito, ergo sum" is supposed to mean that there is one thing that cannot be doubted—doubt itself. "Why doesn't he just say it straight?" I complained. "He just means somehow or other that he has one fact that he knows."

Then it goes on and says things like, "I can only imagine imperfect thoughts, but imperfect can only be understood as referent to the perfect. Hence the perfect must exist somewhere." (He's workin' his way towards God now.)

"Not at all!" I say. "In science you can talk about relative degrees of approximation without having a perfect theory. I don't know what this is all about. I think it's a bunch of baloney."

Arlene understood me. She understood, when she looked at it, that no matter how impressive and important this philosophy stuff was supposed to be, it could be taken lightly—you could just think about the words, instead of worrying about the fact that Descartes said it. "Well, I guess it's okay to take the other side," she said. "My teacher keeps telling us, 'There are two sides to every question, just like there are two sides to every piece of paper.' "

"There's two sides to that, too," I said.

"What do you mean?"

I had read about the Möbius strip in the *Encyclopaedia Britannica*, my wonderful *Britannica!* In those days, things like the Möbius strip weren't so well known to everybody, but they were just as understandable as they are to kids today. The existence of such a surface was so real—it wasn't a wishy-washy political question, or anything that you needed history to understand. Reading about those things was like being way off in a wonderful world that nobody knows about, and you're getting a kick not only from the delight of learning the stuff itself, but also from making yourself unique.

I got a strip of paper, put a half twist in it, and made it into a loop. Arlene was delighted.

The next day, in class, she lay in wait for her teacher. Sure enough, he holds up a piece of paper and says, "There are two sides to every question, just like there are two sides to every piece of paper." Arlene holds up her own strip of paper—with a half twist in it—and says, "Sir, there are even two sides to *that* question: there's paper with only one side!" The teacher and the class got all excited, and Arlene got such a kick out of showing them the Möbius strip that I think she paid more attention to me after that on account of it.

■　■　■

But after Jerome, I had a new competitor—my "good friend" Harold Gast. Arlene was always making up her mind one way or the other. When it came time for graduation, she went with Harold to the senior prom, but sat with my parents for the graduation ceremony.

I was the best in science, the best in mathematics, the best in physics, and the best in chemistry, so I was going up to the stage and receiving honors many times at the ceremony. Harold was the best in English and the best in history, and had written the school play, so that was very impressive.

I was terrible in English—I couldn't stand the subject. It seemed to me ridiculous to worry about whether you spelled something wrong or not, because English spelling is just a human convention—it has nothing to do with anything *real*, anything from nature. Any word can be spelled just as well a different way. I was impatient with all this English stuff.*

There was a series of exams called the Regents, which the state of New York gave to every high school student. A few months before, when we all were taking the Regents examination in English, Harold and the other literary friend of mine, David Leff—the editor of the school newspaper—asked me which books I had chosen to write about. David had chosen something with profound social implications by Sinclair Lewis, and Harold had picked some playwright. I said I chose *Treasure Island* because we had that book in first-year English, and told them what I wrote.

They laughed. "Boy, are *you* gonna flunk, saying such simple stuff about such a simple book!"

There was also a list of questions for an essay. The one I chose was "The Importance of Science in Aviation." I thought, "What a dumb question—the importance of science in aviation is obvious!"

I was about to write a simple theme about this dumb question when I remembered that my literary friends were always "throwing the bull"—building up their sentences to sound complex and sophisticated. I decided to try it, just for the hell of it. I thought, "If the Regents are so silly as to have a subject like the importance of science in aviation, I'm gonna *do* that."

So I wrote stuff like, "Aeronautical science is important in the analysis of the eddies, vortices, and whirlpools formed in the atmosphere behind the aircraft . . ."—I knew that eddies, vortices, and whirlpools are the same thing, but mentioning them three different ways *sounds* better! That was the only thing I would not have ordinarily done on the test.

---

*Case in point: despite reading through the manuscript several times, Feynman never noticed that "Arlene" was not how Arline spelled her own name. —RL

The teacher who corrected my examination must have been impressed by eddies, vortices, and whirlpools, because I got a 91 on the exam—while my literary friends, who chose topics the English teachers could more easily take issue with, both got 88.

That year a new rule came out: if you got 90 or better on a Regents examination, you automatically got honors in that subject at graduation. So while the playwright and the editor of the school newspaper had to stay in their seats, this illiterate fool physics student was called to go up to the stage once again and receive honors in English!

After the graduation ceremony, Arlene was in the hall with my parents and Harold's parents when the head of the math department came over. He was a very strong man—he was also the school disciplinarian—a tall, dominating fellow. Mrs. Gast says to him, "Hello, Dr. Augsberry. I'm Harold Gast's mother. And this is Mrs. Feynman . . ."

He completely ignores Mrs. Gast and immediately turns to my mother. "Mrs. Feynman, I want to impress upon you that a young man like your son comes along only very rarely. The state should support a man of such talent. You must be *sure* that he goes to college, the best college you can afford!" He was concerned that my parents might not be planning to send me to college, for in those days lots of kids had to get a job immediately after graduation to help support the family.

That in fact happened to my friend Robert. He had a lab, too, and taught me all about lenses and optics. (One day he had an accident in his lab. He was opening carbolic acid and the bottle jerked, spilling some acid on his face. He went to the doctor and had bandages put on for a few weeks. The funny thing was, when they took the bandages off his skin was smooth underneath, nicer than it had been before—there were many fewer blemishes. I've since found out that there was, for a while, some kind of a beauty treatment using carbolic acid in a more dilute form.) Robert's mother was poor, and he had to go to work right away to support her, so he couldn't continue his interest in the sciences.

Anyway, my mother reassured Dr. Augsberry: "We're saving money as best we can, and we're trying to send him to Columbia or MIT." And Arlene was listening to all this, so after that I was a little bit ahead.

.   .   .

Arlene was a wonderful girl. She was the editor of the newspaper at Nassau County Lawrence High School; she played the piano beautifully, and was very artistic. She made some decorations for our house, like the parrot on the inside of our closet. As time went on, and our family got to know her better, she would go to the woods to paint with my father, who had taken up painting in later life, as many people do.

Arlene and I began to mold each other's personality. She lived in a family that was very polite, and was very sensitive to other people's feelings. She taught me to be more sensitive to those kinds of things, too. On the other hand, her family felt that "white lies" were okay.

I thought one should have the attitude of "What do *you* care what other people think?" I said, "We should listen to other people's opinions and take them into account. Then, if they don't make sense and we think they're wrong, then that's that!"

Arlene caught on to the idea right away. It was easy to talk her into thinking that, in our relationship, we must be very honest with each other and say everything straight, with absolute frankness. It worked very well, and we became very much in love—a love like no other love that I know of.

After that summer I went away to college at MIT. (I couldn't go to Columbia because of the Jewish quota.) I began getting letters from my friends that said things like, "You should see how Arlene is going out with Harold," or "She's doing this and she's doing that, while you're all alone up there in Boston." Well, I was taking out girls in Boston, but they didn't mean a thing to me, and I knew the same was true with Arlene.

When summer came, I stayed in Boston for a summer job, and worked on measuring friction. The Chrysler Company had developed a new method of polishing to get a super finish, and we were supposed to measure how much better it was. (It turned out that the "super finish" was not significantly better.)

Anyway, Arlene found a way to be near me. She found a summer job in Scituate, about twenty miles away, taking care of children. But my father was concerned that I would become too involved with Arlene and get off the track of my studies, so he talked her out of it—or talked me out of it (I can't remember). Those days were very, very different from now. In those days, you had to go all the way up in your career before marrying.

I was able to see Arlene only a few times that summer, but we promised each other we would marry after I finished school. I had known her for six years by that time. I'm a little tongue-tied trying to describe to you how much our love for each other developed, but we were sure we were right for each other.

Richard and Arlene on the boardwalk in Atlantic City.

■ ■ ■

After I graduated from MIT I went to Princeton, and I would go home on vacations to see Arlene. One time when I went to see her, Arlene had developed a bump on one side of her neck. She was a very beautiful girl, so it worried her a little bit—but it didn't hurt, so she figured it wasn't too serious. She went to her uncle, who was a doctor. He told her to rub it with omega oil.

Then, sometime later, the bump began to change. It got bigger—or maybe it was smaller—and she got a fever. The fever got worse, so the family doctor decided Arlene should go to the hospital. She was told she had typhoid fever. Right away, as I still do today, I looked up the disease in medical books and read all about it.

When I went to see Arlene in the hospital, she was in quarantine— we had to put on special gowns when we entered her room, and so on. The doctor was there, so I asked him how the Wydell test came out—it was an absolute test for typhoid fever that involved checking for bacteria in the feces. He said, "It was negative."

"What? How can that *be?*" I said. "Why all these gowns, when you can't even find the bacteria in an experiment? Maybe she doesn't have typhoid fever!"

The result of that was that the doctor talked to Arlene's parents, who told me not to interfere. "After all, he's the doctor. You're only her fiancé."

I've found out since that such people don't know what they're doing, and get insulted when you make some suggestion or criticism. I realize that *now*, but I wish I had been much stronger then and told her parents that the doctor was an idiot—which he was—and didn't know what he was doing. But as it was, her parents were in charge of it.

Anyway, after a little while Arlene got better, apparently: the swelling went down and the fever went away. But after some weeks the swelling started again, and this time she went to another doctor. This guy feels under her armpits and in her groin, and so on, and notices there's swelling in those places, too. He says the problem is in her lymphatic glands, but he doesn't yet know what the specific disease is. He will consult with other doctors.

As soon as I hear about it I go down to the library at Princeton and look up lymphatic diseases, and find "Swelling of the Lymphatic Glands. (1) Tuberculosis of the lymphatic glands. This is very easy to diagnose . . ."—so I figure this isn't what Arlene has, because the doctors are having trouble trying to figure it out.

I start reading about some other diseases: lymphodenema, lymphodenoma, Hodgkin's disease, all kinds of other things; they're all cancers of one crazy form or another. The only difference between lymphodenema and lymphodenoma was, as far as I could make out by reading it very carefully, that if the patient dies, it's lymphodenoma; if the patient survives—at least for a while—then it's lymphodenema.

At any rate, I read through all the lymphatic diseases, and decided that the most likely possibility was that Arlene had an incurable disease. Then I half smiled to myself, thinking, "I bet everybody who reads through a medical book thinks they have a fatal disease." And yet, after reading everything very carefully, I couldn't find any other possibility. It was serious.

Then I went to the weekly tea at Palmer Hall, and found myself talking to the mathematicians just as I always did, even though I had just found out that Arlene probably had a fatal disease. It was very strange— like having two minds.

When I went to visit her, I told Arlene the joke about the people who don't know any medicine reading the medical book and always assuming they have a fatal disease. But I also told her I thought we were in great difficulty, and that the best I could figure out was that she had an incurable disease. We discussed the various diseases, and I told her what each one was like.

One of the diseases I told Arlene about was Hodgkin's disease. When she next saw her doctor, she asked him about it: "Could it be Hodgkin's disease?"

He said, "Well, yes, that's a possibility."

When she went to the county hospital, the doctor wrote the following diagnosis: "Hodgkin's disease—?" So I realized that the doctor didn't know any more than I did about this problem.

The county hospital gave Arlene all sorts of tests and X-ray treatments for this "Hodgkin's disease—?" and there were special meetings to discuss this peculiar case. I remember waiting for her outside in the hall. When the meeting was over, the nurse wheeled her out in a wheelchair. All of a sudden a little guy comes running out of the meeting room and catches up with us. "Tell me," he says, out of breath, "do you spit up blood? Have you ever coughed up blood?"

The nurse says, "Go away! Go away! What kind of thing is that to ask of a patient!"—and brushes him away. Then she turned to us and said, "That man is a doctor from the neighborhood who comes to the meetings and is always making trouble. That's not the kind of thing to ask of a patient!"

I didn't catch on. The doctor was checking a certain possibility, and if I had been smart, I would have asked him what it was.

Finally, after a lot of discussion, a doctor at the hospital tells me they figure the most likely possibility is Hodgkin's disease. He says, "There will be some periods of improvement, and some periods in the hospital. It will be on and off, getting gradually worse. There's no way to reverse it entirely. It's fatal after a few years."

"I'm sorry to hear that," I say. "I'll tell her what you said."

"No, no!" says the doctor. "We don't want to upset the patient. We're going to tell her it's glandular fever."

"No, no!" I reply. "We've already discussed the possibility of Hodgkin's disease. I know she can adjust to it."

"Her parents don't want her to know. You had better talk to them first."

At home, everybody worked on me: my parents, my two aunts, our family doctor; they were all on me, saying I'm a very foolish young man who doesn't realize what pain he's going to bring to this wonderful girl by telling her she has a fatal disease. "How can you do such a terrible thing?" they asked, in horror.

"Because we have made a pact that we must speak honestly with each other and look at everything directly. There's no use fooling around. She's gonna ask me what she's got, and I cannot lie to her."

"Oh, that's childish!" they said—blah, blah, blah. Everybody kept working on me and said I was wrong. I thought I was definitely right, because I had already talked to Arlene about the disease and knew she could face it—that telling her the truth was the right way to handle it.

But finally, my little sister comes up to me—she was eleven or twelve then—with tears running down her face. She beats me on the chest, telling me that Arlene is such a wonderful girl, and that I'm such a foolish, stubborn brother. I couldn't take it any more. That broke me down.

So I wrote Arlene a goodbye love letter, figuring that if she ever found out the truth after I had told her it was glandular fever, we would be through. I carried the letter with me all the time.

The gods never make it easy; they always make it harder. I go to the hospital to see Arlene—having made this decision—and there she is, sitting up in bed, surrounded by her parents, somewhat distraught. When she sees me, her face lights up and she says, "Now I know how valuable it is that we tell each other the truth!" Nodding at her parents, she continues, "They're telling me I have glandular fever, and I'm not sure whether I believe them or not. Tell me, Richard, do I have Hodgkin's disease or glandular fever?"

"You have glandular fever," I said—and I died inside. It was terrible—just terrible!

Her reaction was completely simple: "Oh! Fine! Then I believe them." Because we had built up so much trust in each other, she was completely relieved. Everything was solved, and all was very nice.

· · ·

She got a little bit better, and went home for a while. About a week later, I get a telephone call. "Richard," she says, "I want to talk to you. Come on over."

"Okay." I made sure I still had the letter with me. I could tell something was the matter.

I go upstairs to her room, and she says, "Sit down." I sit down on the end of her bed. "All right, now tell me," she says, "do I have glandular fever or Hodgkin's disease?"

"You have Hodgkin's disease." And I reached for the letter.

"God!" she says. "They must have put you through hell."

I had just told her she has a fatal disease, and was admitting that I had lied to her as well, and what does she think of? She's worried about *me!* I was terribly ashamed of myself. I gave Arlene the letter.

"You should have stuck by it. We know what we're doing; we are right!"

"I'm sorry. I feel awful."

"I understand, Richard. Just don't do it again."

You see, she was in bed upstairs, and did something she used to do when she was little: She tiptoed out of bed and crawled down the stairs a little bit to listen to what people were doing downstairs. She heard her mother crying a lot, and went back to bed thinking, "If I have glandular fever, why is Mother crying so much? But Richard said I had glandular fever, so it must be right!"

Later she thought, "Could *Richard* have lied to me?" and began to wonder how that might be possible. She concluded that, incredible as it sounded, somebody might have put me through a wringer of some sort.

She was so good at facing difficult situations that she went on to the next problem. "Okay," she says, "I have Hodgkin's disease. What are we going to do now?"

I had a scholarship at Princeton, and they wouldn't let me keep it if I got married. We knew what the disease was like: Sometimes it would get better for some months, and Arlene could be at home; then she would have to be in the hospital for some months—back and forth for two years, perhaps.

So I figure, although I'm in the middle of trying to get my Ph.D., I could get a job at the Bell Telephone Laboratories doing research—it was a very good place to work—and we could get a little apartment in Queens that wasn't too far from the hospital or Bell Labs. We could get married in a few months, in New York. We worked everything out that afternoon.

For some months now Arlene's doctors had wanted to take a biopsy of the swelling on her neck, but her parents didn't want it done—they didn't want to "bother the poor sick girl." But with new resolve, I kept working on them, explaining that it's important to get as much information as possible. With Arlene's help, I finally convinced her parents.

A few days later, Arlene telephones me and says, "They got a report from the biopsy."

"Yeah? Is it good or bad?"

"I don't know. Come over and let's talk about it."

When I got to her house, she showed me the report. It said, "Biopsy shows tuberculosis of the lymphatic gland."

That really got me. I mean, that was the first goddamn thing on the list!

I passed it by, because the book said it was easy to diagnose, and because the doctors were having so much trouble trying to figure out what it was. I assumed they had checked the obvious case. And it *was* the obvious case: the man who had come running out of the meeting room asking "Do you spit up blood?" had the right idea. He knew what it probably was!*

I felt like a jerk, because I had passed over the obvious possibility by using circumstantial evidence—which isn't any good—and by assuming the doctors were more intelligent than they were. Otherwise, I would have suggested it right off, and perhaps the doctor would have diagnosed Arlene's disease way back then as "tuberculosis of the lymphatic gland—?" I was a dope. I've learned, since then.

Anyway, Arlene says, "So I might live as long as seven years. I may even get better."

"So what do you mean, you don't know if it's good or bad?"

"Now we won't be able to get married until later!"

Knowing that she only had two more years to live, we had solved things so perfectly, from her point of view, that she was disturbed to discover she'd live longer! But it didn't take me long to convince her it was a better circumstance.

So we knew we could face things together, from then on. After going through that, we had no difficulty facing any other problem.

◾   ◾   ◾

When the war came, I was recruited to work on the Manhattan Project at Princeton, where I was finishing up my degree. A few months later, as soon as I got my degree, I announced to my family that I wanted to get married.

My father was horrified, because from the earliest times, as he saw me develop, he thought I would be happy as a scientist. He thought it was still too early to marry—it would interfere with my career. He also had this

---

*In 1989 I received a letter from an eighty-year-old retired physics professor at Swarthmore College. The letter read, in part: "When I was a boy in a small town in upstate New York, we got our milk unpasteurized from a nearby farmer. I developed a tubercular lymph gland in my neck, as did my sister. An old-fashioned name for this disease is scrofula. We were both operated on by our family doctor, with another local doctor to handle the ether. This took place on our dining room table, as I recall. Both my sister and I have scars on our necks to show for it, but the operation, and later treatment with silver nitrate, was obviously successful. I am terribly surprised that scrofula was not early diagnosed for Arlene and treated. Incidentally, when NY State passed a law that all cows must be tested for TB, the farmer was wiped out." —RL

crazy idea: If a guy was in some difficulty, he used to always say, "Cherchez la femme"—look for the woman behind it. He felt that women were the great danger to a man, that a man always has to watch out and be tough about women. And when he sees me marrying a girl with tuberculosis, he thinks of the possibility that I'm going to get sick, too.

My whole family was worried about that—aunts, uncles, everyone. They brought the family doctor over to our house. He tried to explain to me that tuberculosis is a dangerous disease, and that I'm bound to get it.

I said, "Just tell me how it's transmitted, and we'll figure it out." We were already very, very careful: We knew we must not kiss, because there's a lot of bacteria in the mouth.

Then they carefully explained to me that when I had promised to marry Arlene, I didn't know the situation. Everybody would understand that I didn't know the situation then, and that it didn't represent a real promise.

I never had that feeling, that crazy idea that they had, that I was getting married because I had promised it. I hadn't even *thought* of that. It wasn't a question of having promised anything; we had stalled around, not getting a piece of paper and not being formally married, but we were in love, and were already married, emotionally.

I said, "Would it be sensible for a husband who learns that his wife has tuberculosis to leave her?"

Only my aunt who ran the hotel thought maybe it would be all right for us to get married. Everybody else was still against it. But this time, since my family had given me this kind of advice before and it had been so wrong, I was in a much stronger position. It was very easy to resist and to just proceed. So there was no problem, really. Although it was a similar circumstance, they weren't going to convince me of anything any more. Arlene and I knew we were right in what we were doing.

Arlene and I worked everything out. There was a hospital in New Jersey just south of Fort Dix where she could stay while I was at Princeton. It was a charity hospital—Deborah was the name of it—supported by the Women's Garment Workers Union of New York. Arlene wasn't a garment worker, but it didn't make any difference. And I was just a young fella working on this project for the government, and the pay was very low. But this way I could take care of her, at last.

We decided to get married on the way to Deborah Hospital. I went to Princeton to pick up a car—Bill Woodward, one of the graduate students there, lent me his station wagon. I fixed it up like a little ambulance, with a mattress and sheets in the back, so Arlene could lie down in case she got tired. Although this was one of the periods when the disease was apparently not so bad and she was at home, Arlene had been in the county hospital a lot, and she was a little weak.

I drove up to Cedarhurst and picked up my bride. Arlene's family waved goodbye, and off we went. We crossed Queens and Brooklyn, then went to Staten Island on the ferry—that was our romantic boat ride—and drove to the city hall for the borough of Richmond to get married.

We went up the stairs, slowly, into the office. The guy there was very nice. He did everything right away. He said, "You don't have any witnesses," so he called the bookkeeper and an accountant from another room, and we were married according to the laws of the state of New York. Then we were very happy, and we smiled at each other, holding hands.

The bookkeeper says to me, "You're married now. You should kiss the bride!"

So the bashful character kissed his bride lightly on the cheek.

On their wedding day.

■ ■ ■

I gave everyone a tip and we thanked them very much. We got back in the car, and drove to Deborah Hospital.

Every weekend I'd go down from Princeton to visit Arlene. One time the bus was late, and I couldn't get into the hospital. There weren't any hotels nearby, but I had my old sheepskin coat on (so I was warm enough), and I looked for an empty lot to sleep in. I was a little worried what it might look like in the morning when people looked out of their windows, so I found a place that was far enough away from houses.

The next morning I woke up and discovered I'd been sleeping in a garbage dump—a landfill! I felt foolish, and laughed.

Arlene's doctor was very nice, but he would get upset when I brought in a war bond for $18 every month. He could see we didn't have much money, and kept insisting we shouldn't contribute to the hospital, but I did it anyway.

One time, at Princeton, I received a box of pencils in the mail. They were dark green, and in gold letters were the words "RICHARD DARLING, I LOVE YOU! PUTSY." It was Arlene. (I called her Putsy.*)

Well, that was nice, and I love her, too, but—you know how you absentmindedly drop pencils around: You're showing Professor Wigner a formula, or something, and leave the pencil on his desk.

In those days we didn't have extra stuff, so I didn't want to waste the pencils. I got a razor blade from the bathroom and cut off the writing on one of them to see if I could use them.

The next morning, I get a letter in the mail. It starts out, "WHAT'S THE IDEA OF TRYING TO CUT THE NAME OFF THE PENCILS?"

It continues: "Aren't you proud of the fact that I love you?" Then: "WHAT DO YOU CARE WHAT OTHER PEOPLE THINK?"

Then came poetry: "If you're ashamed of me, dah dah, then Pecans to you! Pecans to you!" The next verse was the same kind of stuff, with the last line, "Almonds to you! Almonds to you!" Each one was "Nuts to you!" in a different form.

So I had to use the pencils with the names on them. What else could I do?

.   .   .

It wasn't long before I had to go to Los Alamos. Robert Oppenheimer, who was in charge of the project, arranged for Arlene to stay in the nearest hospital, in Albuquerque, about a hundred miles away. I had time off every weekend to see her, so I would hitchhike down on a Saturday, see Arlene in the afternoon, and stay overnight in a hotel there

*Feynman's pronunciation of "Putsy" rhymed with "footsy." —RL

in Albuquerque. Then on Sunday morning I would see Arlene again, and hitchhike back to Los Alamos in the afternoon.

During the week I would often get letters from her. Some of them, like the one written on a jigsaw-puzzle blank and then taken apart and sent in a sack, resulted in little notes from the Army censor, such as "Please tell your wife we don't have time to play games around here!" I didn't tell her anything. I *liked* her to play games—even though she often put me in various uncomfortable but amusing conditions from which I could not escape.

One time, near the beginning of May, newspapers mysteriously appeared in almost everybody's mailbox at Los Alamos. The whole damn place was full of them—hundreds of newspapers. You know the kind—you open it up and there's this headline screaming in thick letters across the front page: ENTIRE NATION CELEBRATES BIRTHDAY OF R. P. FEYNMAN!

Arlene was playing her game with the world. She had a lot of time to think. She would read magazines, and send away for this and that. She was always cooking up something. (She must have got help with the names from Nick Metropolis or one of the other guys at Los Alamos who would often visit her.) Arlene was in her room, but she was in the world, writing me crazy letters and sending away for all kinds of stuff.

One time she sent me a big catalog of kitchen equipment—the kind you need for enormous institutions like prisons, which have a lot of people in them. It showed everything from blowers and hoods for stoves to huge pots and pans. So I'm thinking, "What the hell is this?"

It reminded me of the time I was up at MIT and Arlene sent me a catalog describing huge boats, from warships to ocean liners—great big boats. I wrote to her: "What's the idea?"

She writes back: "I just thought that maybe, when we get married, we could buy a boat."

I write, "Are you crazy? It's all out of proportion!"

Then another catalog comes: it's for big yachts—forty-foot schooners and stuff like that—for very rich people. She writes, "Since you said no to the other boats, maybe we could get one of these."

I write, "Look: you're way out of scale!"

Soon another catalog comes: it's for various kinds of motor boats—Chris-Craft this and that.

I write, "Too expensive!"

Finally, I get a note: "This is your last chance, Richard. You're always saying no." It turns out a friend of hers has a rowboat she wants to sell for $15—a used rowboat—and maybe we could buy it so we could row around in the water next summer.

So, yes. I mean, how can you say no after all that?

Well, I'm still trying to figure out what this big catalog for institutional kitchen equipment is leading to, when another catalog comes: it's for hotels and restaurants—supplies for small and medium-sized hotels and restaurants. Then a few days later, a catalog for the kitchen in your new home comes.

When I go down to Albuquerque the next Saturday, I find out what it's all about. There's a little charcoal broiler in her room—she's bought it through the mail from Sears. It's about eighteen inches across, with little legs.

"I thought we could have steaks," Arlene says.

"How the hell can we use it in the room, here, with all the smoke and everything?"

"Oh, no," she says. "All you have to do is take it out on the lawn. Then you can cook us steaks every Sunday."

The hospital was right on Route 66, the main road across the United States! "I can't do that," I said. "I mean, with all the cars and trucks going by, all the people on the sidewalk walking back and forth, I can't just go out there and start cookin' steaks on the lawn!"

"What do *you* care what other people think?" (Arlene *tortured* me with that!) "Okay," she says, opening a drawer, "we'll compromise: you don't have to wear the chef's hat and the gloves."

She holds up a hat—it's a real chef's hat—and gloves. Then she says, "Try on the apron," as she unfolds it. It has something silly written across it, like BAR-B-Q KING, or something.

"Okay, okay!" I say, horrified. "I'll cook the steaks on the lawn!" So every Saturday or Sunday, I'd go out there on Route 66 and cook steaks.

■　■　■

Then there were the Christmas cards. One day, only a few weeks after I had arrived at Los Alamos, Arlene says, "I thought it would be nice to send Christmas cards to everybody. Would you like to see the ones I picked out?"

They were nice cards, all right, but inside they said Merry Christmas, from Rich & Putsy. "I can't send these to Fermi and Bethe," I protested. "I hardly even know them!"

"What do *you* care what other people think?"—naturally. So we sent them.

Next year comes around, and by this time I know Fermi. I know Bethe. I've been over at their houses. I've taken care of their kids. We're all very friendly.

Somewhere along the line, Arlene says to me, in a very formal tone, "You haven't asked me about our Christmas cards this year, Richard . . ."

Fear goes through me. "Uh, well, let's see the cards."

The cards say Merry Christmas and a Happy New Year, from Richard and Arlene Feynman. "Well, that's fine," I say. "They're very nice. They'll go fine for everybody."

"Oh, no," she says. "They won't do for Fermi and Bethe and all those other famous people." Sure enough, she's got another box of cards.

She pulls one out. It says the usual stuff, and then: From Dr. & Mrs. R. P. Feynman.

So I had to send them those.

"What's this formal stuff, Dick?" they laughed. They were happy that she was having such a good time out of it, and that I had no control over it.

Arlene in the hospital.

* * *

Arlene didn't spend all of her time inventing games. She had sent away for a book called *Sound and Symbol in Chinese*. It was a lovely book—I still have it—with about fifty symbols done in beautiful calligraphy, with explanations like "Trouble: three women in a house." She had the right paper, brushes, and ink, and was practicing calligraphy. She had also bought a Chinese dictionary, to get a lot of other symbols.

One time when I came to visit her, Arlene was practicing these things. She says to herself, "No. That one's wrong."

So I, the "great scientist," say, "What do you mean, 'wrong'? It's only a human convention. There's no law of nature which says how they're supposed to look; you can draw them any way you want."

"I mean, artistically it's wrong. It's a question of balance, of how it feels."

"But one way is just as good as another," I protest.

"Here," she says, and she hands me the brush. "Make one yourself."

So I made one, and I said, "Wait a minute. Let me make another one—it's too blobby." (I couldn't say it was wrong, after all.)

"How do you know how blobby it's supposed to be?" she says.

I learned what she meant. There's a particular way you have to make the stroke for it to look good. An aesthetic thing has a certain set, a certain character, which I can't define. Because it couldn't be defined made me think there was nothing to it. But I learned from that experience that there *is* something to it—and it's a fascination I've had for art ever since.

Just at this moment my sister sends me a postcard from Oberlin, where she's going to college. It's written in pencil, with small symbols—it's in Chinese.

Joan is nine years younger than I am, and studied physics, too. Having me as her older brother was tough on her. She was always looking for something I couldn't do, and was secretly taking Chinese.

Well, I didn't know any Chinese, but one thing I'm good at is spending an infinite amount of time solving a puzzle. The next weekend I took the card with me to Albuquerque. Arlene showed me how to look up the symbols. You have to start in the back of the dictionary with the right category and count the number of strokes. Then you go into the main part of the dictionary. It turns out each symbol has several possible meanings, and you have to put several symbols together before you can understand it.

With great patience I worked everything out. Joan was saying things like, "I had a good time today." There was only one sentence I couldn't figure out. It said, "Yesterday we celebrated mountain-forming day"—obviously an error. (It turned out they did have some crazy thing called "Mountain-Forming Day" at Oberlin, and I had translated it right!)

So it was trivial things like you'd expect to have on a postcard, but I knew from the situation that Joan was trying to floor me by sending me Chinese.

I looked back and forth through the art book and picked out four symbols which would go well together. Then I practiced each one, over and over. I had a big pad of paper, and I would make fifty of each one, until I got it just right.

When I had accidentally made one good example of each symbol, I saved them. Arlene approved, and we glued the four of them end to end, one on top of the other. Then we put a little piece of wood on each end, so you could hang it up on the wall. I took a picture of my masterpiece with Nick Metropolis's camera, rolled up the scroll, put it in a tube, and sent it to Joan.

So she gets it. She unrolls it, and she can't read it. It looks to her as if I simply made four characters, one right after the other, on the scroll. She takes it to her teacher.

The first thing he says is, "This is written rather well! Did you do this?"

"Uh, no. What does it say?"

"Elder brother also speaks."

I'm a real bastard—I would never let my little sister score one on me.

■   ■   ■

When Arlene's condition became much weaker, her father came out from New York to visit her. It was difficult and expensive to travel that far during the war, but he knew the end was near. One day he telephoned me at Los Alamos. "You'd better come down here right away," he said.

I had arranged ahead of time with a friend of mine at Los Alamos, Klaus Fuchs, to borrow his car in case of an emergency, so I could get to Albuquerque quickly. I picked up a couple of hitchhikers to help me in case something happened on the way.

Sure enough, as we were driving into Santa Fe, we got a flat tire. The hitchhikers helped me change the tire. Then on the other side of Santa Fe, the spare tire went flat, but there was a gas station nearby. I remember waiting patiently for the gas station man to take care of some other car, when the two hitchhikers, knowing the situation, went over and explained to the man what it was. He fixed the flat right away. We decided not to get the spare tire fixed, because repairing it would have taken even more time.

We started out again towards Albuquerque, and I felt foolish that I hadn't thought to say anything to the gas station man when time was so precious. About thirty miles from Albuquerque, we got *another* flat! We had to abandon the car, and we hitchhiked the rest of the way. I called up a towing company and told them the situation.

I met Arlene's father at the hospital. He had been there for a few days. "I can't take it any more," he said. "I have to go home." He was so unhappy, he just left.

When I finally saw Arlene, she was very weak, and a bit fogged out. She didn't seem to know what was happening. She stared straight ahead most of the time, looking around a little bit from time to time, and was trying to breathe. Every once in a while her breathing would stop—and she would sort of swallow—and then it would start again. It kept going like this for a few hours.

I took a little walk outside for a while. I was surprised that I wasn't feeling what I thought people were supposed to feel under the circumstances. Maybe I was fooling myself. I wasn't delighted, but I didn't feel terribly upset, perhaps because we had known for a long time that this was going to happen.

It's hard to explain. If a Martian (who, we'll imagine, never dies except by accident) came to Earth and saw this peculiar race of creatures—these humans who live about seventy or eighty years, knowing that death is going to come—it would look to him like a terrible problem of psychology to live under those circumstances, knowing that life is only temporary. Well, we humans somehow figure out how to live despite this problem: we laugh, we joke, we live.

The only difference for me and Arlene was, instead of fifty years, it was five years. It was only a quantitative difference—the psychological problem was just the same. The only way it would have become any different is if we had said to ourselves, "But those other people have it better, because they might live fifty years." But that's crazy. Why make yourself miserable saying things like, "Why do we have such bad luck? What has God done to us? What have we done to deserve this?"—all of which, if you understand reality and take it completely into your heart, are irrelevant and unsolvable. They are just things that nobody can know. Your situation is just an accident of life.

We had a hell of a good time together.

．　．　．

I came back into her room. I kept imagining all the things that were going on physiologically: the lungs aren't getting enough air into the blood, which makes the brain fogged out and the heart weaker, which makes the breathing even more difficult. I kept expecting some sort of avalanching effect, with everything caving in together in a dramatic collapse. But it didn't appear that way at all: She just slowly got more foggy, and her breathing gradually became less and less, until there was no more breath—but just before that, there was a very small one.

The nurse on her rounds came in and confirmed that Arlene was dead, and went out—I wanted to be alone for a moment. I sat there for a while, and then went over to kiss her one last time.

I was very surprised to discover that her hair smelled exactly the same. Of course, after I stopped and thought about it, there was no reason why hair should smell different in such a short time. But to me it was a kind of a shock, because in my mind, something enormous had just happened—and yet nothing had happened.

Then I looked at the clock I had given her seven years before, when she had first become sick with tuberculosis. It was something which in those days was very nice: a digital clock whose numbers would change by turning around mechanically. The clock was very delicate and often stopped for one reason or another—I had to repair it from time to time—but I kept it going for all those years. Now, it had stopped once more—at 9:22 P.M., the time on the death certificate!

I remembered the time I was in my fraternity house at MIT when the idea came into my head completely out of the blue that my grandmother was dead. Right after that there was a telephone call, just like that. It was for Pete Bernays—my grandmother wasn't dead. So I remembered that, in case somebody told me a story that ended the other way. I figured that such things can sometimes happen by luck—after all, my grandmother was very old—although people might think they happened by some sort of supernatural phenomenon.

Arlene had kept this clock by her bedside all the time she was sick, and now it stopped the moment she died. I can understand how a person who half believes in the possibility of such things, and who hasn't got a doubting mind—especially in a circumstance like that—doesn't immediately try to figure out what happened, but instead explains that no one touched the clock, and there was no possibility of explanation by normal phenomena. The clock simply stopped. It would become a dramatic example of these fantastic phenomena.

I saw that the light in the room was low, and then I remembered that the nurse had picked up the clock and turned it toward the light to see the face better. That could easily have stopped it.

The next day, I went to the mortuary. The guy hands me some rings he's taken from her body. "Would you like to see your wife one last time?" he asks.

"What kind of a—no, I don't want to see her, no!" I said. "I just saw her!"

"Yes, but she's been all fixed up," he says.

This mortuary stuff was completely foreign to me. Fixing up a body when there's nothing there? I didn't want to look at Arlene again; that would have made me more upset.

I called the towing company and got the car, and packed Arlene's stuff in the back. I picked up a hitchhiker, and started out of Albuquerque.

It wasn't more than five miles before . . . BANG! Another flat tire. I started to curse.

The hitchhiker looked at me like I was mentally unbalanced. "It's just a tire, isn't it?" he says.

"Yeah, it's just a tire—and another tire, and again another tire, and *another* tire!"

We put the spare tire on, and went very slowly, all the way back to Los Alamos, without getting the other tire repaired.

I didn't know how I was going to face all my friends at Los Alamos. I didn't want people with long faces talking to me about the death of Arlene. Somebody asked me what happened.

"She's dead. And how's the program going?" I said.

They caught on right away that I didn't want to moon over it. Only one guy expressed his sympathy, and it turned out he had been out of town when I came back to Los Alamos.

One night I had a dream, and Arlene came into it. Right away I said to her, "No, no, you can't be in this dream. You're not alive!"

Then later, I had another dream with Arlene in it. I started in again, saying, "You can't be in this dream."

"No, no," she says. "I fooled you. I was tired of you, so I cooked up this ruse so I could go my own way. But now I like you again, so I've come back." My mind was really working against itself. It had to be explained, even in a goddamn *dream*, why it was possible that she was still here.

I must have done something to myself, psychologically. I didn't cry until about a month later, when I was walking past a department store in Oak Ridge and noticed a pretty dress in the window. I thought, "Arlene would like that," and then it hit me.

FEYNMAN, THE MILITARY, AND THE BOMB

Fizzled Fuses

When the war began in Europe but had not yet been declared in the United States, there was a lot of talk about getting ready and being patriotic. The newspapers had big articles on businessmen volunteering to go to Plattsburg, New York, to do military training, and so on.

I began to think I ought to make some kind of contribution, too. After I finished up at MIT, a friend of mine from the fraternity, Maurice Meyer, who was in the Army Signal Corps, took me to see a colonel at the Signal Corps offices in New York.

"I'd like to aid my country, sir, and since I'm technically-minded, maybe there's a way I could help."

"Well, you'd better just go up to Plattsburg to boot camp and go through basic training. Then we'll be able to use you," the colonel said.

"But isn't there some way to use my talent more directly?"

"No, this is the way the Army is organized. Go through the regular way."

I went outside and sat in the park to think about it. I thought and thought: Maybe the best way to make a contribution *is* to go along with their way. But fortunately, I thought a little more, and said, "To hell with it—I'll wait a while. Maybe something will happen where they can use me more effectively."

I went to Princeton to do graduate work, and in the spring I went once again to the Bell Labs in New York to apply for a summer job. I loved to tour the Bell Labs. Bill Shockley, the guy who later invented transistors, would show me around. I remember somebody's room where they had marked a window: the George Washington Bridge was being built, and these guys in the lab were watching its progress. They had plotted the original curve when the main cable was first put up, and they could measure the small differences as the bridge was being suspended from it, as the curve turned into a parabola. It was just the kind of thing I would like to be able to think of doing. I admired those guys; I was always hoping I could work with them one day.

Some guys from the lab took me out to this seafood restaurant for lunch, and they were all pleased that they were going to have oysters. I lived by the ocean and I couldn't look at this stuff; I couldn't eat fish, let alone oysters.

I thought to myself, "I've gotta be brave. I've gotta eat an oyster."

I took an oyster, and it was absolutely terrible. But I said to myself, "That doesn't really prove you're a man. You didn't know how terrible it was gonna be. It was easy enough when it was uncertain."

The others kept talking about how good the oysters were, so I had another oyster, and that really *was* harder than the first one.

This time, which must have been my fourth or fifth time touring the Bell Labs, they accepted me. I was very happy. In those days it was hard to find a job where you could be with other scientists.

But then there was a big excitement at Princeton. General Trichel from the Army came around and spoke to us: "We've got to have physicists! Physicists are very important to us in the Army! We need three physicists!"

You have to understand that, in those days, people hardly knew what a physicist was. Einstein was known as a mathematician, for instance—so it was rare that anybody needed physicists. I thought, "This is my opportunity to make a contribution," and I volunteered to work for the Army.

I asked the Bell Labs if they would let me work for the Army that summer, and they said they had war work, too, if that was what I wanted. But I was caught up in a patriotic fever and lost a good opportunity. It would have been much smarter to work in the Bell Labs, but one gets a little silly during such times.

I went to the Frankfort Arsenal, in Philadelphia, and worked on a dinosaur: a mechanical computer for directing artillery. When airplanes flew by, the gunners would watch them in a telescope, and this mechanical computer, with gears and cams and so forth, would try to predict where the plane was going to be. It was a most beautifully designed and built machine, and one of the important ideas in it was non-circular gears—gears that weren't circular, but would mesh anyway. Because of the changing radii of the gears, one shaft would turn as a function of the other. However, this machine was at the end of the line. Very soon afterwards, electronic computers came in.

After saying all this stuff about how physicists were so important to the Army, the first thing they had me doing was checking gear drawings to see if the numbers were right. This went on for quite a while. Then, gradually, the guy in charge of the department began to see I was useful for other things, and as the summer went on, he would spend more time discussing things with me.

One mechanical engineer at Frankfort was always trying to design things and could never get everything right. One time he designed a box full of gears, one of which was a big, eight-inch-diameter gear wheel that had six spokes. The fella says excitedly, "Well, boss, how is it? How is it?"

"Just fine," the boss replies. "All you have to do is specify a shaft passer on each of the spokes, so the gear wheel can turn!" The guy had designed a shaft that went right between the spokes!

The boss went on to tell us that there *was* such a thing as a shaft passer—I thought he must have been joking. It was invented by the Germans during the war to keep the British minesweepers from catching the cables that held the German mines floating under water at a certain depth. With these shaft passers, the German cables could allow the British cables to pass through as if they were going through a revolving door. So it *was* possible to put shaft passers on all the spokes, but the boss didn't mean that the machinists should go to all that trouble; the guy should instead just redesign it and put the shaft somewhere else.

Every once in a while the Army sent down a lieutenant to check on how things were going. Our boss told us that since we were a civilian section, the lieutenant was higher in rank than any of us. "Don't tell the lieutenant anything," he said. "Once he begins to think he knows what we're doing, he'll be giving us all kinds of orders and screwing everything up."

By that time I was designing some things, but when the lieutenant came by, I pretended I didn't know what I was doing, that I was only following orders.

"What are you doing here, Mr. Feynman?"

"Well, I draw a sequence of lines at successive angles, and then I'm supposed to measure out from the center different distances according to this table, and lay it out . . ."

"Well, what is it?"

"I think it's a cam." I had actually designed the thing, but I acted as if somebody had just told me exactly what to do.

The lieutenant couldn't get any information from anybody, and we went happily along, working on this mechanical computer, without any interference.

One day the lieutenant came by, and asked us a simple question: "Suppose that the observer is not at the same location as the gunner—how do you handle that?"

We got a terrible shock. We had designed the whole business using polar coordinates, using angles and the radius distance. With X and Y coordinates, it's easy to correct for a displaced observer. It's simply a matter of addition or subtraction. But with polar coordinates, it's a terrible mess!

So it turned out that this lieutenant whom we were trying to keep from telling us anything ended up telling us something very important that we had forgotten in the design of this device: the possibility that the gun and the observing station are not at the same place! It was a big mess to fix it.

Near the end of the summer I was given my first real design job: a machine that would make a continuous curve out of a set of points—one point coming in every fifteen seconds—from a new invention developed in England for tracking airplanes, called "radar." It was the first time I had ever done any mechanical designing, so I was a little bit frightened.

I went over to one of the other guys and said, "You're a mechanical engineer; I don't know how to do any mechanical engineering, and I just got this job . . ."

"There's nothin' *to* it," he said. "Look, I'll show you. There's two rules you need to know to design these machines. First, the friction in every bearing is so-and-so much, and in every gear junction so-and-so much. From that, you can figure out how much force you need to drive the thing. Second, when you have a gear ratio, say 2 to 1, and you are wondering whether you should make it 10 to 5 or 24 to 12 or 48 to 24, here's how to decide: You look in the Boston Gear Catalogue, and select those gears that are in the middle of the list. The ones at the high end have so many teeth they're hard to make. If they could make gears with even finer teeth, they'd have made the list go even higher. The gears at the low end of the list have so few teeth they break easy. So the best design uses gears from the middle of the list."

I had a lot of fun designing that machine. By simply selecting the gears from the middle of the list and adding up the little torques with the two numbers he gave me, I could be a mechanical engineer!

The Army didn't want me to go back to Princeton to work on my degree after that summer. They kept giving me this patriotic stuff, and offered a whole project that I could run, if I would stay.

The problem was to design a machine like the other one—what they called a director—but this time I thought the problem was easier, because the gunner would be following behind in another airplane at the same altitude. The gunner would set into my machine his altitude and an estimate of his distance behind the other airplane. My machine would automatically tilt the gun up at the correct angle and set the fuse.

As director of this project, I would be making trips down to Aberdeen to get the firing tables. However, they already had some preliminary data. I noticed that for most of the higher altitudes where these airplanes would be flying, there wasn't any data. So I called up to find out why there wasn't any data and it turned out that the fuses they were going to use were not clock fuses, but powder-train fuses, which didn't work at those altitudes—they fizzled out in the thin air.

I thought I only had to correct for the air resistance at different altitudes. Instead, my job was to invent a machine that would make the shell explode at the right moment, when the fuse won't burn!

I decided that was too hard for me and went back to Princeton.

LoS ALAMOS
FROM BELOW

When I say "Los Alamos from below," I mean that. Although in my field at the present time I'm a slightly famous man, at that time I was not anybody famous at all. I didn't even have a degree when I started to work on the Manhattan Project. Many of the other people who tell you about Los Alamos—people in higher echelons—worried about some big decisions. I worried about no big decisions; I was always flittering about underneath somewhere.

I was working in my room at Princeton one day when Bob Wilson came in and said that he had been funded to do a job that was a secret, and he wasn't supposed to tell anybody, but he was going to tell me because he knew that as soon as I knew what he was going to do, I'd see that I had to go along with it. So he told me about the problem of separating different isotopes of uranium to ultimately make a bomb. He had a process for separating the isotopes of uranium (different from the one which was ultimately used) that he wanted to try to develop. He told me about it, and he said, "There's a meeting . . ."

I said I didn't want to do it.

He said, "All right, there's a meeting at three o'clock. I'll see you there."

I said, "It's all right that you told me the secret because I'm not going to tell anybody, but I'm not going to do it."

So I went back to work on my thesis—for about three minutes. Then I began to pace the floor and think about this thing. The Germans had Hitler and the possibility of developing an atomic bomb was obvious, and the possibility that they would develop it before we did was very much of a fright. So I decided to go to the meeting at three o'clock.

By four o'clock I already had a desk in a room and was trying to calculate whether this particular method was limited by the total amount of current that you get in an ion beam, and so on—I won't go into the details. But I had a desk, and I had paper, and I was working as hard as I could and as fast as I could, so the fellas who were building the apparatus could do the experiment right there.

It was like those moving pictures where you see a piece of equipment go *brrrup, brrrup, brrrup:* Every time I'd look up, the thing was getting bigger. What was happening, of course, was that all the boys had decided to work on this and to stop their research in science. All science stopped during the war except the little bit that was done at Los Alamos—and that was not much science; it was mostly engineering.

All the equipment from different research projects was being put together to make the new apparatus to do the experiment to try to separate the isotopes of uranium. I stopped my own work for the same reason, though I did take a six-week vacation after a while and finished writing my thesis. And I did get my degree just before I went to Los Alamos—so I wasn't quite as far down as I led you to believe.

One of the first interesting experiences I had in this project at Princeton was meeting great men. I had never met very many great men before. But there was an evaluation committee that would help us along, and ultimately decide which way we were going to separate the uranium. This committee had men like Compton and Tolman and Smyth and Urey and Rabi and Oppenheimer on it. I would sit in because I understood the theory of how our process of separating isotopes worked, and so they'd ask me questions and talk about it. In these discussions one man would make a point. Then Compton, for example, would explain a different point of view. He would say it should be *this* way, and he was perfectly right. Another guy would say, well, maybe, but there's this other possibility we have to consider against it.

So everybody is disagreeing, all around the table. I am surprised and disturbed that Compton doesn't repeat and emphasize his point. Finally, at the end, Tolman, who's the chairman, would say, "Well, having heard all these arguments, I guess it's true that Compton's argument is the best of all, and now we have to go ahead."

It was such a shock to me to see that a committee of men could present a whole lot of ideas, each one thinking of a new facet, while remembering what the other fella said, having paid attention, so that, at the end, the decision is made as to which idea was the best—summing it all up—without having to say it three times! So that was a shock—these were very great men indeed.

It was ultimately decided that this project was *not* to be the way they were going to separate uranium. We were told then that we were going to stop, and in Los Alamos, New Mexico, they would be starting the project that would actually make the bomb. We would all go out there to make it. There would be experiments that we would have to do, and theoretical work to do. I was in the theoretical work. All the rest of the fellas around me were in experimental work.

The question was, What to do now? Los Alamos wasn't ready yet. Bob Wilson tried to make use of this time by sending me to Chicago to find out all I could about the bomb and the problems. Then, in our laboratories, we could start to build equipment—counters of various kinds, and so on—that would be useful when we got to Los Alamos. So no time was wasted.

I was sent to Chicago with the instructions to go to each group, tell them I was going to work with them, and have them tell me about a problem in enough detail that I could actually sit down and start to work on it. As soon as I got that far, I was to go to another guy and ask for another problem. That way I would understand the details of everything.

It was a very good idea, but my conscience bothered me a little bit because they would all work so hard to explain things to me, and then I'd go away without helping them. But I was lucky. When one of the guys was explaining a problem, I said, "Why don't you do it by differentiating under the integral sign?" In half an hour he had it solved, and they'd been working on it for three months. So, in the end, I did *something*, using my "different box of tools." Then I came back from Chicago, and I described the situation—how much energy was released, what the bomb was going to be like, and so forth, to the fellas at Princeton.

I remember a friend of mine who worked with me, Paul Olum, a mathematician, came up to me afterwards and said, "When they make a moving picture about this, they'll have the guy coming back from Chicago, telling the Princeton men about the bomb, and he'll be wearing a suit and carrying a briefcase and so on—and here you're in dirty shirt-sleeves and just telling us all about it, in spite of its being such a serious and dramatic thing." So he appreciated the difference between the real world, and that in the movies.

There still seemed to be a delay, and Wilson went to Los Alamos to find out what was holding things up. When he got there, he found that the construction company was working very hard and had finished the theater, and a few other buildings that they understood, but they hadn't gotten instructions clear on how to build a laboratory—how many pipes for gas, how many for water, and so on. So Wilson simply stood around and decided, then and there, how much water, how much gas, and told them to start building the laboratories.

When he came back to us, we were all ready to go and we were getting impatient. So Wilson called John Manley in Chicago, and they all got together and decided we'd go out there anyway, even though it wasn't ready.

We were recruited, by the way, by Oppenheimer, and he was very patient. He paid attention to everybody's problems; he worried about my wife, who had TB, and whether there would be a hospital for her out there. It was the first time I met him in such a personal way; he was a wonderful man.

■   ■   ■

We were told to be very careful not to buy our train tickets in Princeton, because Princeton was a very small station, and if everybody bought train tickets to Albuquerque, New Mexico, in Princeton, there would be some suspicion that something was up. And so everybody bought their tickets somewhere else—except me, because I figured if everybody bought their tickets somewhere else . . .

So when I went to the train station and said, "I want to go to Albuquerque, New Mexico," the man says, "Oh! So all this stuff is for *you!*" We had been shipping out crates full of counters for weeks and expecting that they didn't notice the address was Albuquerque. So at least I explained why it was that we were shipping all those crates: *I* was going out to Albuquerque.

When we arrived, the houses and dormitories and things like that were not ready. In fact, even the laboratories weren't quite ready. We were pushing them by coming down ahead of time. So they just went crazy and rented ranch houses all around the neighborhood. We stayed at first in a ranch house and would drive in in the morning. The first morning I drove in was tremendously impressive. The beauty of the scenery, for a person from the East who didn't travel much, was sensational. There are the great cliffs that you've probably seen in pictures. You'd come up from below and be very surprised to see this high mesa. As we were going up, I said that maybe there had been Indians living here, and the guy who was driving stopped the car and walked around the corner and pointed out some Indian caves that you could inspect. It was very exciting.

When I got up to the site the first time, I saw there was a technical area that was supposed to have a fence around it ultimately, but it was still open. Then there was supposed to be a town, and then a *big* fence further out, around the town. But they were still building, and my friend Paul Olum, who was my assistant, was standing at the gate with a clipboard, checking the trucks coming in and out and telling them which way to go to deliver the materials in different places.

When I went into the laboratory, I would meet men I had heard of by seeing their papers in the *Physical Review*. "This is John Williams," they'd say. Then a guy stands up from a desk that is covered with blueprints, his sleeves all rolled up, and he's calling out the windows, ordering trucks and things going in different directions with building material. In other words, the experimental physicists had nothing to do until their buildings and apparatus were ready, so they just built the buildings—or assisted in building the buildings.

The theoretical physicists, on the other hand, could start working right away, so it was decided that they wouldn't live in the ranch houses, but would live up at the site. We started working immediately. There were no blackboards except for one on wheels, and we'd roll it around. Robert Serber would explain to us all the things that they'd thought of in Berkeley about the atomic bomb, and nuclear physics, and all these things. I didn't know very much about it; I had been doing other kinds of things. So I had to do an awful lot of work.

Every day I would study and read, study and read. It was a very hectic time. But I had some luck. All the big shots except for Hans Bethe happened to be away one time—Viktor Weisskopf had to go back and fix something at MIT, and Edward Teller was away—and what Bethe needed was someone to talk to, to push his ideas against. Well, he comes in to this little squirt in an office and starts to argue, explaining his idea. I say, "No, no, you're crazy: It'll go like this." And he says, "Just a moment," and explains how *he's* not crazy, *I'm* crazy. And we keep on going like this. You see, when I hear about physics, I just think about the physics, and I don't know who I'm talking to, so I say dopey things like, "No, no, you're wrong," or "You're crazy!" But it turned out that's exactly what he needed. I got a notch up on account of that, and I ended up as a group leader under Bethe with four guys under me.*

When I was first there, as I said, the dormitories weren't ready. But the theoretical physicists had to stay up there anyway. The first place

*In this talk Feynman also described how Bethe was good at arithmetic. See "Lucky Numbers," pp. 228–29. —RL

they put us was in an old school building—a boys' school that had been there previously. I lived in a thing called the Mechanics' Lodge. We were all jammed in there in bunk beds, and it wasn't organized very well—Bob Christy and his wife had to go to the bathroom through our bedroom—so that was very uncomfortable.

At last the dormitory was built. I went down to the place where rooms were assigned, and they said, "You can pick your room now." You know what I did? I looked to see where the girls' dormitory was, and then I picked a room that looked right across—though later I discovered a big tree was growing right in front of the window of that room.

They told me there would be two people in a room, but that would only be temporary. Every two rooms would share a bathroom, and there would be double-decker bunks in each room.

The night I got there, nobody else was there, so I decided to try to keep my room for myself. My wife was sick with TB in Albuquerque and I had some boxes of stuff of hers. So I took out a little nightgown, opened the top bed, and threw the nightgown carelessly on it. I took out some slippers, and I threw some powder on the floor in the bathroom. I just made it look like somebody else was there. So, what happened? (It's supposed to be a men's dormitory!) I come home that night, and my pajamas are folded nicely, and put under the pillow at the bottom, and my slippers put nicely at the bottom of the bed. The lady's nightgown is nicely folded under the pillow, the bed is all fixed up and made, and the slippers are put down nicely. The powder is cleaned from the bathroom and *nobody* is sleeping in the upper bed.

Next day, same thing: When I wake up, I rumple up the top bed, I throw the nightgown on it sloppily and scatter the powder in the bathroom, and so on. I went on like this for four nights until everybody was settled and there was no more danger that they would put a second person in my room. Each night, everything was set out very neatly, even though it was a men's dormitory.

I didn't know it then, but this little ruse got me involved in politics. There were all kinds of factions there, of course—the housewives' faction, the mechanics' faction, the technical peoples' faction, and so on. Well, the bachelors and bachelor girls who lived in the dormitory felt they had to have a faction too, because a new rule had been promulgated: NO WOMEN IN THE MEN'S DORMITORY! Well, this is absolutely ridiculous! After all, we are grown people (ha, ha); what kind of nonsense is this? We had to have political action. So we debated this stuff, and I was elected to represent the dormitory people in the town council.

After I'd been on the town council for about a year and a half, I was talking to Hans Bethe about something. He was on the big governing council all this time, and I told him about this trick with my wife's nightgown and bedroom slippers. He started to laugh. "So *that's* how you got on the town council," he said.

It turned out that what happened was this. The woman who cleans the rooms in the dormitory opens this door, and all of a sudden there is trouble: Somebody is sleeping with one of the guys! She reports to the chief charwoman, the chief charwoman reports to the lieutenant, the lieutenant reports to the major. It goes all the way up through the generals to the governing council.

What are they going to do?

They're going to think about it. So in the meantime, what instructions go down through the captains, down through the majors, through the lieutenants, through the chars' chief, through the charwoman? "Just put things back the way they are, clean them up, and see what happens."

Next day, same report. For four days, they worried up there about what they were going to do. Finally they promulgated a rule: No WOMEN IN THE MEN'S DORMITORY! And that caused such a *stink* down below that they had to elect somebody to the town council . . .

■   ■   ■

I would like to tell you something about the censorship that we had there. The Army decided to do something utterly illegal: censor the mail of people inside the United States—which they had no right to do. So it had to be set up very delicately as a voluntary thing: We would all volunteer not to seal the envelopes of the letters we sent out, and it would be all right for the Army censors to open letters coming in to us; that was voluntarily accepted by us. We would leave our letters open, and they would seal them if they were OK. If they weren't OK in their opinion, they would send the letter back to us with a note that there was a violation of such-and-such a paragraph of our understanding.

So, very delicately amongst all these liberal-minded scientific guys, we finally got the censorship set up, with many rules. We were allowed to comment on the character of the administration if we wanted to, so we could write our senator and tell him we didn't like the way things were run, and things like that. They said they would notify us if there were any difficulties.

So it was all set up, and here comes the first day for censorship. Telephone: *Brrrring!*

Me: "What?"

"Please come down."

I come down.

"What's this?"

"It's a letter from my father."

"Well, what *is* it?"

There's lined paper, and there's these lines going out with dots—four dots under, one dot above, two dots under, one dot above . . .

I said, "It's a code."

"Yes, it's a code, but what does it say?"

"I don't know what it says."

"Well, what's the key to the code? How do you decipher it?"

"I don't know!"

Then they said, "And what's this?"

"It's a letter from my wife. It says TJXYWZ TW1X3—another code."

"What's the key to it?"

"I don't know."

"You're receiving codes, and you don't know the key?"

I said, "Precisely! I have a game: I challenge them to send me a code that I can't decipher, so they're making up codes at the other end, and they're sending them in—and they're not going to tell me what the key is."

Now one of the rules of the censorship was that they aren't going to disturb anything that you would ordinarily do, in the mail. So they said, "Well, you're going to have to ask them please to send the key in with the code."

I said, "But I don't want to see the key!"

They said, "Well, all right, we'll take the key out."

So we had that arrangement.

The next day I get a letter from my wife that says, "It's very difficult writing because I feel that the ████ is looking over my shoulder." And where the word had been, there is a splotch made with ink eradicator.

So I went down to the bureau, and I said, "You're not supposed to touch the incoming mail if you don't like it. You can look at it, but you're not supposed to take anything out."

They said, "Don't be ridiculous. Do you think that's the way censors work—with ink eradicator? They cut things out with scissors."

I wrote a letter back to my wife: "Did you use ink eradicator in your letter?"

She writes back: "No, I didn't use ink eradicator in my letter, it must have been the ⬜⬜⬜⬜"—and there's a hole cut out of the paper.

So I went back to the major who was supposed to be in charge of all this and complained. (This took a little time, but I felt I was sort of the representative to get the thing straightened out.) The major tried to explain to me that these people who were the censors had been taught how to do it, but they didn't understand this new way that we had to be so delicate about.

He said, "What's the matter, don't you think I have good will?"

I said, "Yes, you have perfectly good will but I don't think you have *power*."

He says, "We'll see about *that!*" He grabs the telephone, and everything is straightened out. No more is the letter cut.

However, there were a number of other difficulties. For example, one day I got a letter from my wife and a note from the censor that said, "There was a code enclosed without the key, and so we removed it."

So when I went to see my wife in Albuquerque later that day, she said, "Well, where's all the stuff?"

I said, "What stuff?"

"Litharge, glycerine, hot dogs, laundry . . ."

"Wait a minute—that was a list?"

"Yes."

"That was a *code*," I said. They thought it was a code—litharge, glycerine, etc. (She wanted litharge and glycerine to make a cement to fix an onyx box.)

All this went on in the first few weeks before we got it straightened out. Anyway, one day I'm piddling around with the computing machine, and I notice something very peculiar. If you take 1 divided by 243 you get .004115226337 . . . it's quite cute. It goes a little cockeyed after 559 when you're carrying but it soon straightens itself out and repeats itself nicely. I thought it was kind of amusing.

Well, I put that in the mail, and it comes back to me. It doesn't go through, and there's a little note: "Look at Paragraph 17B." I look at Paragraph 17B. It says, "Letters are to be written only in English, Russian, Spanish, Portuguese, Latin, German," and so forth. "Permission to use any other language must be obtained in writing. No codes."

So I wrote back to the censor a little note which said, "Of course this cannot be a code, because if you actually *do* divide 1 by 243, you do, in fact, *get* all that, and therefore there's no more information in the number .004115226337 . . . than there is in the number 243—which is hardly any information at all. I therefore ask for permission to use Arabic numerals in my letters." So I got *that* through all right.

There was always some kind of difficulty with the letters going back and forth. For example, my wife kept mentioning the fact that she felt uncomfortable writing with the feeling that the censor is looking over her shoulder. Now, as a rule, we aren't supposed to mention censorship. *We* aren't, but how can they tell *her?* So they kept sending me a note: "Your wife mentioned censorship." *Certainly* my wife mentioned censorship. So finally they sent me a note that said, "Please inform your wife not to mention censorship in her letters."

So I start my letter: "I have been instructed to inform you not to mention censorship in your letters."

Phoom, phoom! It comes right back.

So I write, "I have been instructed to inform my wife not to mention censorship. How am I going to do it? Furthermore, *why* do I have to instruct her not to mention censorship—are you keeping something from *me?*"

It is very interesting that the censor himself has to tell me to tell my wife not to tell me that she's . . . But they had an answer. They said that they are worried about mail being intercepted on the way from Albuquerque, and that someone might find out that there was censorship if they looked in the mail, so would she please act more normal.

So the next time I went down to Albuquerque, I said, "Now, look, let's not mention censorship any more." But we had had so much trouble that we at last worked out a code, something illegal. If I would put a dot at the end of my signature, it meant I had had trouble again, and she would move on to the next of the moves that she had concocted. (She would sit there all day long, because she was ill, and she would think of things to do.) The last thing she did was to send me an advertisement which she found perfectly legitimately. It said, "Send your boyfriend a letter on a jigsaw puzzle. We sell you the blank, you write the letter on it, take it all apart, put it in a little sack, and mail it." I received that one with a note saying, "We do not have time to play games. Please instruct your wife to confine herself to ordinary letters."

Well, we were ready with the one more dot, but they straightened out just in time and we didn't have to use it. The thing we had ready for the next one was that the letter would start, "I hope you remembered to open this letter carefully because I have included the Pepto-Bismol powder for your stomach as we arranged." It would be a letter full of powder. In the office we expected they would open it quickly, the powder would go all over the floor, and they would get all upset because you are not supposed to upset anything. They'd have to gather up all this Pepto-Bismol . . . But we didn't have to use that one.

As a result of all these experiences with the censor, I knew exactly what could get through and what could not get through—nobody else knew as well as I. And so I made a little money out of all this by making bets.

One day I discovered that the workmen who lived further out and wanted to come in were too lazy to go around through the gate, and so they had cut themselves a hole in the fence. So I went out the gate, went over to the hole and came in, went out again, and so on, until the sergeant at the gate began to wonder why this guy is always going out and never coming in! And, of course, his natural reaction was to call the lieutenant and try to put me in jail for doing this. I explained that there was a hole.

You see, I was always trying to straighten people out. And so I made a bet with somebody that I could tell about the hole in a letter, and mail it out. And sure enough, I did. And the way I did it was I said, "You should see the way they administer this place: There's a hole in the fence seventy-one feet away from such-and-such a place, that's this wide and that tall, that you can walk through."

Now, what can they do? They can't say to me that there is no such hole. I mean, what are they going to do? It's their own hard luck that there's such a hole. They should *fix* the hole. So I got that one through by criticizing the administration.

I also got through a letter that told about how one of the boys who worked in one of my groups, John Kemeny, had been wakened up in the middle of the night and grilled with lights in front of him by some idiots in the Army because they found out something about his father, who was supposed to be a communist or something. Kemeny is a famous man now.

◾   ◾   ◾

There were other things. Like the hole in the fence, I was always trying to point these things out in a non-direct manner. One of the things I wanted to point out was this: At the very beginning we had terribly important secrets—we'd worked out lots of stuff about bombs and uranium and how it worked, and so on—and all this stuff was in documents that were in wooden filing cabinets that had little, ordinary, common padlocks on them. Of course, there were various things made by the shop, like a rod that would go down and then a padlock to hold it, but it was always just a padlock. Furthermore, you could get the stuff out without even opening the padlock. You just tilt the cabinet over backwards. The bottom drawer has a little rod that's supposed to hold the papers together, and there's a long wide hole in the wood underneath. You can pull the papers out from below.

So I used to pick the locks all the time and point out that it was very easy to do. And every time we had a meeting of everybody together, I would get up and say that we have important secrets and we shouldn't keep them in such things; we need better locks.

One day Teller got up at the meeting, and he says to me, "I don't keep my most important secrets in my filing cabinet; I keep them in my desk drawer. Isn't that better?"

I said, "I don't know. I haven't seen your desk drawer."

He's sitting near the front of the meeting, and I'm sitting further back. So the meeting continues, and I sneak out and go down to see his desk drawer.

I don't even have to pick the lock on the desk drawer. It turns out that if you put your hand in the back, underneath, you can pull out the paper like those toilet paper dispensers. You pull out one, it pulls another, it pulls another . . . I empty the whole damn drawer, put everything away to one side, and go back to the meeting.

The meeting is just ending, and everybody's coming out, so I run to catch up with Teller, and I say, "Oh, by the way, let me see your desk drawer."

"Certainly," he says, and he shows me the desk.

I look at it and say, "That looks pretty good to me. Let's see what you have in there."

"I'll be very glad to show it to you," he says, putting in the key and opening the drawer, "if you hadn't already seen it yourself . . ."

The trouble with playing a trick on a highly intelligent man like Mr. Teller is the *time* that it takes him to figure out from the moment he sees there's something wrong until he understands exactly what happened is *too damn small* to give you any pleasure!

■　　■　　■

Some of the special problems I had at Los Alamos were rather interesting. One problem had to do with the safety of the plant at Oak Ridge, Tennessee. Los Alamos was going to make the bomb, but at Oak Ridge they were trying to separate the isotopes of uranium—uranium 238 and uranium 235, the explosive one. They were just beginning to get infinitesimal amounts of U235, and at the same time they were practicing the chemistry. There was going to be a big plant—they were going to have vats of the stuff—and then they were going to take the purified stuff and repurify and get it ready for the next stage. (You have to purify it in several stages.) So they were practicing on the one hand, and they were just getting a little bit of U235 from one of the pieces of apparatus experimentally on the other hand. They were also trying to learn how to assay it, to determine how much uranium 235 there is in it. Though we would send them instructions, they never got it right.

So finally Emil Segrè said that the only possible way to get it right is to go down there and see what they were doing. The Army people said, "No, it is our policy to keep all the information of Los Alamos in one place."

The people in Oak Ridge didn't know anything about what the U235 was to be used for; the higher people knew they were separating uranium, but they didn't know how powerful the bomb was, or exactly how it worked or anything. The people underneath didn't know *at all* what they were doing. The Army wanted to keep it that way—with no information going back and forth—but Segrè insisted they'd never get the assays right, and the whole thing would go up in smoke. So he finally went down to see what they were doing. As he was walking through, he saw them wheeling a big carboy of water—green water—which is uranium nitrate solution.

He said, "Are you going to handle it like that when it's purified, too?"

They said, "Sure—why not?"

"Won't it explode?" he said.

"Huh? *Explode?*"

And so the Army said, "You see! We shouldn't have let any information get to them. Now they are all upset."

It turned out that the Army had realized how much stuff we needed to make a bomb—twenty kilograms or whatever it was—and they realized that this much material, purified, would never be in the plant, so there was no danger. But they did *not* know that the neutrons were enormously more effective when they are slowed down in water. In water it takes less than a hundredth as much material to make a reaction that makes radioactivity. It kills people who are nearby. It was *very* dangerous, and they had not paid any attention to the safety at all.

So a telegram goes from Oppenheimer to Segrè: GO THROUGH THE ENTIRE PLANT. NOTICE WHERE ALL THE CONCENTRATIONS ARE SUPPOSED TO BE, WITH THE PROCESS AS THEY DESIGNED IT. WE WILL CALCULATE HOW MUCH MATERIAL CAN COME TOGETHER BEFORE THERE IS AN EXPLOSION.

Two groups started working on it. Christy's group worked on water solutions, and my group worked on dry powder in boxes. We calculated how much material they could accumulate safely. Christy was going to go down and tell them all at Oak Ridge what the situation was, but Christy got pneumonia—so I had to go.

I had never traveled on an airplane before. They strapped the secrets in a little satchel on my back. The airplane in those days was like a bus, except the stations were further apart. You stopped off every once in a while to wait.

A guy standing there next to me, swinging a chain, said something like, "It must be *terribly* difficult to fly without a priority on airplanes these days."

I couldn't resist. I said, "Well, I don't know. I *have* a priority."

A little bit later he says, "There are some generals coming. It looks like they are going to put off some of us number threes."

"It's all right," I said, "I'm a number two."

He probably wrote to his congressman—if he wasn't a congressman himself—saying, "What are they doing sending these little kids around with number two priorities in the middle of the war?"

At any rate, I arrived at Oak Ridge. The first thing I did was have them take me to the plant, and I said nothing—I just looked at everything. I found out that the situation was even worse than Segrè reported, because he noticed certain boxes in big lots in a room, but he didn't notice a lot of boxes in another room on the other side of the same wall—things like that.

So I went through the entire plant. I have a very bad memory, but when I work intensively I have a good short-term memory, and so I could remember all kinds of crazy things like building 9207, vat number so-and-so, and so forth.

I went to my room that night and went through the whole thing, explained where all the dangers were, and what you would have to do to fix it. It's rather easy: You put cadmium in solution to absorb the neutrons in the water, and you separate the boxes of uranium so they are not too dense, according to certain rules.

The next day there was going to be a big meeting. I forgot to say that, before I left Los Alamos, Oppenheimer said to me, "Now, the following people are technically able at Oak Ridge: Mr. Julian Webb, Mr. So-and-so, and so on. I want you to make sure that these people are at the meeting where you tell them how the plant can be made safe, so that they really *understand*."

I said, "What if they're not at the meeting? What am I supposed to do?"

He said, "Then you should say: *Los Alamos cannot accept the responsibility for the safety of the Oak Ridge plant* unless . . . "

I said, "You mean me, little Richard, is going to go in there and say that?"

He said, "Yes, little Richard, you go and say that."

I really grew up fast.

When I arrived, the big shots in the company and the technical people that I wanted were there, as well as the generals and everyone who was interested in this very serious problem. That was good because the plant would have blown up if nobody had paid attention to it.

There was a Lieutenant Zumwalt who took care of me. He told me that the colonel in charge said I shouldn't tell Oak Ridge how the neutrons work, and all the details, because we want to keep the information separate, so just tell them what to do to keep it safe.

I said, "In my opinion it is impossible for them to obey a bunch of rules unless they understand how it works. It's my opinion that it's only going to work if I tell them, and *Los Alamos cannot accept the responsibility for the safety of the Oak Ridge plant unless they are fully informed as to how it works!*"

It was great. The lieutenant takes me to the colonel and repeats my remark. The colonel says, "Just five minutes," and then he goes to the window and he stops and thinks. That's what they're very good at—making decisions. I thought it was very remarkable how the problem of whether or not information as to how the bomb works should be in the Oak Ridge plant could be decided in five minutes. So I have a great deal of respect for these military guys, because I never can decide anything very important in any length of time at all!

After five minutes he said, "All right, Mr. Feynman, go ahead."

I sat down and I told them all about neutrons, how they worked, how there are too many neutrons together, how you've got to keep the material apart, how cadmium absorbs, and how slow neutrons are more effective than fast neutrons, yak yak—all of which was elementary primer stuff at Los Alamos—but they had never heard of any of it. So I appeared to be a tremendous genius to them: I was a god coming down from the sky! All these phenomena that they never heard of before, I knew all about—I could give them facts, and numbers, and everything else—so by being rather primitive at Los Alamos, I was a super-genius at the other end.

The result was that they decided to set up groups to make their own calculations and learn how to do it. The designers of the plant were there—the construction designers, engineers, and chemical engineers—for the new plant that was going to handle the separated material.

They told me to come back in a few months, when the engineers had finished the design of the plant.

A few months later, it was time for me to look at the plant.

How do you look at a plant that isn't built yet? I don't know. Lieutenant Zumwalt, who was always coming around with me because I had to have an escort everywhere, takes me into this room where there are two engineers from the Stone and Webster Company, and a *loooooong* table covered with a stack of blueprints representing the various floors of the proposed plant.

I took mechanical drawing when I was in school, but I am not good at reading blueprints. So they unroll the stack of blueprints and start to explain it to me, thinking I am a genius. Now, one of the things they had to avoid in the plant was accumulation: They had problems like when there's an evaporator working, which is trying to accumulate the stuff, if the valve gets stuck and too much stuff accumulates, it'll explode. So they explained to me that this plant is designed so that if any *one* valve gets stuck nothing will happen. It needs at least *two* valves everywhere.

Then they explain how it works. The carbon tetrachloride comes in here, the uranium nitrate from here comes in here, it goes up and down, it goes up through the floor, comes up through the pipes, coming up from the second floor, *brrrrrup*—going through the stack of blueprints, down-up-down-up, talking very fast, explaining the very, very complicated chemical plant.

I'm completely dazed. Worse: I don't know what the symbols on the blueprint mean. There is some kind of a thing that at first I think is a window: It's a square with a little cross in the middle, all over the damn place. I think it's a window, but no, it can't be a window, because it isn't always at the edge. I want to ask them what it is.

Now, you must have been in a situation like this, when you didn't ask them right away. Right away it would have been OK. But now they've been talking a little bit too long. You hesitated too long. If you ask them now they'll say, "What are you wasting my time all this time for?"

What am I going to do? I get an idea. Maybe it's a valve. I take my finger and I put it down on one of the mysterious little crosses in the middle of one of the blueprints on page three, and I say, "What happens if *this* valve gets stuck?"—figuring they're going to say, "That's not a valve, Sir, that's a window."

So one looks at the other and says, "Well, if *that* valve gets stuck—" and he goes up and down the blueprint, up and down, the other guy goes up and down, back and forth, back and forth, and they both look at each other. They turn around to me and they open their mouths like astonished fish and say, "You're absolutely right, Sir!"

So they rolled up the blueprints and away they went, and we walked out. And Mr. Zumwalt, who had been following me all the way through, said, "You're a genius. I got the idea you were a genius when you went through the plant once and you could tell them about evaporator C-21 in building 9207 the next morning," he says, "and when you knew all about the neutrons, you were a genius. But what you have just done is so *fantastic,* I want to know how—*how*—do you do something like *that?*"

I told him you try to find out whether it's a valve or not.

• • •

Another kind of problem I worked on was this: We had to do lots of calculations, and we did them on Marchant calculating machines. By the way, just to give you an idea of what Los Alamos was like, we had these Marchant "computers"—hand calculators with numbers. You push them, and they multiply, divide, add, and so on, but not easy like they do now. They were mechanical gadgets, failing often, and they had to be sent back to the factory to be repaired. Pretty soon we were running out of machines. A few of us started to take the covers off. (We weren't supposed to. The rules read: "You take the covers off, we cannot be responsible . . .") We took the covers off and we got a nice series of lessons on how to fix the machines, and we got better and better. When we got something too complicated, we sent it back to the factory, but we'd do the easy ones and kept the things going. I ended up doing all the Marchant computers and there was a guy in the machine shop who took care of the typewriters.

Anyway, we decided that the big problem—which was to figure out exactly what happened during the bomb's implosion (when you push the stuff in by an explosion and it goes out again), so you can figure out exactly how much energy was released and so on—required much more calculating than we were capable of. A clever fellow by the name of Stanley Frankel realized that it could possibly be done on IBM machines. The IBM company had machines for business purposes—adding machines called tabulators for listing sums, and a multiplier—that you put cards in and it would take two numbers from a card and add or multiply them. There were also collators and sorters and so on.

So Frankel figured out a nice program: If we got enough of these machines in a room, we could take the cards and put them through a cycle. Everybody who does numerical calculations now knows exactly what I'm talking about, but this was a new thing then—mass-production calculating with machines. Usually you go across, doing everything yourself. But this was different: You go first to the adder, then to the multiplier, then to the adder, and so on. So Frankel designed this system and ordered the machines from the IBM company, because we realized it was a good way of solving our problems.

We needed a man to repair the IBM machines, to keep them going, and the Army was going to send this fellow they had, but he was always delayed. Now, we always were in a hurry. *Everything* we did, we tried to do as quickly as possible. In this particular case, we worked out all the numerical steps that the machines were supposed to do—multiply this, and then do this, and subtract that. In other words, we worked out the program—but we didn't have any machine to test it on. So we set up this room with girls in it. Each one had a Marchant: one girl was the multiplier, another was the adder. This one cubed—all she did was cube a number on an index card and send it to the next girl.

We went through our cycle this way until we got all the bugs out. It turned out that the speed at which we were able to do it was a hell of a lot faster than the other way, where a single person did all the steps. We got speed with this system that was the predicted speed for the IBM machine! The only difference was that the IBM machines didn't get tired and could work three shifts—but the girls got tired after a while.

Anyway, we got the bugs out during this process, and finally the machines arrived, but not the repairman. These were some of the most complicated machines of the technology of those days—big things that came partially disassembled, with lots of wires and blueprints of what to do. We went down and we put them together, Stan Frankel and I and another fellow, and we had our troubles. Most of the trouble was the big shots coming in all the time and saying, "You're going to break something!"

We put them together, and sometimes they would work—and sometimes they were put together wrong and they didn't work. Finally I was working on some multiplier and I saw a bent part inside, but I was afraid to straighten it because it might snap off—and they were always telling us we were going to bust something irreversibly. When the repairman finally got there, he fixed the machines we hadn't got ready, and everything was going. But he had trouble with the one that I had had trouble with. After three days he was still working on that one last machine.

I said, "Oh, I noticed that part there was bent."

He said, "Oh, of course. That's all there is *to* it!" *Bend!* It was all right.

Well, Mr. Frankel, who started this program, began to suffer from the computer disease that anybody who works with computers now knows about. It's a very serious disease and it interferes completely with the work. The trouble with computers is you *play* with them—they are so wonderful. You have these switches—if it's an even number you do this, if it's an odd number you do that—and pretty soon you can do more and more elaborate things, if you are clever enough, on one machine.

After a while the whole system broke down. Frankel wasn't paying any attention; he wasn't supervising anybody. The system was going very, very slowly, while he was sitting in a room figuring out how to make one tabulator automatically print arctangent x, and then it would start and it would print columns and then *bitsi, bitsi, bitsi,* and calculate the arctangent automatically by integrating as it went along and make a whole table in one operation.

Absolutely useless! We *had* tables of arctangents. But if you've ever worked with computers, you understand the disease—the *delight* in being able to see how much you can do. But he got the disease for the first time, the poor fellow who invented the program.

I was asked to stop working on the stuff I was doing in my group and take over the IBM group, so I tried to avoid the disease. And, although they had done only three problems in nine months, I had a very good group.

The trouble was that no one had ever told these fellows anything. The Army had selected from all over the country a thing called Special Engineer Detachment—clever boys from high school who had engineering ability. They were sent up to Los Alamos, put into barracks, and were told *nothing*.

What they had to do was work on IBM machines—punching holes, numbers that they didn't understand. Nobody told them what it was. The thing was going very slowly.

I said the first thing there has to be is that these technical guys know what we're doing. Oppenheimer went and talked to the security and got special permission so I could give a nice lecture about what we were doing, and they were all excited: "We're fighting a war! We see what it is!" Now they knew what the numbers meant: If the pressure came out higher, that meant there was more energy released, and so on. They now knew what they were doing.

Complete transformation! *They* began to invent ways of doing it better. They improved the scheme. They worked at night. They didn't need supervising; they didn't need anything. They understood everything; they invented several of the programs that we used.

So my boys really came through, and all that had to be done was to tell them what it was they were doing. As a result, although it took them nine months to do three problems before, they now did nine problems in *three* months, which is nearly ten times as fast.

One of the secret ways we did our problems faster was this: The problems consisted of a bunch of cards that had to go through a cycle— first add, then multiply—so it went through the cycle of machines in this room, slowly, as it went around and around. Now, we figured a way to put a different-colored set of cards through a cycle too, but out of phase. We'd do two or three problems at a time that way.

But this got us into another problem. Near the end of the war, just before we had to make a test in Albuquerque, the question was: How much energy would be released? We had been calculating the release from various designs, but we hadn't computed for the specific design that was ultimately used. So Bob Christy came down and said, "We would like the results for how this thing is going to work in one month"—or some very short time, like three weeks.

I said, "It's impossible."

He said, "But you're putting out two or three problems a month!"

I said, "I know. It really takes much longer to do each problem, because we're doing them in *parallel*. As it goes through, it takes a long time and there's no way to make it go around faster."

He went out, and I began to think: Is there a way to make it go around faster? What if we did nothing else on the machine, so nothing else was interfering? I put a challenge to the boys on the blackboard— CAN WE DO IT? They all start yelling, "Yes, we'll work double shifts, we'll work overtime," all this kind of thing. "We'll *try* it!"

And so the rule was: all other problems *out;* only one problem in, and just concentrate on this one. So they started to work.

My wife, Arlene, was ill with tuberculosis—very ill indeed. It looked as if something might happen at any minute, so I arranged ahead of time with a friend of mine in the dormitory to borrow his car in an emergency so I could get to Albuquerque quickly. His name was Klaus Fuchs.

He was the spy, and he used his automobile to take the atomic secrets away from Los Alamos down to Santa Fe. But nobody knew that.

The emergency arrived. I borrowed Fuchs's car and got three flat tires along the way. I finally had to abandon the car, and hitchhiked the last thirty miles into Albuquerque.

Arlene died a few hours after I got there. A nurse came in to fill out the death certificate, and went out again. I spent a little more time with my wife.

I went for a walk outside. Maybe I was fooling myself, but I was surprised how I didn't feel what I thought people would expect to feel under the circumstances. I wasn't delighted, but I didn't feel terribly upset, perhaps because I had known for seven years that this was going to happen.

When I went back to work on the calculation program, I found it in a mess: There are white cards, there are blue cards, there are yellow cards, and I start to say, "You're not supposed to do more than one problem—only one problem!" They said, "Get out, get out, get out. Wait—we'll explain everything later."

So I waited, and what happened was this. As the cards went through, sometimes the machine made a mistake, or they put a wrong number in. What we used to have to do when that happened was to stop, go back, and do it over again. But they noticed that a mistake made at some point in one cycle only affects the nearby cards, the next cycle affects the nearby cards, and so on. It works its way slowly through the pack of cards. If you have a deck of fifty cards and you make a mistake at card number 38, it affects 37, 38, and 39. The next time, it affects cards 36, 37, 38, 39, and 40—it spreads like a disease.

So when they found an error back a ways in the white deck, they got an idea. They would only compute a small deck of ten blue cards around the error. And because ten cards could be put through the machines faster than the deck of fifty cards, they would go rapidly through with this smaller deck while they continued with the disease slowly spreading in the deck of fifty cards. But the smaller deck was computing faster, and they would seal it all up and correct it. Very clever!

That was the way those guys worked to get speed. There was no other way: If they had stopped to try to fix it, we'd have lost time—we couldn't have gotten a result.

Of course, you know what happened while they were doing that: They found an error in the blue deck! And so they had a yellow deck with even fewer cards; it was going around faster than the blue deck. And just when they are going crazy—because after they get the blue deck straightened out, they have to fix the white deck—the *boss* comes walking in.

"Leave us alone!" they said. So I left them alone and everything came out. We solved the problem in time and that's the way it was.

. . .

I was an underling at the beginning; later I became a group leader, and I met some very great men. It is one of the great experiences of my life to have met all these wonderful physicists.

There was, of course, Enrico Fermi. He came down once from Chicago to consult a little bit, to help us if we had some problems. We had a meeting with him, and I had been doing some calculations and gotten some results. The calculations were so elaborate it was very difficult. Now, usually I was the expert at this; I could always tell you what the answer was going to look like, or when I got it I could explain why. But this thing was so complicated I couldn't explain *why* it was like that.

So I told Fermi I was doing this problem, and I started to describe the results. He said, "Wait. Before you tell me the result, let me think. It's going to come out like this (he was right), and it's going to come out like this because of so and so."

He was doing what I was supposed to be good at, ten times better. That was quite a lesson to me.

Then there was John Von Neumann, the great mathematician. We used to go for walks on Sunday. We'd walk in the canyons, often with Bethe and Bob Bacher. It was a great pleasure. Von Neumann gave me an interesting idea: that you don't have to be responsible for the world that you're in. So I have developed a very powerful sense of "social irresponsibility" as a result of Von Neumann's advice. It's made me a very happy man ever since. But it was Von Neumann who put the seed in that grew into my *active* "irresponsibility!"

I also met Niels Bohr. His code name was Nicholas Baker in those days, and he came to Los Alamos with Jim Baker, his son, whose name is really Aage Bohr. They came from Denmark, and they were *very* famous physicists, as you know. Even to the big shot guys, Bohr was the great god.

We were at a meeting once, the first time he came, and everybody wanted just to *see* the great Bohr. So there were a lot of people there as we were discussing the problems of the bomb. I was back in a corner somewhere. He came and went, and all I could see of him was from between people's heads.

Early in the morning of the day he's due to come next time, I get a telephone call.

"Hello—Feynman?"

"Yes."

"This is Jim Baker. My father and I would like to speak to you . . ."

"Me? I'm *Feynman*, I'm just a—."

"That's right. Is eight o'clock OK?"

So, at eight o'clock in the morning, before anybody's awake, we go into an office in the technical area and the great Bohr says, "We have been thinking how we could make the bomb more efficient and we think of the following idea . . ."

I say, "No, it's not going to work. It's not good on account of this and that."

He says, "How about so and so?"

I said, "That sounds a bit better, but it's got this damn fool idea in it."

This went on for about two hours, going back and forth over lots of ideas, back and forth, arguing. The great Niels kept lighting his pipe; it always went out. And he talked in a way that was mumble, mumble, hard to understand. His son I could understand better.

"Well," he said finally, lighting his pipe once again, "I guess we can call in the big shots *now*." So then they called all the other guys and had a discussion with them.

Aage Bohr told me what happened. The last time he was there, Niels Bohr said to his son, "Remember the name of that little fellow in the back over there—he's the only guy who's not afraid of me, and will say when I've got a crazy idea. So next time when we want to discuss ideas, we're not going to be able to do it with these guys who say everything is yes, yes, Dr. Bohr. Get that guy and we'll talk with him first."

I was always dumb in that way. I never knew who I was talking to. I was only worried about the physics. If the idea looked lousy, I said it looked lousy. If it looked good, I said it looked good—simple proposition.

I've always lived that way. It's nice, it's pleasant—if you can do it. I'm lucky in my life that I can do this.

■   ■   ■

After we'd made the calculations, the next thing that happened, of course, was the test. I was actually at home on a short vacation at that time, after my wife died, when I got a message that said THE BABY IS EXPECTED ON JULY 16.

I flew back, and I arrived just when the buses were leaving, so I went straight out to the site and we waited out there, twenty miles away. We had a radio, and they were supposed to tell us when the bomb was going to go off, but the radio wouldn't work, so we never knew what was happening. But just a few minutes before it was supposed to go off the radio started to work, and they told us there was twenty seconds to go.

They gave out dark glasses that you could watch it with. Dark glasses? Twenty miles away, you couldn't see a damn thing through dark glasses! I figured the only thing that could really hurt your eyes (bright light can never hurt your eyes) is ultraviolet light, so I got behind a truck windshield, because the ultraviolet can't go through glass, so I could *see* the damn thing.

Time comes, and this *tremendous* flash out there is so bright that I duck, and I see this purple splotch on the floor of the truck. I say to myself, "That ain't it—that's an after-image." So I look back up, and I see this white light changing into yellow and then into orange. Clouds form and disappear again—from the compression and expansion of the shock wave.

Finally, a big ball of orange, the center that was so bright, becomes a ball of orange that starts to rise and billow a little bit and get a little black around the edges, and then you see it's a big ball of smoke with flashes on the inside, from the heat and fire going out.

All this took about one minute. It was a series from bright to dark, and I had *seen* it. I'm the only guy who actually looked at the damn thing—the first Trinity test. Everybody else at twenty miles had dark glasses, and the people at six miles couldn't see it because they were all told to lie on the ground. I'm the only guy who saw it with the human eye.

Finally, after about a minute and a half, there's suddenly a tremendous noise—BANG, and then a rumble, like thunder—and that's what convinced me. Nobody had said a word during this whole time—we were all just watching quietly. But this sound released everybody—it released me particularly—because the solidity of the sound at that distance meant that it had really worked.

The man standing next to me said, "What's *that?*"

I said, "That was the Bomb."

The man was William Laurence. He was there to write an article describing the whole situation. I had been the one who was supposed to have taken him around. Then it was found that it was too technical for him, and so later H. D. Smyth came and I showed him around. One thing we did, we went into a room and there on the end of a narrow pedestal was a small silver-plated ball. You could put your hand on it: it was warm; it was radioactive—it was plutonium. We stood at the door of this room, talking about it: Here was a new element that was made by man, that had never existed on the earth before, except for a very short period possibly at the very beginning. And here it was, all isolated and radioactive, and had these properties. And we had made it. It was *tremendously* valuable.

Meanwhile, you know how people do when they talk—you kind of jiggle around and so forth. Mr. Smyth was kicking the doorstop, and I said, "Yes, the doorstop certainly is appropriate for this door." The doorstop was a ten-inch hemisphere of yellowish metal—gold, as a matter of fact.

What had happened was that we needed to do an experiment to see how many neutrons were reflected by different materials, in order to save the neutrons so we didn't use so much material. We had tested many different materials: we had tested platinum, we had tested zinc, we had tested brass, we had tested gold. So, in making the tests with the gold, we had these pieces of gold left over, and somebody had the clever idea of using that great ball of gold for a doorstop for the door of the room that contained the plutonium.

After the bomb went off, there was tremendous excitement at Los Alamos. Everybody had parties; we all ran around. I sat on the end of a jeep and beat drums. But one man, I remember—Bob Wilson—was just sitting there moping.

I said, "What are you moping about?"

He said, "It's a terrible thing that we made."

I said, "But you started it. You got us into it."

You see, what happened to me—what happened to the rest of us—is we *started* for a good reason. Then you're working very hard to accomplish something, and it's a pleasure, it's excitement. And you stop thinking —you just stop. Bob Wilson was the only one who was still thinking about it at that moment.

I returned to civilization shortly after that and went to Cornell to teach, and my first impression was a very strange one. I can't understand it any more, but I felt it very strongly then. I sat in a restaurant in New York, for example, and I looked out at the buildings and I began to think about how much the radius of the Hiroshima bomb damage was— from here to 34th Street—all those buildings, all smashed. I would go along and I would see people building a bridge, or they'd be making a new road, and I'd think "They're *crazy*, they just don't understand. Why are they making new things? It's useless."

But, fortunately, it's been useless for almost thirty years now. So I've been wrong about it being useless building bridges, and I'm glad those other people had the sense to go ahead.

SAFECRACKER
MEETS SAFECRACKER

I learned to pick locks from a guy named Leo Lavatelli. It turns out that picking ordinary tumbler locks—like Yale locks—is easy. You try to turn the lock by putting a screwdriver sideways in the hole—you have to push from the side in order to leave the hole open. It doesn't turn because there are some pins inside which have to be lifted to just the right height (normally by the key). Because it is not made perfectly, the lock is held more by one pin than the others. Now, if you push a little wire gadget—maybe a paper clip with a slight bump at the end—and jiggle it back and forth inside the lock, you'll eventually push the one pin that's doing the most holding up to the right height. The lock gives just a little bit, so the first pin stays up—it's caught on the edge. Now most of the load is held by another pin, and you repeat the same random process for a few more minutes, until all the pins are pushed up.

What often happens is that the screwdriver will slip and you hear tic-tic-tic, and it makes you mad. There are little springs that push the pins back down when a key is removed, and you can hear them click when you let go of the screwdriver. (Sometimes you intentionally let go of the screwdriver to see if you're getting anywhere—you might be pushing the wrong way, for instance.) The process is something like Sisyphus: you're always falling back downhill.

It's a simple process, but practice helps a lot. You learn how hard to push on things—hard enough so the pins will stay up, but not so hard that they won't go up in the first place. What is not really appreciated by most people is that they're perpetually locking themselves in with locks everywhere, and it's not very hard to pick them.

▪ ▪ ▪

When we started to work on the atomic bomb project at Los Alamos, everything was in such a hurry that it wasn't really ready. All the secrets of the project—everything about the atomic bomb—were kept in filing cabinets which, if they had locks at all, were locked with padlocks that had maybe only three pins: they were as easy as pie to open.

To improve security the shop outfitted every filing cabinet with a long steel rod that went down through the handles of the drawers, and that rod was fastened by a padlock.

Some guy said to me, "Look at this new thing the shop put on—can you open the cabinet now?"

I looked at the back of the cabinet and saw that the drawers didn't have a solid bottom. There was a slot with a wire rod in each one that held a slidable piece (which holds the papers up inside the drawer). I poked in from the back, slid the piece back, and began pulling the papers out through the slot. "Look!" I said. "I don't even have to pick the lock."

Los Alamos was a very cooperative place, and we felt it our responsibility to point out things that should be improved. I'd keep complaining that the stuff was unsafe, and although everybody *thought* it was safe because there were steel rods and padlocks, it didn't mean a damn thing.

To demonstrate that the locks meant nothing, whenever I wanted somebody's report and they weren't around, I'd just go in their office, open the filing cabinet, and take it out. When I was finished I would give it back to the guy: "Thanks for your report."

"Where'd you get it?"

"Out of your filing cabinet."

"But I *locked* it!"

"I *know* you locked it. The locks are no good."

■   ■   ■

Finally some filing cabinets came that had combination locks on them made by the Mosler Safe Company. They had three drawers. Pulling the top drawer out would release the other drawers by a catch. The top drawer was opened by turning a combination wheel to the left, right, and left for the combination, and then right to number 10, which would draw back a bolt inside. The whole filing cabinet could be locked by closing the bottom drawers first, then the top drawer, and spinning the combination wheel away from number 10, which pushed up the bolt.

These new filing cabinets were an immediate challenge. I love puzzles: one guy tries to make something to keep another guy out; there must be a way to beat it.

I had first to understand how the lock worked, so I took apart the one in my office. The way it worked is this: There are three discs on a single shaft, one behind the other; each has a notch in a different place. The idea is to line up the notches so that when you turn the wheel to 10, the little friction drive will draw the bolt down into the slot generated by the notches of the three discs.

Now, to turn the discs, there's a pin sticking out from the back of the combination wheel, and a pin sticking up from the first disc at the same radius. Within one turn of the combination wheel, you've picked up the first disc.

On the back of the first disc there's a pin at the same radius as a pin on the front of the second disc, so by the time you've spun the combination wheel around twice, you've picked up the second disc as well.

Keep turning the wheel, and a pin on the back of the second disc will catch a pin on the front of the third disc, which you now set into the proper position with the first number of the combination.

Now you have to turn the combination wheel the other way one full turn to catch the second disc from the other side, and then continue to the second number of the combination to set the second disc.

Again you reverse direction and set the first disc to its proper place. Now the notches are lined up, and by turning the wheel to 10, you open the cabinet.

Well, I struggled, and I couldn't get anywhere. I bought a couple of safecracker books, but they were all the same. In the beginning of the book there are some stories describing the fantastic achievements of the safecracker, such as the woman caught in a meat refrigerator who is freezing to death, but the safecracker, hanging upside down, opens it in two minutes. Or there are some precious furs or gold bullion under water, down in the sea, and the safecracker dives down and opens the chest.

In the second part of the book, they tell you how to crack a safe. And there you find all kinds of ninny-pinny, dopey things, like "It might be a good idea to try a date for the combination, because lots of people like to use dates." Or "Think of the psychology of the owner of the safe, and what he might use for the combination." And "The secretary is often worried that she might forget the combination of the safe, so she will write it down in one of the following places: along the edge of her desk drawer, on a list of names and addresses . . ." and so on.

They *did* tell me something sensible about how to open ordinary safes, and it's easy to understand. Ordinary safes have an extra handle, so if you push down on the handle while you're turning the combination

wheel, things being unequal (as with locks), the force of the handle trying to push the bolt down into the notches (which are not lined up) is
held up more by one disc than another. When the notch on that disc
comes under the bolt, there's a tiny click that you can hear with a stetho-
scope, or a slight decrease in friction that you can feel (you don't have to
sandpaper your fingertips), so you know, "There's *one* number!"

You don't know whether it's the first, second, or third number, but
you can get a pretty good idea of that by finding out how many times you
have to turn the wheel the other way to hear the same click again. If it's a
little less than once, it's the first disc; if it's a little less than twice, it's the
second disc (you have to make a correction for the thickness of the pins).

But this useful trick only works on ordinary safes, which have the
extra handle, so I was stymied.

I tried all kinds of subsidiary tricks with the cabinets, such as finding
out how to release the latches on the lower drawers, without opening
the top drawer, by taking off a screw in front and poking around with a
piece of hanger wire.

I tried spinning the combination wheel very rapidly and then going to
10, thus putting a little friction on, which I hoped would stop a disc at the
right point in some manner. I tried all *kinds* of things. I was desperate.

I also did a certain amount of systematic study. For instance, a typical combination was 69-32-21. How far off could a number be when
you're opening the safe? If the number was 69, would 68 work? Would
67 work? On the particular locks we had, the answer was yes for both,
but 66 wouldn't work—you could be off by two in either direction. That
meant you only had to try one out of five numbers, so you could try 0,
5, 10, 15, and so on. With twenty such numbers on a wheel of 100, that
was 8,000 possibilities instead of the 1,000,000 you would get if you
had to try every single number.

Now the question was, how long would it take me to try the 8,000
combinations? Suppose I've got the first two numbers right of a combination I'm trying to get. Say the numbers are 69-32, but I don't know
it—I've got them as 70-30. Now I can try the twenty possible third numbers without having to set up the first two numbers each time. Now let's
suppose I have only the first number of the combination right. After trying the twenty numbers on the third disc, I move the second wheel only
a little bit, and then do another twenty numbers on the third wheel.

I practiced all the time on my own safe so I could do this process as
fast as I could and not get lost in my mind as to which number I was
pushing and mess up the first number. Like a guy who practices sleight

of hand, I got it down to an absolute rhythm so I could try the 400 possible back numbers in less than half an hour. That meant I could open a safe in a maximum of eight hours—with an average time of four hours.

There was another guy there at Los Alamos named Staley who was also interested in locks. We talked about it from time to time, but we weren't getting anywhere much. After I got this idea how to open a safe in an average time of four hours, I wanted to show Staley how to do it, so I went into a guy's office over in the computing department and asked, "Do you mind if I use your safe? I'd like to show Staley something."

Meanwhile some guys in the computing department came around and one of them said, "Hey, everybody, Feynman's gonna show Staley how to open a safe, ha, ha, ha!" I wasn't going to actually open the safe; I was just going to show Staley this way of quickly trying the back two numbers without losing your place and having to set up the first number again.

I began, "Let's suppose that the first number is 40, and we're trying 15 for the second number. We go back and forth, 10; back five more and forth, 10; and so on. Now we've tried all the possible third numbers. Now we try 20 for the second number: we go back and forth, 10; back five more and forth, 10; back five more and forth . . ." CLICK! My jaw dropped: The first number happened to be right!

Nobody saw my expression because my back was towards them. Staley looked very surprised, but both of us caught on very quickly as to what happened, so I pulled the top drawer out with a flourish and said, "And there you are!"

Staley said, "I see what you mean; it's a very good scheme"—and we walked out. Everybody was amazed. It was complete luck. Now I *really* had a reputation for opening safes.

■　■　■

It took me about a year and a half to get that far (of course, I was working on the bomb, too!), but I figured that now I had the safes beaten in the sense that if there was a real difficulty—if somebody was lost, or dead, and nobody else knew the combination but the stuff in the filing cabinet was needed—I could open it. After reading what preposterous things the safecrackers claimed, I thought that was a rather respectable accomplishment.

We had no entertainment there at Los Alamos, and we had to amuse ourselves somehow, so fiddling with the Mosler lock on my filing cabinet was one of my entertainments.

One day I made an interesting observation: When the lock is open and the drawer has been pulled out and the wheel is left on 10 (which is what people do when they've opened their filing cabinet and are taking papers out of it), the bolt is still down. Now what does that mean, the bolt is still down? It means the bolt is in the slot made by the three discs, which are still properly lined up. Ahhhh!

Now, if I turn the wheel away from 10 a little bit, the bolt comes up; if I immediately go back to 10, the bolt goes back down again, because I haven't yet disturbed the slot. If I keep going away from 10 in steps of five, at some point the bolt won't go back down when I go back to 10—the slot has just been disturbed. The number just before, which still let the bolt go down, is the last number of the combination!

I realized that I could do the same thing to find the second number: As soon as I know the last number, I can turn the wheel around the other way and again, in lumps of five, push the second disc bit by bit until the bolt doesn't go down. The number just before would be the second number.

If I were *very* patient I would be able to pick up all three numbers that way, but the amount of work involved in picking up the first number of the combination by this elaborate scheme would be much more than just trying the twenty possible first numbers with the other two numbers that you already know, when the filing cabinet is closed.

I practiced and I practiced until I could get the last two numbers off an open filing cabinet, hardly looking at the dial. Then, when I'd be in some guy's office discussing some physics problem, I'd lean against his opened filing cabinet, and just like a guy who's jiggling keys absent-mindedly while he's talking, I'd just wobble the dial back and forth, back and forth. Sometimes I'd put my finger on the bolt so I wouldn't have to look to see if it's coming up. In this way I picked off the last two numbers of various filing cabinets. When I got back to my office I would write the two numbers down on a piece of paper that I kept inside the lock of my filing cabinet. I took the lock apart each time to get the paper—I thought that was a very safe place.

After a while my reputation began to sail, because things like this would happen: Somebody would say, "Hey, Feynman! Christy's out of town and we need a document from his safe—can you open it?"

If it was a safe I knew I didn't have the last two numbers of, I would simply say, "I'm sorry, but I can't do it now; I've got this work that I have to do." Otherwise, I would say, "Yeah, but I gotta get my tools." I didn't need any tools, but I'd go back to my office, open my filing cabinet, and look at my little piece of paper: "Christy—35, 60." Then I'd get a screwdriver and go over to Christy's office and close the door behind me—obviously not everybody should be allowed to know how to do this!

I'd be in there alone and I'd open the safe in a few minutes. All I had to do was try the first number at most twenty times, then sit around, reading a magazine or something, for fifteen or twenty minutes. There was no use trying to make it look too easy; somebody would figure out there was a trick to it. After a while I'd open the door, sweating a bit, and say, "It's open."

People thought I was opening the safes from scratch. Now I could maintain the idea, which began with that accident with Staley, that I could open safes cold. Nobody figured out that I was picking the last two numbers off their safes, even though—or perhaps because—I was doing it all the time, like a card sharp walking around all the time with a deck of cards.

■   ■   ■

I often went to Oak Ridge to check up on the safety of the uranium plant. Everything was always in a hurry because it was wartime, and one time I had to go there on a weekend. It was Sunday, and we were in this fella's office—a general, a vice president of some company, a couple of other big muck-a-mucks, and me. We were gathered together to discuss a report that was in the fella's safe—a secret safe—when suddenly he realized that he didn't know the combination. His secretary was the only one who knew it, so he called her home and it turned out she had gone on a picnic up in the hills.

While all this was going on, I asked, "Do you mind if I fiddle with the safe?"

"Ha, ha, ha—not at all!" So I went over to the safe and started to fool around.

They began to discuss how they could get a car to try to find the secretary, and the guy was getting more and more embarrassed because he had all these people waiting, and he was such a jackass because he didn't know how to open his own safe. Everybody was all tense and getting mad at him, when CLICK!—the safe opened.

In ten minutes I had opened the safe that contained all the secret documents about the plant. They were astonished. The safes were apparently not very safe! It was a terrible shock: All this "eyes only" stuff, top secret, locked in this wonderful secret safe, and this guy from Los Alamos opens it in ten minutes!

Of course I was able to open the safe because of my perpetual habit of taking the last two numbers off. While in Oak Ridge the month before, I was in the same office when the safe was open and I took the numbers off in an absent-minded way—I was always practicing. Although I hadn't written them down, I was able to vaguely remember what they were. First I tried 40-15, then 15-40, but neither of those worked. Then I tried 10-45 with all the first numbers, and it opened.

A similar thing happened on another weekend when I was visiting Oak Ridge. I had written a report that had to be OK'd by a colonel, and it was in his safe. Everybody else kept their documents in filing cabinets like the ones at Los Alamos, but *he* was a colonel, so he had a much fancier, two-door safe with big handles that pull four $\frac{3}{4}$-inch-thick steel bolts back from the frame. The great brass doors swung open and he took out my report to read.

Not having had an opportunity to see any really *good* safes, I said to him, "Would you mind, while you're reading my report, if I looked at your safe?"

"Go right ahead," he said, convinced that there was nothing I could do. I looked at the back of one of the solid brass doors, and I discovered that the combination wheel was connected to a little lock that looked exactly the same as the little unit that was in my filing cabinet at Los Alamos. Same company, same little bolt, except that when the bolt came down, the big handles on the safe could then move some rods sideways, and with a bunch of levers you could pull back all those $\frac{3}{4}$-inch steel rods. The whole lever system, it appeared, depended on the same little bolt that locks filing cabinets.

Just for the sake of professional perfection, to make sure it was the same, I took the two numbers off the same way I did with the filing cabinet safes.

Meanwhile, he was reading the report. When he'd finished he said, "All right, it's fine." He put the report in the safe, grabbed the big handles, and swung the great brass doors together. It sounds so good when they close, but I knew it's all psychological, because it's nothing but the same damn lock.

I couldn't help but needle him a little bit (I always had a thing about military guys, in such wonderful uniforms) so I said, "The way you close that safe, I get the idea that you think things are safe in there."

"Of course."

"The only reason you think they're safe in there is because *civilians* call it a 'safe.' " (I put the word "civilians" in there to make it sound as if he'd been had by civilians.)

He got very angry. "What do you mean—it's not safe?"

"A good safecracker could open it in thirty minutes."

"Can *you* open it in thirty minutes?"

"I said a *good* safecracker. It would take me about forty-five."

"Well!" he said. "My wife is waiting at home for me with supper, but I'm gonna stay here and watch you, and *you're* gonna sit down there and work on that damn thing for forty-five minutes and *not* open it!" He sat down in his big leather chair, put his feet up on his desk, and started reading.

I picked up a chair, carried it over to the safe and sat down in front of it. I began to turn the wheel at random, just to make some action.

After about five minutes, which is quite a long time when you're just sitting and waiting, he lost some patience: "Well, are you making any progress?"

"With a thing like this, you either open it or you don't."

I figured one or two more minutes would be about time, so I began to work in earnest and two minutes later, CLINK—it opened.

The colonel's jaw dropped and his eyes bugged out.

"Now, Colonel," I said, in a serious tone, "let me tell you something about these locks: When the door to the safe or the top drawer of the filing cabinet is left open, it's very easy for someone to get the combination. That's what I did while you were reading my report, just to demonstrate the danger. You should insist that everybody keep their filing cabinet drawers locked while they're working, because when they're open, they're very, very vulnerable."

"I see what you mean. That's very interesting!" We were on the same side after that.

The next time I went to Oak Ridge, all the secretaries and people who knew who I was were telling me, "Don't come through here! Don't come through here!"

The colonel had sent a note around to everyone in the plant that said, "During his last visit, was Mr. Feynman at any time in your office, near your office, or walking through your office?" Some people answered yes; others said no. The ones who said yes got another note: "Please change the combination of your safe."

That was his solution: *I* was the danger. So they all had to change their combinations on account of me. It's a pain in the neck to change a combination and remember the new one, so they were all mad at me and didn't want me to come near them—they might have to change their combination once again. Of course, their filing cabinets were still left open while they were working.

Recounting the safecracker story at Caltech's Winnett Student Center, 1964.

■ ■ ■

The main library at Los Alamos held all of the documents we had ever worked on: It was a solid, concrete room with a big, beautiful door which had a metal wheel that turns—like a safe-deposit vault. During the war I had tried to look at it closely. I knew the girl who was the librarian, and I begged her to let me play with it a little bit. I was fascinated by it—it was the biggest lock I ever saw! I discovered that I could never use my method of picking off the last two numbers to get in. In fact, while turning the knob while the door was open, I made the lock close, so it was sticking out, and they couldn't close the door again until the girl came and opened the lock again. That was the end of my fiddling around with *that* lock. I didn't have time to figure out how it worked; it was way beyond my capacity.

During the summer after the war I had some documents to write and work to finish up, so I went back to Los Alamos from Cornell, where I had taught during the year. In the middle of my work I had to refer to a document that I had written before but couldn't remember, and it was down in the library.

I went down to get the document, and there was a soldier walking back and forth, with a gun. It was a Saturday, and after the war the library was closed on Saturdays.

Then I remembered what a good friend of mine, Frederic de Hoffman, had done. He was in the Declassification Section. After the war the Army was thinking of declassifying some documents, and he had to go back and forth to the library so much—look at this document, look at that document, check this, check that—that he was going nuts. So he had a copy of every document—all the secrets to the atomic bomb—in nine filing cabinets in his office.

I went down to his office, and the lights were on. It looked as if whoever was there—perhaps his secretary—had just stepped out for a few minutes, so I waited. While I was waiting I started to fiddle around with the combination wheel on one of the filing cabinets. (By the way, I didn't have the last two numbers for de Hoffman's safes; they were put in after the war, after I had left.)

I started to play with one of the combination wheels and began to think about the safecracker books. I thought to myself, "I've never been much impressed by the tricks described in those books, so I've never tried them—but let's see if I can open de Hoffman's safe by following the book."

First trick, the secretary: She's afraid she's going to forget the combination, so she writes it down somewhere. I started to look in some of the places mentioned in the book. The desk drawer was locked, but it was an ordinary lock like Leo Lavatelli taught me how to open—*ping!* I look along the edge: nothing.

Then I looked through the secretary's papers. I found a sheet of paper that all the secretaries had, with the Greek letters carefully made—so they could recognize them in mathematical formulas—and named. And there, carelessly written along the top of the paper, was pi = 3.14159. Now, that's six digits, and why does a secretary have to know the numerical value of pi? It was obvious; there was no other reason.

I went over to the filing cabinets and tried the first one: 31-41-59. It didn't open. Then I tried 59-41-31. That didn't work either. Then 95-14-13. Backwards, forwards, upside down, turn it this way, turn it that—nothing!

I closed the secretary's desk drawer and started to walk out the door, when I thought of the safecracker books again: Next, try the psychology method. I said to myself, "Freddy de Hoffman is *just* the kind of guy to use a mathematical constant for a safe combination."

The mathematical constant second in importance to pi is the base of natural logarithms, e: 2.71828 . . . I went back to the first filing cabinet and tried 27-18-28—CLICK—it opened!

There were nine filing cabinets, and I had opened the first one, but the document I wanted was in another one—they were in alphabetical order by author. I tried the second filing cabinet: 27-18-28—CLICK—it opened with the same combination. I thought, "This is *wonderful:* I've opened the secrets to the atomic bomb, but if I'm ever going to tell this story, I've got to make sure that all the combinations are really the same." Some of the filing cabinets were in the next room, so I tried 27-18-28 on one of them, and it opened. Now I'd opened three safes—all the same.

I thought to myself, "Now *I* could write a safecracker book that would beat every one, because at the beginning I would tell how I opened safes whose contents were bigger and more valuable than what any safecracker anywhere had opened—except for a life, of course—but compared to the furs or the gold bullion, I had them all beat: I opened the safes which contained all the secrets to the atomic bomb—the schedules for the production of the plutonium, the purification procedures, how much material is needed, how the bomb works, how the neutrons are generated, what the design is, the dimensions—the entire information that was known at Los Alamos: *the whole schmeer!*"

I went back to the second filing cabinet and took out the document I wanted. Then I took a red grease pencil and a piece of yellow paper that was lying around in the office and wrote, "I borrowed document no. LA4312—Feynman the Safecracker." I put the note on top of the papers in the filing cabinet and closed it.

Then I went to the first one I had opened and wrote another note: "This one was no harder to open than the other one—Wise Guy" and shut the cabinet.

Then in the other cabinet, in the other room, I wrote, "When the combinations are all the same, one is no harder to open than another—Same Guy" and I shut that one. I went back to my office and wrote my report.

∎   ∎   ∎

That evening I went to the cafeteria and ate supper. There was Freddy de Hoffman. He said he was going over to his office to work, so just for fun I went with him.

He started to work, and soon he went into the other room to open one of the filing cabinets in there—something I hadn't counted on—and he happened to open the filing cabinet I had put the third note in, first.

He opened the drawer, and he saw this foreign object in there—this bright yellow paper with something scrawled on it in bright red crayon.

I had read in books that when somebody is afraid, his face gets sallow, but I had never seen it before. Well, it's absolutely true: His face turned a gray, yellow green—it was really frightening to see. He picked up the paper, and his hand was shaking. "L-l-look at this!" he said, trembling.

The note said, "When the combinations are all the same, one is no harder to open than another—Same Guy."

"What does it mean?" I said.

"All the c-c-combinations of my safes are the s-s-same!" he stammered.

"That ain't such a good idea."

"I-I know that n-now!" he said, completely shaken.

Another effect of the blood draining from the face must be that the brain doesn't work right. "He signed who it was! He signed who it was!" he said.

"*What?*" (I hadn't put my name on that one.)

"Yes," he said, "it's the *same guy* who's been trying to get into Building Omega!"

All during the war, and even after, there were these perpetual rumors: "Somebody's been trying to get into Building Omega!" You see, during the war they were doing experiments for the bomb in which they wanted to get enough material together for the chain reaction to just get started. They would drop one piece of material *through* another, and when it went through, the reaction would start and they'd measure how many neutrons they got. The piece would fall through so fast that nothing should build up and explode. Enough of a reaction would begin, however, so they could tell that things were really starting correctly, that the rates were right, and everything was going according to prediction—a *very* dangerous experiment.

Naturally, they were not doing this experiment in the middle of Los Alamos, but off several miles, in a canyon several mesas over, all isolated. This Building Omega had its own fence around it with guard towers. In the middle of the night when everything's quiet, some rabbit comes out of the brush and smashes against the fence and makes a noise. The guard shoots. The lieutenant in charge comes around. What's the guard going to say—that it was only a rabbit? No. "Somebody's been trying to get into Building Omega, and I scared him off!"

So de Hoffman was pale and shaking, and he didn't realize there was a flaw in his logic: it was not clear that the same guy who'd been trying to get into Building Omega was the same guy who was standing next to him.

He asked me what to do.

"Well, see if any documents are missing."

"It looks all right," he said. "I don't see any missing."

I tried to steer him to the filing cabinet I took my document out of. "Well, uh, if all the combinations are the same, perhaps he's taken something from another drawer."

"Right!" he said, and he went back into his office and opened the first filing cabinet and found the second note I wrote: "This one was no harder to open than the other one—Wise Guy."

By that time it didn't make any difference whether it was "Same Guy" or "Wise Guy": It was completely clear to him that it was the guy who was trying to get into Building Omega. So to convince him to open the filing cabinet with my first note in it was particularly difficult, and I don't remember how I talked him into it.

He started to open it, so I began to walk down the hall, because I was a little bit afraid that when he found out who did it to him, I was going to get my throat cut.

Sure enough, he came running down the hall after me—but instead of being angry, he practically put his arms around me because he was so completely relieved that this terrible burden of the atomic secrets being stolen was only me doing my usual mischief.

. . . .

A few days later de Hoffman told me that he needed something from Kerst's safe. Donald Kerst had gone back to Illinois and was hard to reach. "If you can open all *my* safes using the psychological method," de Hoffman said (I had told him how I did it), "maybe you could open Kerst's safe that way."

By now the story had gotten around, so several people came to watch this fantastic process where I was going to open Kerst's safe—cold. There was no need for me to be alone. I didn't have the last two numbers to Kerst's safe, and to use the psychology method I needed people around who knew Kerst.

We all went over to Kerst's office and I checked the drawers for clues; there was nothing. Then I asked them, "What kind of a combination would Kerst use—a mathematical constant?"

"Oh, no!" de Hoffman said. "Kerst would do something very simple."

I tried 10-20-30, 20-40-60, 60-40-20, 30-20-10. Nothing.

Then I said, "Do you think he would use a date?"

"Yeah!" they said. "He's just the kind of guy to use a date."

We tried various dates: 8-6-45, when the bomb went off; 86-19-45; this date; that date; when the project started. Nothing worked.

By this time most of the people had drifted off. They didn't have the patience to watch me do this, but the only way to solve such a thing is patience.

Then I decided to try everything from around 1900 until now. That sounds like a lot, but it's not: the first number is a month, 1 through 12, and I can try that using only three numbers: 10, 5, and 0. The second number is a day, from 1 to 31, which I can try with six numbers. The third number is the year, which was only forty-seven numbers at that time, which I could try with nine numbers. So the 8,000 combinations had been reduced to 162, something I could try in fifteen or twenty minutes.

Unfortunately I started with the high end of the numbers for the months, because when I finally opened it, the combination was 0-5-35.

I turned to de Hoffman. "What happened to Kerst around January 5, 1935?"

"His daughter was born in 1936," de Hoffman said. "It must be her birthday."

I had just opened two safes cold. I was getting good. Now I was professional.

That same summer after the war, the guy from the property section was trying to take back some of the things the government had bought, to sell again as surplus. One of the things was the Captain's safe. We all knew about this safe. The Captain, when he arrived during the war, decided that the filing cabinets weren't safe enough for the secrets *he* was going to get, so he had to have a special safe.

The Captain's office was on the second floor of one of the flimsy wooden buildings that we all had our offices in, and the safe he ordered was a heavy steel safe. The workmen had to put down platforms of wood and use special jacks to get it up the steps. Since there wasn't much amusement, we all watched this big safe being moved up to his office with great effort, and we all made jokes about what kind of secrets he was going to keep in there. Some fella said we ought to put our stuff in *his* safe, and let him put his stuff in ours. So everyone knew about this safe.

The property section man wanted it for surplus, but first it had to be emptied, and the only people who knew the combination were the

Captain, who was in Bikini, and Alvarez, who'd forgotten it. The man asked me to open it.

I went up to his old office and said to the secretary, "Why don't you phone the Captain and ask him the combination?"

"I don't want to bother him," she said.

"Well, you're gonna bother *me* for maybe eight hours. I won't do it unless you make an attempt to call him."

"OK, OK," she said. She picked up the telephone and I went into the other room to look at the safe. There it was—that huge, steel Captain's safe, and its doors were wide open!

I went back to the secretary. "It's open."

"Marvelous!" she said, as she put down the phone.

"No," I said, "it was *already* open."

"Oh! I guess the property section was able to open it after all."

I went down to the man in the property section. "I went up to the safe and it was already open."

"Oh, yeah," he said, "I'm sorry I didn't tell you: I sent our regular locksmith up there to drill it, but before he drilled it he tried to open it, and he opened it."

So! First information: Los Alamos now has a regular locksmith. Second information: This man knows how to drill safes, something I know nothing about. Third information: He can open a safe cold—in a few minutes. This is a *real* professional, a *real* source of information. This guy I have to meet.

I found out he was a locksmith they had hired after the war (when they weren't as concerned about security) to take care of such things. It turned out that he didn't have enough work to do opening safes, so he also repaired the Marchant calculators we had used. During the war I repaired those things all the time—so I had a way to meet him.

Now, I have never been surreptitious or tricky about meeting somebody; I just go right up and introduce myself. But in this case it was so important to meet this man, and I knew that before he would tell me any of his secrets on how to open safes, I would have to prove myself first.

I found out where his room was—in the basement of the theoretical physics section, where I worked—and I knew he worked in the evening, when the machines weren't being used. So, at first I would walk past his door on my way to my office in the evening. That's all; I'd just walk past.

A few nights later, just a "Hi." After a while, when he saw it was the same guy walking past, he'd say "Hi," or "Good evening."

A few weeks of this slow process and I see he's working on the Marchant calculators. I say nothing about them; it isn't time yet.

We gradually say a little more: "Hi! I see you're working pretty hard . . ."

"Yeah, pretty hard . . . "—that kind of stuff.

Finally, a breakthrough: He invites me for soup. It's going very good now. Every evening we have soup together. Now I begin to talk a little bit about the adding machines, and he tells me he has a problem. He's been trying to put a succession of spring-loaded wheels back onto a shaft, and he doesn't have the right tool, or something; he's been working on it for a week. I tell him that I used to work on those machines during the war, and "I'll tell you what: You just leave the machine out tonight, and I'll have a look at it tomorrow."

"OK," he says, because he's desperate.

The next day I looked at the damn thing and tried to load it by holding all the wheels in my hand. It kept snapping back. I thought to myself, "If he's been trying the same thing for a week, and I'm trying it and can't do it, that ain't the way to *do* it!" I stopped and looked at it very carefully, and I noticed that each wheel had a little hole—just a little hole. Then it dawned on me: I sprung the first one; then I put a piece of wire through the little hole. Then I sprung the second one and put the wire through it. Then the next one, the next one—like putting beads on a string—and I sprung the whole thing the first time I tried it, got it all in line, pulled the wire out, and everything was OK.

That night I showed him the little hole and how I did it, and from then on we talked a lot about machines; we got to be good friends. Now, in his office there were a lot of little cubbyholes that contained locks half taken apart, and pieces from safes, too. Oh, they were beautiful! But I still didn't say a word about locks and safes.

Finally, I figured the day was coming, so I decided to put out a little bit of bait about safes. "Hey!" I said, looking over at the cubbyholes. "I see you're working on Mosler safes."

"Yeah."

"You know, those locks are weak: If they're open, you can take the last two numbers off . . ."

"You can?" he said, finally showing some interest.

"Yeah."

"Show me how," he said. I showed him how to do it, and he turned to me. "What's your name?" All this time we had never exchanged names.

"Dick Feynman," I said.

"God! You're Feynman!" he said in awe. "The great safecracker! I've heard about you; I've wanted to meet you for so long! I want to learn how to crack a safe from you."

"What do you mean? You know how to open safes cold."

"I don't."

"Listen, I heard about the Captain's safe, and I've been working pretty hard all this time because I wanted to meet *you*. And you tell me you don't know how to open a safe cold?"

"That's right."

"Well you must know how to drill a safe."

"I don't know how to do that either."

"*What?*" I exclaimed. "The guy in the property section said you picked up your tools and went up to drill the Captain's safe."

"Suppose you had a job as a locksmith," he said, "and a guy comes down and asks you to drill a safe. What would you do?"

"Well," I replied, "I'd make a fancy thing of putting my tools together, pick them up and take them to the safe. Then I'd put my drill up against the safe somewhere at random and I'd go *vvvvvvvvvvv*, so I'd save my job."

"That's exactly what I was going to do."

"But you opened it! You must know how to crack safes."

"I don't. But I knew that the locks come from the factory set at 25-0-25 or 50-25-50, so I thought, 'Who knows—maybe the guy didn't bother to change the combination,' and the second one worked."

So I *did* learn something from him—that he cracked safes by the same miraculous methods that I did. But even funnier was that this big shot Captain had to have a super heavy steel safe, and had people go to all that trouble to hoist the thing up into his office—and he didn't even bother to set the combination.

I went from office to office in my building, trying those two factory combinations, and I opened about one safe in five.

Uncle Sam Doesn't Need You!

After the war the Army was scraping the bottom of the barrel to get the guys for the occupation forces in Germany. Up until then the Army deferred people for some reason *other* than physical first (I was deferred because I was working on the bomb), but now they reversed that and gave everybody a physical first.

That summer I was working for Hans Bethe at General Electric in Schenectady, New York, and I remember that I had to go some distance—I think it was to Albany—to take the physical.

I get to the draft place, and I'm handed a lot of forms to fill out, and then I start going around to all these different booths. They check your vision at one, your hearing at another, they take your blood sample at another, and so forth.

Anyway, finally you come to booth number 13: psychiatrist. There you wait, sitting on one of the benches, and while I'm waiting I can see what is happening. There are three desks, with a psychiatrist behind each one, and the "culprit" sits across from the psychiatrist in his BVDs and answers various questions.

At that time there were a lot of movies about psychiatrists. For example, there was Alfred Hitchcock's *Spellbound;* there was also a movie in which a woman who used to be a great piano player has her hands stuck in some awkward position and she can't move them, and her family calls in a psychiatrist to try to help her, and the psychiatrist goes upstairs into a room with her, and you see the door close behind them, and downstairs the family is discussing what's going to happen, and then she comes out of the room, hands still stuck in the horrible position, walks dramatically down the stairs over to the piano and sits down, lifts her hands over the keyboard, and suddenly—*dum diddle dum diddle dum, dum, dum*—she can play again. Well, I can't stand this kind of baloney, and I had decided that psychiatrists are fakers, and I'll have nothing to do with them. So that was the mood I was in when it was my turn to talk to the psychiatrist.

I sit down at the desk, and the psychiatrist starts looking through my papers. "Hello, Dick!" he says in a cheerful voice. "Where do you work?"

I'm thinking, "Who does he think he is, calling me by my first name?" and I say coldly, "Schenectady."

"Who do you work for, Dick?" says the psychiatrist, smiling again.

"General Electric."

"Do you like your work, Dick?" he says, with that same big smile on his face.

"So-so." I just wasn't going to have anything to do with him.

Three nice questions, and then the fourth one is completely different: "Do you think people talk about you?" he asks, in a low, serious tone.

I light up and say, "Sure! When I go home, my mother often tells me how she was telling her friends about me." He isn't listening to the explanation; instead, he's writing something down on my paper.

Then again, in a low, serious tone, he says, "Do you think people *stare* at you?"

I'm all ready to say no, when he says, "For instance, do you think any of the boys waiting on the benches are staring at you now?"

While I had been waiting to talk to the psychiatrist, I had noticed there were about twelve guys on the benches waiting for the three psychiatrists, and they've got nothing else to look at, so I divide twelve by three—that makes four each—but I'm conservative, so I say, "Yeah, maybe two of them are looking at us."

He says, "Well just turn around and look"—and *he's* not even bothering to look himself!

So I turn around, and sure enough, two guys are looking. So I point to them and I say, "Yeah—there's *that* guy, and that guy over *there* looking at us." Of course, when I'm turned around and pointing like that, other guys start to look at us, so I say, "Now him, and those two over there—and now the whole bunch." He still doesn't look up to check. He's busy writing more things on my paper.

Then he says, "Do you ever hear voices in your head?"

"Very rarely," and I'm about to describe the two occasions on which it happened when he says, "Do you talk to yourself?"

"Yeah, sometimes when I'm shaving, or thinking; once in a while." He's writing down more stuff.

"I see you have a deceased wife—do you talk to *her*?"

This question really annoyed me, but I contained myself and said, "Sometimes, when I go up on a mountain and I'm thinking about her."

More writing. Then he asks, "Is anyone in your family in a mental institution?"

"Yeah, I have an aunt in an insane asylum."

"Why do you call it an insane asylum?" he says, resentfully. "Why don't you call it a mental institution?"

"I thought it was the same thing."

"Just what do you think insanity is?" he says, angrily.

"It's a strange and peculiar disease in human beings," I say honestly.

"There's nothing any more strange or peculiar about it than appendicitis!" he retorts.

"I don't think so. In appendicitis we understand the causes better, and something about the mechanism of it, whereas with insanity it's much more complicated and mysterious." I won't go through the whole debate; the point is that I meant insanity is *physiologically* peculiar, and he thought I meant it was *socially* peculiar.

Up until this time, although I had been unfriendly to the psychiatrist, I had nevertheless been honest in everything I said. But when he asked me to put out my hands, I couldn't resist pulling a trick a guy in the "bloodsucking line" had told me about. I figured nobody was ever going to get a chance to do this, and as long as I was halfway under water, I would do it. So I put out my hands with one palm up and the other one down.

The psychiatrist doesn't notice. He says, "Turn them over."

I turn them over. The one that was up goes down, and the one that was down goes up, and he *still* doesn't notice, because he's always looking very closely at only one hand to see if it is shaking. So the trick had no effect.

Finally, at the end of all these questions, he becomes friendly again. He lights up and says, "I see you have a Ph.D., Dick. Where did you study?"

"MIT and Princeton. And where did *you* study?"

"Yale and London. And what did you study, Dick?"

"Physics. And what did *you* study?"

"Medicine."

"And *this* is *medicine*?"

"Well, yes. What do you *think* it is? You go and sit down over there and wait a few minutes."

So I sit on the bench again, and one of the other guys waiting sidles up to me and says, "Gee! You were in there twenty-five minutes! The other guys were in there only five minutes."

"Yeah."

"Hey," he says. "You wanna know how to fool the psychiatrist? All you have to do is pick your nails, like this."

"Then why don't *you* pick *your* nails like that?"

"Oh," he says, "I wanna get in the Army!"

"You wanna fool the psychiatrist?" I say. "You just tell him that."

∎ ∎ ∎

After a while I was called over to a different desk to see another psychiatrist. While the first psychiatrist had been rather young and innocent-looking, this one was gray-haired and distinguished-looking—obviously the superior pyschiatrist. I figure all of this is now going to get straightened out, but no matter what happens, I'm not going to become friendly.

The new psychiatrist looks at my papers, puts a big smile on his face, and says, "Hello, Dick. I see you worked at Los Alamos during the war."

"Yeah."

"There used to be a boys' school there, didn't there?"

"That's right."

"Were there a lot of buildings in the school?"

"Only a few."

Three questions—same technique—and the next question is completely different. "You said you hear voices in your head. Describe that, please."

"It happens very rarely, when I've been paying attention to a person with a foreign accent. As I'm falling asleep I can hear his voice very clearly. The first time it happened was while I was a student at MIT. I could hear old professor Vallarta say, 'Dee-a dee-a electric field-a.' And the other time was in Chicago during the war, when Professor Teller was explaining to me how the bomb worked. Since I'm interested in all kinds of phenomena, I wondered how I could hear these voices with accents so precisely, when I couldn't imitate them that well . . . Doesn't everybody have something like that happen once in a while?"

The psychiatrist put his hand over his face, and I could see through his fingers a little smile.

Then the psychiatrist checked into something else. "You said that you talk to your deceased wife. What do you say to her?"

I got angry. I figure it's none of his damn business, and I say, "I tell her I love her, if it's all right with you!"

After some more bitter exchanges he says, "Do you believe in the supernormal?"

I say, "I don't know what the 'supernormal' is."

"What? You, a Ph.D. in physics, don't know what the supernormal is?"

"That's right."

"It's what Sir Oliver Lodge and his school believe in."

That's not much of a clue, but I knew it. "You mean the *supernatural.*"

"You can call it that if you want."

"All right, I will."

"Do you believe in mental telepathy?"

"No. Do you?"

"Well, I'm keeping an open mind."

"What? You, a psychiatrist, keeping an *open mind?* Ha!" It went on like this for quite a while.

Then at some point near the end he says, "How much do you value life?"

"Sixty-four."

"Why did you say 'sixty-four'?"

"How are you *supposed* to measure the value of life?"

"No, I mean, why did you say 'sixty-four,' and not 'seventy-three,' for instance?"

"If I had said 'seventy-three,' you would have asked me the same question!"

The psychiatrist finished with three friendly questions, just as the other psychiatrist had done, handed me my papers, and I went off to the next booth.

While I'm waiting in the line, I look at the paper which has the summary of all the tests I've taken so far. And just for the hell of it I show my paper to the guy next to me, and I ask him in a rather stupid-sounding voice, "Hey! What did you get in 'Psychiatric'? Oh! You got an 'N.' I got an 'N' in everything else, but I got a 'D' in 'Psychiatric.' What does *that* mean?" I knew what it meant: "N" is normal, and "D" is deficient.

The guy pats me on the shoulder and says, "Buddy, it's perfectly all right. It doesn't mean anything. Don't worry about it." Then he walks way over to the other corner of the room, frightened: It's a lunatic!

I started looking at the papers the psychiatrists had written, and it looked pretty serious. The first guy wrote:

Thinks people talk about him.

Thinks people stare at him.

Auditory hypnogogic hallucinations.

Talks to self.

Talks to deceased wife.

Maternal aunt in mental institution.

Very peculiar stare. (I knew what *that* was—that was when I said, "And *this* is *medicine?*")

The second psychiatrist was obviously more important, because his scribble was harder to read. His notes said things like "auditory hypnogogic hallucinations confirmed." ("Hypnogogic" means you get them while you're falling asleep.)

He wrote a lot of other technical-sounding notes, and I looked them over, and they looked pretty bad. I figured I'd have to get all of this straightened out with the Army somehow.

At the end of the whole physical examination there's an Army officer who decides whether you're in or you're out. For instance, if there's something the matter with your hearing, *he* has to decide if it's serious enough to keep you out of the Army. And because the Army was scraping the bottom of the barrel for new recruits, this officer wasn't going to take anything from anybody—he was tough as nails. For instance, the fellow ahead of me had two bones sticking out from the back of his neck—some kind of displaced vertebra, or something—and this Army officer had to get up from his desk and *feel* them—he had to make sure they were real!

I figure *this* is the place I'll get this whole misunderstanding straightened out. When it's my turn, I hand my papers to the officer, and I'm ready to explain everything—but the officer doesn't look up. He sees the "D" next to "Psychiatric," immediately reaches for the rejection stamp, doesn't ask me any questions, doesn't say anything; he just stamps my papers REJECTED, and hands me my 4F paper, still looking at his desk.

So I went out and got on the bus for Schenectady. While I was riding on the bus I thought about the crazy thing that had happened, and I started to laugh—out loud—and I said to myself, "My god! If they saw me now, they would be *sure!*"

When I finally got back to Schenectady I went in to see Hans Bethe. He was sitting behind his desk, and he said to me in a joking voice, "Well, Dick, did you pass?"

I made a long face and shook my head slowly. "No."

Then he suddenly felt terrible, thinking that they had discovered some serious medical problem with me, so he said in a concerned voice, "What's the matter, Dick?"

I touched my finger to my forehead.

He said, "No."

"Yes!"

He cried, "No-o-o-o-o-o!!!" and he laughed so hard that the roof of the General Electric Company nearly came off.

*   *   *

I told the story to many other people, and everybody laughed, with a few exceptions.

When I got back to New York, my father, mother, and sister called for me at the airport, and on the way home in the car I told them all the story. At the end of it my mother said, "Well, what should we do, Mel?"

My father said, "Don't be ridiculous, Lucille. It's absurd!"

So that was that, but my sister told me later that when we got home and they were alone, my father said, "Now, Lucille, you shouldn't have said anything in front of him. What *should* we do?"

By that time my mother had sobered up, and she said, "Don't be ridiculous, Mel!"

One other person was bothered by the story. It was at a Physical Society meeting dinner, and Professor Slater, my old professor at MIT, said, "Hey, Feynman, tell us that story about the draft I heard."

I told the whole story to all these physicists—I didn't know any of them except Slater—and they were all laughing throughout, but at the end one guy said, "Well, maybe the psychiatrist had something in mind."

I said resolutely, "And what profession are *you*, sir?" Of course, that was a dumb question, because we were all physicists at a professional meeting. But I was surprised that a physicist would say something like that.

He said, "Well, uh, I'm really not supposed to be here, but I came as the guest of my brother, who's a physicist. I'm a psychiatrist." I smoked him right out.

After a while I began to worry. Here's a guy who's been deferred all during the war because he's working on the bomb, and the draft board gets letters saying he's important, and now he gets a "D" in "Psychiatric"—it turns out he's a nut? Obviously he *isn't* a nut; he's just trying to make us *believe* he's a nut—we'll get him!

The situation didn't look good to me, so I had to find a way out. After a few days, I figured out a solution. I wrote a letter to the draft board that went something like this:

Dear Sirs:

I do not think I should be drafted because I am teaching science students, and it is partly in the strength of our future scientists that the national welfare lies. Nevertheless, you may decide that I should be deferred because of the result of my medical report, namely, that I am psychiatrically unfit. I feel that no weight whatsoever should be attached to this report because I consider it to be a gross error.

I am calling this error to your attention because I am insane enough not to wish to take advantage of it.

Sincerely,

R. P. Feynman

Result: DEFERRED 4F MEDICAL REASONS

FROM CORNELL TO CALTECH WITH A TOUCH OF BRAZIL

THE
DIGNIFIED PROFESSOR

I don't believe I can really do without teaching. The reason is, I have to have something so that when I don't have any ideas and I'm not getting anywhere I can say to myself, "At least I'm living; at least I'm *doing* something; I'm making *some* contribution"—it's just psychological.

When I was at Princeton in the 1940s I could see what happened to those great minds at the Institute for Advanced Study who had been specially selected for their tremendous brains and were now given this opportunity to sit in this lovely house by the woods there, with no classes to teach, with no obligations whatsoever. These poor bastards could now sit and think clearly all by themselves, OK? So they don't get an idea for a while: They have every opportunity to do something, and they're not getting any ideas. I believe that in a situation like this a kind of guilt or depression worms inside of you, and you begin to *worry* about not getting any ideas. And nothing happens. Still no ideas come.

Nothing happens because there's not enough real activity and challenge: You're not in contact with the experimental guys. You don't have to think how to answer questions from the students. Nothing.

In any thinking process there are moments when everything is going good and you've got wonderful ideas. Teaching is an interruption, and so it's the greatest pain in the neck in the world. And then there are the *longer* periods of time when not much is coming to you. You're not getting any ideas, and if you're doing nothing at all, it drives you nuts. You can't even say, "Well, at least I'm teaching my class."

If you're teaching a class, you can think about the elementary things that you know very well. These things are kind of fun and delightful. It doesn't do any harm to think them over again: Is there a better way to present them? Are there any new problems associated with them? Are there any new thoughts you can make about them? The elementary things are *easy* to think about; if you can't think of a new thought, no harm done—what you thought about it before is good enough for the class. If you *do* think of something new, you're rather pleased that you have a new way of looking at it.

The questions of the students are often the source of new research. They often ask profound questions that I've thought about at times and then given up on for a while. It wouldn't do me any harm to think about them again and see if I can go any further now. The students may not be able to see the thing I want to answer, or the subtleties I want to think about, but they *remind* me of a problem by asking questions in the *neighborhood* of that problem. It's not so easy to remind yourself of these things.

So I find that teaching and the students keep life going, and I would *never* accept any position in which somebody has invented a happy situation for me where I don't have to teach. Never.

But once I *was* offered such a position.

During the war, when I was still at Los Alamos, Hans Bethe got me this job at Cornell, for $3700 a year. I got an offer from some other place for more, but I like Bethe, and I had decided to go to Cornell and wasn't worried about the money. But Bethe was always watching out for me, and when he found out that others were offering more, he got Cornell to give me a raise to $4000 even before I started.

Cornell told me that I would be teaching a course in mathematical methods of physics, and they told me what day I should come—November 6, I think, but it sounds funny that it could be so late in the year. I took the train from Los Alamos to Ithaca, and spent most of my time writing final reports for the Manhattan Project. I still remember that it was on the night train from Buffalo to Ithaca that I began to work on my course.

You have to understand the pressures at Los Alamos. You did everything as fast as you could; everybody worked very, very hard, and everything was finished at the last minute. So, working out my course on the train a day or two before the first lecture seemed natural to me.

Mathematical methods of physics was an ideal course for me to teach. It was what I had done during the war—apply mathematics to physics. I knew which methods were *really* useful, and which were not. I had lots of experience by that time, working so hard for four years using mathematical tricks. So I laid out the different subjects in mathematics and how to deal with them, and I still have the papers—the notes I made on the train.

I got off the train in Ithaca, carrying my heavy suitcase on my shoulder, as usual. A guy called out, "Want a taxi, sir?"

I had never wanted to take a taxi: I was always a young fella, short on money, wanting to be my own man. But I thought to myself, "Now I'm a *professor*—I must be dignified." So I took my suitcase down from my shoulder and carried it in my hand, and said "Yes."

"Where to?"

"The hotel."

"Which hotel?"

"One of the hotels you've got in Ithaca."

"Have you got a reservation?"

"No."

"It's not so easy to get a room."

"We'll just go from one hotel to another. Stay and wait for me."

I try the Hotel Ithaca: no room. We go over to the Traveller's Hotel: They don't have any room either. I say to the taxi guy, "No use driving around town with me; it's gonna cost a lot of money. I'll walk from hotel to hotel." I leave my suitcase in the Traveller's Hotel and I start to wander around, looking for a room. That shows you how much preparation I had, a new professor.

I found some other guy wandering around looking for a room too. It turned out that the hotel room situation was utterly impossible. After a while we wandered up some sort of a hill, and gradually realized we were coming near the campus of the university.

We saw something that looked like a rooming house, with an open window, and you could see bunk beds in there. By this time it was night, so we decided to ask if we could sleep there. The door was open, but there was nobody in the whole place. We walked up into one of the rooms, and the other guy said, "Come on, let's just sleep here."

I didn't think that was so good. It seemed like stealing to me. Somebody had made the beds; they might come home and find us sleeping in their beds, and we'd get into trouble.

So we go out. We walk a little further, and we see, under a streetlight, an enormous mass of leaves that had been collected—it was autumn—from the lawns. I say, "Hey! We could crawl in these leaves and sleep here!" I tried it; they were rather soft. I was tired of walking around, and if the pile of leaves hadn't been right under a streetlight, it would have been perfectly all right. But I didn't want to get into trouble right away. Back at Los Alamos people had teased me—when I played drums and so on—about what kind of "professor" Cornell was going to get. They said I'd get a reputation right off by doing something silly, so I was trying to be a little dignified. I reluctantly gave up the idea of sleeping in the pile of leaves.

We wandered around a little more, and came to a big building, some important building of the campus. We went in, and there were two couches in the hallway. The other guy said, "I'm sleeping here!" and collapsed onto the couch.

I didn't want to get into trouble, so I found a janitor down in the basement and asked him whether I could sleep on the couch, and he said "Sure."

The next morning I woke up, found a place to eat breakfast, and started rushing around as fast as I could to find out when my first class was going to be. I ran into the physics department: "What time is my first class? Did I miss it?"

The guy said, "You have nothing to worry about. Classes don't start for eight days."

That was a *shock* to me. The first thing I said was, "Well, why did you tell me to be here a week ahead?"

"I thought you'd like to come and get acquainted, find a place to stay and settle down before you begin your classes."

I was back to civilization, and I didn't know what it was.

Professor Gibbs sent me to the Student Union to find a place to stay. It's a big place, with lots of students milling around. I go up to a big desk that says HOUSING and I say, "I'm new, and I'm looking for a room."

The guy says, "Buddy, the housing situation in Ithaca is tough. In fact, it's so tough that, believe it or not, a *professor* had to sleep on a couch in this lobby last night!"

I look around, and I suddenly realize it's the same lobby! I turn to him and I say, "Well, I'm that professor, and the professor doesn't want to do it again!"

■ · ■

My early days at Cornell as a new professor were interesting and sometimes amusing. A few days after I got there, Professor Gibbs came into my office and explained to me that ordinarily we don't accept students this late in the term, but in a few cases, when the applicant is very, very good, we can accept him. He handed me the application and asked me to look it over.

He comes back. "Well, what do you think?"

"I think he's first rate, and I think we ought to accept him. I think we're lucky to get him here."

"Yes, but did you look at his picture?"

"*What possible difference could that make?*" I exclaimed.

"Absolutely none, sir! Glad to hear you say that. I wanted to see what kind of a man we had for our new professor." Gibbs liked the way I came right back at him without thinking to myself, "He's the head of the department, and I'm new here, so I'd better be careful what I say." I haven't got the speed to think like that; my first reaction is immediate, and I say the first thing that comes into my mind.

Then another guy came into my office. He wanted to talk to me about philosophy, and I can't really quite remember what he said, but he wanted me to join some kind of a club of professors. The club was some sort of anti-Semitic club that thought the Nazis weren't so bad. He tried to explain to me how there were too many Jews doing this and that—some crazy thing. So I waited until he got all finished, and said to him, "You know, you made a big mistake: I was brought up in a Jewish family." He went out, and that was the beginning of my loss of respect for some of the professors in the humanities, and other areas, at Cornell University.

I was starting over, after my wife's death, and I wanted to meet some girls. In those days there was a lot of social dancing. So there were a lot of dances at Cornell, mixers to get people together, especially for the freshmen and others returning to school.

I remember the first dance that I went to. I hadn't been dancing for three or four years while I was at Los Alamos; I hadn't even been in society. So I went to this dance and danced as best I could, which I thought was reasonably all right. You can usually tell when somebody's dancing with you and they feel pretty good about it.

As we danced I would talk with the girl a little bit; she would ask me some questions about myself, and I would ask some about her. But when I wanted to dance with her again, I had to look for her. When I finally found her, she'd say, "No, I'm sorry; I need some air." Or, "Well, I have to go to the ladies' room"—this and that excuse, from two or three girls in a row.

What was the matter with me? Was my dancing lousy? Was my personality lousy?

I danced with another girl, and again came the usual questions: "Are you a student, or a graduate student?" (There were a lot of students who looked old then because they had been in the Army.)

"No, I'm a professor."

"Oh? A professor of what?"

"Theoretical physics."

"I suppose you worked on the atomic bomb."

"Yes, I was at Los Alamos during the war."

She said, "You're a damn liar!"—and walked off.

That relieved me a great deal. It explained everything. I had been telling all the girls the simple-minded, stupid truth, and I never knew what the trouble was. It was perfectly obvious that I was being shunned by one girl after another when I did everything perfectly nice and natural and was polite, and answered the questions. Everything would look very pleasant, and then *thwoop*—it wouldn't work. I didn't understand it until this woman fortunately called me a damn liar.

So then I tried to avoid all the questions, and it had the opposite effect: "Are you a freshman?"

"Well, no."

"Are you a graduate student?"

"No."

"What *are* you?"

"I don't want to say."

"Why won't you tell us what you are?"

"I don't want to . . ."—and they'd keep working on me!

I ended up with two girls over at my house and one of them told me that I really shouldn't feel uncomfortable about being a freshman; there were plenty of guys my age who were starting out in college, and it was really all right. They were sophomores, and were being quite motherly, the two of them. They worked very hard on my psychology, but I didn't want the situation to get so distorted and so misunderstood, so I let them know I was a professor. They were very upset that I had fooled them. I had a lot of trouble being a young professor at Cornell.

Anyway, I began to teach the course in mathematical methods in physics, and I think I also taught another course—electricity and magnetism, perhaps. I also intended to do research. Before the war, while I was getting my degree, I had many ideas: I had invented new methods of doing quantum mechanics with path integrals, and I had a lot of stuff I wanted to do.

■   ■   ■

At Cornell, I'd work on preparing my courses, and I'd go over to the library a lot and read through the *Arabian Nights* and ogle the girls that would go by. But when it came time to do some research, I couldn't get to work. I was always a little tired; I was often not interested; I just couldn't do research. This went on for what I felt was a few years, but when I go back and calculate the timing, it couldn't have been that long. Perhaps nowadays I wouldn't think it was such a long time, but then, it seemed to go on for a *very* long time. I simply couldn't get started on any problem. I remember writing one or two sentences about some problem in gamma rays and then I couldn't go any further. I was convinced that between the war and the death of my wife, I had simply burned myself out.

I now understand it much better. First of all, a young man doesn't realize how much time it takes to prepare good lectures—for the first time, especially—to give the lectures, to make up exam problems, and to check that they're sensible ones. I was giving good courses, the kind of courses where I put a lot of thought into each lecture. But I didn't realize that that's a *lot* of work. So here I was, "burned out," reading the *Arabian Nights* and feeling depressed about myself.

During this period I would get offers from different places—universities and industry—with salaries higher than my own. And each time I got something like that I would get a little more depressed. I would say to myself, "Look, they're giving me these wonderful offers, but they don't realize that I'm burned out. Of course I can't accept them: They expect me to accomplish something, and I can't accomplish *anything*."

Finally there came in the mail an invitation from the Institute for Advanced Study: Einstein . . . von Neumann . . . Wyl . . . all these great minds. *They* write to me, and invite me to be a professor *there!* And not just a regular professor: Somehow they knew my feelings about the Institute—how it's too theoretical, how there's not enough *real* activity and challenge. So they write, "We appreciate that you have a considerable interest in experiments and in teaching, so we have made arrangements to create a special type of professorship, if you wish: half professor at Princeton University, and half at the Institute."

Institute for Advanced Study! Special exception! A position better than Einstein, even! It was ideal, it was perfect, it was absurd.

It *was* absurd. The other offers had made me feel worse, up to a point. They were expecting me to accomplish something. But this offer was so ridiculous, so impossible for me ever to live up to, so ridiculously out of proportion. The other ones were just mistakes; this was an absurdity! I laughed at it while I was shaving, thinking about it.

Then I thought to myself, "You know, what they think of you is so fantastic, it's impossible to live up to it. You have *no responsibility* to live up to it!"

It was a brilliant idea: You have no responsibility to live up to what other people think you ought to accomplish. I have no responsibility to be like they expect me to be: it's their mistake, not my failing.

It wasn't a failure on *my* part that the Institute for Advanced Study expected me to be that good; it was impossible. It was clearly a mistake—and the moment I appreciated the possibility that they might be wrong, I realized that it was also true of all the other places, including my own university. I am what I am, and if they expected me to be good and they're offering me some money for it, it's their hard luck.

Then, within the day, by some strange miracle—perhaps he overheard me talking about it, or maybe he just understood me—Bob Wilson, who was head of the laboratory there at Cornell, called me in to see him. He said, in a serious tone, "Feynman, you're teaching your classes well; you're doing a good job, and we're very satisfied. Any other expectations we might have are a matter of luck. When we hire a professor, we're taking all the risks. If it comes out good, all right. If it doesn't, too bad. But you shouldn't worry about what you're doing or not doing." He said it much better than that, and it released me from the feeling of guilt.

Then I had another thought: Physics disgusts me a little bit now, but I used to *enjoy* doing physics. Why did I enjoy it? I used to *play* with it. I used to do whatever I felt like doing—it didn't have to do with whether it was important for the development of nuclear physics, but whether it was interesting and amusing for me to play with. When I was in high school, I'd see water running out of a faucet growing narrower, and wonder if I could figure out what determines that curve. I found it was rather easy to do. I didn't *have* to do it; it wasn't important for the future of science; somebody else had already done it. That didn't make any difference: I used to invent things and play with things for my own entertainment.

So I got this new attitude. Now that I *am* burned out and I'll never accomplish anything, I've got this nice position at the university teaching classes which I rather enjoy, and just like I read the *Arabian Nights* for pleasure, I'm going to *play* with physics, whenever I want to, without worrying about any importance whatsoever.

Within a week I was in the cafeteria and some guy, fooling around, throws a plate in the air. As the plate went up in the air I saw it wobble, and I noticed the red medallion of Cornell on the plate going around. It was pretty obvious to me that the medallion went around faster than the wobbling.

I had nothing to do, so I start to figure out the motion of the rotating plate. I discover that when the angle is very slight, the medallion rotates twice as fast as the wobble rate—two to one.* It came out of a complicated equation! Then I thought, "Is there some way I can see in a more fundamental way, by looking at the forces or the dynamics, why it's two to one?"

I don't remember how I did it, but I ultimately worked out what the motion of the mass particles is, and how all the accelerations balance to make it come out two to one.

I still remember going to Hans Bethe and saying, "Hey, Hans! I noticed something interesting. Here the plate goes around so, and the reason it's two to one is . . ." and I showed him the accelerations.

He says, "Feynman, that's pretty interesting, but what's the importance of it? Why are you doing it?"

"Ha!" I say. "There's no importance whatsoever. I'm just doing it for the fun of it." His reaction didn't discourage me; I had made up my mind I was going to enjoy physics and do whatever I liked.

I went on to work out equations of wobbles. Then I thought about how electron orbits start to move in relativity. Then there's the Dirac Equation in electrodynamics. And then quantum electrodynamics, QED. And before I knew it (it was a very short time) I was "playing"—working, really—with the same old problems that I loved so much, that I had stopped working on when I went to Los Alamos: my thesis-type problems, all those old-fashioned, wonderful things.

It was effortless. It was easy to play with these things. It was like uncorking a bottle: Everything flowed out effortlessly. I almost tried to resist it! There was no importance to what I was doing, but ultimately there was: The diagrams and the whole business that I got the Nobel Prize for came from that piddling around with the wobbling plate.

---

*Lowell C. Thelin of New Jersey had a hunch that Feynman intentionally reversed the ratio to inspire readers to try the experiment themselves. Thelin videotaped a spinning, wobbling plate, confirming two wobbles to one rotation. In truth Feynman had missed this error, even after proofreading. What tantalized him was such a simple proportion hiding inside such complex motion. —RL

Any
Questions?

When I was at Cornell I was asked to give a series of lectures once a week at an aeronautics laboratory in Buffalo. Cornell had made an arrangement with the laboratory which included evening lectures in physics to be given by somebody from the university. There was some guy already doing it, but there were complaints, so the physics department came to me. I was a young professor at the time and I couldn't say no very easily, so I agreed to do it.

To get to Buffalo they had me go on a little airline which consisted of one airplane. It was called Robinson Airlines (it later became Mohawk Airlines) and I remember the first time I flew to Buffalo, Mr. Robinson was the pilot. He knocked the ice off the wings and we flew away.

All in all, I didn't enjoy the idea of going to Buffalo every Thursday night. The university was paying me $35 in addition to my expenses. I was a Depression kid, and I figured I'd save the $35, which was a sizable amount of money in those days.

Suddenly I got an idea: I realized that the purpose of the $35 was to make the trip to Buffalo more attractive, and the way to do that is to spend the money. So I decided to spend the $35 to entertain myself each time I went to Buffalo, and see if I could make the trip worthwhile.

I didn't have much experience with the rest of the world. Not knowing how to get started, I asked the taxi driver who picked me up at the airport to guide me through the ins and outs of entertaining myself in Buffalo. He was very helpful, and I still remember his name—Marcuso, who drove car number 169. I would always ask for him when I came into the airport on Thursday nights.

As I was going to give my first lecture I asked Marcuso, "Where's an interesting bar where lots of things are going on?" I thought that things went on in bars.

"The Alibi Room," he said. "It's a lively place where you can meet lots of people. I'll take you there after your lecture."

After the lecture Marcuso picked me up and drove me to the Alibi Room. On the way, I say, "Listen, I'm gonna have to ask for some kind of drink. What's the name of a good whiskey?"

"Ask for Black and White, water on the side," he counseled.

The Alibi Room was an elegant place with lots of people and lots of activity. The women were dressed in furs, everybody was friendly, and the telephones were ringing all the time.

I walked up to the bar and ordered my Black and White, water on the side. The bartender was very friendly, quickly found a beautiful woman to sit next to me, and introduced her. I bought her drinks. I liked the place and decided to come back the following week.

Every Thursday night I'd come to Buffalo and be driven in car number 169 to my lecture and then to the Alibi Room. I'd walk into the bar and order my Black and White, water on the side. After a few weeks of this it got to the point where as soon as I would come in, before I reached the bar, there would be a Black and White, water on the side, waiting for me. "Your regular, sir," was the bartender's greeting.

I'd take the whole shot glass down at once, to show I was a tough guy, like I had seen in the movies, and then I'd sit around for about twenty seconds before I drank the water. After a while I didn't need the water.

The bartender always saw to it that the empty chair next to mine was quickly filled by a beautiful woman, and everything would start off all right, but just before the bar closed, they all had to go off somewhere. I thought it was possibly because I was getting pretty drunk by that time.

One time, as the Alibi Room was closing, the girl I was buying drinks for that night suggested we go to another place where she knew a lot of people. It was on the second floor of some other building which gave no hint that there was a bar upstairs. All the bars in Buffalo had to close at two o'clock, and all the people in the bars would get sucked into this big hall on the second floor, and keep right on going—illegally, of course.

I tried to figure out a way that I could stay in bars and watch what was going on without getting drunk. One night I noticed a guy who had been there a lot go up to the bar and order a glass of milk. Everybody knew what his problem was: He had an ulcer, the poor fella. That gave me an idea.

The next time I come into the Alibi Room the bartender says, "The usual, sir?"

"No. Coke. Just plain Coke," I say, with a disappointed look on my face.

The other guys gather around and sympathize: "Yeah, I was on the wagon three weeks ago," one says. "It's really tough, Dick, it's really tough," says another.

They all honored me. I was "on the wagon" now, and had the *guts* to enter that bar, with all its "temptations," and just order Coke—because, of course, I had to see my friends. I maintained that for a month—I was a real tough bastard.

· · ·

One time I was in the men's room of the bar and there was a guy at the urinal. He was kind of drunk, and said to me in a mean-sounding voice, "I don't like your face. I think I'll push it in."

I was scared green. I replied in an equally mean voice, "Get out of my way, or I'll pee right through ya!"

He said something else, and I figured it was getting pretty close to a fight now. I had never been in a fight. I didn't know what to do, exactly, and I was afraid of getting hurt. I did think of one thing: I moved away from the wall, because I figured if I got hit, I'd get hit from the back, too.

Then I felt a sort of funny crunching in my eye—it didn't hurt much—and the next thing I know, I'm slamming the son of a gun right back, automatically. It was remarkable for me to discover that I didn't have to think; the "machinery" knew what to do.

"OK. That's one for one," I said. "Ya wanna keep on goin'?"

The other guy backed off and left. We would have killed each other if the other guy was as dumb as I was.

I went to wash up. My hands are shaking, blood is leaking out of my gums—I've got a weak place in my gums—and my eye hurts. After I calmed down I went back into the bar and swaggered up to the bartender: "Black and White, water on the side," I said. I figured it would calm my nerves.

I didn't realize it, but the guy I socked in the men's room was over in another part of the bar, talking with three other guys. Soon these three guys—big, tough guys—came over to where I was sitting and leaned over me. They looked down threateningly, and said, "What's the idea of pickin' a fight with our friend?"

Well I'm so dumb I don't realize I'm being intimidated; all I know is right and wrong. I simply whip around and snap at them, "Why don't ya find out who started what first, before ya start makin' trouble?"

The big guys were so taken aback by the fact that their intimidation didn't work that they backed away and left.

After a while one of the guys came back and said to me, "You're right, Curly's always doin' that. He's always gettin' into fights and askin' us to straighten it out."

"You're damn tootin' I'm right!" I said, and the guy sat down next to me.

Curly and the other two fellas came over and sat down on the other side of me, two seats away. Curly said something about my eye not looking too good, and I said his didn't look to be in the best of shape either—I continue talking tough, because I figure that's the way a real man is supposed to act in a bar.

The situation's getting tighter and tighter, and people in the bar are worrying about what's going to happen. The bartender says, "No fighting in here, boys! Calm down!"

Curly hisses, "That's OK; we'll get 'im when he goes out."

Then a genius comes by. Every field has its first-rate experts. This fella comes over to me and says, "Hey, Dan! I didn't know you were in town! It's good to see you!"

Then he says to Curly, "Say, Paul! I'd like you to meet a good friend of mine, Dan, here. I think you two guys would like each other. Why don't you shake?"

We shake hands. Curly says, "Uh, pleased to meet you."

Then the genius leans over to me and very quietly whispers, "Now get out of here fast!"

"But they said they would . . ."

"Just go!" he says.

I got my coat and went out quickly. I walked along near the walls of the buildings, in case they went looking for me. Nobody came out, and I went to my hotel. It happened to be the night of the last lecture, so I never went back to the Alibi Room, at least for a few years.

(I did go back to the Alibi Room about ten years later, and it was all different. It wasn't nice and polished like it was before; it was sleazy and had seedy-looking people in it. I talked to the bartender, who was a different man, and told him about the old days. "Oh, yes!" he said. "This was the bar where all the bookmakers and their girls used to hang out." I understood then why there were so many friendly and elegant-looking people there, and why the telephones were ringing all the time.)

The next morning, when I got up and looked in the mirror, I discovered that a black eye takes a few hours to develop fully. When I got back to Ithaca that day, I went to deliver some stuff over to the dean's office. A professor of philosophy saw my black eye and exclaimed, "Oh, Mr. Feynman! Don't tell me you got that walking into a door . . ."

"Not at all," I said. "I got it in a fight in the men's room of a bar in Buffalo."

"Ha, ha, ha!" he laughed.

Then there was the problem of giving the lecture to my regular class. I walked into the lecture hall with my head down, studying my notes. When I was ready to start, I lifted my head and looked straight at them, and said what I always said before I began my lecture—but this time, in a tougher tone of voice: "Any questions?"

I Want
My Dollar!

When I was at Cornell I would often come back home to Far Rockaway to visit. One time when I happened to be home, the telephone rings: it's LONG DISTANCE, from California. In those days, a long distance call meant it was something very important, especially a long distance call from this marvelous place, California, a million miles away.

The guy on the other end says, "Is this Professor Feynman, of Cornell University?"

"That's right."

"This is Mr. So-and-so from the Such-and-such Aircraft Company." It was one of the big airplane companies in California, but unfortunately I can't remember which one. The guy continues: "We're planning to start a laboratory on nuclear-propelled rocket airplanes. It will have an annual budget of so-and-so-many million dollars"—big numbers.

I said, "Just a moment, sir; I don't know why you're telling me all this."

"Just let me speak to you," he says; "just let me explain everything. Please let me do it my way." So he goes on a little more, and says how many people are going to be in the laboratory, so-and-so-many people at this level, and so-and-so-many Ph.D.'s at that level . . .

"Excuse me, sir," I say, "but I think you have the wrong fella."

"Am I talking to Richard Feynman, Richard P. Feynman?"

"Yes, but you're . . ."

"Would you *please* let me present what I have to say, sir, and *then* we'll discuss it."

I sit down and close my eyes to listen to all this stuff, all these details about this big project, and I still haven't the slightest idea why he's giving me all this information.

Finally, when he's all finished, he says, "I'm telling you about our plans because we want to know if you would like to be the director of the laboratory."

"Have you *really* got the right fella?" I say. "I'm a professor of theoretical physics. I'm not a rocket engineer, or an airplane engineer, or anything like that."

"We're sure we have the right fellow."

"Where did you get my name then? Why did you decide to call *me*?"

"Sir, your name is on the patent for nuclear-powered, rocket-propelled airplanes."

"Oh," I said, and I realized *why* my name was on the patent, and I'll have to tell you the story. I told the man, "I'm sorry, but I would like to continue as a professor at Cornell University."

*   *   *

What had happened was, during the war, at Los Alamos, there was a very nice fella in charge of the patent office for the government, named Captain Smith. Smith sent around a notice to everybody that said something like, "We in the patent office would like to patent every idea you have for the United States government, for which you are working now. Any idea you have on nuclear energy or its application that you may think everybody knows about, everybody *doesn't* know about: Just come to my office and tell me the idea."

I see Smith at lunch, and as we're walking back to the technical area, I say to him, "That note you sent around, that's kind of crazy to have us come in and tell you *every* idea."

We discussed it back and forth—by this time we're in his office—and I say, "There are so many ideas about nuclear energy that are so perfectly obvious, that I'd be here all *day* telling you stuff."

"Like *what*?"

"Nothin' to it!" I say. "Example: nuclear reactor . . . under water . . . water goes in . . . steam goes out the other side . . . *Pshshshsht*—it's a submarine. Or: nuclear reactor . . . air comes rushing in the front . . . heated up by nuclear reaction . . . out the back it goes . . . *Boom* through the air—it's an airplane. Or: nuclear reactor . . . you have hydrogen go through the thing . . . *Zoom*—it's a rocket. Or: nuclear reactor . . . only instead of using ordinary uranium, you use enriched uranium with beryllium oxide at high temperature to make it more efficient—it's an electrical power plant. There's a *million* ideas!" I said, as I went out the door.

Nothing happened.

About three months later, Smith calls me in the office and says,

"Feynman, the submarine has already been taken. But the other three are yours." So when the guys at the airplane company in California are planning their laboratory, and try to find out who's an expert in rocket-propelled whatnots, there's nothing to it: They look at who's got the patent on it!

Anyway, Smith told me to sign some papers for the three ideas I was giving to the government to patent. Now, it's some dopey legal thing, but when you give the patent to the government, the document you sign is not a legal document unless there's some exchange, so the paper I signed said, "For the sum of one dollar, I, Richard P. Feynman, give this idea to the government . . ."

I hand the pen to Smith: "Where's my dollar?"

"That's just a formality," he says. "We haven't got any funds set up to give a dollar."

"You've got it all set up that I'm *signing* for the dollar," I say.

"This is silly," Smith protests.

"No, it's not," I say. "It's a legal document. You made me sign it, and I'm an honest man. If I sign something that says I get a dollar, I've gotta get a dollar. There's no fooling around about it."

"All right, all right!" he says, exasperated. "I'll *give* you a dollar, from my *pocket!*"

"OK."

I take the dollar, and I realize what I'm going to do: I go down to the grocery store, and I buy a dollar's worth—which was pretty good, then—of cookies and goodies, those chocolate goodies with marshmallow inside, a whole lot of stuff.

I come back to the theoretical laboratory, and I give them out: "I got a prize, everybody! Have a cookie! I got a prize! A dollar for my patent! I got a dollar for my patent!"

Everybody who had one of those patents—a lot of people had been sending them in—everybody comes down to Captain Smith saying, "I want my dollar!"

He starts shelling them out of his pocket, but soon realizes that it's going to be a hemorrhage. He went crazy trying to set up a fund where he could get the dollars these guys were insisting on. I don't know how he settled up.

You Just Ask
Them?

When I was first at Cornell I corresponded with a girl I had met in New Mexico while I was working on the bomb. I got to thinking, when she mentioned some other fella she knew, that I had better go out there quickly at the end of the school year and try to save the situation. But when I got out there, I found out that it was too late, so I ended up in a motel in Albuquerque with a free summer and nothing to do.

The Casa Grande Motel was on Route 66, the main highway through town. About three places further down the road there was a little nightclub that had entertainment. Since I had nothing to do, and since I enjoyed watching and meeting people in bars, I often went to this nightclub.

When I first went there I was talking with some guy at the bar, and we noticed a whole table full of nice young ladies—TWA hostesses, I think they were—who were having some sort of birthday party. The other guy said, "Come on, let's get up our nerve and ask them to dance."

So we asked two of them to dance, and afterwards they invited us to sit with the other girls at the table. After a few drinks, the waiter came around: "Anybody *want* anything?"

I liked to imitate being drunk, so although I was completely sober, I turned to the girl I'd been dancing with and asked her in a drunken voice, "YaWANanything?"

"What can we have?" she asks.

"Annnnnnnnnnnnnnything you want—*anything!*"

"All right, we'll have champagne!" she says happily.

So I say in a loud voice that everybody in the bar can hear, "OK! Ch-ch-champagne for evvverybody!"

Then I hear my friend talking to my girl, saying what a dirty trick it is to "take all that dough from him because he's drunk," and I'm beginning to think maybe I made a mistake.

Well, nicely enough, the waiter comes over to me, leans down, and says in a low voice, "Sir, that's *sixteen dollars a bottle.*"

I decide to drop the idea of champagne for everybody, so I say in an even louder voice than before, "NEVER MIND!"

I was therefore quite surprised when, a few moments later, the waiter came back to the table with all his fancy stuff—a white towel over his arm, a tray full of glasses, an ice bucket full of ice, and a bottle of champagne. He thought I meant "Never mind the *price*," when I meant "Never mind the *champagne!*"

The waiter served champagne to everybody, I paid out the sixteen dollars, and my friend was mad at my girl because he thought she had got me to pay all this dough. But as far as I was concerned, that was the end of it—though it turned out later to be the beginning of a new adventure.

* * *

I went to that nightclub quite often and as the weeks went by, the entertainment changed. The performers were on a circuit that went through Amarillo and a lot of other places in Texas, and god knows where else. There was also a permanent singer who was at the nightclub, whose name was Tamara. Every time a new group of performers came to the club, Tamara would introduce me to one of the girls from the group. The girl would come and sit down with me at my table, I would buy her a drink, and we'd talk. Of course I would have liked to do more than just talk, but there was always something the matter at the last minute. So I could never understand why Tamara always went to the trouble of introducing me to all these nice girls, and then, even though things would start out all right, I would always end up buying drinks, spending the evening talking, but that was it. My friend, who didn't have the advantage of Tamara's introductions, wasn't getting anywhere either—we were both clunks.

After a few weeks of different shows and different girls, a new show came, and as usual Tamara introduced me to a girl from the group, and we went through the usual thing—I'm buying her drinks, we're talking, and she's being very nice. She went and did her show, and afterwards she came back to me at my table, and I felt pretty good. People would look around and think, "What's he got that makes this girl come to *him?*"

But then, at some stage near the close of the evening, she said something that by this time I had heard many times before: "I'd like to have you come over to my room tonight, but we're having a party, so perhaps tomorrow night . . ."—and I knew what this "perhaps tomorrow night" meant: nothing.

Well, I noticed throughout the evening that this girl—her name was Gloria—talked quite often with the master of ceremonies during the show, and on her way to and from the ladies' room. So one time, when she was in the ladies' room and the master of ceremonies happened to be walking near my table, I impulsively took a guess and said to him, "Your wife is a very nice woman."

He said, "Yes, thank you," and we started to talk a little. He figured she had told me. And when Gloria returned, she figured *he* had told me. So they both talked to me a little bit, and invited me to go over to their place that night after the bar closed.

At two o'clock in the morning I went over to their motel with them. There wasn't any party, of course, and we talked a long time. They showed me a photo album with pictures of Gloria when her husband first met her in Iowa, a corn-fed, rather fattish-looking woman; then other pictures of her as she reduced, and now she looked really nifty! He had taught her all kinds of stuff, but *he* couldn't read or write, which was especially interesting because he had the job, as master of ceremonies, of reading the names of the acts and the performers who were in the amateur contest, and I hadn't even noticed that he couldn't *read* what he was "reading." (The next night I saw what they did. While she was bringing a person on or off the stage, she glanced at the slip of paper in his hand and whispered the names of the next performers and the title of the act to him as she went by.)

They were a very interesting, friendly couple, and we had many interesting conversations. I recalled how we had met, and I asked them why Tamara was always introducing the new girls to me.

Gloria replied, "When Tamara was about to introduce me to you, she said, 'Now I'm going to introduce you to the real *spender* around here!' "

I had to think a moment before I realized that the sixteen-dollar bottle of champagne bought with such a vigorous and misunderstood "*never mind!*" turned out to be a good investment. I apparently had the reputation of being some kind of eccentric who always came in *not* dressed up, *not* with a neat suit, but *always* ready to spend lots of money on the girls.

Eventually I told them that I was struck by something: "I'm fairly intelligent," I said, "but probably only about physics. But in that bar there are lots of intelligent guys—oil guys, mineral guys, important businessmen, and so forth—and all the time they're buying the girls drinks, and they get nothin' *for* it." (By this time I had deduced that nobody else was getting anything out of all those drinks either.) "How is it possible," I asked, "that an 'intelligent' guy can be such a goddamn fool when he gets into a bar?"

The master said, "*This* I know all about. I know exactly how it all works. I will give you lessons, so that hereafter you can get something from a girl in a bar like this. But before I give you the lessons, I must demonstrate that I really know what I'm talking about. So to do that, Gloria will get a *man* to buy *you* a champagne cocktail."

I say, "OK," though I'm thinking, "How the hell are they gonna *do* it?"

The master continued: "Now you must do exactly as we tell you. Tomorrow night you should sit some distance from Gloria in the bar, and when she gives you a sign, all you have to do is walk by."

"Yes," says Gloria. "It'll be easy."

The next night I go to the bar and sit in the corner, where I can keep my eye on Gloria from a distance. After a while, sure enough, there's some guy sitting with her, and after a little while longer the guy's happy and Gloria gives me a wink. I get up and nonchalantly saunter by. Just as I'm passing, Gloria turns around and says in a real friendly and bright voice, "Oh, hi, Dick! When did you get back into town? Where have you been?"

At this moment the guy turns around to see who this "Dick" is, and I can see in his eyes something I understand completely, since I have been in that position so often myself.

First look: "Oh-oh, competition coming up. He's gonna take her away from me after I bought her a drink. What's gonna happen?"

Next look: "No, it's just a casual friend. They seem to know each other from some time back." I could *see* all this. I could read it on his face. I knew exactly what he was going through.

Gloria turns to him and says, "Jim, I'd like you to meet an old friend of mine, Dick Feynman."

Next look: "I know what I'll do; *I'll be kind to this guy so that she'll like me more.*"

Jim turns to me and says, "Hi, Dick. How about a drink?"

"Fine!" I say.

"What'll ya have?"

"Whatever she's having."

"Bartender, another champagne cocktail, please."

■   ■   ■

That night after the bar closed I went again over to the master and Gloria's motel. They were laughing and smiling, happy with how it worked out. "All right," I said, "I'm absolutely convinced that you two know exactly what you're talking about. Now, what about the lessons?"

"OK," he says. "The whole principle is this: The guy wants to be a gentleman. He doesn't want to be thought of as impolite, crude, or especially a cheapskate. As long as the girl knows the guy's motives so well, it's easy to steer him in the direction she wants him to go.

"Therefore," he continued, "under *no circumstances* be a gentleman: You must *disrespect* the girls. Furthermore, the very first rule is, don't buy a girl *anything*—not even a pack of cigarettes—until you've *asked* her if she'll sleep with you, and you're convinced that she *will*, and that she's not lying."

"Uh . . . you mean . . . you don't . . . uh . . . you just *ask* them?"

"OK," he says, "I know this is your first lesson, and it may be hard for you to be so blunt. So you might buy her one thing—just one little something—before you ask. But on the other hand, it will only make it more difficult!"

Well, someone only has to give me the principle, and I get the idea. All during the next day I built up my psychology differently: I adopted the attitude that those bar girls are all bitches, that they aren't *worth* anything, that all they're in there for is to get you to buy them a drink and they're not going to give you a goddamn thing; I'm not going to be a gentleman to such worthless bitches, and so on. I practiced till it was automatic.

Then that night I was ready to try it out. I go into the bar as usual, and right away my friend says, "Hey, Dick! Wait'll you see the girl I got tonight! She had to go change her clothes, but she's coming right back."

"Yeah, yeah," I say, unimpressed, and I sit at another table to watch the show. My friend's girl comes in just as the show starts, and I'm thinking, "I don't give a damn *how* pretty she is; all she's doing is getting him to buy her drinks, and she's going to give him *nothing!*"

After the first act my friend says, "Hey, Dick! I want you to meet Ann. Ann, this is a good friend of mine, Dick Feynman."

I say "Hi" and keep looking at the show.

A few moments later Ann says to me, "Why don't you come and sit at the table here with us?"

I think to myself, "Typical bitch: *he's* buying her drinks, and *she's* inviting somebody *else* to the table." I say, "I can see fine from here."

A little while later a lieutenant from the military base nearby comes in, dressed in a nice uniform. It isn't long before we notice that Ann is sitting over on the other side of the bar with the lieutenant.

Later that evening I'm sitting at the bar, Ann is dancing with the lieutenant, and when the lieutenant's back is toward me and she's facing me, she smiles very pleasantly to me. I think again, "Some bitch: now she's doing this trick on the *lieutenant* even!"

Then I get a good idea: I don't look at her until the lieutenant can also see me, and *then* I smile back at her, so the lieutenant will know what's going on. So her trick didn't work for long.

A few minutes later she's not with the lieutenant any more, but asking the bartender for her coat and handbag, saying in a loud, obvious voice, "I'd like to go for a walk. Does anybody want to go for a walk with me?"

I think to myself, "You can keep saying no and pushing them off, but you can't do it permanently, or you won't get anywhere. There comes a time when you have to go along." So I say coolly, "*I'll* walk with you." So we go out. We walk down the street a few blocks and see a café, and she says, "I've got an idea—let's get some coffee and sandwiches, and go over to my place and eat them."

The idea sounds pretty good, so we go into the café and she orders three coffees and three sandwiches and I pay for them.

As we're going out of the café, I think to myself, "Something's wrong: too many sandwiches!"

On the way to her motel she says, "You know, I won't have time to eat these sandwiches with you, because a lieutenant is coming over . . ."

I think to myself, "See, I flunked. The master gave me a lesson on what to do, and I flunked. I bought her $1.10 worth of sandwiches, and hadn't asked her anything, and now I *know* I'm gonna get nothing! I have to recover, if only for the pride of my teacher."

I stop suddenly and I say to her, "You . . . are worse than a *whore!*"

"Whaddya mean?"

"*You* got *me* to buy these sandwiches, and what am I going to get for it? *Nothing!*"

"Well, you cheapskate!" she says. "If that's the way you feel, *I'll* pay you *back* for the sandwiches!"

I called her bluff: "Pay me back, then."

She was astonished. She reached into her pocketbook, took out the little bit of money that she had and gave it to me. I took my sandwich and coffee and went off.

After I was through eating, I went back to the bar to report to the master. I explained everything; I told him how I flunked, but tried to recover.

He said very calmly, "It's OK, Dick; it's all right. Since you ended up not buying her anything, she's gonna sleep with you tonight."

"What?"

"That's right," he said confidently; "she's gonna sleep with you. I *know* that."

"But she isn't even *here!* She's at *her* place with the lieu—"

"It's all right."

Two o'clock comes around, the bar closes, and Ann hasn't appeared. I ask the master and his wife if I can come over to their place again. They say sure.

Just as we're coming out of the bar, here comes Ann, running across Route 66 toward me. She puts her arm in mine, and says, "Come on, let's go over to my place."

The master was right. So the lesson was terrific!

*   *   *

When I was back at Cornell in the fall, I was dancing with the sister of a grad student, who was visiting from Virginia. She was very nice, and suddenly I got this idea: "Let's go to a bar and have a drink," I said.

On the way to the bar I was working up nerve to try the master's lesson on an *ordinary* girl. After all, you don't feel so bad disrespecting a bar girl who's trying to get you to buy her drinks—but a nice, ordinary, Southern girl?

We went into the bar, and before I sat down, I said, "Listen, before I buy you a drink, I want to know one thing: Will you sleep with me tonight?"

"Yes."

So it worked even with an ordinary girl! But no matter how effective the lesson was, I never really used it after that. I didn't enjoy doing it that way. But it was interesting to know that things worked much differently from how I was brought up.*

---

*As a "commentary in the margin" added in 2005, I feel compelled to point out—as a possible explanation for the disturbing behavior recounted at his insistence (not because he was proud of it, but because he wanted to show that this purported hero had feet of clay)—that during the years in which these episodes occurred, Feynman could well have been still reeling from the effects of his work on the atomic bomb, and from the concomitant loss of his beloved Arline. His sojourns in Brazil can be seen in the same light, I believe. —RL

O Americano,
Outra Vez!

One time, a few years after the war, I picked up a hitchhiker who told me how interesting South America was, and that I ought to go there. I complained that the language is different, but he said just go ahead and learn it—it's no big problem. So I thought, that's a good idea: I'll go to South America.

Cornell had some foreign language classes that followed a method used during the war, in which small groups of about ten students and one native speaker speak only the foreign language—nothing else. Since I was a rather young-looking professor there at Cornell, I decided to take the class as if I were a regular student. And since I didn't know yet where I was going to end up in South America, I decided to take Spanish, because the great majority of the countries there speak Spanish.

When it was time to register for the class, we were standing outside, ready to go into the classroom, when this pneumatic blonde came along. You know how once in a while you get this feeling, *wow!*—she looked terrific. I said to myself, "Maybe she's going to be in the Spanish class—that'll *be great!*" But no, she walked into the Portuguese class. So I figured, what the hell—I might as well learn Portuguese.

I started walking right after her when this Anglo-Saxon attitude that I have said, "No, that's not a good reason to decide which language to speak." So I went back and signed up for the Spanish class, to my utter regret.

Some time later I was at a Physics Society meeting in New York, and I found myself sitting next to Jaime Tiomno, from Brazil, and he asked, "What are you going to do next summer?"

"I'm thinking of visiting South America."

"Oh! Why don't you come to Brazil? I'll get a position for you at the Center for Physical Research."

So now I had to convert all that Spanish into Portuguese!

I found a Portuguese graduate student at Cornell, and twice a week he gave me lessons, so I was able to alter what I had learned.

On the plane to Brazil I started out sitting next to a guy from Colombia who spoke only Spanish. (I didn't talk to him because I didn't want to get confused again.) But sitting in front of me were two guys who were talking Portuguese. I had never heard *real* Portuguese; I had only had this teacher who had talked very slowly and clearly. So here are these two guys talking a blue streak, *brrrrrr-a-ta brrrrrrr-a-ta*, and I can't even hear the word for "I," or the word for "the," or *anything*.

Finally, when we made a refueling stop in Trinidad, I went up to the two fellas and said very slowly in Portuguese, or what I thought was Portuguese, "Excuse me . . . can you understand . . . what I am saying to you now?"

"*Pois não, porque não?*"—"Sure, why not?" they replied.

So I explained as best I could that I had been learning Portuguese for some months now, but I had never heard it spoken in conversation, and I was listening to them on the airplane, but couldn't understand a word they were saying.

"Oh," they said with a laugh, "*Não e Portugues! E Ladão! Judeo!*" What they were speaking was to Portuguese as Yiddish is to German, so you can imagine a guy who's been studying German sitting behind two guys talking Yiddish, trying to figure out what's the matter. It's obviously German, but it doesn't work—he thinks he must not have learned German very well.

When we got back on the plane, they pointed out another man who did speak Portuguese, so I sat next to him. He had been studying neurosurgery in Maryland, so it was very easy to talk with him—as long as it was about *cirurgia neural, o cérebro*, and other such "complicated" things. The long words are actually quite easy to translate into Portuguese because the only difference is their endings: "-tion" in English is "-ção" in Portuguese; "-ly" is "-mente," and so on. But when he looked out the window and said something simple, I was lost: I couldn't decipher "the sky is blue."

I got off the plane in Recife (the Brazilian government was going to pay the part from Recife to Rio) and was met by the father-in-law of Cesar Lattes, who was the director of the Center for Physical Research in Rio, his wife, and another man. As the men were off getting my luggage, the lady started talking to me in Portuguese: "You speak Portuguese? How nice! How was it that you learned Portuguese?"

I replied slowly, with great effort. "First, I started to learn Spanish . . .

then I discovered I was going to Brazil . . ." Now I wanted to say, "So, I learned Portuguese," but I couldn't think of the word for "so." I knew how to make BIG words, though, so I finished the sentence like this: "CON-SEQUENTEMENTE, *aprendi Portugues!*"

When the two men came back with the baggage, she said, "Oh, he speaks Portuguese! And with such wonderful words: CONSEQUENTE-MENTE!"

Then an announcement came over the loudspeaker. The flight to Rio was canceled, and there wouldn't be another one till next Tuesday—and I had to be in Rio on Monday, at the latest.

I got all upset. "Maybe there's a cargo plane. I'll travel in a cargo plane," I said.

"Professor!" they said, "It's really quite nice here in Recife. We'll show you around. Why don't you relax—you're in *Brazil!*"

That evening I went for a walk in town, and came upon a small crowd of people standing around a great big rectangular hole in the road—it had been dug for sewer pipes, or something—and there, sitting exactly in the hole, was a car. It was marvelous: It fitted absolutely perfectly, with its roof level with the road. The workmen hadn't bothered to put up any signs at the end of the day, and the guy had simply driven into it. I noticed a difference: When *we'd* dig a hole, there'd be all kinds of detour signs and flashing lights to protect us. There, they dig the hole, and when they're finished for the day, they just leave.

Anyway, Recife *was* a nice town, and I *did* wait until next Tuesday to fly to Rio.

When I got to Rio I met Cesar Lattes. The national TV network wanted to make some pictures of our meeting, so they started filming, but without any sound. The cameramen said, "Act as if you're talking. Say something—anything."

So Lattes asked me, "Have you found a sleeping dictionary yet?"

That night, Brazilian TV audiences saw the director of the Center for Physical Research welcome the Visiting Professor from the United States, but little did they know that the subject of their conversation was finding a girl to spend the night with!

When I got to the center, we had to decide when I would give my lectures—in the morning, or afternoon.

Lattes said, "The students prefer the afternoon."

"So let's have them in the afternoon."

"But the beach is nice in the afternoon, so why don't you give the lectures in the morning, so you can enjoy the beach in the afternoon."

"But you said the students prefer to have them in the afternoon."

"Don't worry about that. Do what's most convenient for *you*—enjoy the beach in the afternoon!"

So I learned how to look at life in a way that's different from the way it is where I come from: First, they weren't in the same hurry that I was; and second, if it's better for you, never mind! So I gave the lectures in the morning and enjoyed the beach in the afternoon. Had I learned that lesson earlier, I would have learned Portuguese in the first place, instead of Spanish.

I thought at first that I would give my lectures in English, but I noticed something: When the students were explaining something to me in Portuguese, I couldn't understand it very well, even though I knew a certain amount of Portuguese. It was not exactly clear to me whether they had said "increase," or "decrease," or "not increase," or "not decrease," or "decrease slowly." But when they struggled with English, they'd say "ahp" or "doon," and I knew which way it was, even though the pronunciation was lousy and the grammar was all screwed up. So I realized that if I was going to talk to them and try to teach them, it would be better for me to talk in Portuguese, poor as it was. It would be easier for them to understand.

During that first time in Brazil, which lasted six weeks, I was invited to give a talk at the Brazilian Academy of Sciences about some work in quantum electrodynamics that I had just done. I thought I would give the talk in Portuguese, and two students at the center said they would help me with it. I began by writing out my talk in absolutely lousy Portuguese. I wrote it myself, because if they had written it, there would be too many words I didn't know and couldn't pronounce correctly. So I wrote it, and they fixed up all the grammar, fixed up the words and made it nice, but it was still at the level that I could read easily and know more or less what I was saying. They practiced with me to get the pronunciations absolutely right: the "de" should be in between "deh" and "day"—it had to be just so.

I got to the Brazilian Academy of Sciences meeting, and the first speaker, a chemist, got up and gave his talk—in English. Was he trying to be polite? I couldn't understand what he was saying because his pronunciation was so bad, but maybe everybody else had the same accent so *they* could understand him—I don't know. Then the next guy gets up, and gives *his* talk in English.

When it was my turn, I got up and said, "I'm sorry; I hadn't realized that the official language of the Brazilian Academy of Sciences was

English, and therefore I did not prepare my talk in English. So please excuse me, but I'm going to have to give it in Portuguese."

So I read the thing, and everybody was very pleased with it.

The next guy to get up said, "Following the example of my colleague from the United States, I also will give my talk in Portuguese." So, for all I know, I changed the tradition of what language is used in the Brazilian Academy of Sciences.

Some years later, I met a man from Brazil who quoted to me the exact sentences I had used at the beginning of my talk to the Academy. So apparently it made quite an impression on them.

But the language was always difficult for me, and I kept working on it all the time, reading the newspaper, and so on. I kept on giving my lectures in Portuguese—what I call "Feynman's Portuguese," which I knew couldn't be the same as real Portuguese, because while I could understand what *I* was saying, I couldn't understand what the people in the street were saying.

* * *

Because I liked it so much that first time in Brazil, I went again a year later, this time for ten months. This time I lectured at the University of Rio, which was supposed to pay me, but they never did, so the center kept giving me the money I was supposed to get from the university.

I finally ended up staying in a hotel right on the beach at Copacabana, called the Miramar. For a while I had a room on the thirteenth floor, where I could look out the window at the ocean and watch the girls on the beach.

It turned out that this hotel was the one that the airline pilots and the stewardesses from Pan American Airlines stayed at when they would "lay over"—a term that always bothered me a little bit. Their rooms were always on the fourth floor, and late at night there would often be a certain amount of sheepish sneaking up and down in the elevator.

One time I went away for a few weeks on a trip, and when I came back the manager told me he had to book my room to somebody else, since it was the last available empty room, and that he had moved my stuff to a new room.

It was a room right over the kitchen, that people usually didn't stay in very long. The manager must have figured that I was the only guy who could see the advantages of that room sufficiently clearly that I would tolerate the smells and not complain. I didn't complain: It was on the fourth floor, near the stewardesses. It saved a lot of problems.

The people from the airlines were somewhat bored with their lives, strangely enough, and at night they would often go to bars to drink. I liked them all, and in order to be sociable, I would go with them to the bar to have a few drinks, several nights a week.

One day, about 3:30 in the afternoon, I was walking along the sidewalk opposite the beach at Copacabana past a bar. I suddenly got this tremendous, strong feeling: "That's *just* what I want; that'll fit just right: I'd just love to have a drink *right now!*"

I started to walk into the bar, and I suddenly thought to myself, "Wait a minute! It's the middle of the afternoon. There's nobody here. There's no social reason to drink. Why do you have such a terribly strong feeling that you *have* to have a drink?"—and I got scared.

I never drank ever again, since then. I suppose I really wasn't in any danger, because I found it very easy to stop. But that strong feeling that I didn't understand frightened me. You see, I get such fun out of *thinking* that I don't want to destroy this most pleasant machine that makes life such a big kick. It's the same reason that, much later on, I was reluctant to try LSD in spite of my curiosity about hallucinations.

Near the end of that year in Brazil I took one of the air hostesses—a very lovely girl with braids—to the museum. As we went through the Egyptian section, I found myself telling her things like, "The wings on the sarcophagus mean such-and-such, and in these vases they used to put the entrails, and around the corner there oughta be a so-and-so . . ." and I thought to myself, "You know where you learned all that stuff? From Mary Lou"—and I got lonely for her.

I met Mary Lou at Cornell and later, when I came to Pasadena, I found that she had come to Westwood, nearby. I liked her for a while, but we used to argue a bit; finally we decided it was hopeless, and we separated. But after a year of taking out these air hostesses and not really getting anywhere, I was frustrated. So when I was telling this girl all these things, I thought Mary Lou really was quite wonderful, and we shouldn't have had all those arguments.

I wrote a letter to her and proposed. Somebody who's wise could have told me that was dangerous: When you're away and you've got nothing but paper, and you're feeling lonely, you remember all the good things and you can't remember the reasons you had the arguments. And it didn't work out: The arguments started again right away, and the marriage lasted for only two years.

There was a man at the U.S. Embassy who knew I liked samba music. I told him that when I had been in Brazil the first time, I had heard a samba band practicing in the street, and I wanted to learn more about Brazilian music.

He said a small group, called a "regional," practiced at his apartment every week, and I could come over and listen to them play.

There were three or four people—one was the janitor from the apartment house—and they played rather quiet music up in his apartment; they had no other place to play. One guy had a tambourine that they called a *pandeiro*, and another guy had a small guitar. I kept hearing the beat of a drum somewhere, but there was no drum! Finally I figured out that it was the tambourine, which the guy was playing in a complicated way, twisting his wrist and hitting the skin with his thumb. I found that interesting, and learned how to play the *pandeiro*, more or less.

Then the season for *Carnaval* began to come around. That's the season when new music is presented. They don't put out new music and records all the time; they put them all out during *Carnaval* time, and it's very exciting.

It turned out that the janitor was the composer for a small samba "school"—not a school in the sense of education, but in the sense of fish—from Copacabana Beach, called *Farçantes de Copacabana*, which means "Fakers from Copacabana," which was just right for me, and he invited me to be in it.

Now this samba school was a thing where guys from the *favelas*—the poor sections of the city, up on the steep hillsides—would come down and meet behind a construction lot where some apartment houses were being built, and practice the new music for *Carnaval*.

I chose to play a thing called a "*frigideira,*" which is a toy frying pan made of metal, about six inches in diameter, with a little metal stick to beat it with. It's an accompanying instrument that makes a tinkly, rapid noise that goes with the main samba music and rhythm and fills it out. So I tried to play this thing and thought everything was going all right. We were practicing, the music was roaring along and we were going like sixty, when all of a sudden the head of the *bateria* section, a great big black man, yelled out, "STOP! Hold it, hold it—wait a minute!" And everybody stopped. "Something's wrong with the *frigideiras!*" he boomed out. "O Americano, *outra vez!*" ("The American again!")

I felt uncomfortable, so I practiced all the time: I'd walk along the beach holding two sticks that I had picked up, getting the twisty motion of the wrists, practicing, practicing, practicing. I kept working on it, but

I always felt inferior, that I was some kind of trouble, and wasn't really up to it.

Well, it was getting closer to *Carnaval* time, and one evening there was a conversation between the leader of the band and another guy, and then the leader started coming around, picking people out: "You!" he said to a trumpeter. "You!" he said to a singer. "You!"—and he pointed to me. I figured we were finished. He said, "Go out in front!"

We went out to the front of the construction site—the five or six of us—and there was an old Cadillac convertible, with its top down. "Get in!" the leader said.

There wasn't enough room for us all, so some of us had to sit up on the back. I said to the guy next to me, "What's he doing—is he putting us out?"

"*Não sei, não sei.*" ("I don't know.")

We drove off way up high on a road which ended near the edge of a cliff overlooking the sea. The car stopped and the leader said, "Get out!"—and they walked us right up to the edge of the cliff!

And sure enough, he said, "Now line up! You first, you next, you next! Start playing! Now march!"

We would have marched right off the edge of the cliff—except for a steep trail that went down. So our little group goes down the trail—the trumpet, the singer, the guitar, the *pandeiro*, and the *frigideira*—to an outdoor party in the woods. We weren't picked out because the leader wanted to get rid of us; he was sending us to this private party that wanted some samba music! And afterwards he collected money to pay for some costumes for our band.

After that I felt a little better, because I realized that when he picked the *frigideira* player, he picked *me!*

Another thing happened to increase my confidence. Some time later, a guy came from another samba school, in Leblon, a beach further on. He wanted to join our school.

The boss said, "Where're you from?"

"Leblon."

"What do you play?"

"*Frigideira.*"

"OK. Let me hear you play the *frigideira.*"

So this guy picked up his *frigideira* and his metal stick and goes "*brrra-dup-dup; chick-a-chick.*" Gee whiz! It was wonderful!

The boss said to him, "You go over there and stand next to O Americano, and you'll learn how to play the *frigideira!*"

My theory is that it's like a person who speaks French who comes to America. At first they're making all kinds of mistakes, and you can hardly understand them. Then they keep on practicing until they speak rather well, and you find there's a delightful twist to their way of speaking—their accent is rather nice, and you love to listen to it. So I must have had some sort of accent playing the *frigideira*, because I couldn't compete with those guys who had been playing it all their lives; it must have been some kind of dumb accent. But whatever it was, I became a rather successful *frigideira* player.

One day, a week or so before *Carnaval*, the leader of the samba school said, "OK, we're going to practice marching in the street."

We all went out from the construction site to the street, and it was full of traffic. The streets of Copacabana were always a big mess. Believe it or not, there was a trolley line in which the trolley cars went one way, and the automobiles went the other way. Here it was rush hour in Copacabana, and we were going to march down the middle of Avenida Atlantica.

I said to myself, "Geesus! The boss didn't get a license, he didn't OK it with the police, he didn't do anything. He's decided we're just going to go out."

So we started to go out into the street, and everybody, all around, was excited. Some volunteers from a group of bystanders took a rope and formed a big square around our band, so the pedestrians wouldn't walk through our lines. People started to lean out of the windows. Everybody wanted to hear the new samba music. It was very exciting!

As soon as we started to march, I saw a policeman, way down at the other end of the road. He looked, saw what was happening, and started diverting traffic! Everything was informal. Nobody made any arrangements, but it worked fine. The people were holding the ropes around us, the policeman was diverting the traffic, the pedestrians were crowded and the traffic was jammed, but we were going along great! We walked down the street, around the corners, and all over Copacabana, at *random!*

Finally we ended up in a little square in front of the apartment where the boss's mother lived. We stood there in this place, playing, and the guy's mother, and aunt, and so on, came down. They had aprons on; they had been working in the kitchen, and you could see their excitement—they were almost crying. It was really nice to do that human stuff. And all the people leaning out of the windows—that was terrific! I remembered the time I had been in Brazil before, and had seen one of these samba schools—how I loved the music and nearly went crazy over it—and now I was *in* it!

By the way, when we were marching around the streets of Copacabana that day, I saw in a group on the sidewalk two young ladies from the embassy. Next week I got a note from the embassy saying, "It's a great thing you are doing, yak, yak, yak . . ." as if my purpose was to improve relations between the United States and Brazil. So it was a "great thing" I was doing.

Well, in order to go to these rehearsals, I didn't want to go dressed in my regular clothes that I wore to the university. The people in the band were very poor, and had only old, tattered clothes. So I put on an old undershirt, some old pants, and so forth, so I wouldn't look too peculiar. But then I couldn't walk out of my luxury hotel on Avenida Atlantica in Copacabana Beach through the lobby. So I always took the elevator down to the bottom and went out through the basement.

A short time before *Carnaval*, there was going to be a special competition between the samba schools of the beaches—Copacabana, Ipanema, and Leblon; there were three or four schools, and we were going to march in costume down Avenida Atlantica. I felt a little uncomfortable about marching in one of those fancy *Carnaval* costumes, since I wasn't a Brazilian. But we were supposed to be dressed as Greeks, so I figured I'm as good a Greek as they are.

On the day of the competition, I was eating at the hotel restaurant, and the head waiter, who had often seen me tapping on the table when there was samba music playing, came over to me and said, "Mr. Feynman, this evening there's going to be something you will *love*! It's *tipico Brasileiro*—typical Brazilian: There's going to be a march of the samba schools right in front of the hotel! And the music is so good—you *must* hear it."

I said, "Well, I'm kind of busy tonight. I don't know if I can make it."

"Oh! But you'd love it so much! You must not miss it! It's *tipico Brasileiro!*"

He was very insistent, and as I kept telling him I didn't think I'd be there to see it, he became disappointed.

That evening I put on my old clothes and went down through the basement, as usual. We put on the costumes at the construction lot and began marching down Avenida Atlantica, a hundred Brazilian Greeks in papier-mâché, and I was in the back, playing away on the *frigideira*.

Big crowds were along both sides of the Avenida; everybody was leaning out of the windows, and we were coming up to the Miramar Hotel, where I was staying. People were standing on the tables and chairs, and there were crowds and crowds of people. We were playing along, going like sixty, as our band started to pass in front of the hotel. Suddenly I saw one of the waiters shoot up in the air, pointing with his arm, and through all this *noise* I can hear him scream, "O PROFES-SOOOOOR!" So the head waiter found out why I wasn't able to be there that evening to see the competition—I was *in* it!

The next day I saw a lady I knew from meeting her on the beach all the time, who had an apartment overlooking the Avenida. She had some friends over to watch the parade of the samba schools, and when we went by, one of her friends exclaimed, "Listen to that guy play the *frigideira—he is good!*" I had succeeded. I got a kick out of succeeding at something I wasn't supposed to be able to do.

When the time came for *Carnaval* itself, not very many people from our school showed up. There were some special costumes that were made just for the occasion, but not enough people. Maybe they had the attitude that we couldn't win against the really big samba schools from the city; I don't know. I thought we were working day after day, practicing and marching for *Carnaval*, but when *Carnaval* came, a lot of the band didn't show up, and we didn't compete very well. Even as we were marching around in the street, some of the band wandered off. Funny result! I never did understand it very well, but maybe the main excitement and fun was trying to win the contest of the beaches, where most people felt their level was. (And we did win, by the way.)

■　　■　　■

During that ten-month stay in Brazil I got interested in the energy levels of the lighter nuclei. I worked out all the theory for it in my hotel room, but I wanted to check how the data from the experiments looked. This was new stuff that was being worked out at the Kellogg Laboratory by the experts at Caltech, so I made contact with them—the timing was all arranged—by ham radio. I found an amateur radio operator in Brazil, and about once a week I'd go over to his house. He'd make contact with a ham radio operator in Pasadena, and then, because there was something slightly illegal about it, he'd give me some call letters and would say, "Now I'll turn you over to WKWX, who's sitting next to me and would like to talk to you."

So I'd say, "This is WKWX. Could you please tell me the spacing between the certain levels in boron we talked about last week," and so on. I would use the data from the experiments to adjust my constants and check whether I was on the right track.

The first guy went on vacation, but he gave me another amateur radio operator to go to. This second guy was blind and operated his station. They were both very nice, and the contact I had with Caltech by ham radio was very effective and useful to me.

As for the physics itself, I worked out quite a good deal, and it was sensible. It was worked out and verified by other people later. I decided, though, that I had so many parameters that I had to adjust—too much "phenomenological adjustment of constants" to make everything fit— that I couldn't be sure it was very useful. I wanted a rather deeper understanding of the nuclei, and I was never quite convinced it was very significant, so I never did anything with it.

. . .

In regard to education in Brazil, I had a very interesting experience. I was teaching a group of students who would ultimately become teachers, since at that time there were not many opportunities in Brazil for a highly trained person in science. These students had already had many courses, and this was to be their most advanced course in electricity and magnetism—Maxwell's equations, and so on.

The university was located in various office buildings throughout the city, and the course I taught met in a building which overlooked the bay.

I discovered a very strange phenomenon: I could ask a question, which the students would answer immediately. But the next time I would ask the question—the same subject, and the same question, as far as I could tell—they couldn't answer it at all! For instance, one time I was talking about polarized light, and I gave them all some strips of polaroid.

Polaroid passes only light whose electric vector is in a certain direction, so I explained how you could tell which way the light is polarized from whether the polaroid is dark or light.

We first took two strips of polaroid and rotated them until they let the most light through. From doing that we could tell that the two strips were now admitting light polarized in the same direction—what passed through one piece of polaroid could also pass through the other. But then I asked them how one could tell the *absolute* direction of polarization, from a *single* piece of polaroid.

They hadn't any idea.

I knew this took a certain amount of ingenuity, so I gave them a hint: "Look at the light reflected from the bay outside."

Nobody said anything.

Then I said, "Have you ever heard of Brewster's Angle?"

"Yes, sir! Brewster's Angle is the angle at which light reflected from a medium with an index of refraction is completely polarized."

"And which way is the light polarized when it's reflected?"

"The light is polarized perpendicular to the plane of reflection, sir." Even now, I have to think about it; they knew it cold—they even knew the tangent of the angle equals the index!

I said, "Well?"

Still nothing. They had just told me that light reflected from a medium with an index, such as the bay outside, was polarized; they had even told me which *way* it was polarized.

I said, "Look at the bay outside, through the polaroid. Now turn the polaroid."

"Ooh, it's polarized!" they said.

After a lot of investigation, I finally figured out that the students had memorized everything, but they didn't know what anything meant. When they heard "light that is reflected from a medium with an index," they didn't know that it meant a material *such as water*. They didn't know that the "direction of the light" is the direction in which you *see* something when you're looking at it, and so on. Everything was entirely memorized, yet nothing had been translated into meaningful words. So if I asked, "What is Brewster's Angle?" I'm going into the computer with the right keywords. But if I say, "Look at the water," nothing happens—they don't have anything under "Look at the water."

Later I attended a lecture at the engineering school. The lecture went like this, translated into English: "Two bodies . . . are considered equivalent . . . if equal torques . . . will produce . . . equal acceleration. Two bodies, are considered equivalent, if equal torques, will produce equal acceleration." The students were all sitting there taking dictation, and when the professor repeated the sentence, they checked it to make sure they wrote it down all right. Then they wrote down the next sentence, and on and on. I was the only one who knew the professor was talking about objects with the same moment of inertia, and it was hard to figure out.

I didn't see how they were going to learn anything from that. Here he was talking about moments of inertia, but there was no discussion about how hard it is to push a door open when you put heavy weights on the outside, compared to when you put them near the hinge—*nothing!*

After the lecture, I talked to a student: "You take all those notes—what do you do with them?"

"Oh, we study them," he says. "We'll have an exam."

"What will the exam be like?"

"Very easy. I can tell you now one of the questions." He looks at his notebook and says, " 'When are two bodies equivalent?' And the answer is, 'Two bodies are considered equivalent if equal torques will produce equal acceleration.' " So, you see, they could pass the examinations, and "learn" all this stuff, and not *know* anything at all, except what they had memorized.

Then I went to an entrance exam for students coming into the engineering school. It was an oral exam, and I was allowed to listen to it. One of the students was absolutely super: He answered everything nifty! The examiners asked him what diamagnetism was, and he answered it perfectly. Then they asked, "When light comes at an angle through a sheet of material with a certain thickness, and a certain index N, what happens to the light?"

"It comes out parallel to itself, sir—displaced."

"And how much is it displaced?"

"I don't know, sir, but I can figure it out." So he figured it out. He was very good. But I had, by this time, my suspicions.

After the exam I went up to this bright young man, and explained to him that I was from the United States, and that I wanted to ask him some questions that would not affect the result of his examination in any way. The first question I ask is, "Can you give me some example of a diamagnetic substance?"

"No."

Then I asked, "If this book was made of glass, and I was looking at something on the table through it, what would happen to the image if I tilted the glass?"

"It would be deflected, sir, by twice the angle that you've turned the book."

I said, "You haven't got it mixed up with a mirror, have you?"

"No, sir!"

He had just told me in the examination that the light would be displaced, parallel to itself, and therefore the image would move over to one side, but would not be turned by any angle. He had even figured out how *much* it would be displaced, but he didn't realize that a piece of glass is a material with an index, and that his calculation had applied to my question.

I taught a course at the engineering school on mathematical methods in physics, in which I tried to show how to solve problems by trial and error. It's something that people don't usually learn, so I began with some simple examples of arithmetic to illustrate the method. I was surprised that only about eight out of the eighty or so students turned in the first assignment. So I gave a strong lecture about having to actually *try* it, not just sit back and watch *me* do it.

After the lecture some students came up to me in a little delegation, and told me that I didn't understand the backgrounds that they have, that they can study without doing the problems, that they have already learned arithmetic, and that this stuff was beneath them.

So I kept going with the class, and no matter how complicated or obviously advanced the work was becoming, they were never handing a damn thing in. Of course I realized what it was: They couldn't *do* it!

One other thing I could never get them to do was to ask questions. Finally, a student explained it to me: "If I ask you a question during the lecture, afterwards everybody will be telling me, 'What are you wasting our time for in the class? We're trying to *learn* something. And you're stopping him by asking a question.' "

It was a kind of one-upmanship, where nobody knows what's going on, and they'd put the other one down as if they *did* know. They all fake that they know, and if one student admits for a moment that something is confusing by asking a question, the others take a high-handed attitude, acting as if it's not confusing at all, telling him that he's wasting their time.

I explained how useful it was to work together, to discuss the questions, to talk it over, but they wouldn't do that either, because they would be losing face if they had to ask someone else. It was pitiful! All the work they did, intelligent people, but they got themselves into this funny state of mind, this strange kind of self-propagating "education" which is meaningless—utterly meaningless!

At the end of the academic year, the students asked me to give a talk about my experiences of teaching in Brazil. At the talk there would be not only students, but professors and government officials, so I made them promise that I could say whatever I wanted. They said, "Sure. Of course. It's a free country."

So I came in, carrying the elementary physics textbook that they used in the first year of college. They thought this book was especially good because it had different kinds of typeface—bold black for the most important things to remember, lighter for less important things, and so on.

Right away somebody said, "You're not going to say anything bad about the textbook, are you? The man who wrote it is here, and everybody thinks it's a good textbook."

"You promised I could say whatever I wanted."

The lecture hall was full. I started out by defining science as an understanding of the behavior of nature. Then I asked, "What is a good reason for teaching science? Of course, no country can consider itself civilized unless . . . yak, yak, yak." They were all sitting there nodding, because I know that's the way they think.

Then I say, "That, of course, is absurd, because why should we feel we have to keep up with another country? We have to do it for a *good* reason, a *sensible* reason; not just because other countries do." Then I talked about the utility of science, and its contribution to the improvement of the human condition, and all that—I really teased them a little bit.

Then I say, "The main purpose of my talk is to demonstrate to you that *no* science is being taught in Brazil."

I can see them stir, thinking, "What? No science? This is absolutely crazy! We have all these classes."

So I tell them that one of the first things to strike me when I came to Brazil was to see elementary school kids in bookstores, buying physics books. There are so many kids learning physics in Brazil, beginning much earlier than kids do in the United States, that it's amazing you don't find many physicists in Brazil—why is that? So many kids are working so hard, and nothing comes of it.

Then I gave the analogy of a Greek scholar who loves the Greek language, who knows that in his own country there aren't many children studying Greek. But he comes to another country, where he is delighted to find everybody studying Greek—even the smaller kids in the elementary schools. He goes to the examination of a student who is coming to get his degree in Greek, and asks him, "What were Socrates' ideas on the relationship between Truth and Beauty?"—and the student can't answer. Then he asks the student, "What did Socrates say to Plato in the Third Symposium?" The student lights up and goes, "*Brrrrrrrr-up*"—he tells you everything, word for word, that Socrates said, in beautiful Greek.

But what Socrates was talking about in the Third Symposium was the relationship between Truth and Beauty!

What this Greek scholar discovers is, the students in another country learn Greek by first learning to pronounce the letters, then the words, and then sentences and paragraphs. They can recite, word for word, what Socrates said, without realizing that those Greek words actually *mean* something. To the student they are all artificial sounds. Nobody has ever translated them into words the students can understand.

I said, "That's how it looks to me, when I see you teaching the kids 'science' here in Brazil." (Big blast, right?)

Then I held up the elementary physics textbook they were using. "There are no experimental results mentioned anywhere in this book, except in one place where there is a ball, rolling down an inclined plane, in which it says how far the ball got after one second, two seconds, three seconds, and so on. The numbers have 'errors' in them—that is, if you look at them, you think you're looking at experimental results, because the numbers are a little above, or a little below, the theoretical values. The book even talks about having to correct the experimental errors—very fine. The trouble is, when you calculate the value of the acceleration constant from these values, you get the right answer. But a ball rolling down an inclined plane, *if it is actually done*, has an inertia to get it to turn, and will, *if you do the experiment*, produce five-sevenths of the right answer, because of the extra energy needed to go into the rotation of the ball. Therefore this single example of experimental 'results' is obtained from a *fake* experiment. Nobody had rolled such a ball, or they would never have gotten those results!

"I have discovered something else," I continued. "By flipping the pages at random, and putting my finger in and reading the sentences on that page, I can show you what's the matter—how it's not science, but memorizing, in *every* circumstance. Therefore I am brave enough to flip through the pages now, in front of this audience, to put my finger in, to read, and to show you."

So I did it. *Brrrrrrrup*—I stuck my finger in, and I started to read: "Triboluminescence. Triboluminescence is the light emitted when crystals are crushed . . ."

I said, "And there, have you got science? No—you have only told what a word means in terms of other words. You haven't told anything about nature—*which* crystals produce light when you crush them, *why* they produce light. Did you see any student go home and *try* it? He can't.

"But if, instead, you were to write, 'When you take a lump of sugar and crush it with a pair of pliers in the dark, you can see a bluish flash. Some other crystals do that, too. Nobody knows why. The phenomenon is called "triboluminescence." ' Then someone will go home and try it; then there's an experience of nature." I used that example to show them, but it didn't make any difference where I would have put my finger in the book—it was like that everywhere.

Finally, I said that I couldn't see how anyone could be educated by this self-propagating system in which people pass exams, and teach others to pass exams, but nobody knows anything. "However," I said, "I must be wrong. There were two students in my class who did very well, and one of the physicists I know was educated entirely in Brazil. Thus, it must be possible for some people to work their way through the system, bad as it is."

Well, after I gave the talk, the head of the science education department got up and said, "Mr. Feynman has told us some things that are very hard for us to hear, but it appears that he really loves science, and is sincere in his criticism. Therefore, I think we should listen to him. I came here knowing we have some sickness in our system of education; what I have learned is that we have a *cancer!*"—and he sat down.

That gave other people the freedom to speak out, and there was a big excitement. Everybody was getting up and making suggestions. The students got a committee together to mimeograph the lectures in advance, and they got other committees organized to do this and that.

Then something happened which was totally unexpected for me. One of the students got up and said, "I'm one of the two students whom Mr. Feynman referred to at the end of his talk. I was not educated in Brazil; I was educated in Germany, and I've just come to Brazil this year."

The other student who had done well in class had a similar thing to say. And the professor I had mentioned got up and said, "I was educated here in Brazil during the war, when, fortunately, all of the professors had left the university, so I learned everything by reading alone. Therefore I was not really educated under the Brazilian system."

I didn't expect that. I knew the system was bad, but 100 percent—that was terrible!

Since I had gone to Brazil under a program sponsored by the U.S. government, I was asked by the State Department to write a report about my experiences in Brazil, so I wrote out the essentials of the speech I had just given. I found out later through the grapevine that the reaction of somebody in the State Department was, "That shows you how dangerous it is to send somebody to Brazil who is so naïve. Foolish fellow, he can only cause trouble: He didn't understand the problems."

Quite the contrary! I think this person in the State Department was naïve to think that because he saw a university with a list of courses and descriptions, that's what it was.

Getting
Ahead

One time, back in the fifties, when I was returning from Brazil by boat, we stopped off in Trinidad for a day, so I decided to see the main city, Port of Spain. In those days, when I visited a city I was most interested in seeing the poorest sections—to see how life works at the bottom end.

I spent some time off in the hills, in the black section of town, wandering around on foot. On the way back a taxi stopped and the driver said, "Hey, mon! You want to see the city? It only cost five Biwi."

I said, "Okay," and got in the taxi.

The driver started right off to go up and see some palace, saying, "I'll show you all the fancy places."

I said, "No, thank you; that's similar in every city. I want to see the bottom part of the city, where the poor people live. I've already seen the hills up there."

"Oh!" he said, impressed. "I'll be glad to show you around. And I have a question for you when we're through, so I want you to look at everything carefully."

So he took me to an East Indian neighborhood—it must have been some housing project—and he stopped in front of a house made of concrete blocks. There was practically nothing inside. A man was sitting on the front steps. "You see that man?" he said. "He has a son studyin' medicine in Maryland."

Then he picked up someone from the neighborhood so I could better see what they were like. It was a woman whose teeth had a lot of decay.

Further along we stopped and he introduced me to two women he admired. "They got enough money together to buy a sewing machine, and now they do sewing and tailoring work for people in the neighborhood," he said, proudly. When he introduced me to them, he said, "This man is a professor, and what's interesting is, he wants to see our neighborhoods."

We saw many things, and finally the taxi driver said to me, "Now, Professor, here is my question: you see the Indian people are just as poor, and sometimes even poorer than the black people, but they're getting somewhere, somehow—this man has sent his son to college; those women are building up a sewing business. But my people aren't getting anywhere. Why is that?"

I told him, of course, that I didn't know—which is my answer to almost every question—but he wouldn't accept that, coming from a professor. I tried to guess at something which I thought was possible. I said, "There's a long tradition behind life in India that comes from a religion and philosophy that is thousands of years old. And although these people are not in India, they still pass on those traditions about what's important in life—trying to build for the future and supporting their children in the effort—which have come down to them for centuries."

I continued, "I think that your people have unfortunately not had a chance to develop such a long tradition, or if they did, they lost it through conquest and slavery." I don't know if it's true, but it was my best guess.

The taxi driver felt that it was a good observation, and said he was planning to build for the future, too: He had some money on the horses, and if he won, he would buy his own taxicab, and *really* do well.

I felt very sorry. I told him that betting on the horses was a bad idea, but he insisted it was the only way he could do it. He had such good intentions, but his method was going to be luck.

I wasn't going to go on philosophizing, so he took me to a place where there was a steel band playing some great calypso music, and I had an enjoyable afternoon.

LUCKY
NUMBERS

One day at Princeton I was sitting in the lounge and overheard some mathematicians talking about the series for e^x, which is $1 + x + x^2/2$ factorial + $x^3/3$ factorial—each term you get by multiplying the preceding term by x and dividing by the next number. For example, to get the next term after $x^4/4$ factorial you multiply that term by x and divide by 5. It's very simple.

When I was a kid I was excited by series, and had played with this thing. I had computed e using that series, and had seen how quickly the new terms became very small.

I mumbled something about how it was easy to calculate e to any power using that series—you just substitute the power for x.

"Oh yeah?" they said, "Well, then, what's e to the 3.3?" said some joker—I think it was John Tukey.

I say, "That's easy. It's 27.11."

Tukey knows it isn't so easy to compute all that in your head. "Hey! How'd you do that?"

Another guy says, "You know Feynman, he's just faking it. It's not really right."

They go to get a table, and while they're doing that, I put on a few more figures: "27.1126," I say.

They find it in the table. "It's right! But how'd you *do* it!"

"I just summed the series."

"Nobody can sum the series that fast. You must just happen to know that one. How about e to the 3?"

"Look," I say. "It's hard work! Only one a day!"

"Hah! It's a fake!" they say, happily.

"All right," I say. "It's 20.085."

They look in the book as I put a few more figures on. They're all excited now, because I got another one right.

Here are these great mathematicians of the day, puzzled at how I can compute *e* to any power! One of them says, "He just *can't* be substituting and summing—it's too hard. There's some trick. You couldn't do just any old number like *e* to the 1.4."

I say, "It's hard work, but for you, OK. It's 4.05."

As they're looking it up, I put on a few more digits and say, "And that's the last one for the day!" and walk out.

What happened was this: I happened to know three numbers—the logarithm of 10 to the base *e* (needed to convert numbers from base 10 to base *e*), which is 2.3026 (so I knew that *e* to the 2.3 is very close to 10), and because of radioactivity (mean-life and half-life), I knew the log of 2 to the base *e*, which is .69315 (so I also knew that *e* to the .7 is nearly equal to 2). I also knew *e* (to the 1), which is 2.71828.

The first number they gave me was *e* to the 3.3, which is *e* to the 2.3—ten—times *e*, or 27.18. While they were sweating about how I was doing it, I was correcting for the extra .0026—2.3026 is a little high.

I knew I couldn't do another one; that was sheer luck. But then the guy said *e* to the 3: that's *e* to the 2.3 times *e* to the .7, or ten times two. So I knew it was 20.something, and while they were worrying how I did it, I adjusted for the .693.

Now I was *sure* I couldn't do another one, because the last one was again by sheer luck. But the guy said *e* to the 1.4, which is *e* to the .7 times itself. So all I had to do is fix up 4 a little bit!

They never did figure out how I did it.

. . . .

When I was at Los Alamos I found out that Hans Bethe was absolutely top-notch at calculating. For example, one time we were putting some numbers into a formula, and got to 48 squared. I reach for the Marchant calculator, and he says, "That's 2300." I begin to push the buttons, and he says, "If you want it exactly, it's 2304."

The machine says 2304. "Gee! That's pretty remarkable!" I say.

"Don't you know how to square numbers near 50?" he says. "You square 50—that's 2500—and subtract 100 times the difference of your number from 50 (in this case it's 2), so you have 2300. If you want the correction, square the difference and add it on. That makes 2304."

A few minutes later we need to take the cube root of $2\frac{1}{2}$. Now, to take cube roots on the Marchant you had to use a table for the first approximation. I open the drawer to get the table—it takes a little longer this time—and he says, "It's about 1.35."

I try it out on the Marchant and it's right. "How did you do *that* one?" I ask. "Do you have a secret for taking cube roots of numbers near $2\frac{1}{2}$?"

"Oh," he says, "the log of $2\frac{1}{2}$ is so-and-so. Now one-third of that log is between the logs of 1.3, which is this, and 1.4, which is that, so I interpolated."

So I found out something: first, he knows the log tables; second, the amount of arithmetic he did to make the interpolation alone would have taken me longer to do than reach for the table and punch the buttons on the calculator. I was very impressed.

After that, I tried to do those things. I memorized a few logs, and began to notice things. For instance, if somebody says, "What is 28 squared?" you notice that the square root of 2 is a bit more than 1.4, and 28 is 20 times 1.4, so the square of 28 must be on the low side of 400 times 2, or 800.

If somebody comes along and wants to divide 1 by 1.73, you can tell them immediately that it's .577, because you notice that 1.73 is nearly the square root of 3, so 1/1.73 must be one-third of the square root of 3. And if it's 1/1.75, that's equal to 4 over 7, and you've memorized the repeating decimals for sevenths: .571428 . . .

I had a lot of fun trying to do arithmetic fast, by tricks, with Hans. It was very rare that I'd see something he didn't see—like if you have 174 times 140, it's like 173 by 141, which is like the square root of 3 times the square root of 2, which is the square root of 6, which is 245—and beat him to the answer, and he'd laugh his hearty laugh when I'd get one. He was nearly always able to get the answer to any problem within a percent. It was easy for him—every number was near something he knew.

◾ ◾ ◾

One day I was feeling my oats. It was lunchtime in the technical area, and I don't know how I got the idea, but I announced, "I can work out in sixty seconds the answer to any problem that anybody can state in ten seconds, to 10 percent!"

People started giving me problems they thought were difficult, such as integrating a function like $1/(1+x^4)$, which hardly changed over the range they gave me. The hardest one somebody gave me was the binomial coefficient of x^{10} in $(1+x)^{20}$; I got that just in time.

They were all giving me problems and I was feeling great, when Paul Olum walked by in the hall. Paul had worked with me for a while at Princeton before coming out to Los Alamos, and he was always cleverer than I was. For instance, one day I was absentmindedly playing with one of those measuring tapes that snap back into your hand when you push a button. The tape would always slap over and hit my hand, and it hurt a little bit. "Geez!" I exclaimed. "What a *dope* I am. I keep playing with this thing, and it hurts me every time."

He said, "You don't hold it right," and took the damn thing, pulled out the tape, pushed the button, and it came right back. No hurt.

"Wow! How do you *do* that?" I exclaimed.

"Figure it out."

For the next two weeks I'm walking all around Princeton, snapping this tape back until my hand is absolutely raw. Finally I can't take it any longer. "Paul! I give up! How the hell do you hold it so it doesn't hurt?"

"Who says it doesn't hurt? It hurts me, too!"

I felt so stupid. He had gotten me to go around and hurt my hand for two weeks!

So Paul is walking past the lunch place and these guys are all excited. "Hey, Paul!" they call out. "Feynman's terrific! We give him a problem that can be stated in ten seconds, and in a minute he gets the answer to 10 percent. Why don't you give him one?"

Hardly stopping, he says, "The tangent of 10 to the 100th."

I was sunk: you have to divide by pi to 100 decimal places! It was hopeless.

One time I boasted, "I can do by other methods any integral anybody else needs contour integration to do."

So Paul puts up this tre*men*dous damn integral he had obtained by starting out with a complex function that he knew the answer to, taking out the real part of it and leaving only the complex part. He had unwrapped it so it was *only* possible by contour integration. He was always deflating me like that. He was a very smart fellow.

*   *   *

The first time I was in Brazil I was eating a noon meal at I don't know what time—I was always in the restaurants at the wrong time—and I was the only customer in the place. I was eating rice with steak (which I loved), and there were about four waiters standing around.

A Japanese* man came into the restaurant. I had seen him before, wandering around; he was trying to sell abacuses. He started to talk to the waiters, and challenged them: He said he could add numbers faster than any of them could do.

---

*Brazil has a significant native population of Japanese descent. —RL

The waiters didn't want to lose face, so they said, "Yeah, yeah. Why don't you go over and challenge the customer over there?"

The man came over. I protested, "But I don't speak Portuguese well!"

The waiters laughed. "The numbers are easy," they said.

They brought me a pencil and paper.

The man asked a waiter to call out some numbers to add. He beat me hollow, because while I was writing the numbers down, he was already adding them as he went along.

I suggested that the waiter write down two identical lists of numbers and hand them to us at the same time. It didn't make much difference. He still beat me by quite a bit.

However, the man got a little bit excited: he wanted to prove himself some more. "*Multiplicação!*" he said.

Somebody wrote down a problem. He beat me again, but not by much, because I'm pretty good at products.

The man then made a mistake: he proposed we go on to division. What he didn't realize was, the harder the problem, the better chance I had.

We both did a long division problem. It was a tie.

This bothered the hell out of the Japanese man, because he was apparently very well trained on the abacus, and here he was almost beaten by this customer in a restaurant.

"*Raios cubicos!*" he says, with a vengeance. Cube roots! He wants to do cube roots by arithmetic! It's hard to find a more difficult fundamental problem in arithmetic. It must have been his topnotch exercise in abacus-land.

He writes a number on some paper—any old number—and I still remember it: 1729.03. He starts working on it, mumbling and grumbling: "*Mmmmmmagmmmmmbrrr*"—he's working like a demon! He's poring away, doing this cube root.

Meanwhile I'm just sitting there.

One of the waiters says, "What are you doing?"

I point to my head. "Thinking!" I say. I write down 12 on the paper. After a little while I've got 12.002.

The man with the abacus wipes the sweat off his forehead: "Twelve!" he says.

"Oh, no!" I say. "More digits! More digits!" I know that in taking a cube root by arithmetic, each new digit is even more work than the one before. It's a hard job.

He buries himself again, grunting "*Rrrrgrrrrmmmmmmm*," while I add on two more digits. He finally lifts his head to say, "12.0!"

The waiters are all excited and happy. They tell the man, "Look! He does it only by thinking, and you need an abacus! He's got more digits!"

He was completely washed out, and left, humiliated. The waiters congratulated each other.

How did the customer beat the abacus? The number was 1729.03. I happened to know that a cubic foot contains 1728 cubic inches, so the answer is a tiny bit more than 12. The excess, 1.03, is only one part in nearly 2000, and I had learned in calculus that for small fractions, the cube root's excess is one-third of that fraction times the cube root. So all I had to do is find the fraction 1/1728, and multiply by 4 (divide by 3 and multiply by 12). So I was able to pull out a whole lot of digits that way.

A few weeks later the man came into the cocktail lounge of the hotel I was staying at. He recognized me and came over. "Tell me," he said, "how were you able to do that cube-root problem so fast?"

I started to explain that it was an approximate method, and had to do with the percentage of error. "Suppose you had given me 28. Now, the cube root of 27 is 3 . . ."

He picks up his abacus: *zzzzzzzzzzzzzzz*— "Oh yes," he says.

I realized something: he doesn't *know* numbers. With the abacus, you don't have to memorize a lot of arithmetic combinations; all you have to do is learn how to push the little beads up and down. You don't have to memorize 9 + 7 = 16; you just know that when you add 9, you push a "tens" bead up and pull a "ones" bead down. So I'm slower at basic arithmetic, but I know numbers.

Furthermore, the whole idea of an approximate method was beyond him, even though a cube root often cannot be computed exactly by any method. So I never could teach him how I did cube roots or explain how lucky I was that he happened to choose 1729.03.

CERTAINLY,
MR. BIG!

I used to cross the United States in my automobile every summer, trying to make it to the Pacific Ocean. But, for various reasons, I would always get stuck somewhere—usually in Las Vegas.

I remember the first time, particularly, I liked it very much. Then, as now, Las Vegas made its money on the people who gamble, so the whole problem for the hotels was to get people to come there to gamble. So they had shows and dinners which were very inexpensive, almost free. You didn't have to make any reservations for anything: You could walk in, sit down at one of the many tables, and enjoy the show. It was just *wonderful* for a man who didn't gamble, because I was enjoying all the advantages: the rooms were inexpensive, the meals were next to nothing, the shows were good—and I liked the girls.

One day I was lying around the pool at my motel, and some guy came up and started to talk to me. I can't remember how he got started, but his idea was that I presumably worked for a living, and it was really quite silly to do that. "Look how easy it is for me," he said. "I just hang around the pool all the time and enjoy life in Las Vegas."

"How the hell do you do that without working?"

"Simple: I bet on the horses."

"I don't know anything about horses, but I don't see how you can make a living betting on the horses," I said, skeptically.

"Of course you can," he said. "That's how I live! I'll tell you what: I'll teach *you* how to do it. We'll go down and I'll guarantee that you'll win a hundred dollars."

"How can you do that?"

"I'll *bet* you a hundred dollars that you'll win," he said. "So if you win it doesn't cost you anything, and if you lose, you get a hundred dollars!"

So I think, "Gee! That's right! If I win a hundred dollars on the horses and I have to pay him, I don't lose anything; it's just an exercise—

it's just proof that his system works. And if he fails, I win a hundred dollars. It's quite wonderful!"

He takes me down to some betting place where they have a list of horses and racetracks all over the country. He introduces me to other people who say, "Geez, he's great! I won a hunerd dollas!"

I gradually realize that I have to put up some of my own money for the bets, and I begin to get a little nervous. "How much money do I have to bet?" I ask.

"Oh, three or four hundred dollars."

I haven't got that much. Besides, it begins to worry me: Suppose I lose all the bets?

So then he says, "I'll tell you what: My advice will cost *you* only *fifty* dollars, and *only if it works*. In other words, if my system works and you win a hundred dollars, we'll split it fifty-fifty. If it doesn't work, I'll give you the hundred dollars you would have won anyway."

I figure, "Wow! Now I win both ways—either fifty or a hundred dollars! How the heck can he *do* that?" Then I realize that if you have a reasonably even game—forget the little losses from the take for the moment in order to understand it—the chance that you'll win a hundred dollars versus losing your four hundred dollars is four to one. So out of five times that he tries this on somebody, four times they're going to win a hundred dollars, and he gets two hundred (and points out to them how smart he is); the fifth time he has to *pay* a hundred dollars—while the fool who took his advice loses four hundred. So he receives *two* hundred, on the average, when he's paying out *one* hundred. So I finally understood how he could do that.

This process went on for a few days. He would invent some scheme that sounded like a terrific deal at first, but after I thought about it for a while I'd slowly figure out how it worked. Finally, in some sort of desperation he says, "All right, I'll tell you what: You pay me fifty dollars for the advice, and if you lose, I'll pay you back *all* your money."

Now I *can't lose* on that! So I say, "All right, you've got a deal!"

"Fine!" he says. "But unfortunately, I have to go to San Francisco this weekend, so you just mail me the results, and if you lose your four hundred dollars, I'll send you the money."

The first schemes were designed to make him money by honest arithmetic. Now, he's going to be out of town. The only way he's going to make money on *this* scheme is *not* to send it.

So I never accepted any of his offers. But it was very entertaining to see how he operated.

. . .

The other thing that was fun in Las Vegas was meeting show girls. I guess they were supposed to hang around the bar between shows to attract customers. I met several of them that way, and talked to them, and found them to be nice people. People who say, "Show girls, eh?" have already made up their mind what they are. But in any group, if you look at it, there's all kinds of variety. For example, there was the daughter of a dean of an Eastern university. She had a talent for dancing and liked to dance; she had the summer off and dancing jobs were hard to find, so she worked as a chorus girl in Las Vegas. Most of the show girls were very nice, friendly people. They were all beautiful, and I just *love* beautiful women. In fact, show girls were my real reason for liking Las Vegas so much.

At first I was a little bit afraid: the girls were so beautiful, they had such a reputation, and so forth. I would try to meet them, and I'd choke a little bit when I talked. It was difficult at first, but gradually it got easier, and finally I had enough confidence that I wasn't afraid of anybody.

I had a way of having adventures which is hard to explain: It's like fishing, where you put a line out and then you have to have patience. When I would tell someone about some of my adventures, they might say, "Oh, come on—let's *do* that!" So we would go to a bar to see if something will happen, and they would lose patience after twenty minutes or so. You have to spend a couple of *days* before something happens, on average. I spent a lot of time talking to show girls. One would introduce me to another, and often after a while, something interesting would happen.

I remember one girl who liked to drink Gibsons. She danced at the Flamingo Hotel, and I got to know her rather well. When I'd come into town, I'd order a Gibson put at her table before she sat down, to announce my arrival.

One time I went over and sat next to her and she said, "I'm with a man tonight—a high-roller from Texas." (I had already heard about this guy. Whenever he'd play at the craps table, everybody would gather around to see him gamble.) He came back to the table where we were sitting, and my show girl friend introduced me to him.

The first thing he said to me was, "You know somethin'? I lost sixty thousand dollars here last night."

I knew what to do: I turned to him, completely unimpressed, and I said, "Is that supposed to be smart, or stupid?"

We were eating breakfast in the dining room. He said, "Here, let me sign your check. They don't charge me for all these things because I gamble so much here."

"I've got enough money that I don't need to worry about who pays for my breakfast, thank you." I kept putting him down each time he tried to impress me.

He tried everything—how rich he was, how much oil he had in Texas—but nothing worked, because I knew the formula.

We ended up having quite a bit of fun together.

One time when we were sitting at the bar he said to me, "You see those girls at the table over there? They're whores from Los Angeles."

They looked very nice; they had a certain amount of class.

He said, "Tell you what I'll do: I'll introduce them to you, and then I'll pay for the one you want."

I didn't feel like meeting the girls, and I knew he was saying that to impress me, so I began to tell him no. But then I thought, "This is something! This guy is trying so hard to impress me, he's willing to *buy* this for me. If I'm ever going to tell the story . . ." So I said to him, "Well, OK, introduce me."

We went over to their table and he introduced me to the girls and then went off for a moment. A waitress came around and asked us what we wanted to drink. I ordered some water, and the girl next to me said, "Is it all right if I have a champagne?"

"You can have whatever you want," I replied, coolly, " 'cause *you're* payin' for it."

"What's the matter with you?" she said. "Cheapskate, or something?"

"That's right."

"You're certainly not a gentleman!" she said, indignantly.

"You figured me out immediately!" I replied. I had learned in New Mexico *not* to be a gentleman.

Pretty soon they were offering to buy *me* drinks—the tables were turned completely! (By the way, the Texas oilman never came back.)

After a while, one of the girls said, "Let's go over to the El Rancho. Maybe things are livelier over there." We got in their car. It was a nice car, and they were nice people. On the way, they asked me my name.

"Dick Feynman."

"Where are you from, Dick? What do you do?"

"I'm from Pasadena; I work at Caltech."

One of the girls said, "Oh, isn't that the place where that scientist Pauling comes from?"

I had been in Las Vegas many times, over and over, and there was *nobody* who ever knew anything about science. I had talked to businessmen of all kinds, and to them, a scientist was a nobody. "Yeah!" I said, astonished.

"And there's a fella named Gellan, or something like that—a physicist." I couldn't believe it. I was riding in a car full of prostitutes and they know all this stuff!

"Yeah! His name is Gell-Mann! How did you happen to know that?"

"Your pictures were in *Time* magazine." It's true, they had pictures of ten U.S. scientists in *Time* magazine, for some reason. I was in it, and so were Pauling and Gell-Mann.

"How did you remember the names?" I asked.

"Well, we were looking through the pictures, and we picked out the youngest and the handsomest!" (Gell-Mann is younger than I am.)

We got to the El Rancho Hotel and the girls continued this game of acting towards me like everybody normally acts towards them: "Would you like to gamble?" they asked. "We'll pay for it, and you can keep half the winnings." I gambled a little bit with their money and we all had a good time.

After a while they said, "Look, we see a live one, so we'll have to leave you now," and they went back to work.

■　　■　　■

One time I was sitting at a bar and I noticed two girls with an older man. Finally he walked away, and they came over and sat next to me: the prettier and more active one next to me, and her duller friend, named Pam, on the other side.

Things started going along very nicely right away. She was very friendly. Soon she was leaning against me, and I put my arm around her. Two men came in and sat at a table nearby. Then, before the waitress came, they walked out.

"Did you see those men?" my new-found "friend" said.

"Yeah."

"They're friends of my husband."

"Oh? What *is* this?"

"You see, I just married John Big"—she mentioned a big name in the newspaper publishing business—"and we've had a little argument. We're on our honeymoon, and John is always gambling. He doesn't pay any attention to me, so I go off and enjoy myself, but he keeps sending spies around to check on what I'm doing."

She asked me to take her to her motel room, so we went in my car. On the way I asked her, "Well, what about John?"

She said, "Don't worry. Just look around for a big red car with two antennas. If you don't see it, he's not around."

The next night I took the "Gibson girl" and a friend of hers to the late show at the Silver Slipper, which had a show later than all the other hotels. The girls who worked in the other shows liked to go there, and the master of ceremonies announced the arrival of the various dancers as they came in. So in I went with these two *lovely* dancers on my arm, and he said, "And here come Miss So-and-so and Miss So-and-so from the Flamingo!" Everybody looked around to see who was coming in. I felt *great!*

We sat down at a table near the bar, and after a little while there was a bit of a flurry—waiters moving tables around, security guards, with guns, coming in. They were making room for a celebrity. JOHN BIG was coming in!

He came over to the bar, right next to our table, and right away two guys wanted to dance with the girls I brought. They went off to dance, and I was sitting alone at the table when John came over and sat down at my table. "How *are* yah?" he said. "Whattya doin' in Vegas?"

I was sure he'd found out about me and his wife. "Just foolin' around . . ." (I've gotta act tough, right?)

"How long ya been here?"

"Four or five nights."

"I know ya," he said. "Didn't I see you in Florida?"

"Well, I really don't know . . ."

He tried this place and that place, and I didn't know what he was getting at. "I know," he said; "It was in El Morocco." (El Morocco was a big nightclub in New York, where a lot of big operators go—like professors of theoretical physics . . .)

"That must have been it," I said. I was wondering when he was going to get *to* it. Finally he leaned over to me and said, "Hey, will you introduce me to those girls you're with when they come back from dancing?"

That's all he wanted; he didn't know me from a hole in the wall. So I introduced him, but my show girl friends said they were tired and wanted to go home.

The next afternoon, I saw John Big at the Flamingo, standing at the bar, talking to the bartender about cameras and taking pictures. He must be an amateur photographer: He's got all these bulbs and cameras, but he says the dumbest things about them. I decided he wasn't an amateur photographer after all; he was just a rich guy who bought himself some cameras.

I figured by that time that he didn't know I had been fooling around with his wife; he only wanted to talk to me because of the girls I had. So I thought I would play a game. I'd invent a part for myself: John Big's assistant.

"Hi, John," I said. "Let's take some pictures. I'll carry your flash-bulbs."

I put the flashbulbs in my pocket, and we started off taking pictures. I'd hand him flashbulbs and give him advice here and there; he *likes* that stuff.

We went over to the Last Frontier to gamble, and he started to win. The hotels don't like a high roller to leave, but I could see he wanted to go. The problem was how to do it gracefully.

"John, we have to leave now," I said in a serious voice.

"But I'm winning."

"Yes, but we *have* made an appointment this afternoon."

"OK, get my car."

"Certainly, Mr. Big!" He handed me the keys and told me what it looked like—I didn't let on that I knew.

I went out to the parking lot, and sure enough, there was this big, fat, wonderful red car with the two antennas. I climbed into it and turned the key—and it wouldn't start. It had an automatic transmission; they had just come out and I didn't know anything about them. After a bit I accidentally shifted it into PARK and it started. I drove it very carefully, like a million-dollar car, to the hotel entrance. I got out and went inside to the table where John Big was still gambling, and said, "Your car is ready, Sir!"

"I have to quit," he announced, and we left.

He had me drive the car. "I want to go to the El Rancho," he said. "Do you know any girls there?"

I knew one girl there rather well, so I said "Yeah." By this time I felt confident enough that the only reason he was going along with this game I had invented was that he wanted to meet some girls, so I brought up a delicate subject: "I met your wife the other night . . ."

"My wife? My wife's not here in Las Vegas."

I told him about the girl I met in the bar.

"Oh! I know who you mean; I met that girl and her friend in Los Angeles and brought them to Las Vegas. The first thing they did was use my phone for an hour to talk to their friends in Texas. I got mad and threw 'em out! So she's been going around telling everybody that she's my wife, eh?"

So *that* was cleared up.

We went into the El Rancho, and the show was going to start in about fifteen minutes. The place was packed; there wasn't a seat in the house. John went over to the majordomo and said, "I want a table."

"Yes, Sir, Mr. Big! It will be ready in a few minutes."

John tipped him and went off to gamble. Meanwhile I went around to the back, where the girls were getting ready for the show, and asked for my friend. She came out and I explained to her that John Big was with me, and he'd like some company after the show.

"Certainly, Dick," she said. "I'll bring some friends and we'll see you after the show."

I went around to the front to find John. He was still gambling. "Just go in without me," he said. "I'll be there in a minute."

There were two tables at the very front, right at the edge of the stage. Every other table in the place was packed. I sat down by myself. The show started before John came in, and the show girls came out. They could see me at the table, all by myself. Before, they thought I was some small-time professor; now they see I'm a Big Operator.

Finally John came in, and soon afterwards some people sat down at the table next to us—John's "wife" and her friend Pam, with two men!

I leaned over to John: "She's at the other table."

"Yeah."

She saw I was taking care of John, so she leaned over to me from the other table and asked, "Could I talk to John?"

I didn't say a word. John didn't say anything either.

I waited a little while, then I leaned over to John: "She wants to talk to you."

Then he waited a little bit. "All right," he said.

I waited a little more, and then I leaned over to her: "John will speak to you now."

She came over to our table. She started working on "Johnnie," sitting very close to him. Things were beginning to get straightened out a little bit, I could tell.

I love to be mischievous, so every time they got things straightened out a little bit, I reminded John of something: "The telephone, John . . ."

"Yeah!" he said. "What's the idea, spending an hour on the telephone?"

She said it was Pam who did the calling.

Things improved a little bit more, so I pointed out that it was her idea to *bring* Pam.

"Yeah!" he said. (I was having a great time playing this game; it went on for quite a while.)

When the show was over, the girls from the El Rancho came over to our table and we talked to them until they had to go back for the next show. Then John said, "I know a nice little bar not too far away from here. Let's go over there."

I drove him over to the bar and we went in. "See that woman over there?" he said. "She's a really good lawyer. Come on, I'll introduce you to her."

John introduced us and excused himself to go to the restroom. He never came back. I think he wanted to get back with his "wife" and I was beginning to interfere.

I said "Hi" to the woman and ordered a drink for myself, still playing this game of not being impressed and not being a gentleman.

"You know," she said to me, "I'm one of the better lawyers here in Las Vegas."

"Oh, no, you're not," I replied coolly. "You might be a lawyer during the day, but you know what you are right now? You're just a barfly in a small bar in Vegas."

She liked me, and we went to a few places dancing. She danced very well, and I *love* to dance, so we had a great time together.

Then, all of a sudden in the middle of a dance, my back began to hurt. It was some kind of big pain, and it started suddenly. I know now what it was: I had been up for three days and nights having these crazy adventures, and I was completely exhausted.

She said she would take me home. As soon as I got into her bed I went BONGO! I was out.

The next morning I woke up in this beautiful bed. The sun was shining, and there was no sign of her. Instead, there was a maid. "Sir," she said, "are you awake? I'm ready with breakfast."

"Well, uh . . ."

"I'll bring it to you. What would you like?" and she went through a whole menu of breakfasts.

I ordered breakfast and had it in bed—in the bed of a woman I didn't know; I didn't know who she was or where she came from!

I asked the maid a few questions, and she didn't know anything about this mysterious woman either: she had just been hired, and it was her first day on the job. She thought I was the man of the house, and found it curious that I was asking *her* questions. I got dressed, finally, and left. I never saw the mysterious woman again.

■　■　■

The first time I was in Las Vegas I sat down and figured out the odds for everything, and I discovered that the odds for the crap table were something like .493. If I bet a dollar, it would only cost me 1.4 cents. So I thought to myself, "Why am I so reluctant to bet? It hardly costs anything!"

So I started betting, and right away I lost five dollars in succession— one, two, three, four, five. I was supposed to be out only seven cents; instead, I was five dollars behind! I've never gambled since then—with my own money, that is. I'm very lucky that I started off losing.

One time I was eating lunch with one of the show girls. It was a quiet time in the afternoon; there was not the usual big bustle, and she said, "See that man over there, walking across the lawn? That's Nick the Greek. He's a professional gambler."

Now I knew damn well what all the odds were in Las Vegas, so I said, "How can he be a professional gambler?"

"I'll call him over."

Nick came over and she introduced us. "Marilyn tells me that you're a professional gambler."

"That's correct."

"Well, I'd like to know how it's possible to make your living gambling, because at the table, the odds are .493."

"You're right," he said, "and I'll explain it to you. I don't bet on the table, or things like that. I only bet when the odds are in my favor."

"Huh? When are the odds ever in your favor?" I asked incredulously.

"It's really quite easy," he said. "I'm standing around a table, when some guy says, 'It's comin' out nine! It's gotta be a nine!' The guy's excited; he thinks it's going to be a nine, and he wants to bet. Now I know the odds for all the numbers inside out, so I say to him, 'I'll bet you four to three it's *not* a nine,' and I win in the long run. I don't bet on the table; instead, I bet with people around the table who have prejudices—superstitious ideas about lucky numbers."

Nick continued: "Now that I've got a reputation, it's even easier, because people will bet with me even when they *know* the odds aren't very good, just to have the chance of telling the story, if they win, of how they beat Nick the Greek. So I really do make a living gambling, and it's wonderful!"

So Nick the Greek was really an educated character. He was a very nice and engaging man. I thanked him for the explanation; now I understood it. I have to understand the world, you see.

An Offer
You Must Refuse

Cornell had all kinds of departments that I didn't have much interest in. (That doesn't mean there was anything wrong with them; it's just that I didn't happen to have much interest in them.) There was domestic science, philosophy (the guys from this department were particularly inane), and there were the cultural things—music and so on. There were quite a few people I did enjoy talking to, of course. In the math department there was Professor Kac and Professor Feller; in chemistry, Professor Calvin; and a great guy in the zoology department, Dr. Griffin, who found out that bats navigate by making echoes. But it was hard to find enough of these guys to talk to, and there was all this other stuff which I thought was low-level baloney. And Ithaca was a small town.

The weather wasn't really very good. One day I was driving in the car, and there came one of those quick snow flurries that you don't expect, so you're not ready for it, and you figure, "Oh, it isn't going to amount to much; I'll keep on going."

But then the snow gets deep enough that the car begins to skid a little bit, so you have to put the chains on. You get out of the car, put the chains out on the snow, and it's *cold*, and you're beginning to shiver. Then you roll the car back onto the chains, and you have this problem—or we had it in those days; I don't know what there is now—that there's a hook on the inside that you have to hook first. And because the chains have to go on pretty tight, it's hard to get the hook to hook. Then you have to push this clamp down with your fingers, which by this time are nearly frozen. And because you're on the outside of the tire, and the hook is on the inside, and your hands are cold, it's very difficult to control. It keeps slipping, and it's *cold*, and the snow's coming down, and you're trying to push this clamp, and your hand's hurting, and the damn thing's not going down—well, I remember that *that* was the moment when I decided that *this is insane;* there must be a part of the world that doesn't have this problem!

I remembered the couple of times I had visited Caltech at the invitation of Professor Bacher, who had previously been at Cornell. He was very smart when I visited. He knew me inside out, so he said, "Feynman, I have this extra car, which I'm gonna lend you. Now here's how you go to Hollywood and the Sunset Strip. Enjoy yourself."

So I drove his car every night down to the Sunset Strip—to the nightclubs and the bars and the action. It was the kind of stuff I liked from Las Vegas—pretty girls, big operators, and so on. So Bacher knew how to get me interested in Caltech.

You know the story about the donkey who is standing exactly in the middle of two piles of hay, and doesn't go to either one, because it's balanced? Well, that's nothing. Cornell and Caltech started making me offers, and as soon as I would move, figuring that Caltech was really better, they would up their offer at Cornell; and when I thought I'd stay at Cornell, they'd up something at Caltech. So you can imagine this donkey between the two piles of hay, with the extra complication that as soon as he moves toward one, the other one gets higher. That makes it very difficult!

The argument that finally convinced me was my sabbatical leave. I wanted to go to Brazil again, this time for ten months, and I had just earned my sabbatical leave from Cornell. I didn't want to lose that, so now that I had invented a reason to come to a decision, I wrote Bacher and told him what I had decided.

Caltech wrote back: "We'll hire you immediately, and we'll give you your first year as a sabbatical year." That's the way they were acting: No matter what I decided to do, they'd screw it up. So my first year at Caltech was really spent in Brazil. I came to Caltech to teach on my second year. That's how it happened.

■ ■ ■

Now that I have been at Caltech since 1951, I've been very happy here. It's *exactly* the thing for a one-sided guy like me. There are all these people who are close to the top, who are very interested in what they are doing, and who I can talk to. So I've been very comfortable.

But one day, when I hadn't been at Caltech very long, we had a bad attack of smog. It was worse then than it is now—at least your eyes smarted much more. I was standing on a corner, and my eyes were watering, and I thought to myself, "This is crazy! This is absolutely *insane!* It was all right back at Cornell. I'm getting out of here."

So I called up Cornell, and asked them if they thought it was possible for me to come back. They said, "Sure! We'll set it up and call you back tomorrow."

The next day, I had the greatest luck in making a decision. God must have set it up to help me decide. I was walking to my office, and a guy came running up to me and said, "Hey, Feynman! Did you hear what happened? Baade found that there are *two* different populations of stars! All the measurements we had been making of the distances to the galaxies had been based on Cephid variables of *one* type, but there's *another* type, so the universe is twice, or three, or even four times as old as we thought!"

I knew the problem. In those days, the earth appeared to be older than the universe. The earth was four and a half billion, and the universe was only a couple, or three billion years old. It was a great puzzle. And this discovery resolved all that: The universe was now demonstrably older than was previously thought. And I got this information right away—the guy came running up to me to tell me all this.

I didn't even make it across the campus to get to my office, when *another* guy came up—Matt Meselson, a biologist who had minored in physics. (I had been on the committee for his Ph.D.) He had built the first of what they call a density gradient centrifuge—it could measure the density of molecules. He said, "Look at the results of the experiment I've been doing!"

He had proved that when a bacterium makes a new one, there's a whole molecule, intact, which is passed from one bacterium to another—a molecule we now know as DNA. You see, we always think of everything dividing, dividing. So we think *everything* in the bacterium divides and gives half of it to the new bacterium. But that's impossible: Somewhere, the smallest molecule that contains genetic information *can't* divide in half; it has to make a *copy* of itself, and send one copy to the new bacterium, and keep one copy for the old one. And he had proved it in this way: He first grew the bacteria in heavy nitrogen, and later grew them all in ordinary nitrogen. As he went along, he weighed the molecules in his density gradient centrifuge.

The first generation of new bacteria had all of their chromosome molecules at a weight exactly in between the weight of molecules made with heavy nitrogen, and molecules made with ordinary nitrogen—a result that could occur if everything divided, including the chromosome molecules.

But in succeeding generations, when one might expect that the weight of the chromosome molecules would be one-fourth, one-eighth, and one-sixteenth of the difference between the heavy and ordinary molecules, the weights of the molecules fell into only two groups. One group was the same weight as the first new generation (halfway between the heavier and the lighter molecules), and the other group was lighter—the weight of molecules made in ordinary nitrogen. The *percentage* of heavier molecules was cut in half in each succeeding generation, but not their weights. That was tremendously exciting, and very important—it was a fundamental discovery. And I realized, as I finally got to my office, that this is where I've got to be: where people from all different fields of science would tell me stuff, and it was all exciting. It was exactly what I wanted, really.

So when Cornell called a little later, and said they were setting everything up, and it was nearly ready, I said, "I'm sorry, I've changed my mind again." But I decided then *never* to decide again. Nothing—absolutely nothing—would ever change my mind again.

When you're young, you have all these things to worry about—should you go there, what about your mother. And you worry, and try to decide, but then something else comes up. It's much easier to just plain *decide*. Never mind—*nothing* is going to change your mind. I did that once when I was a student at MIT. I got sick and tired of having to decide what kind of dessert I was going to have at the restaurant, so I decided it would *always* be chocolate ice cream, and never worried about it again—I had the solution to *that* problem. Anyway, I decided it would always be Caltech.

* * *

One time someone tried to change my mind about Caltech. Fermi had just died a short time before, and the faculty at Chicago were looking for someone to take his place. Two people from Chicago came out and asked to visit me at my home—I didn't know what it was about. They began telling me all the good reasons why I ought to go to Chicago: I could do this, I could do that, they had lots of great people there, I had the opportunity to do all kinds of wonderful things. I didn't ask them how much they would pay, and they kept hinting that they would tell me if I asked. Finally, they asked me if I wanted to know the salary. "Oh, no!" I said. "I've already decided to stay at Caltech. My wife Mary Lou is in the other room, and if she hears how much the salary is, we'll get into an argument. Besides, I've decided not to decide any more; I'm staying at Caltech for good." So I didn't let them tell me the salary they were offering.

About a month later I was at a meeting, and Leona Marshall came over and said, "It's funny you didn't accept our offer at Chicago. We were so disappointed, and we couldn't understand how you could turn down such a terrific offer."

"It was easy," I said, "because I never let them tell me what the offer was."

A week later I got a letter from her. I opened it, and the first sentence said, "The salary they were offering was _____"—a *tremendous* amount of money, three or four times what I was making. Staggering! Her letter continued, "I told you the salary before you could read any further. Maybe now you want to reconsider, because they've told me the position is still open, and we'd very much like to have you."

So I wrote them back a letter that said, "After reading the salary, I've decided that I *must* refuse. The reason I have to refuse a salary like that is I would be able to do what I've always wanted to do—get a wonderful mistress, put her up in an apartment, buy her nice things. . . . With the salary you have offered, I could actually *do* that, and I know what would happen to me. I'd worry about her, what she's doing; I'd get into arguments when I come home, and so on. All this bother would make me uncomfortable and unhappy. I wouldn't be able to do physics well, and it would be a big mess. What I've always wanted to do would be bad for me, so I've decided that I can't accept your offer."

MAN OF
A THOUSAND
TONGUES

When I was in Brazil I had struggled to learn the local language, and decided to give my physics lectures in Portuguese. Soon after I came to Caltech, I was invited to a party hosted by Professor Bacher. Before I arrived at the party, Bacher told the guests, "This guy Feynman thinks he's smart because he learned a little Portuguese, so let's fix him good: Mrs. Smith, here, grew up in China. Let's have her greet Feynman in Chinese."

I walk into the party innocently, and Bacher introduces me to all these people: "Mr. Feynman, this is Mr. So-and-so."

"Pleased to meet you, Mr. Feynman."

"And this is Mr. Such-and-such."

"My pleasure, Mr. Feynman."

"And this is Mrs. Smith."

"*Ai, choong, ngong jia!*" she says, bowing.

This is such a surprise to me that I figure the only thing to do is to reply in the same spirit. I bow politely to her, and with complete confidence I say, "*Ah ching, jong jien!*"

"Oh, my God!" she exclaims, losing her own composure. "I knew this would happen: I speak Mandarin and he speaks Cantonese!"

THE
WORLD OF
ONE PHYSICIST

◈

WOULD YOU ʃOLVE
THE DIRAC EQUATION?

Near the end of the year I was in Brazil I received a letter from Professor Wheeler which said that there was going to be an international meeting of theoretical physicists in Japan, and might I like to go? Japan had some famous physicists before the war—Professor Yukawa (with a Nobel Prize), Tomonaga, and Nishina—but this was the first sign of Japan coming back to life after the war, and we all thought we ought to go and help them along.

Wheeler enclosed an Army phrasebook and wrote that it would be nice if we would all learn a little Japanese. I found a Japanese woman in Brazil to help me with the pronunciation, I practiced lifting little pieces of paper with chopsticks, and I read a lot about Japan. At that time Japan was very mysterious to me, and I thought it would be interesting to go to such a strange and wonderful country, so I worked very hard.

When we got there, we were met at the airport and taken to a hotel in Tokyo designed by Frank Lloyd Wright. It was an imitation of a European hotel, right down to the little bellhop dressed in an outfit like the Philip Morris guy. We weren't in Japan; we might as well have been in Europe or America! The guy who showed us to our rooms stalled around, pulling the shades up and down, waiting for a tip. Everything was just like America.

Our hosts had everything organized. That first night we were served dinner up at the top of the hotel by a woman dressed Japanese, but the menus were in English. I had gone to a lot of trouble to learn a few phrases in Japanese, so near the end of the meal, I said to the waitress, *"Kohi-o motte kite kudasai."* She bowed and walked away.

My friend Marshak did a double take: "What? What?"

"I talk Japanese," I said.

"Oh, you faker! You're always kidding around, Feynman."

"What are you talkin' about?" I said, in a serious tone.

"OK," he said. "What did you ask?"

"I asked her to bring us coffee."

Marshak didn't believe me. "I'll make a bet with you," he said. "If she brings us coffee . . ."

The waitress appeared with our coffee, and Marshak lost his bet.

It turned out I was the only guy who had learned some Japanese—even Wheeler, who had told everybody they ought to learn Japanese, hadn't learned any—and I couldn't stand it any more. I had read about the Japanese-style hotels, which were supposed to be very different from the hotel we were staying in.

The next morning I called the Japanese guy who was organizing everything up to my room. "I would like to stay at a Japanese-style hotel."

"I am afraid that it is impossible, Professor Feynman."

I had read that the Japanese are very polite, but very obstinate—you have to keep working on them. So I decided to be as obstinate as they, and equally polite. It was a battle of minds: It took thirty minutes, back and forth.

"Why do you want to go to a Japanese-style hotel?"

"Because in this hotel, I don't feel like I'm in Japan."

"Japanese-style hotels are no good. You have to sleep on the floor."

"That's what I want; I want to see how it is."

"And there are no chairs—you sit on the floor at the table."

"It's OK. That will be delightful. That's what I'm looking for."

Finally he owns up to what the situation is: "If you're in another hotel, the bus will have to make an extra stop on its way to the meeting."

"No, no!" I say. "In the morning, I'll come to this hotel, and get on the bus here."

"Well, then, OK. That's fine." That's all there was to it—except it took half an hour to get to the real problem.

He's walking over to the telephone to make a call to the other hotel when suddenly he stops—everything is blocked up again. It takes another fifteen minutes to discover that this time it's the mail. If there are any messages from the meeting, they already have it arranged where to deliver them.

"It's OK," I say. "When I come in the morning to get the bus, I'll look for any messages for me here at this hotel."

"All right. That's fine." He gets on the telephone and at last we're on our way to the Japanese-style hotel.

As soon as I got there, I knew it was worth it: It was so lovely! There was a place at the front where you take your shoes off, then a girl dressed in the traditional outfit—the obi—with sandals comes shuffling out, and takes your stuff; you follow her down a hallway which has mats on the floor, past sliding doors made of paper, and she's going *cht-cht-cht-cht* with little steps. It was all very wonderful.

We went into my room and the guy who arranged everything got all the way down, prostrated, and touched his nose to the floor; she got down and touched her nose to the floor. I felt very awkward. Should *I* touch my nose to the floor, too?

They said greetings to each other, he accepted the room for me, and went out. It was a *really* wonderful room. There were all the regular, standard things that you know of now, but it was all new to me. There was a little alcove with a painting in it, a vase with pussywillows nicely arranged, a table along the floor with a cushion nearby, and at the end of the room were two sliding doors which opened onto a garden.

The lady who was supposed to take care of me was a middle-aged woman. She helped me undress and gave me a *yukata*, a simple blue and white robe, to wear at the hotel.

I pushed open the doors and admired the lovely garden, and sat down at the table to do a little work.

I wasn't there more than fifteen or twenty minutes when something caught my eye. I looked up, out towards the garden, and I saw, sitting at the entrance to the door, draped in the corner, a *very* beautiful young Japanese woman, in a most lovely outfit.

I had read a lot about the customs of Japan, and I had an idea of why she was sent to my room. I thought, "This might be very interesting!"

She knew a little English. "Would you rike to see the garden?" she asked.

I put on the shoes that went with the *yukata* I was wearing, and we went out into the garden. She took my arm and showed me everything.

It turned out that because she knew a little English, the hotel manager thought I would like her to show me the garden—that's all it was. I was a bit disappointed, of course, but this was a meeting of cultures, and I knew it was easy to get the wrong idea.

Sometime later the woman who took care of my room came in and said something—in Japanese—about a bath. I knew that Japanese baths were interesting and was eager to try it, so I said, "*Hai.*"

I had read that Japanese baths are very complicated. They use a lot of water that's heated from the outside, and you aren't supposed to get soap into the bathwater and spoil it for the next guy.

I got up and walked into the lavatory section, where the sink was, and I could hear some guy in the next section with the door closed, taking a bath. Suddenly the door slides open: the man taking the bath looks to see who is intruding. "Professor!" he says to me in English. "That's a very bad error to go into the lavatory when someone else has the bath!" It was Professor Yukawa!

He told me that the woman had no doubt asked do I *want* a bath, and if so, she would get it ready for me and tell me when the bathroom was free. But of all the people in the world to make that serious social error with, I was lucky it was Professor Yukawa.

That Japanese-style hotel was delightful, especially when people came to see me there. The other guys would come in to my room and we'd sit on the floor and start to talk. We wouldn't be there more than five minutes when the woman who took care of my room would come in with a tray of candies and tea. It was as if you were a host in your own home, and the hotel staff was helping you to entertain your guests. Here, when you have guests at your hotel room, nobody cares—you have to call up for service, and so on.

Eating meals at the hotel was also different. The girl who brings in the food stays with you while you eat, so you're not alone. I couldn't have too good a conversation with her, but it was all right. And the food is wonderful. For instance, the soup comes in a bowl that's covered. You lift the cover and there's a beautiful picture: little pieces of onion floating in the soup just so; it's gorgeous. How the food looks on the plate is very important.

I had decided that I was going to live Japanese as much as I could. That meant eating fish. I never liked fish when I was growing up, but I found out in Japan that it was a childish thing: I ate a lot of fish, and enjoyed it. (When I went back to the United States the first thing I did was go to a fish place. It was horrible—just like it was before; I couldn't stand it. I later discovered the answer: The fish has to be very, very fresh—if it isn't, it gets a certain taste that bothers me.)

One time when I was eating at the Japanese-style hotel I was served a round, hard thing, about the size of an egg yolk, in a cup with some yellow liquid. So far I had eaten everything in Japan, but this thing frightened me: It was all convoluted, like a brain looks. When I asked the girl what it was, she replied "*kuri*." That didn't help much. I figured it was probably an octopus egg, or something. I ate it, with some trepidation, because I wanted to be as much in Japan as possible. (I also remembered the word "*kuri*" as if my life depended on it—I haven't forgotten it in thirty years.)

The next day I asked a Japanese guy at the conference what this convoluted thing was. I told him I had found it very difficult to eat. What the hell was "*kuri?*"

"It means 'chestnut,' " he replied.

. . .

Some of the Japanese I had learned had quite an effect. One time, when the bus was taking a long time to get started, some guy says, "Hey, Feynman! You know Japanese; tell 'em to get going!"

I said, *"Hayaku! Hayaku! Ikimasho! Ikimasho!"*—which means, "Let's go! Let's go! Hurry! Hurry!"

I realized my Japanese was out of control. I had learned these phrases from a military phrase book, and they must have been very rude, because everyone at the hotel began to scurry like mice, saying, "Yes, sir! Yes, sir!" and the bus left right away.

The meeting in Japan was in two parts: one was in Tokyo, and the other was in Kyoto. In the bus on the way to Kyoto I told my friend Abraham Pais about the Japanese-style hotel, and he wanted to try it. We stayed at the Hotel Miyako, which had both American-style and Japanese-style rooms, and Pais shared a Japanese-style room with me.

The next morning the young woman taking care of our room fixes the bath, which was right in our room. Sometime later she returns with a tray to deliver breakfast. I'm partly dressed. She turns to me and says, politely, *"Ohayo, gozai masu,"* which means, "Good morning."

Pais is just coming out of the bath, sopping wet and completely nude. She turns to him and with equal composure says, *"Ohayo, gozai masu,"* and puts the tray down for us.

Pais looks at me and says, "God, are we uncivilized!"

We realized that in America if the maid was delivering breakfast and the guy's standing there, stark naked, there would be little screams and a big fuss. But in Japan they were completely used to it, and we felt that they were much more advanced and civilized about those things than we were.

. . .

I had been working at that time on the theory of liquid helium, and had figured out how the laws of quantum dynamics explain the strange phenomena of super-fluidity. I was very proud of this achievement, and was going to give a talk about my work at the Kyoto meeting.

The night before I gave my talk there was a dinner, and the man who sat down next to me was none other than Professor Onsager, a topnotch expert in solid-state physics and the problems of liquid helium. He was one of these guys who doesn't say very much, but any time he said anything, it was significant.

"Well, Feynman," he said in a gruff voice, "I hear you think you have understood liquid helium."

"Well, yes . . ."

"Hoompf." And that's all he said to me during the whole dinner! So that wasn't much encouragement.

The next day I gave my talk and explained all about liquid helium. At the end, I complained that there was still something I hadn't been able to figure out: that is, whether the transition between one phase and the other phase of liquid helium was first-order (like when a solid melts or a liquid boils—the temperature is constant) or second-order (like you see sometimes in magnetism, in which the temperature keeps changing).

Then Professor Onsager got up and said in a dour voice, "Well, Professor Feynman is new in our field, and I think he needs to be educated. There's something he ought to know, and we should tell him."

I thought, "Geesus! What did I do wrong?"

Onsager continued, "We should tell Feynman that *nobody* has ever figured out the order of *any* transition correctly from first principles, so the fact that his theory does not allow him to work out the order correctly does *not* mean that he hasn't understood all the other aspects of liquid helium satisfactorily." It turned out to be a compliment, but from the way he started out, I thought I was really going to get it!

It wasn't more than a day later when I was in my room and the telephone rang. It was *Time* magazine. The guy on the line said, "We're very interested in your work. Do you have a copy of it you could send us?"

I had never been in *Time* and was very excited. I was proud of my work, which had been received well at the meeting, so I said, "Sure!"

"Fine. Please send it to our Tokyo bureau." The guy gave me the address. I was feeling great.

I repeated the address, and the guy said, "That's right. Thank you very much, Mr. Pais."

"Oh, no!" I said, startled. "I'm not Pais; it's Pais you want? Excuse me. I'll tell him that you want to speak to him when he comes back."

A few hours later Pais came in. "Hey, Pais! Pais!" I said, excited. "*Time* magazine called! They want you to send 'em a copy of the paper you're giving."

"Aw," he says. "Publicity is a whore!"

I was doubly taken aback.

I've since found out that Pais was right, but in those days, I thought it would be wonderful to have my name in *Time* magazine.

That was the first time I was in Japan. I was eager to go back, and said I would go to any university they wanted me to. So the Japanese arranged a whole series of places to visit for a few days at a time.

By this time I was married to Mary Lou, and we were entertained wherever we went. At one place they put on a whole ceremony with dancing, usually performed only for large groups of tourists, especially for us. At another place we were met right at the boat by all the students. At another place, the mayor met us.

One particular place we stayed was a little, modest place in the woods, where the emperor would stay when he came by. It was a very lovely place, surrounded by woods, just beautiful, the stream selected with care. It had a certain calmness, a quiet elegance. That the emperor would go to such a place to stay showed a greater sensitivity to nature, I think, than what we were used to in the West.

      ■   ■   ■

At all these places everybody working in physics would tell me what they were doing and I'd discuss it with them. They would tell me the general problem they were working on, and would begin to write a bunch of equations.

"Wait a minute," I would say. "Is there a particular example of this general problem?"

"Why yes; of course."

"Good. Give me one example." That was for me: I can't understand anything in general unless I'm carrying along in my mind a specific example and watching it go. Some people think in the beginning that I'm kind of slow and I don't understand the problem, because I ask a lot of these "dumb" questions: "Is a cathode plus or minus? Is an anion this way, or that way?"

But later, when the guy's in the middle of a bunch of equations, he'll say something and I'll say, "Wait a minute! There's an error. That can't be right!"

The guy looks at his equations, and sure enough, after a while, he finds the mistake and wonders, "How the hell did this guy, who hardly understood at the beginning, find that mistake in the mess of all these equations?"

He thinks I'm following the steps mathematically, but that's not what I'm doing. I have the specific, physical example of what he's trying to analyze, and I know from instinct and experience the properties of the thing. So when the equation says it should behave so-and-so, and I know that's the wrong way around, I jump up and say, "Wait! There's a mistake!"

So in Japan I couldn't understand or discuss anybody's work unless they could give me a physical example, and most of them couldn't find one. Of those who could, it was often a weak example, one which could be solved by a much simpler method of analysis.

Since I was perpetually asking *not* for mathematical equations, but for physical circumstances of what they were trying to work out, my visit was summarized in a mimeographed paper circulated among the scientists (it was a modest but effective system of communication they had cooked up after the war) with the title, "Feynman's Bombardments, and Our Reactions."

After visiting a number of universities I spent some months at the Yukawa Institute in Kyoto. I really enjoyed working there. Everything was so nice: You'd come to work, take your shoes off, and someone would come and serve you tea in the morning when you felt like it. It was very pleasant.

While in Kyoto I tried to learn Japanese with a vengeance. I worked much harder at it, and got to a point where I could go around in taxis and do things. I took lessons from a Japanese man every day for an hour.

One day he was teaching me the word for "see." "All right," he said. "You want to say, 'May I see your garden?' What do you say?"

I made up a sentence with the word that I had just learned.

"No, no," he said. "When you say to someone, 'Would you like to see my garden?' you use the first 'see.' But when you want to see someone else's garden, you must use another 'see,' which is more polite."

"Would you like to *glance at* my lousy garden?" is essentially what you're saying in the first case, but when you want to look at the other fella's garden, you have to say something like, "May I *observe* your gorgeous garden?" So there's two different words you have to use.

Then he gave me another one: "You go to a temple, and you want to look at the gardens . . ."

I made up a sentence, this time with the polite "see."

"No, no," he said. "In the temple, the gardens are much more elegant. So you have to say something that would be equivalent to 'May I *hang my eyes* on your most exquisite gardens?'"

Three or four different words for one idea, because when *I'm* doing it, it's miserable; when *you're* doing it, it's elegant.

I was learning Japanese mainly for technical things, so I decided to check if this same problem existed among the scientists.

At the institute the next day, I said to the guys in the office, "How would I say in Japanese, 'I solve the Dirac Equation'?"

They said such-and-so.

"OK. Now I want to say, 'Would *you* solve the Dirac Equation?'—how do I say that?"

"Well, you have to use a different word for 'solve,' " they say.

"Why?" I protested. "When *I* solve it, I do the same damn thing as when *you* solve it!"

"Well, yes, but it's a different word—it's more polite."

I gave up. I decided that wasn't the language for me, and stopped learning Japanese.

Is
Electricity
Fire?

In the early fifties I suffered temporarily from a disease of middle age:
I used to give philosophical talks about science*—how science satisfies
curiosity, how it gives you a new world view, how it gives man the ability to do things, how it gives him power—and the question is, in view of
the recent development of the atomic bomb, is it a good idea to give man
that much power? I also thought about the relation of science and religion, and it was about this time when I was invited to a conference in
New York that was going to discuss "the ethics of equality."

There had already been a conference among the older people, somewhere on Long Island, and this year they decided to have some younger
people come in and discuss the position papers they had worked out in
the other conference.

Before I got there, they sent around a list of "books you might find
interesting to read, and please send us any books you want others to
read, and we will store them in the library so that others may read them."

So here comes this wonderful list of books. I start down the first
page: I haven't read a single one of the books, and I feel very uneasy—I
hardly belong. I look at the second page: I haven't read a single one. I
found out, after looking through the whole list, that I haven't read *any*
of the books. I must be an idiot, an illiterate! There were wonderful
books there, like Thomas Jefferson *On Freedom*, or something like that,
and there were a few *authors* I had read. There was a book by
Heisenberg, one by Schrödinger, and one by Einstein, but they were
something like Einstein, *My Later Years* and Schrödinger, *What Is
Life*—different from what I had read. So I had a feeling that I was out of

*For a prime example, see "The Value of Science," pp. 483–89. —RL my depth, and that I shouldn't be *in* this. Maybe I could just sit quietly and listen.

I go to the first big introductory meeting, and a guy gets up and explains that we have two problems to discuss. The first one is fogged up a little bit—something about ethics and equality, but I don't understand what the problem *exactly* is. And the second one is, "We are going to demonstrate by our efforts a way that we can have a dialogue among people of different fields." There was an international lawyer, a historian, a Jesuit priest, a rabbi, a scientist (me), and so on.

Well, right away my logical mind goes like this: The second problem I don't have to pay any attention to, because if it works, it works; if it doesn't work, it doesn't work—we don't have to *prove* that we can have a dialogue, and *discuss* that we can have a dialogue, if we haven't got any dialogue to talk about. So the primary problem is the first one, which I didn't understand.

I was ready to put my hand up and say, "Would you please define the problem better," but then I thought, "No, *I'm* the ignoramus; I'd better listen. I don't want to start trouble right away."

The subgroup I was in was supposed to discuss the "ethics of equality in education." In the meetings of our subgroup the Jesuit priest was always talking about "the fragmentation of knowledge." He would say, "The real problem in the ethics of equality in education is the fragmentation of knowledge." This Jesuit was looking back into the thirteenth century when the Catholic Church was in charge of all education, and the whole world was simple. There was God, and everything came from God; it was all organized. But today, it's not so easy to understand everything because knowledge has become fragmented. I felt that "the fragmentation of knowledge" had nothing to do with "it," but "it" had never been defined, so there was no way for me to prove that.

Finally I said, "What is the *ethical* problem associated with the fragmentation of knowledge?" He would only answer me with great clouds of fog, and I'd say, "I don't understand," and everybody else would say they *did* understand, and *they* tried to explain it to me, but they couldn't explain it to me either.

So the others in the group told me to write down why I thought the fragmentation of knowledge was not a problem of ethics. I went back to my dormitory room and I wrote out carefully, as best I could, what I thought the subject of "the ethics of equality in education" might be, and I gave some examples of the kinds of problems I thought we might be talking about. For instance, in education, you increase differences. If someone's good at something, you try to develop his ability, which results in differences, or inequalities. So if education increases inequality, is this ethical? Then, after giving some more examples, I went on to say that while "the fragmentation of knowledge" is a difficulty because the complexity of the world makes it hard to learn things, in light of my definition of the *realm* of the subject, I couldn't see how the fragmentation of knowledge had anything to do with anything *approximating* what the ethics of equality in education might more or less be.

The next day I brought my paper into the meeting, and the guy said, "Yes, Mr. Feynman has brought up some very interesting questions we ought to discuss, and we'll put them aside for some possible future discussion." They completely missed the point. I was trying to define the problem, and then show how "the fragmentation of knowledge" didn't have anything to do with it. And the reason that nobody got anywhere in that conference was that they hadn't clearly defined the subject of "the ethics of equality in education," and therefore no one knew exactly what they were supposed to talk about.

There was a sociologist who had written a paper for us all to read—something he had written ahead of time. I started to read the damn thing, and my eyes were coming out: I couldn't make head nor tail of it! I figured it was because I hadn't read any of the books on that list. I had this uneasy feeling of "I'm not adequate," until finally I said to myself, "I'm gonna stop, and read *one sentence* slowly, so I can figure out what the hell it means."

So I stopped—at random—and read the next sentence very carefully. I can't remember it precisely, but it was very close to this: "The individual member of the social community often receives his information via visual, symbolic channels." I went back and forth over it, and translated. You know what it means? "People read."

Then I went over the next sentence, and I realized that I could translate that one also. Then it became a kind of empty business: "Sometimes people read; sometimes people listen to the radio," and so on, but written in such a fancy way that I couldn't understand it at first, and when I finally deciphered it, there was nothing to it.

There was only one thing that happened at that meeting that was pleasant or amusing. At this conference, *every word* that every guy said at the plenary session was so important that they had a stenotypist there, typing every goddam thing. Somewhere on the second day the stenotypist came up to me and said, "What profession are you? Surely not a professor."

"I *am* a professor," I said.

"Of what?"

"Of physics—science."

"Oh! *That* must be the reason," he said.

"Reason for what?"

He said, "You see, I'm a stenotypist, and I type everything that is said here. Now, when the other fellas talk, I type what they say, but I don't understand what they're saying. But every time *you* get up to ask a question or to say something, I understand exactly what you mean— what the question is, and what you're saying—so I thought you *can't* be a professor!"

■ ■ ■

There was a special dinner at some point, and the head of the theology place, a very nice, very Jewish man gave a speech. It was a good speech, and he was a very good speaker, so while it sounds crazy now, when I'm telling about it, at that time his main idea sounded completely obvious and true. He talked about the big differences in the welfare of various countries, which cause jealousy, which leads to conflict, and now that we have atomic weapons, any war and we're doomed; therefore, the right way out is to strive for peace by making sure there are no great differences from place to place, and since we have so much in the United States, we should give up nearly everything to the other countries until we're all even. Everybody was listening to this, and we were all full of sacrificial feeling, thinking we ought to do this. But I came back to my senses on the way home.

The next day one of the guys in our group said, "I think that speech last night was so good that we should all endorse it, and it should be the summary of our conference."

I started to say that the idea of distributing everything evenly is based on a *theory* that there's only X amount of stuff in the world, that somehow we took it away from the poorer countries in the first place, and therefore we should give it back to them. But this theory doesn't take into account the *real* reason for the differences between countries— that is, the development of new techniques for growing food, the development of machinery to grow food and to do other things, and the fact that all this machinery requires the concentration of capital. It isn't the *stuff*, but the power to *make* the stuff, that is important. But I realize now that these people were not in science; they didn't understand it. They didn't understand technology; they didn't understand their time.

The conference made me so nervous that a girl I knew in New York had to calm me down. "Look," she said, "you're shaking! You've gone absolutely nuts! Just take it easy, and don't take it so seriously. Back away a minute and look at what it is." So I thought about the conference, how crazy it was, and it wasn't so bad. But if someone were to ask me to participate in something like that again, I'd shy away from it like mad—I mean zero! Absolutely not! And I still get invitations for this kind of thing today.

When it came time to evaluate the conference at the end, the others told how much they got out of it, how successful it was, and so on. When they asked me, I said, "This conference was worse than a Rorschach test: There's a meaningless inkblot, and the others ask you what you think you see, but when you tell them, they start arguing with you!"

Even worse, at the end of the conference they were going to have another meeting, but this time the public would come, and the guy in charge of our group has the *nerve* to say that since we've worked out so much, there won't be any time for public discussion, so we'll just *tell* the public all the things we've worked out. My eyes bugged out: I didn't think we had worked out a damn thing!

Finally, when we were discussing the question of whether we had developed a way of having a dialogue among people of different disciplines—our second basic "problem"—I said that I noticed something interesting. Each of us talked about what *we* thought the "ethics of equality" was, from our own point of view, without paying any attention to the other guy's point of view. For example, the historian proposed that the way to understand ethical problems is to look historically at how they evolved and how they developed; the international lawyer suggested that the way to do it is to see how in fact people actually act in different situations and make their arrangements; the Jesuit priest was always referring to "the fragmentation of knowledge"; and I, as a scientist, proposed that we should isolate the problem in a way analogous to Galileo's techniques for experiments; and so on. "So, in my opinion," I concluded, "we had no dialogue at all. Instead, we had nothing but chaos."

Of course I was attacked, from all around. "Don't you think that order can come from chaos?"

"Uh, well, as a general principle, or . . ." I didn't understand what to do with a question like "Can order come from chaos?" Yes, no, what of it?

There were a lot of fools at that conference—pompous fools—and pompous fools drive me up the wall. Ordinary fools are all right; you can talk to them, and try to help them out. But pompous fools—guys who are fools and are covering it all over and impressing people as to how wonderful they are with all this hocus pocus—THAT, I CANNOT STAND! An ordinary fool isn't a faker; an honest fool is all right. But a dishonest fool is terrible—and that's what I got at the conference, a bunch of pompous fools, and I got very upset. I'm not going to get upset like that again, so I won't participate in interdisciplinary conferences any more.

■   ■   ■

A footnote: While I was at the conference, I stayed at the Jewish Theological Seminary, where young rabbis—I think they were Orthodox—were studying. Since I have a Jewish background, I knew of some of the things they told me about the Talmud, but I had never seen the Talmud.

It was very interesting: It's got big pages, and in a little square in the corner of the page is the original Talmud, and then in a sort of L-shaped margin, around this square, are commentaries written by different people. The Talmud has evolved, and everything has been discussed again and again, all very carefully, in a medieval kind of reasoning. I think the commentaries were shut down in the Middle Ages—there hasn't been any modern commentary. The Talmud is a wonderful book, a great, big potpourri of things: trivial questions, and difficult questions—for example, problems of teachers, and how to teach—and then some trivia again, and so on. The students told me that the Talmud was never translated, something I thought was curious, since the book is so valuable.

One day, two or three of the young rabbis came to me and said, "We realize that we can't study to be rabbis in the modern world without knowing something about science, so we'd like to ask you some questions."

Of course there are thousands of places to find out about science, and Columbia University was right near there, but I wanted to know what kinds of questions they were interested in.

They said, "Well, for instance, is electricity fire?"

"No," I said, "but . . . what is the problem?"

They said, "In the Talmud it says you're not supposed to make fire on a Saturday, so our question is, can we use electrical things on Saturdays?"

I was shocked. They weren't interested in science at all: The only way science was influencing their lives was so they might be able to interpret better the Talmud! They weren't interested in the world outside, in natural phenomena; they were only interested in resolving some question brought up in the Talmud.

And then one day—I guess it was a Saturday—I want to go up in the elevator, and there's a guy standing near the elevator. The elevator comes, I go in, and he goes in with me. I say, "Which floor?" and my hand's ready to push one of the buttons.

"No, no!" he says, "*I'm* supposed to push the buttons for *you*."

"*What?*"

"The boys here can't push the buttons on Saturday, so I have to do it for them. You see, I'm not Jewish, so it's all right for *me* to push the buttons. I stand near the elevator, and they tell me what floor, and I push the button for them."

Well, this really bothered me, so I decided to trap the students in a logical discussion. I had been brought up in a Jewish home, so I knew the kind of nitpicking logic to use, and I thought, "Here's fun!"

My plan went like this: I'd start off by asking, "Is the Jewish viewpoint a viewpoint that *any* man can have? Because if it is not, then it's certainly not something that is truly valuable for humanity . . . yak, yak, yak." And then they would have to say, "Yes, the Jewish viewpoint is good for any man."

Then I would steer them around a little more by asking, "Is it ethical for a man to hire another man to do something which is unethical for him to do? Would you hire a man to rob for you, for instance?" And I keep working them into the channel, very slowly, and very carefully, until I've got them—trapped!

You know what happened: They're *rabbinical* students—they were ten times better than I was! As soon as they saw I could put them in a hole, they went twist, turn, twist—I can't remember how—and they were free! I thought I had come up with an original idea—phooey! It had been discussed in the Talmud for ages! So they cleaned me up just as easy as pie—they got right out.

Finally I tried to assure the rabbinical students that the electric spark that was bothering them when they pushed the elevator buttons was not fire. I said, "Electricity is *not* fire. It's not a chemical process, as fire is."

"Oh?" they said.

"Of course, there's electricity in amongst the *atoms* in a fire."

"Aha!" they said.

"And in every *other* phenomenon that occurs in the world."

I even proposed a practical solution for eliminating the spark. "If that's what's bothering you, you can put a condensor across the switch, so the electricity will go on and off without any spark whatsoever—anywhere." But for some reason, they didn't like that idea either.

It really was a disappointment. Imagine! In modern times like this, guys are studying to go into society and *do* something—to be a rabbi—and the only way they think that science might be interesting is because their ancient, provincial, medieval problems are being confounded slightly by some new phenomena.

Something else happened at that time which is worth mentioning here. One of the questions the rabbinical students and I discussed at some length was why it is that in academic things, such as theoretical physics, there is a higher proportion of Jewish kids than their proportion in the general population. The rabbinical students thought the reason was that the Jews have a history of respecting learning: They respect their rabbis, who are really teachers, and they respect education. The Jews pass on this tradition in their families all the time, so that if a boy is a good student, it's as good as, if not better than, being a good football player.

It was the same afternoon that I was reminded how true it is. I was invited to one of the rabbinical students' home, and he introduced me to his mother, who had just come back from Washington, D.C. She clapped her hands together, in ecstasy, and said, "Oh! My day is complete. Today I met a general, and a professor!"

I realized that there are not many people who think it's just as important, and just as nice, to meet a professor as to meet a general. So I guess there's something in what they said.

HOTEL CITY

One time, when I was in Geneva, Switzerland, for a Physical Society meeting, I was walking around and happened to go past the United Nations buildings. I thought to myself, "Gee! I think I'll go in and look around." I wasn't particularly dressed for it—I was wearing dirty pants and an old coat—but it turned out there were tours you could go on where a guide would show you around.

The tour was quite interesting, but the most striking part was the great big auditorium. You know how everything is overdone for these big international characters, so what would ordinarily be a stage or a dais was in several layers: You have to climb up whole sequences of steps to this great, big, monstrous wooden thing that you stand behind, with a big screen in back of you. In front of you are the seats. The carpets are elegant, and the big doors with brass handles at the back are beautiful. On each side of the great auditorium, up above, are windowed booths for the translators of different languages to work in. It's a fantastic place, and I kept thinking to myself, "Gee! How it must be to give a talk in a place like this!"

Right after that, we were walking along the corridor just outside the auditorium when the guide pointed through the window and said, "You see those buildings over there that are under construction? They'll be used for the first time at the Atoms for Peace Conference, in about six weeks."

I suddenly remembered that Murray Gell-Mann and I were supposed to give talks at that conference on the present situation of high-energy physics. My talk was set for the plenary session, so I asked the guide, "Sir, where would the talks for the *plenary* session of that conference be?"

"Back in that room that we just came through."

"Oh!" I said in delight. "Then I'm gonna give a speech in that room!"

The guide looked down at my dirty pants and my sloppy shirt. I realized how dumb that remark must have sounded to him, but it was genuine surprise and delight on my part.

We went along a little bit farther, and the guide said, "This is a lounge for the various delegates, where they often hold informal discussions." There were some small, square windows in the doors to the lounge that you could look through, so people looked in. There were a few men sitting there talking.

I looked through the windows and saw Igor Tamm, a physicist from Russia that I know. "Oh!" I said. "I know that guy!" and I started through the door.

The guide screamed, "No, no! Don't go in there!" By this time he was *sure* he had a maniac on his hands, but he couldn't chase me because he wasn't allowed to go through the door himself!

Tamm's face lit up when he recognized me, and we talked a little bit. The guide was relieved and continued the tour without me, and I had to run to catch up.

*   *   *

At the Physical Society meeting my good friend Bob Bacher said to me, "Listen: it's going to be hard to get a room when that Atoms for Peace Conference is going on. Why don't you have the State Department arrange a room for you, if you haven't already made a reservation?"

"Naw," I said. "I'm not gonna have the State Department do a damn thing for me—I'll do it myself."

When I returned to my hotel I told them that I would be leaving in a week, but I'd be coming back at the end of summer: "Could I make a reservation now for that time?"

"Certainly! When will you be returning?"

"The second week in September . . ."

"Oh, we're terribly sorry, Professor Feynman; we are already completely booked for that time."

So I wandered off, from one hotel to another, and found they were all booked solid, six weeks ahead of time!

Then I remembered a trick I used once when I was with a physicist friend of mine, a quiet and dignified English fellow.

We were going across the United States by car, and when we got just beyond Tulsa, Oklahoma, there were supposed to be big floods up ahead. We came into this little town and we saw cars parked everywhere, with people and families in them, trying to sleep. He says, "We had better stop here. It's clear we can go no further."

"Aw, come on," I say. "How do you know? Let's see if we can *do* it: Maybe by the time we get there, the water will be down."

"We shouldn't waste time," he replies. "Perhaps we can find a room in a hotel if we look for it now."

"Aw, don't worry about that," I say. "Let's go!"

We drive out of town about ten or twelve miles and come to an arroyo. Yes, even for me, there's too much water. There's no question: We aren't going to try to get through *that*.

We turn around, and my friend's muttering about how we'll have no chance of finding a room in a hotel now, and I tell him not to worry.

Back in town, it's absolutely *blocked* with people sleeping in their cars, obviously because there are no more rooms—all the hotels must be packed. I see a small sign over a door: it says HOTEL. It was the kind of hotel I was familiar with in Albuquerque, when I would wander around town looking at things, waiting to see my wife at the hospital: You have to go up a flight of stairs and the office is on the first landing.

We go up the stairs to the office and I say to the manager, "We'd like a room."

"Certainly, sir. We have one with two beds on the third floor."

My friend is amazed: The town is packed with people sleeping in cars, and here's a hotel that has room!

We go up to our room, and gradually it becomes clear to him: there's no door on the room, only a hanging cloth in the doorway. The room was fairly clean, it had a sink; it wasn't so bad. We get ready for bed.

He says, "I've got to pee."

"The bathroom is down the hall."

We hear girls giggling and walking back and forth in the hall outside, and he's nervous. He doesn't want to go out there.

"That's all right; just pee in the sink," I say.

"But that's unsanitary."

"Naw, it's okay; you just turn the water on."

"I can't pee in the sink," he says.

We're both tired, so we lie down. It's so hot that we don't use any covers, and my friend can't get to sleep because of the noises in the place. I kind of fall asleep a little bit.

A little later I hear a creaking of the floor nearby, and I open one eye slightly. There he is, in the dark, quietly stepping over to the sink.*

■   ■   ■

*For the "physicist friend's" version of the story, see Chapter 6 of *Disturbing the Universe* by Freeman Dyson (1979). —RL

Anyway, I knew a little hotel in Geneva called the Hotel City, which was one of those places with just a doorway on the street and a flight of stairs leading up to the office. There were usually some rooms available, and nobody made reservations.

I went up the stairs to the office and told the desk clerk that I'd be back in Geneva in six weeks, and I'd like to stay in their hotel: "Could I make a reservation?"

"Certainly, sir. Of course!"

The clerk wrote my name on a piece of paper—they hadn't any book to write reservations in—and I remember the clerk trying to find a hook to put the paper on, to remember. So I had my "reservation," and everything was fine.

I came back to Geneva six weeks later, went to the Hotel City, and they *did* have the room ready for me; it was on the top floor. Although the place was cheap, it was clean. (It's Switzerland; it was clean.) There were a few holes in the bedspread, but it was a clean bedspread. In the morning they served a European breakfast in my room; they were rather delighted to have this guest who had made a reservation six weeks in advance.

Then I went over to the U.N. for the first day of the Atoms for Peace Conference. There was quite a line at the reception desk, where everyone was checking in: A woman was taking down everybody's address and phone number so they could be reached in case there were any messages.

"Where are you staying, Professor Feynman?" she asks.

"At the Hotel City."

"Oh, you must mean the Hotel Cité."

"No, it's called 'City': C-I-T-Y." (Why not? We would call it "Cité" here in America, so they called it "City" in Geneva.)

"But it isn't on our list of hotels. Are you *sure* it's 'City'?"

"Look in the telephone book for the number. You'll find it."

"Oh!" she said, after checking the phone book. "My list is incomplete! Some people are still looking for a room, so perhaps I can recommend the Hotel City to them."

She must have got the word about the Hotel City from someone, because nobody else from the conference ended up staying there. Once in a while the people at the Hotel City would receive telephone calls for me from the U.N., and would *run up* the two flights of stairs from the office to tell me, with some awe and excitement, to come down and answer the phone.

There's an amusing scene I remember from the Hotel City. One night I was looking through my window out into the courtyard. Something, in a building across the courtyard, caught the corner of my eye: It looked like an upside-down bowl on the windowsill. I thought it had moved, so I watched it for a while, but it didn't move any. Then, after a bit, it moved a little to one side. I couldn't figure out what this thing was.

After a while I figured it out: It was a man with a pair of binoculars that he held against the windowsill for support, looking across the courtyard to the floor below me.

There's another scene at the Hotel City which I'll always remember, that I'd love to be able to paint: I was returning one night from the conference and opened the door at the bottom of the stairway. There was the proprietor, standing there, trying to look nonchalant with a cigar in one hand while he pushed something up the stairs with the other. Farther up, the woman who brought me breakfast was pulling on this same heavy object with both hands. And at the top of the stairs, at the landing, there *she* was, with her fake furs on, bust sticking out, hand on her hip, *imperiously waiting*. Her customer was a bit drunk, and was not very capable of walking up the steps. I don't know whether the proprietor knew that *I* knew what this was all about; I just walked past everything. He was perhaps ashamed of his hotel—but, of course, to me, it was delightful.

It Sounds Greek to Me!

I don't know why, but I'm always very careless, when I go on a trip, about the address or telephone number or anything of the people who invited me. I figure I'll be met, or somebody else will know where we're going; it'll get straightened out somehow.

One time, in 1957, I went to a gravity conference at the University of North Carolina. I was supposed to be an expert in a different field who looks at gravity.

I landed at the airport a day late for the conference (I couldn't make it the first day), and I went out to where the taxis were. I said to the dispatcher, "I'd like to go to the University of North Carolina."

"Which do you mean," he said, "the State University of North Carolina at Raleigh, or the University of North Carolina at Chapel Hill?"

Needless to say, I hadn't the slightest idea. "Where are they?" I asked, figuring that one might be near the other.

"One's north of here, and the other is south of here, about the same distance."

I had nothing with me that showed which one it was, and there was nobody else going to the conference a day late like I was.

That gave me an idea. "Listen," I said to the dispatcher. "The main meeting began yesterday, so there were a whole lot of guys going to the meeting who must have come through here yesterday. Let me describe them to you: They would have their heads kind of in the air, and they would be talking to each other, not paying attention to where they were going, saying things to each other, like 'G-mu-nu. G-mu-nu.' "

His face lit up. "Ah, yes," he said. "You mean Chapel Hill!" He called the next taxi waiting in line. "Take this man to the university at Chapel Hill."

"Thank you," I said, and I went to the conference.

THE 7 PERCENT
∫OLUTION

The problem was to find the right laws of beta decay. There appeared to be two particles, which were called a tau and a theta. They seemed to have almost exactly the same mass, but one disintegrated into two pions, and the other into three pions. Not only did they seem to have the same mass, but they also had the same lifetime, which is a funny coincidence. So everybody was concerned about this.

At a meeting I went to, it was reported that when these two particles were produced in a cyclotron at different angles and different energies, they were always produced in the same proportions—so many taus compared to so many thetas.

Now, one possibility, of course, was that it was the same particle, which sometimes decayed into two pions, and sometimes into three pions. But nobody would allow that, because there is a law called the parity rule, which is based on the assumption that all the laws of physics are mirror-image-symmetrical, and says that a thing that can go into two pions can't also go into three pions.

At that particular time I was not really quite up on things: I was always a little behind. Everybody seemed to be smart, and I didn't feel I was keeping up. Anyway, I was sharing a room with a guy named Martin Block, an experimenter. And one evening he said to me, "Why are you guys so insistent on this parity rule? Maybe the tau and theta are the same particle. What would be the consequences if the parity rule were wrong?"

I thought a minute and said, "It would mean that nature's laws are different for the right hand and the left hand, that there's a way to define the right hand by physical phenomena. I don't know that that's so terrible, though there must be some bad consequences of that, but I don't know. Why don't you ask the experts tomorrow?"

He said, "No, they won't listen to me. *You* ask."

So the next day, at the meeting, when we were discussing the tau-theta puzzle, Oppenheimer said, "We need to hear some new, wilder ideas about this problem."

So I got up and said, "I'm asking this question for Martin Block: What would be the consequences if the parity rule was wrong?"

Murray Gell-Mann often teased me about this, saying I didn't have the nerve to ask the question for myself. But that's not the reason. I thought it might very well be an important idea.

Lee, of Lee and Yang, answered something complicated, and as usual I didn't understand very well. At the end of the meeting, Block asked me what he said, and I said I didn't know, but as far as I could tell, it was still open—there was still a possibility. I didn't think it was likely, but I thought it was possible.

Norm Ramsey asked me if I thought he should do an experiment looking for parity law violation, and I replied, "The best way to explain it is, I'll bet you only fifty to one you don't find anything."

He said, "That's good enough for me." But he never got to do the experiment.

*   *   *

Anyway, the discovery of parity law violation was made, experimentally, by Wu, and this opened up a whole bunch of new possibilities for beta decay theory. It also unleashed a whole host of experiments immediately after that. Some showed electrons coming out of the nuclei spun to the left, and some to the right, and there were all kinds of experiments, all kinds of interesting discoveries about parity. But the data was so confusing that nobody could put things together.

At one point there was a meeting in Rochester—the yearly Rochester Conference. I was still always behind, and Lee was giving his paper on the violation of parity. He and Yang had come to the conclusion that parity was violated, and now he was giving the theory for it.

During the conference I was staying with my sister in Syracuse. I brought the paper home and said to her, "I can't understand these things that Lee and Yang are saying. It's all so complicated."

"No," she said, "what you mean is *not* that you can't understand it, but that you didn't *invent* it. You didn't figure it out your *own* way, from hearing the clue. What you should do is imagine you're a student again, and take this paper upstairs, read every line of it, and check the equations. Then you'll understand it very easily."

I took her advice, and checked through the whole thing, and found it to be very obvious and simple. I had been afraid to read it, thinking it was too difficult.

It reminded me of something I had done a long time ago with left and right unsymmetrical equations. Now it became kind of clear, when I looked at Lee's formulas, that the solution to it all was much simpler: Everything comes out coupled to the left. For the electron and the muon, my predictions were the same as Lee's, except I changed some signs around. I didn't realize it at the time, but Lee had taken only the simplest example of muon coupling, and hadn't proved that all muons would be full to the right, whereas according to my theory, all muons would have to be full automatically. Therefore, I had, in fact, a prediction on top of what he had. I had different signs, but I didn't realize that I also had this quantity right.

I predicted a few things that nobody had experiments for yet, but when it came to the neutron and proton, I couldn't make it fit well with what was then known about neutron and proton coupling—it was kind of messy.

The next day, when I went back to the meeting, a very kind man named Ken Case, who was going to give a paper on something, gave me five minutes of his allotted time to present my idea. I said I was convinced that everything was coupled to the left, and that the signs for the electron and muon are reversed, but I was struggling with the neutron. Later, the experimenters asked me some questions about my predictions, and then I went to Brazil for the summer.

When I came back to the United States, I wanted to know what the situation was with beta decay. I went to Professor Wu's laboratory at Columbia, and she wasn't there, but another lady was there who showed me all kinds of data, all kinds of chaotic numbers that didn't fit with anything. The electrons, which in my model would have all come out spinning to the left in the beta decay, came out on the right in some cases. Nothing fit anything.

When I got back to Caltech, I asked some of the experimenters what the situation was with beta decay. I remember three guys, Hans Jensen, Aaldert Wapstra, and Felix Boehm, sitting me down on a little stool, and starting to tell me all these facts: experimental results from other parts of the country, and their own experimental results. Since I knew those guys, and how careful they were, I paid more attention to their results than to the others. Their results, alone, were not so inconsistent; it was all the others *plus* theirs.

Finally they get all this stuff into me, and they say, "The situation is so mixed up that even some of the things they've established for *years* are being questioned—such as the beta decay of the neutron is S and T. It's so messed up, Murray says it might even be V and A."

I jump up from the stool and say, "Then I understand EVVVVVERY-THING!"

They thought I was joking. But the thing that I had trouble with at the Rochester meeting—the neutron and proton disintegration—everything fit *but* that, and if it was V and A instead of S and T, *that* would fit too. Therefore I had the whole theory!

■   ■   ■

That night I calculated all kinds of things with this theory. The first thing I calculated was the rate of disintegration of the mu and the neutron. They should be connected together, if this theory was right, by a certain relationship, and it was right to 9 percent. That's pretty close, 9 percent. It should have been more perfect than that, but it was close enough.

I went on and checked some other things, which fit, and new things fit, new things fit, and I was very excited. It was the first time, and the only time, in my career that I knew a law of nature that nobody else knew. (Of course it wasn't true, but finding out later that at least Murray Gell-Mann—and also Sudarshan and Marshak—had worked out the same theory didn't spoil my fun.)

The other things I had done before were to take somebody else's theory and improve the method of calculating, or take an equation, such as the Schrödinger Equation, to explain a phenomenon, such as helium. We know the equation, and we know the phenomenon, but how does it work?

I thought about Dirac, who had his equation for a while—a new equation which told how an electron behaved—and I had this new equation for beta decay, which wasn't as vital as the Dirac Equation, but it was good. It's the only time I ever discovered a new law.

I called up my sister in New York to thank her for getting me to sit down and work through that paper by Lee and Yang at the Rochester Conference. After feeling uncomfortable and behind, now I was *in;* I had made a discovery, just from what she suggested. I was able to enter physics again, so to speak, and I wanted to thank her for that. I told her that everything fit, except for the 9 percent.

I was very excited, and kept on calculating, and things that fit kept on tumbling out—they fit automatically, without a strain. I had begun to forget about the 9 percent by now, because everything else was coming out right.

I worked very hard, late into the night, sitting at a small table in the kitchen next to a window. I'm getting all these calculations packed solid with things that fit, and I'm thinking, and concentrating, and it's dark, and it's quiet . . . when suddenly there's a TAC-TAC-TAC-TAC—loud, on the window. I look, and there's this *white face*, right at the window, only inches away, and I *scream* with shock and surprise!

It was a lady I knew who was angry at me because I had come back from vacation and didn't immediately call her up to tell her I was back. I let her in, and tried to explain that I was just now very busy, that I had just discovered something, and it was very important. I said, "Please go out and let me finish it."

She said, "No, I don't want to bother you. I'll just sit here in the living room."

I said, "Well, all right, but it's very difficult."

She didn't exactly *sit* in the living room. The best way to say it is she sort of squatted in a corner, holding her hands together, not wanting to "bother" me. Of course her purpose was to bother the *hell* out of me! And she succeeded—I couldn't ignore her. I got angry and upset. I had to do this calculating; I was making a big discovery and was terribly excited, and somehow it was more important to me than this lady—at least at that moment. I don't remember how I finally got her out of there, but it was very difficult.

After working some more, very intensely, I was hungry. I walked up the main street of Altadena to a little restaurant that was open all night, as I had often done before.

On earlier occasions I was sometimes stopped by the police, because I would be walking along, thinking, and then I'd stop—sometimes an idea comes that's difficult enough that you can't keep walking; you have to make sure of something. So I'd stop, and sometimes I'd hold my hands out in the air, saying to myself, "The distance between these is that way, and then this would turn over *this* way . . ."

I'd be moving my hands, standing in the street, when the police would come: "What is your name, sir? Where do you live? What are you doing?"

"Oh! I was thinking. I'm sorry; I live here, and go often to the restaurant . . ." After a bit they knew I was harmless, and they didn't stop me any more.

So I went to the restaurant, and while I'm eating I'm so excited that

I tell a lady that I just made a discovery. She starts in: She's the wife of a fireman, or forester, or something. And she's very lonely . . .

.　.　.

The next morning when I got to work I went to Wapstra, Boehm, and Jensen, and told them, "I've got it all worked out. Everything fits."

Bob Christy, who was there, too, said, "What beta-decay constant did you use?"

"The one from So-and-So's book."

"But that's been found out to be wrong. Recent measurements have shown it's off by 7 percent."

Then I remember the 9 percent. It was like a prediction for me: I went home and got this theory that says the neutron decay should be off by 9 percent, and they tell me the next *morning* that, as a matter of fact, it's 7 percent changed. But is it changed from 9 to 16, which is bad, or from 9 to 2, which is good?

Just then my sister calls from New York: "How about the 9 per-cent—what's happened?"

"I've just discovered that there's new data: 7 percent. . . ."

"*Which way?*"

"I'm trying to find out. I'll call you back."

I was so excited that I couldn't think. It's like when you're rushing for an airplane, and you don't know whether you're late or not, and you just can't make it, when somebody says, "It's Daylight Saving Time!" Yes, but *which way?* You can't think in the excitement.

So Christy went into one room, and I went into another room, each of us to be quiet, so we could think it through: This moves *this* way, and that moves *that* way—it wasn't very difficult, really; it's just exciting.

Christy came out, and I came out, and we both agreed: It's 2 per-cent, which is well within experimental error. After all, if they just changed the constant by 7 percent, the 2 percent could have been an error. I called my sister back: "Two percent." The theory was right.

(Actually, it was wrong: It was off, really, by 1 percent, for a reason we hadn't appreciated, which was only understood later by Nicola Cabibbo. So that 2 percent was not all experimental.)

Murray Gell-Mann and I compared and combined our ideas and wrote a paper on the theory. The theory was rather neat; it was rela-tively simple, and it fit a lot of stuff. But as I told you, there was an awful lot of chaotic data. And in some cases, we even went so far as to state that the experiments were in error.

A good example of this was an experiment by Valentine Telegdi, in which he measured the number of electrons that go out in each direction when a neutron disintegrates. Our theory had predicted that the number should be the same in all directions, whereas Telegdi found that 11 percent more came out in one direction than the others. Telegdi was an excellent experimenter, and very careful. And once, when he was giving a talk somewhere, he referred to our theory and said, "The trouble with theorists is, they never pay attention to the experiments!"

Telegdi also sent us a letter, which wasn't exactly scathing, but nevertheless showed he was convinced that our theory was wrong. At the end he wrote, "The F-G theory of beta decay is no F-G."*

Murray says, "What should we do about this? You know, Telegdi's pretty good."

I say, "We just wait." (I knew that Telegdi was excellent, and it would be hard to go upstream against him. But I was convinced by that time that something must be wrong with his experiment, and that *he* would find it—he's much better at finding it than we would be.)

Two days later there's another letter from Telegdi. He's a complete convert. He found out from our theory that he had disregarded the possibility that the proton recoiling from the neutron is not the same in all directions. He had assumed it was the same. By putting in corrections that our theory predicted instead of the ones *he* had been using, the results straightened out and were in complete agreement.

■   ■   ■

I went to Professor Bacher and told him about our success, and he said, "Yes, you come out and say that the neutron-proton coupling is V instead of T. Everybody used to think it was T. Where is the fundamental experiment that says it's T? Why don't you look at the early experiments and find out what was wrong with them?"

I went out and found the original article on the experiment that said the neutron-proton coupling is T, and I was *shocked* by something: I remembered reading that article once before (back in the days when I read every article in the *Physical Review*—it was small enough), and I *remembered*, when I saw this article again, looking at that curve and thinking, "That doesn't prove *anything!*"

You see, it depended on one or two points at the very edge of the

---

*Incomplete translation: "The Feynman–Gell-Mann theory of beta decay is no . . . good."
—RL

range of the data, and there's a principle that a point on the edge of the range of the data—the last point—isn't very good, because if it was, they'd have another point further along. And I had realized that the whole idea (that neutron-proton coupling is T) was based on the last point, which wasn't very good, and therefore it's not proved. I remembered *noticing* that!

And when I became interested in beta decay, directly, I read all these reports by the "beta-decay experts," which said it's T. I never looked at the original data; I only read those reports, like a dope. Had I been a *good* physicist, when I thought of the original idea back at the Rochester Conference I would have immediately looked up "how strong do we know it's T?"—that would have been the sensible thing to do. I would have recognized right away that I had already *noticed* it wasn't satisfactorily proved.

Since then I never pay any attention to anything by "experts." I calculate everything myself. When people said the quark theory was pretty good, I got two Ph.D.s, Finn Ravndal and Mark Kislinger, to go through the *whole works* with me, just so I could check that the thing was really giving results that fit fairly well, and that it was a significantly good theory. I'll never make that mistake again, reading the experts' opinions. Of course, you only live one life: you make all your mistakes, and learn what not to do—and that's the end of you.

THE
AMATEUR SCIENTIST

When I was a kid I had a "lab." It wasn't a laboratory in the sense that I would measure, or do important experiments. Instead, I would play: I'd make a motor, I'd make a gadget that would go off when something passed a photocell, I'd play around with selenium; I was piddling around all the time. I did calculate a little bit for the lamp bank, a series of switches and bulbs I used as resistors to control voltages. But all that was for application. I never did any laboratory kind of experiments.

I also had a microscope and *loved* to watch things under the microscope. It took patience: I would get something under the microscope and I would watch it interminably. I saw many interesting things, like everybody sees—a diatom slowly making its way across the slide, and so on.

But one day I was watching a paramecium and I saw something that was not described in the books I got in school—in college, even. These books always simplify things so the world will be more like *they* want it to be: When they're talking about the behavior of animals, they always start out with, "The paramecium is extremely simple; it has a simple behavior. It turns as its slipper shape moves through the water until it hits something, at which time it recoils, turns through an angle, and then starts out again."

It isn't really right. First of all, as everybody knows, the paramecia, from time to time, conjugate with each other—they meet and exchange nuclei. How do they decide when it's time to do that? (Never mind; that's not my observation.)

I watched these paramecia hit something, recoil, turn through an angle, and go again. The idea that it's mechanical, like a computer program —it doesn't look that way. They go different distances, they recoil different distances, they turn through angles that are different in various cases; they don't always turn to the right; they're very irregular. It looks random, because you don't know what they're hitting; you don't know all the chemicals they're smelling, or what.

One of the things I wanted to watch was what happens to the paramecium when the water that it's in dries up. It was claimed that the paramecium can dry up into a sort of hardened seed. I had a drop of water on the slide under my microscope, and in the drop of water was a paramecium and some "grass"—at the scale of the paramecium, it looked like a network of jackstraws. As the drop of water evaporated, over a time of fifteen or twenty minutes, the paramecium got into a tighter and tighter situation: there was more and more of this back-and-forth until it could hardly move. It was stuck between these "sticks," almost jammed.

Then I saw something I had never seen or heard of: the paramecium lost its shape. It could flex itself, like an amoeba. It began to push itself against one of the sticks, and began dividing into two prongs until the division was about halfway up the paramecium, at which time it decided *that* wasn't a very good idea, and backed away.

So my impression of these animals is that their behavior is much too simplified in the books. It is not so utterly mechanical or one-dimensional as they say. They should describe the behavior of these simple animals correctly. Until we see how many dimensions of behavior even a one-celled animal has, we won't be able to fully understand the behavior of more complicated animals.

■   ■   ■

I also enjoyed watching bugs. I had an insect book when I was about thirteen. It said that dragonflies are not harmful; they don't sting. In our neighborhood it was well known that "darning needles," as we called them, were very dangerous when they'd sting. So if we were outside somewhere playing baseball, or something, and one of these things would fly around, everybody would run for cover, waving their arms, yelling, "A darning needle! A darning needle!"

So one day I was on the beach, and I'd just read this book that said dragonflies don't sting. A darning needle came along, and everybody was screaming and running around, and I just sat there. "Don't worry!" I said. "Darning needles don't sting!"

The thing landed on my foot. Everybody was yelling and it was a big mess, because this darning needle was sitting on my foot. And there I was, this scientific wonder, saying it wasn't going to sting me.

You're *sure* this is a story that's going to come out that it stings me—but it didn't. The book was right. But I did sweat a bit.

I also had a little hand microscope. It was a toy microscope, and I pulled the magnification piece out of it, and would hold it in my hand like a magnifying glass, even though it was a microscope of forty or fifty power. With care you could hold the focus. So I could go around and look at things right out in the street.

When I was in graduate school at Princeton, I once took it out of my pocket to look at some ants that were crawling around on some ivy. I had to exclaim out loud, I was so excited. What I saw was an ant and an aphid, which ants take care of—they carry them from plant to plant if the plant they're on is dying. In return the ants get partially digested aphid juice, called "honeydew." I knew that; my father had told me about it, but I had never seen it.

So here was this aphid and sure enough, an ant came along, and patted it with its feet—all around the aphid, pat, pat, pat, pat, pat. This was terribly exciting! Then the juice came out of the back of the aphid. And because it was magnified, it looked like a big, beautiful, glistening ball, like a balloon, because of the surface tension. Because the microscope wasn't very good, the drop was colored a little bit from chromatic aberration in the lens—it was a gorgeous thing!

The ant took this ball in its two front feet, lifted it off the aphid, and *held* it. The world is so different at that scale that you can pick up water and hold it! The ants probably have a fatty or greasy material on their legs that doesn't break the surface tension of the water when they hold it up. Then the ant broke the surface of the drop with its mouth, and the surface tension collapsed the drop right into his gut. It was *very* interesting to see this whole thing happen.

．　．　．

In my room at Princeton I had a bay window with a U-shaped windowsill. One day some ants came out on the windowsill and wandered around a little bit. I got curious as to how they found things. I wondered, how do they know where to go? Can they tell each other where food is, like bees can? Do they have any sense of geometry?

This is all amateurish; everybody knows the answer, but *I* didn't know the answer, so the first thing I did was to stretch some string across the U of the bay window and hang a piece of folded cardboard with sugar on it from the string. The idea of this was to isolate the sugar from the ants, so they wouldn't find it accidentally. I wanted to have everything under control.

Next I made a lot of little strips of paper and put a fold in them, so I could pick up ants and ferry them from one place to another. I put the folded strips of paper in two places: Some were by the sugar (hanging from the string), and the others were near the ants in a particular location. I sat there all afternoon, reading and watching, until an ant happened to walk onto one of my little paper ferries. Then I took him over to the sugar. After a few ants had been ferried over to the sugar, one of them accidentally walked onto one of the ferries nearby, and I carried him back.

I wanted to see how long it would take the other ants to get the message to go to the "ferry terminal." It started slowly, but rapidly increased until I was going mad ferrying the ants back and forth.

But suddenly, when everything was going strong, I began to deliver the ants from the sugar to a *different* spot. The question now was, does the ant learn to go back to where it just came from, or does it go where it went the time before?

After a while there were practically no ants going to the first place (which would take them to the sugar), whereas there were many ants at the second place, milling around, trying to find the sugar. So I figured out so far that they went where they just came from.

In another experiment, I laid out a lot of glass microscope slides, and got the ants to walk on them, back and forth, to some sugar I put on the windowsill. Then, by replacing an old slide with a new one, or by rearranging the slides, I could demonstrate that the ants had no sense of geometry: they couldn't figure out where something was. If they went to the sugar one way, and there was a shorter way back, they would never figure out the short way.

It was also pretty clear from rearranging the glass slides that the ants left some sort of trail. So then came a lot of easy experiments to find out how long it takes a trail to dry up, whether it can be easily wiped off, and so on. I also found out the trail wasn't directional. If I'd pick up an ant on a piece of paper, turn him around and around, and then put him back onto the trail, he wouldn't know that he was going the wrong way until he met another ant. (Later, in Brazil, I noticed some leaf-cutting ants and tried the same experiment on them. They *could* tell, within a few steps, whether they were going toward the food or away from it—presumably from the trail, which might be a series of smells in a pattern: A, B, space, A, B, space, and so on.)

I tried at one point to make the ants go around in a circle, but I didn't have enough patience to set it up. I could see no reason, other than lack of patience, why it couldn't be done.

One thing that made experimenting difficult was that breathing on the ants made them scurry. It must be an instinctive thing against some animal that eats them or disturbs them. I don't know if it was the warmth, the moisture, or the smell of my breath that bothered them, but I always had to hold my breath and kind of look to one side so as not to confuse the experiment while I was ferrying the ants.

One time the ants found my larder, where I had jelly and bread and stuff, which was quite a distance from the window. A long line of ants marched along the floor across the living room. I thought to myself, "What can I do to stop them from coming to my larder without killing any ants? No poison; you gotta be humane to the ants!"

What I did was this: In preparation, I put a bit of sugar about six or eight inches from their entry point into the room, that they didn't know about. Then I made those ferry things again, and whenever an ant returning with food walked onto my little ferry, I'd carry him over and put him on the sugar. Any ant coming toward the larder that walked onto a ferry I also carried over to the sugar. Eventually the ants found their way from the sugar to their hole, so this new trail was being doubly reinforced, while the old trail was being used less and less. I knew that after half an hour or so the old trail would dry up, and in an hour they were out of my larder. I didn't wash the floor; I didn't do anything but ferry ants.

*   *   *

One question I wondered about was why the ant trails look so straight and nice. The ants look as if they know what they're doing, as if they have a good sense of geometry. Yet the experiments that I did to try to demonstrate their sense of geometry didn't work.

Many years later, when I was at Caltech and lived in a little house on Alameda Street, some ants came out around the bathtub. I thought, "This is a great opportunity." I put some sugar on the other end of the bathtub, and sat there the whole afternoon until an ant finally found the sugar—it's only a question of patience.

The moment the ant found the sugar, I picked up a colored pencil that I had ready (I had previously done experiments indicating that the ants don't give a damn about pencil marks—they walk right over them—so I knew I wasn't disturbing them), and behind where the ant went I drew a line so I could tell where his trail was. The ant wandered a little bit wrong to get back to the hole, so the line was quite wiggly, unlike a typical ant trail.

When the next ant to find the sugar began to go back, I marked his trail with another color. (By the way, he followed the first ant's return trail back, rather than his own incoming trail. My theory is that when an ant has found some food, he leaves a much stronger trail than when he's just wandering around.)

This second ant was in a great hurry and followed, pretty much, the original trail. But because he was going so fast he would go straight out, as if he were coasting, when the trail was wiggly. Often, as the ant was "coasting," he would find the trail again. Already it was apparent that the second ant's return was slightly straighter. With successive ants the same "improvement" of the trail by hurriedly and carelessly "following" it occurred.

I followed eight or ten ants with my pencil until their trails became a neat line right along the bathtub. It's something like sketching: You draw a lousy line at first; then you go over it a few times and it makes a nice line after a while.

I remember that when I was a kid my father would tell me how wonderful ants are, and how they cooperate. I would watch very carefully three or four ants carrying a little piece of chocolate back to their nest. At first glance it looks like efficient, marvelous, brilliant cooperation. But if you look at it carefully, you'll see that it's nothing of the kind: They're all behaving as if the chocolate is held up by something else. They pull at it one way or the other way. An ant may crawl over it while it's being pulled at by the others. It wobbles, it wiggles, the directions are all confused. The chocolate doesn't move in a nice way toward the nest.

The Brazilian leaf-cutting ants, which are otherwise so marvelous, have a very interesting stupidity associated with them that I'm surprised hasn't evolved out. It takes considerable work for the ant to cut the circular arc in order to get a piece of leaf. When the cutting is done, there's a fifty-fifty chance that the ant will pull on the wrong side, letting the piece he just cut fall to the ground. Half the time, the ant will yank and pull and yank and pull on the wrong part of the leaf, until it gives up and starts to cut another piece. There is no attempt to pick up a piece that it, or any other ant, has already cut. So it's quite obvious, if you watch very carefully, that it's not a brilliant business of cutting leaves and carrying them away; they go to a leaf, cut an arc, and pick the wrong side half the time while the right piece falls down.

TEƧTING
BLOODHOUNDƧ

When I was at Los Alamos and would get a little time off, I would
often go visit my wife, who was in a hospital in Albuquerque, a few
hours away. One time I went to visit her and couldn't go in right away,
so I went to the hospital library to read.

I read an article in *Science* about bloodhounds, and how they could
smell so very well. The authors described the various experiments that
they did—the bloodhounds could identify which items had been touched
by people, and so on—and I began to think: It *is* very remarkable how
good bloodhounds are at smelling, being able to follow trails of people,
and so forth, but how good are *we*, actually?

When the time came that I could visit my wife, I went to see her and
I said, "We're gonna do an experiment. Those Coke bottles over there
(she had a six-pack of empty Coke bottles that she was saving to send
out)—now you haven't touched them in a couple of days, right?"

"That's right."

I took the six-pack over to her without touching the bottles, and
said, "OK. Now I'll go out, and you take out one of the bottles, handle
it for about two minutes, and then put it back. Then I'll come in, and try
to tell which bottle it was."

So I went out, and she took out one of the bottles and handled it for
quite a while—lots of time, because I'm no bloodhound! According to
the article, they could tell if you just touched it.

Then I came back, and it was absolutely obvious: I didn't even have
to smell the damn thing, because, of course, the temperature was different. And it was also obvious from the smell. As soon as you put it up
near your face, you could smell it was dampish and warmer. So that
experiment didn't work because it was too obvious.

Then I looked at the bookshelf and said, "Those books you haven't looked at for a while, right? This time, when I go out, take one book off the shelf, and just open it—that's all—and close it again; then put it back."

So I went out again, she took a book, opened it and closed it, and put it back. I came in—and, again, nothing *to* it! It was easy. You just smell the books. It's hard to explain, because we're not used to saying things about it. You put each book up to your nose and sniff a few times, and you can tell. It's very different. A book that's been standing there a while has a dry, uninteresting kind of smell. But when a hand has touched it, there's a dampness and a smell that's very distinct.

We did a few more experiments, and I discovered that while bloodhounds are indeed quite capable, humans are not as *in*capable as they think they are—it's just that they carry their nose so high off the ground!

(I've noticed that my dog can correctly tell which way I've gone in the house, especially if I'm barefoot, by smelling my footprints. So I tried to do that: I crawled around the rug on my hands and knees, sniffing, to see if I could tell the difference between where I walked and where I didn't, and I found it impossible. So the dog is much better than I am.)

Many years later, when I was first at Caltech, there was a party at Professor Bacher's house, and there were a lot of people from Caltech. I don't know how it came up, but I was telling them this story about smelling the bottles and the books. They didn't believe a word, naturally, because they always thought I was a faker. I had to demonstrate it.

We carefully took eight or nine books off the shelf without touching them directly with our hands, and then I went out. Three different people touched three different books: they picked one up, opened it, closed it, and put it back.

Then I came back, and smelled everybody's hands, and smelled all the books—I don't remember which I did first—and found all three books correctly; I got one person wrong.

People's hands smell very different—that's why dogs can identify people; you have to *try* it. All hands have a sort of moist smell, and a person who smokes has a very different smell on his hands from a person who doesn't; ladies often have different kinds of perfumes, and so on. If somebody happened to have some coins in his pocket and happened to be handling them, you can smell that.

They still didn't believe me; they thought it was some sort of magic trick. They kept trying to figure out how I did it. There's a famous trick of this kind, where you have a confederate in the group who gives you signals as to what it is, and they were trying to figure out who the confederate was. Since then I've often thought that it would be a good card trick to take a deck of cards and tell someone to pick a card and put it back, while you're in the other room. You come back and say, "Now I'm going to tell you which card it is, because I'm a bloodhound: I'm going to *smell* all these cards and tell you which card you picked." Of course, with that kind of patter, people wouldn't believe for a minute that that's what you were actually doing.

A Map
of the Cat?

In the Graduate College dining room at Princeton everybody used to sit with his own group. I sat with the physicists, but after a bit I thought: It would be nice to see what the rest of the world is doing, so I'll sit for a week or two in each of the other groups.

When I sat with the philosophers I listened to them discuss very seriously a book called *Process and Reality* by Whitehead. They were using words in a funny way, and I couldn't quite understand what they were saying. I didn't want to interrupt them in their own conversation and keep asking them to explain something, and on the few occasions that I did, they'd try to explain it to me, but I still didn't get it. Finally they invited me to come to their seminar.

They had a seminar that was like a class. It had been meeting once a week to discuss a new chapter out of *Process and Reality*—some guy would give a report on it and then there would be a discussion. I went to this seminar promising myself to keep my mouth shut, reminding myself that I didn't know anything about the subject, and I was going there just to watch.

What happened there was typical—so typical that it was unbelievable, but true. First of all, I sat there without saying anything, which is almost unbelievable, but also true. A student gave a report on the chapter to be studied that week. In it Whitehead kept using the words "essential object" in a particular technical way that presumably he had defined, but that I didn't understand.

After some discussion as to what "essential object" meant, the professor leading the seminar said something meant to clarify things and drew something that looked like lightning bolts on the blackboard. "Mr. Feynman," he said, "would you say an electron is an 'essential object'? "

Well, now I was in trouble. I admitted that I hadn't read the book, so I had no idea of what Whitehead meant by the phrase; I had only come to watch. "But," I said, "I'll try to answer the professor's question if you will first answer a question from me, so I can have a better idea of what 'essential object' means. Is a *brick* an essential object?"

What I had intended to do was to find out whether they thought theoretical constructs were essential objects. The electron is a *theory* that we use; it is so useful in understanding the way nature works that we can almost call it real. I wanted to make the idea of a theory clear by analogy. In the case of the brick, my next question was going to be, "What about the *inside* of the brick?"—and I would then point out that no one has ever seen the inside of a brick. Every time you break the brick, you only see a surface. That the brick has an inside is a simple theory which helps us understand things better. The theory of electrons is analogous. So I began by asking, "Is a brick an essential object?"

Then the answers came out. One man stood up and said, "A brick as an individual, specific brick. *That* is what Whitehead means by an essential object."

Another man said, "No, it isn't the individual brick that is an essential object; it's the general character that all bricks have in common—their 'brickiness'—that is the essential object."

Another guy got up and said, "No, it's not in the bricks themselves. 'Essential object' means the idea in the mind that you get when you think of bricks."

Another guy got up, and another, and I tell you I have never heard such ingenious different ways of looking at a brick before. And, just like it should in all stories about philosophers, it ended up in complete chaos. In all their previous discussions they hadn't even asked themselves whether such a simple object as a brick, much less an electron, is an "essential object."

.   .   .

After that I went around to the biology table at dinnertime. I had always had some interest in biology, and the guys talked about very interesting things. Some of them invited me to come to a course they were going to have in cell physiology. I knew something about biology, but this was a graduate course. "Do you think I can handle it? Will the professor let me in?" I asked.

They asked the instructor, E. Newton Harvey, who had done a lot of research on light-producing bacteria. Harvey said I could join this special, advanced course provided one thing—that I would do all the work, and report on papers just like everybody else.

Before the first class meeting, the guys who had invited me to take the course wanted to show me some things under the microscope. They had some plant cells in there, and you could see some little green spots called chloroplasts (they make sugar when light shines on them) circulating around. I looked at them and then looked up: "How do they circulate? What pushes them around?" I asked.

Nobody knew. It turned out that it was not understood at that time. So right away I found out something about biology: it was very easy to find a question that was very interesting, and that nobody knew the answer to. In physics you had to go a little deeper before you could find an interesting question that people didn't know.

When the course began, Harvey started out by drawing a great, big picture of a cell on the blackboard and labeling all the things that are in a cell. He then talked about them, and I understood most of what he said.

After the lecture, the guy who had invited me said, "Well, how did you like it?"

"Just fine," I said. "The only part I didn't understand was the part about lecithin. What is lecithin?"

The guy begins to explain in a monotonous voice: "All living creatures, both plant and animal, are made of little brick-like objects called 'cells' . . ."

"Listen," I said, impatiently, "I *know* all that; otherwise I wouldn't be in the course. What is *lecithin?*"

"I don't know."

I had to report on papers along with everyone else, and the first one I was assigned was on the effect of pressure on cells—Harvey chose that topic for me because it had something that had to do with physics. Although I understood what I was doing, I mispronounced everything when I read my paper, and the class was always laughing hysterically when I'd talk about "blastospheres" instead of "blastomeres," or some other such thing.

The next paper selected for me was by Adrian and Bronk. They demonstrated that nerve impulses were sharp, single-pulse phenomena. They had done experiments with cats in which they had measured voltages on nerves.

I began to read the paper. It kept talking about extensors and flexors, the gastrocnemius muscle, and so on. This and that muscle were named, but I hadn't the foggiest idea of where they were located in relation to the nerves or to the cat. So I went to the librarian in the biology section and asked her if she could find me a map of the cat.

"A *map* of the *cat*, sir?" she asked, horrified. "You mean a *zoological chart!*" From then on there were rumors about some dumb biology graduate student who was looking for a "map of the cat."

When it came time for me to give my talk on the subject, I started off by drawing an outline of the cat and began to name the various muscles.

The other students in the class interrupt me: "We *know* all that!"

"Oh," I say, "you *do?* Then no *wonder* I can catch up with you so fast after you've had four years of biology." They had wasted all their time memorizing stuff like that, when it could be looked up in fifteen minutes.

*   *   *

After the war, every summer I would go traveling by car somewhere in the United States. One year, after I was at Caltech, I thought, "This summer, instead of going to a different place, I'll go to a different *field.*"

It was right after Watson and Crick's discovery of the DNA helix. There were some very good biologists at Caltech because Delbrück had his lab there, and Watson came to Caltech to give some lectures on the coding systems of DNA. I went to his lectures and to seminars in the biology department and got full of enthusiasm. It was a very exciting time in biology, and Caltech was a wonderful place to be.

I didn't think I was up to doing actual research in biology, so for my summer visit to the field of biology I thought I would just hang around the biology lab and "wash dishes," while I watched what they were doing. I went over to the biology lab to tell them my desire, and Bob Edgar, a young post-doc who was sort of in charge there, said he wouldn't let me do that. He said, "You'll have to really do some research, just like a graduate student, and we'll give you a problem to work on." That suited me fine.

I took a phage course, which told us how to do research with bacteriophages (a phage is a virus that contains DNA and attacks bacteria). Right away I found that I was saved a lot of trouble because I knew some physics and mathematics. I knew how atoms worked in liquids, so there was nothing mysterious about how the centrifuge worked. I knew enough statistics to understand the statistical errors in counting little spots in a dish. So while all the biology guys were trying to understand these "new" things, I could spend my time learning the biology part.

(There was one useful lab technique I learned in that course which I still use today. They taught us how to hold a test tube and take its cap off with one hand—you use your middle and index fingers—while leaving the other hand free to do something else, like hold a pipette that you're sucking cyanide up into. I can now hold my toothbrush in one hand, and with the other hand, hold the tube of toothpaste, twist the cap off, and put it back on.)

It had been discovered that phages could have mutations which would affect their ability to attack bacteria, and we were supposed to study those mutations. There were also some phages that would have a second mutation which would reconstitute their ability to attack bacteria. Some phages which mutated back were exactly the same as they were before. Others were not: There was a slight difference in their effect on bacteria—they would act faster or slower than normal, and the bacteria would grow slower or faster than normal. In other words, there were "back mutations," but they weren't always perfect; sometimes the phage would recover only part of the ability it had lost.

Bob Edgar suggested that I do an experiment that would try to find out if the back mutations occurred in the same place on the DNA spiral. With great care and a lot of tedious work I was able to find three examples of back mutations which had occurred very close together—closer than anything seen so far—and which partially restored the phage's ability to function. It was a slow job. It was sort of accidental: You had to wait around until you got a double mutation, which was very rare.

I kept trying to think of ways to make a phage mutate more often, and how to detect mutations more quickly, but before I could come up with a good technique the summer was over, and I didn't feel like continuing on that problem.

However, my sabbatical year was coming up, so I decided to work in the same biology lab but on a different subject. I worked with Matt Meselson to some extent, and then with a nice fella from England named J. D. Smith. The problem had to do with ribosomes, the "machinery" in the cell that makes protein from what we now call messenger RNA. Using radioactive substances, we demonstrated that the RNA could come out of the ribosomes and could be put back in.

I did a very careful job in measuring and trying to control everything, but it took me eight months to realize that there was one step that was sloppy. In preparing the bacteria to get the ribosomes out, in those days you ground it up with alumina in a mortar. Everything else was chemical and under control, but you could never repeat the way you pushed the pestle around when you were grinding the bacteria. So nothing ever came of the experiment.

Then I guess I have to tell about the time I tried with Hildegarde Lamfrom to discover whether peas could use the same ribosomes as bacteria. The question was whether the ribosomes of bacteria can manufacture the proteins of humans or other organisms. She had just developed a scheme for getting the ribosomes out of peas and giving them messenger RNA so that they would make pea proteins. We realized that a very dramatic and important question was whether ribosomes from bacteria, when given the peas' messenger RNA, would make pea protein or bacteria protein. It was to be a very dramatic and fundamental experiment.

Hildegarde said, "I'll need a lot of ribosomes from bacteria."

Meselson and I had extracted enormous quantities of ribosomes from *E. coli* for some other experiment. I said, "Hell, I'll just give you the ribosomes we've got. We have plenty of them in my refrigerator at the lab."

It would have been a fantastic and vital discovery if I had been a good biologist. But I wasn't a good biologist. We had a good idea, a good experiment, the right equipment, but I screwed it up: I gave her infected ribosomes—the grossest possible error that you could make in an experiment like that. My ribosomes had been in the refrigerator for almost a month, and had become contaminated with some other living things. Had I prepared those ribosomes promptly over again and given them to her in a serious and careful way, with everything under control, that experiment would have worked, and we would have been the first to demonstrate the uniformity of life: the machinery of making proteins, the ribosomes, is the same in every creature. We were there at the right place, we were doing the right things, but I was doing things as an amateur—stupid and sloppy.

You know what it reminds me of? The husband of Madame Bovary in Flaubert's book, a dull country doctor who had some idea of how to fix club feet, and all he did was screw people up. I was similar to that unpracticed surgeon.

The other work on the phage I never wrote up—Edgar kept asking me to write it up, but I never got around to it. That's the trouble with not being in your own field: you don't take it seriously.

I did write something informally on it. I sent it to Edgar, who laughed when he read it. It wasn't in the standard form that biologists use—procedures first, and so forth. I spent a lot of time explaining things that all the biologists knew. Edgar made a shortened version, but I couldn't understand it. I don't think they ever published it. I never published it directly.*

---

*A paper was published in 1962. It can be found on the Internet using the keywords "Edgar," "Feynman," and "phage." —RL

Watson thought the stuff I had done with phages was of some interest, so he invited me to come to Harvard and give a talk to the biology department about the double mutations which occurred so close together. I told them my guess was that one mutation made a change in the protein, such as changing the pH of an amino acid, while the other mutation made the opposite change on a different amino acid in the same protein, so that it partially balanced the first mutation—not perfectly, but enough to let the phage operate again. I thought they were two changes in the same protein that chemically compensated each other.

That turned out not to be the case. It was found out a few years later by people who undoubtedly developed a technique for producing and detecting the mutations faster, that what happened was, the first mutation was a mutation in which an entire DNA base was missing. Now the "code" was shifted and could not be "read" anymore. The second mutation was either one in which an extra base was put back in, or two more were taken out. Now the code could be read again. The closer the second mutation occurred to the first, the less message would be altered by the double mutation, and the more completely the phage would recover its lost abilities. The fact that there are three "letters" to code each amino acid was thus demonstrated.

While I was at Harvard that week, Watson suggested something and we did an experiment together for a few days. It was an incomplete experiment, but I learned some new lab techniques from one of the best men in the field.

But that was my big moment: I gave a seminar to the biology department at Harvard University! I always do that—get into something and see how far I can go.

I learned a lot of things in biology, and I gained a lot of experience. I got better at pronouncing the words, knowing what not to include in a paper or a seminar, and detecting a weak technique in an experiment. But I love physics, and I love to go back to it.

BUT
Is It Art?

Once I was at a party playing bongos, and I got going pretty good. One of the guys was particularly inspired by the drumming. He went into the bathroom, took off his shirt, smeared shaving cream in funny designs all over his chest, and came out dancing wildly, with cherries hanging from his ears. Naturally, this crazy nut and I became good friends right away. His name is Jirayr Zorthian; he's an artist.

We often had long discussions about art and science. I'd say things like, "Artists are lost; they don't have any subject: They used to have the religious subjects, but they lost their religion and now they haven't got anything. They don't understand the technical world they live in; they don't know anything about the beauty of the *real* world—the scientific world—so they don't have anything in their hearts to paint."

Jerry would reply that artists don't need to have a physical subject; there are many emotions that can be expressed through art. Besides, art can be abstract. Furthermore, scientists destroy the beauty of nature when they pick it apart and turn it into mathematical equations.

One time I was over at Jerry's for his birthday, and one of these dopey arguments lasted until 3:00 A.M. The next morning I called him up: "Listen, Jerry," I said, "the reason we have these arguments that never get anywhere is that you don't know a damn thing about science, and I don't know a damn thing about art. So, on alternate Sundays, I'll give you a lesson in science, and you give me a lesson in art."

"OK," he said. "I'll teach you how to draw."

"That will be *impossible,*" I said, because when I was in high school, the only thing I could draw was pyramids on deserts—consisting mainly of straight lines—and from time to time I would attempt a palm tree and put in a sun. I had absolutely no talent. I sat next to a guy who was equally adept. When he was permitted to draw anything, it consisted of two flat, elliptical blobs, like tires stacked on one another, with a stalk coming out of the top, culminating in a green triangle. It was supposed to be a tree. So I bet Jerry that he wouldn't be able to teach me to draw.

"Of course you'll have to work," he said.

I promised to work, but still bet that he couldn't teach me to draw. I wanted very much to learn to draw, for a reason that I kept to myself: I wanted to convey an emotion I have about the beauty of the world. It's difficult to describe because it's an emotion. It's analogous to the feeling one has in religion that has to do with a god that controls everything in the whole universe: There's a generality aspect you feel when you think about how things that appear so different and behave so differently are all run "behind the scenes" by the same organization, the same physical laws. It's an appreciation of the mathematical beauty of nature, of how she works inside; a realization that the phenomena we see result from the complexity of the inner workings between atoms; a feeling of how dramatic and wonderful it is. It's a feeling of awe—of scientific awe—which I felt could be communicated through a drawing to people who had also had this emotion. It could remind them, for a moment, of this feeling about the glories of the universe.

Jerry turned out to be a very good teacher. He told me first to go home and draw anything. So I tried to draw a shoe; then I tried to draw a flower in a pot. It was a mess!

The next time we met I showed him my attempts: "Oh, look!" he said. "You see, around in back here, the line of the flower pot doesn't touch the leaf." (I had meant the line to come up to the leaf.) "That's very good. It's a way of showing depth. That's very clever of you.

"And the fact that you don't make all the lines the same thickness" (which I didn't mean to do) "is good. A drawing with all the lines the same thickness is dull." It continued like that: he used everything that I thought was a mistake to teach me something in a positive way. He never said it was wrong; he never put me down. So I kept on trying, and I gradually got a little bit better, but I was never satisfied.

To get more practice I also signed up for a correspondence school course, with International Correspondence Schools, and I must say they were very good. They started me off drawing pyramids and cylinders, shading them and so on. We covered many areas: drawing, pastels, watercolors, and paints. Near the end I petered out: I made an oil painting for them, but I never sent it in.

I practiced drawing all the time, and became very interested in it. If I was at a meeting that wasn't getting anywhere—like the one where Carl Rogers came to Caltech to discuss with us whether Caltech should develop a psychology department—I would draw the other people. I had a little pad of paper I kept with me and I practiced drawing wherever I went. So, as Jerry taught me, I worked very hard.

Jerry, on the other hand, didn't learn much physics. His mind wandered too easily. I tried to teach him something about electricity and magnetism, but as soon as I mentioned "electricity," he'd tell me about some motor he had that didn't work, and how might he fix it. When I tried to show him how an electromagnet works by making a little coil of wire and hanging a nail on a piece of string, I put the voltage on, the nail swung into the coil, and Jerry said, "Ooh! It's just like fucking!" So that was the end of that.

So now we have a new argument: whether he's a better teacher than I was, or I'm a better student than he was.

Because Jerry was such a poor student (or I was such a bad teacher), I gave up the idea of trying to get an artist to appreciate the feeling I had about nature so *he* could portray it. I would now have to double my efforts in learning to draw so I could do it myself. It was a very ambitious undertaking, and I kept the idea entirely to myself, because the odds were I would never be able to do it.

■   ■   ■

Early on in the process of learning to draw, some lady I knew saw my attempts and said, "You should go down to the Pasadena Art Museum. They have drawing classes there, with models—nude models."

"No," I said; "I can't draw well enough—I'd feel very embarrassed."

"You're good enough; you should see some of the others!"

So I worked up enough courage to go down there. In the first lesson they told us about newsprint—very large sheets of low-grade paper, the size of a newspaper—and the various kinds of pencils and charcoal to get. For the second class a model came, and she started off with a ten-minute pose.

I started to draw the model, and by the time I'd done one leg, the ten minutes were up. I looked around and saw that everyone else had already drawn a complete picture, with shading in the back—the whole business.

I realized I was way out of my depth. But finally, at the end, the model was going to pose for thirty minutes. I worked very hard, and with great effort I was able to draw her whole outline. This time there was half a hope. So this time I didn't cover up my drawing, as I had done with all the previous ones.

We went around to look at what the others had done, and I discovered what they could *really* do: They draw the model, with details and shadows, the pocketbook that's on the bench she's sitting on, the platform—everything! They've all gone *zip, zip, zip, zip, zip* with the charcoal, all over, and I figure it's hopeless—utterly hopeless.

I go back to cover up my drawing, which consists of a few lines crowded into the upper left-hand corner of the newsprint—I had, until then, only been drawing on $8\frac{1}{2} \times 11$ paper—but some others in the class are standing nearby: "Oh, look at this one," one of them says. "Every line counts!"

I didn't know what that meant, exactly, but I felt encouraged enough to come to the next class. In the meantime, Jerry kept telling me that drawings that are too full aren't any good. His job was to teach me not to worry about the others, so he'd tell me they weren't so hot.

I noticed that the teacher didn't tell people much—the only thing he told me was my picture was too small on the page. Instead, he tried to inspire us to experiment with new approaches. I thought of how we teach physics: We have so many techniques—so many mathematical methods—that we never stop telling the students how to do things. On the other hand, the drawing teacher is afraid to tell you anything. If your lines are very heavy, the teacher can't say, "Your lines are too heavy," because *some* artist has figured out a way of making great pictures using heavy lines. The teacher doesn't want to push you in some particular direction. So the drawing teacher has this problem of communicating how to draw by osmosis and not by instruction, while the physics teacher has the problem of always teaching techniques, rather than the spirit, of how to go about solving physical problems.

They were always telling me to "loosen up," to become more relaxed about drawing. I figured that made no more sense than telling someone who's just learning to drive to "loosen up" at the wheel—it isn't going to work. Only after you know how to do it carefully can you begin to loosen up. So I resisted this perennial "loosen-up" stuff.

One exercise they had invented for loosening us up was to draw without looking at the paper. Don't take your eyes off the model; just look at her and make the lines on the paper without looking at what you're doing.

One of the guys says, "I can't help it. I have to cheat. I bet everybody's cheating!"

"*I'm* not cheating!" I say.

"Aw, baloney!" they say.

I finish the exercise and they come over to look at what I had drawn. They found that, indeed, I was *not* cheating; at the very beginning my pencil point had busted, and there was nothing but impressions on the paper.

When I finally got my pencil to work, I tried it again. I found that my drawing had a kind of strength—a funny, semi-Picasso-like strength—which appealed to me. The reason I felt good about that drawing was, I knew it was impossible to draw well that way, and therefore it didn't have to be good—and that's really what the loosening up was all about. I had thought that "loosen up" meant "make sloppy drawings," but it really meant to relax and not worry about how the drawing is going to come out.

I made a lot of progress in the class, and I was feeling pretty good. Up until the last session, all the models we had were rather heavy and out of shape. But in the last class we had a model who was a nifty blonde, perfectly proportioned. It was then that I discovered that I still didn't know how to draw: I couldn't make anything come out that looked anything *like* this beautiful girl! With the other models, if you draw something a little too big or bit too small, it doesn't make any difference because it's all out of shape anyway. But when you're trying to draw something that's so well put together, you can't fool yourself—it's got to be just right.

. . .

During one of the breaks I overheard a guy who could *really* draw asking this model whether she posed privately. She said yes. "Good. But I don't have a studio yet, so I'll have to work that out first."

I figured I could learn a lot from this guy, and I'd never get another chance to draw this nifty model unless I did something. "Excuse me," I said to him, "I have a room downstairs in my house that could be used as a studio."

They both agreed. I took a few of the guy's drawings to my friend Jerry, but he was aghast. "Those aren't so good," he said. He tried to explain why, but I never really understood.

Until I began to learn to draw, I was never much interested in looking at art. I had very little appreciation for things artistic, and only very rarely, such as once when I was in a museum in Japan. I saw a painting of bamboo done on brown paper, and what was beautiful about it to me was that it was perfectly poised between being just some brush strokes and being bamboo—I could make it go back and forth.

The summer after the drawing class I was in Italy for a science conference and I thought I'd like to see the Sistine Chapel. I got there very early in the morning, bought my ticket before anybody else, and *ran* up the stairs as soon as the place opened. I therefore had the unusual pleasure of looking at the whole chapel for a moment, in silent awe, before anybody else came in.

Soon the tourists came, and there were crowds of people milling around, talking different languages, pointing at this and that. I'm walking around, looking at the ceiling for a while. Then my eye came down a little bit and I saw some big, framed pictures, and I thought, "Gee! I never knew about these."

Unfortunately I'd left my guidebook at the hotel, but I thought to myself, "I know why these panels aren't famous; they aren't any good." But then I looked at another one, and I said, "Wow! That's a *good one*." I looked at the others. "That's good too, so is that one, but that one's lousy." I had never heard of these panels, but I decided that they were all good except for two.

I went into a place called the Sala de Raphael—the Raphael Room— and I noticed the same phenomenon. I thought to myself, "Raphael is irregular. He doesn't always succeed. Sometimes he's very good. Sometimes it's just junk."

When I got back to the hotel, I looked up the Sistene Chapel in my guidebook: "Below the paintings by Michelangelo there are fourteen panels by Botticelli, Perugino"—all these great artists—"and two by So-and-so, which are of no significance." This was a terrific excitement to me: I, too, could tell the difference between a beautiful work of art and one that's not, without being able to define it. As a scientist you always think you know what you're doing, so you tend to distrust the artist who says, "It's great," or "It's no good," and then is not able to explain to you why, as Jerry did with those drawings I took him. But here I was, sunk: I could do it too!

In the Raphael Room the secret turned out to be that only some of the paintings were made by the great master; the rest were made by students. I had liked the ones by Raphael. This was a big jab for my self-confidence in my ability to appreciate art.

Anyway, the guy from the art class and the nifty model came over to my house a number of times and I tried to draw her and learn from him. After many attempts I finally drew what I felt was a really nice picture—it was a portrait of her head—and I got very excited about this first success.

I had enough confidence to ask an old friend of mine named Steve Demitriades if his beautiful wife would pose for me, and in return I would give him the portrait. He laughed. "If she wants to waste her time posing for you, it's all right with me, ha, ha, ha."

I worked very hard on her portrait, and when he saw it, he turned over to my side completely: "It's *just wonderful!*" he exclaimed. "Can you get a photographer to make copies of it? I want to send one to my mother in Greece!" His mother had never seen the girl he married. That was very exciting to me, to think that I had improved to the point where someone wanted one of my drawings.

A similar thing happened at a small art exhibit that some guy at Caltech had arranged, where I contributed two drawings and a painting. He said, "We oughta put a price on the drawings."

I thought, "That's silly! I'm not trying to sell them."

"It makes the exhibition more interesting. If you don't mind parting with them, just put a price on."

After the show the guy told me that a girl had bought one of my drawings and wanted to speak to me to find out more about it.

The drawing was called "The Magnetic Field of the Sun." For this particular drawing I had borrowed one of those beautiful pictures of the solar prominences taken at the solar laboratory in Colorado. Because I understood how the sun's magnetic field was holding up the flames and had, by that time, developed some technique for drawing magnetic field lines (it was similar to a girl's flowing hair), I wanted to draw something beautiful that no artist would think to draw: the rather complicated and twisting lines of the magnetic field, close together here and spreading out there.

I explained all this to her, and showed her the picture that gave me the idea.

She told me this story: She and her husband had gone to the exhibit, and they both liked the drawing very much. "Why don't we buy it?" she suggested.

Her husband was the kind of a man who could never do anything right away. "Let's think about it a while," he said.

She realized his birthday was a few months ahead, so she went back the same day and bought it herself.

That night when he came home from work, he was depressed. She finally got it out of him: He thought it would be nice to buy her that picture, but when he went back to the exhibit, he was told that the picture had already been sold. So she had it to surprise him on his birthday.

What *I* got out of that story was something still very new to me: I understood at last what art is really for, at least in certain respects. It gives somebody, individually, pleasure. You can make something that somebody likes *so much* that they're depressed, or they're happy, on account of that damn thing you made! In science, it's sort of general and large: You don't know the individuals who have appreciated it directly.

I understood that to sell a drawing is not to make money, but to be sure that it's in the home of someone who really wants it; someone who would feel bad if they didn't have it. This was interesting.

So I decided to sell my drawings. However, I didn't want people to buy my drawings because the professor of physics isn't supposed to be able to draw, isn't that wonderful, so I made up a false name. My friend Dudley Wright suggested "Au Fait," which means "It is done" in French. I spelled it O-f-e-y, which turned out to be a name blacks used for "whitey." But after all, I was whitey, so it was all right.

One of my models wanted me to make a drawing for her, but she didn't have the money. (Models don't have money; if they did, they wouldn't be modeling.) She offered to pose three times free if I would give her a drawing.

"On the contrary," I said. "I'll give you three drawings if you'll pose once for nothing."

She put one of the drawings I gave her on the wall in her small room, and soon her boyfriend noticed it. He liked it so much that he wanted to commission a portrait of her. He would pay me sixty dollars. (The money was getting pretty good now.)

Then she got the idea to be my agent: She could earn a little extra money by going around selling my drawings, saying, "There's a new artist in Altadena . . ." It was *fun* to be in a different world: She arranged to have some of my drawings put on display at Bullock's, Pasadena's most elegant department store. She and the lady from the art section picked out some drawings—drawings of plants that I had made early on (that I didn't like)—and had them all framed. Then I got a signed document from Bullock's saying that they had such-and-such drawings on consignment. Of course nobody bought *any* of them, but otherwise I was a big success: I had my drawings on sale at Bullock's! It was fun to have them there, just so I could say one day that I had reached that pinnacle of success in the art world.

■   ■   ■

Most of my models I got through Jerry, but I also tried to get models on my own. Whenever I met a young woman who looked as if she would be interesting to draw, I would ask her to pose for me. It always ended up that I would draw her face, because I didn't know exactly how to bring up the subject of posing nude.

Once when I was over at Jerry's, I said to his wife Dabney, "I can never get the girls to pose nude: I don't know how Jerry does it!"

"Well, did you ever *ask* them?"

"Oh! I never thought of that."

The next girl I met that I wanted to pose for me was a Caltech student. I asked her if she would pose nude. "Certainly," she said, and there we were—so it was easy. I guess there was so much in the back of my mind that I thought it was somehow wrong to ask.

I've done a lot of drawing by now, and I've gotten so I like to draw nudes best. For all I know it's not art, exactly; it's a mixture. Who knows the percentages?

One model I met through Jerry had been a *Playboy* playmate. She was tall and gorgeous. Every girl in the world, looking at her, would have been jealous. However, she thought she was *too* tall. When she would come into a room, she'd be half stooped over. I tried to teach her, when she was posing, to *please stand up*, because she was so elegant and striking. I finally talked her into that.

Then she had another worry: She's got "dents" near her groin. I have to get out a book of anatomy to show her that it's the attachment of the muscles to the ilium, and to explain to her that you can't see these dents on everybody; to see them, everything must be just right, in perfect proportion, like she was. I learned from her that every woman is worried about her looks, no matter how beautiful she is.

I wanted to draw a picture of this model in color, in pastels, just to experiment. I thought I would first make a sketch in charcoal, which would be later covered with the pastel. When I got through with this charcoal drawing that I had made without worrying how it was going to look, I realized that it was one of the best drawings I had ever made. I decided to leave it, and forget about the pastels for that one.

My "agent" looked at it and wanted to take it around.

"You can't sell that," I said, "it's on newsprint."

"Oh, never mind," she said.

A few weeks later she came back with this picture in a beautiful wooden frame with a red band and a gold edge. It's a funny thing which must make artists, generally, unhappy—how much improved a drawing gets when you put a frame around it. My agent told me that a particular lady got all excited about the drawing and they took it to a picture framer. He told them that there were special techniques for mounting drawings on newsprint: Impregnate it with plastic, do this, do that. So this lady goes to all that trouble over this drawing I had made, and then has my agent bring it back to me. "I think the artist would like to see how lovely it is, framed," she said.

I certainly did. There was another example of the direct pleasure somebody got out of one of my pictures. So it was a real kick selling the drawings.

. . .

There was a period when there were topless restaurants in town: You could go there for lunch or dinner, and the girls would dance without a top, and after a while without anything. One of these places, it turned out, was only a mile and a half away from my house, so I went there very often. I'd sit in one of the booths and work a little physics on the paper placemats with the scalloped edges, and sometimes I'd draw one of the dancing girls or one of the customers, just to practice.

My wife, Gweneth, who is English, had a good attitude about my going to this place. She said, "The Englishmen have clubs they go to." So it was something like my club.

There were pictures hanging around the place, but I didn't like them much. They were these fluorescent colors on black velvet—kind of ugly—a girl taking off her sweater, or something. Well, I had a rather nice drawing I had made of my model Kathy, so I gave it to the owner of the restaurant to put up on the wall, and he was delighted.

Giving him the drawing turned out to produce some useful results. The owner became very friendly to me, and would give me free drinks all the time. Now, every time I would come in to the restaurant a waitress would come over with my free 7-Up. I'd watch the girls dance, do a little physics, prepare a lecture, or draw a little bit. If I got a little tired, I'd watch the entertainment for a while, and then do a little more work. The owner knew I didn't want to be disturbed, so if a drunk man came over and started to talk to me, right away a waitress would come and get the guy out of there. If a girl came over, he would do nothing. We had a very good relationship. His name was Gianonni.

The other effect of my drawing on display was that people would ask him about it. One day a guy came over to me and said, "Gianonni tells me you made that picture."

"Yeah."

"Good. I'd like to commission a drawing."

"All right; what would you like?"

"I want a picture of a nude toreador girl being charged by a bull with a man's head."

"Well, uh, it would help me a little if I had some idea of what this drawing is for."

"I want it for my business establishment."

"What kind of business establishment?"

"It's for a massage parlor: you know, private rooms, masseuses—get the idea?"

"Yeah, I get the idea." I didn't want to draw a nude toreador girl being charged by a bull with a man's head, so I tried to talk him out of it. "How do you think that looks to the customers, and how does it make the girls feel? The men come in there and you get 'em all excited with this picture. Is that the way you want 'em to treat the girls?"

He's not convinced.

"Suppose the cops come in and they see this picture, and you're claiming it's a massage parlor."

"OK, OK," he says; "You're right. I've gotta change it. What I want is a picture that, if the cops look at it, is perfectly OK for a massage parlor, but if a customer looks at it, it gives him ideas."

"OK," I said. We arranged it for sixty dollars, and I began to work on the drawing. First, I had to figure out how to do it. I thought and I thought, and I often felt I would have been better off drawing the nude toreador girl in the first place!

Finally I figured out how to do it: I would draw a slave girl in imaginary Rome, massaging some important Roman—a senator, perhaps. Since she's a slave girl, she has a certain look on her face. She knows what's going to happen next, and she's sort of resigned to it.

I worked very hard on this picture. I used Kathy as the model. Later, I got another model for the man. I did lots of studies, and soon the cost for the models was already eighty dollars. I didn't care about the money; I liked the challenge of having to do a commission. Finally I ended up with a picture of a muscular man lying on a table with the slave girl massaging him: she's wearing a kind of toga that covers one breast—the other one was nude—and I got the expression of resignation on her face just right.

I was just about ready to deliver my commissioned masterpiece to the massage parlor when Gianonni told me that the guy had been arrested and was in jail. So I asked the girls at the topless restaurant if they knew any good massage parlors around Pasadena that would like to hang my drawing in the lobby.

They gave me names and locations of places in and around Pasadena and told me things like "When you go to the Such-and-such massage parlor, ask for Frank—he's a pretty good guy. If he's not there, don't go in." Or "Don't talk to Eddie. Eddie would never understand the value of a drawing."

The next day I rolled up my picture, put it in the back of my station wagon, and Gweneth wished me good luck as I set out to visit the brothels of Pasadena to sell my drawing.

Just before I went to the first place on my list, I thought to myself, "You know, before I go anywhere else, I oughta check at the place he used to have. Maybe it's still open, and perhaps the new manager wants my drawing." I went over there and knocked on the door. It opened a little bit, and I saw a girl's eye. "Do we know you?" she asked.

"No, you don't, but how would you like to have a drawing that would be appropriate for your entrance hall?"

"I'm sorry," she said, "but we've already contracted an artist to make a drawing for us, and he's working on it."

"I'm the artist," I said, "and your drawing is ready!"

It turns out that the guy, as he was going to jail, told his wife about our arrangement. So I went in and showed them the drawing.

The guy's wife and his sister, who were now running the place, were not entirely pleased with it—they wanted the girls to see it. I hung it up on the wall, there in the lobby, and all the girls came out from the various rooms in the back and started to make comments.

One girl said she didn't like the expression on the slave girl's face. "She doesn't look happy," she said. "She should be smiling."

I said to her, "Tell me—while you're massaging a guy, and he's not lookin' at you, are you smiling?"

"Oh, no!" she said. "I feel exactly like she looks! But it's not right to put it in the picture."

I left it with them, but after a week of worrying about it back and forth, they decided they didn't want it. It turned out that the real reason that they didn't want it was the one nude breast. I tried to explain that my drawing was a tone-down of the original request, but they said they had different ideas about it than the guy did. I thought the irony of people running such an establishment being prissy about one nude breast was amusing, and I took the drawing home.

My businessman friend Dudley Wright saw the drawing and I told him the story about it. He said, "You oughta triple its price. With art, nobody is really sure of its value, so people often think, 'If the price is higher, it must be more valuable!' "

I said, "You're crazy!" but, just for fun, I bought a twenty-dollar frame and mounted the drawing so it would be ready for the next customer.

Some guy from the weather forecasting business saw the drawing I had given Gianonni and asked if I had others. I invited him and his wife to my "studio" downstairs in my home, and they asked about the newly framed drawing. "That one is two hundred dollars." (I had multiplied sixty by three and added twenty for the frame.) The next day they came back and bought it. So the massage parlor drawing ended up in the office of a weather forecaster.

One day there was a police raid on Gianonni's, and some of the dancers were arrested. Someone wanted to stop Gianonni from putting on topless dancing shows, and Gianonni didn't want to stop. So there was a big court case about it; it was in all the local papers.

Gianonni went around to all the customers and asked them if they would testify in support of him. Everybody had an excuse: "I run a day camp, and if the parents see that I'm going to this place, they won't send their kids to my camp . . . ." Or, "I'm in the such-and-such business, and if it's publicized that I come down here, we'll lose customers."

I think to myself, "I'm the only free man in here—I haven't any excuse! I *like* this place, and I'd like to see it continue. I don't see anything wrong with topless dancing." So I said to Gianonni, "Yes, I'll be glad to testify."

In court the big question was, is topless dancing acceptable to the community—do community standards allow it? The lawyer from the defense tried to make me into an expert on community standards. He asked me if I went into other bars.

"Yes."

"And how many times per week would you typically go to Gianonni's?"

"Five, six times a week." (That got into the papers: The Caltech professor of physics goes to see topless dancing six times a week.)

"What sections of the community were represented at Gianonni's?"

"Nearly every section: There were guys from the real estate business, a guy from the city governing board, workmen from the gas station, guys from engineering firms, a professor of physics . . . ."

"So would you say that topless entertainment is acceptable to the community, given that so many sections of it are watching it and enjoying it?"

"I need to know what you mean by 'acceptable to the community.' Nothing is accepted by *everybody*, so what *percentage* of the community must accept something in order for it to be 'acceptable to the community?' "

The lawyer suggests a figure. The other lawyer objects. The judge calls a recess, and they all go into chambers for 15 minutes before they can decide that "acceptable to the community" means accepted by 50% of the community.

In spite of the fact that I made them be precise, I had no precise numbers as evidence, so I said, "I believe that topless dancing is accepted by more than 50% of the community, and is therefore acceptable to the community."

Gianonni temporarily lost the case, and his, or another one very similar to it, went ultimately to the Supreme Court. In the meantime, his place stayed open, and I got still more free 7-Ups.

■   ■   ■

Around that time there were some attempts to develop an interest in art at Caltech. Somebody contributed the money to convert an old plant sciences building into some art studios. Equipment and supplies were bought and provided for the students, and they hired an artist from South Africa to coordinate and support the art activities around Caltech.

Various people came in to teach classes. I got Jerry Zorthian to teach a drawing class, and some guy came in to teach lithography, which I tried to learn.

The South African artist came over to my house one time to look at my drawings. He said he thought it would be fun to have a one-man show. This time I was cheating: If I hadn't been a professor at Caltech, they would have never thought my pictures were worth it.

"Some of my better drawings have been sold, and I feel uncomfortable calling the people," I said.

"You don't have to worry, Mr. Feynman," he reassured me. "You won't have to call them up. We will make all the arrangements and operate the exhibit officially and correctly."

I gave him a list of people who had bought my drawings, and they soon received a telephone call from him: "We understand that you have an Ofey."

"Yes . . ."

"We are planning to have an exhibition of Ofeys, and we're wondering if you would consider lending it to us."

"Yes, of course!"

They were delighted.

The exhibition was held in the basement of the Athenaeum, the Caltech faculty club. Everything was like the real thing: All the pictures had titles, and those that had been taken on consignment from their owners had due recognition: "Lent by Mr. Gianonni," for instance.

One drawing was a portrait of the beautiful blonde model from the art class, which I had originally intended to be a study of shading: I put a light at the level of her legs a bit to the side and pointed it upwards. As she sat, I tried to draw the shadows as they were—her nose cast its shadow rather unnaturally across her face—but so they wouldn't look so bad. I drew her torso as well, so you could also see her breasts and the shadows they made. I stuck it in with the other drawings in the exhibit and called it "Madame Curie Observing the Radiations from Radium." The message I intended to convey was that nobody thinks of Madame Curie as a woman, as feminine, with beautiful hair, bare breasts, and all that—they only think of the radium part.

A prominent industrial designer named Henry Dreyfuss invited various people to a reception at his home after the exhibition—the woman who had contributed money to support the arts, the president of Caltech and his wife, and so on.

One of these art-lovers came over and started up a conversation with me; "Tell me, Professor Feynman, do you draw from photographs or from models?"

"I always draw directly from a posed model."

"Then how did you get Madame Curie to pose for you?"

■   ■   ■

Around that time the Los Angeles County Museum of Art had a similar idea to the one I had, that artists are far away from an understanding of science. My idea was that artists don't understand the underlying generality and beauty of nature and her laws, and therefore cannot portray this in their art. The museum's idea was that artists should know more about technology: they should become more familiar with machines and other applications of science.

The art museum organized a scheme in which they would get some of the really good artists of the day to go to various companies that volunteered some time and money to the project. The artists would visit these companies and snoop around until they saw something interesting that they could use in their work. The museum thought it might help if someone who knew something about technology could be a sort of liaison with the artists from time to time as they visited the companies. Since they knew I was fairly good at explaining things to people and I wasn't a complete jackass when it came to art (actually, I think they knew I was trying to learn to draw)—they asked me if I would do that, and I agreed.

It was lots of fun visiting the companies with the artists. What typically happened was, some guy would show us a tube that discharged sparks in beautiful blue, twisting patterns. The artists would get all excited and ask me how they could use it in an exhibit: What were the necessary conditions to make it work?

The artists were very interesting people. Some of them were absolute fakes: They would claim to be an artist, and everybody agreed they were an artist, but when you'd sit and talk to them, they'd make no sense whatsoever. One guy in particular, the biggest faker, always dressed funny; he had a big black bowler hat. He would answer your questions in an incomprehensible way, and when you'd try to find out more about what he said by asking him about some of the words he used, off we'd be in another direction. The only thing he contributed, ultimately, to the exhibit for art and technology was a portrait of himself.

Other artists I talked to would say things that made no sense at first, but they would go to great lengths to explain their ideas to me. One time I went somewhere, as a part of this scheme, with Robert Irwin. It was a two-day trip, and after a great effort of discussing back and forth, I finally understood what he was trying to explain to me, and I thought it was quite interesting and wonderful.

Then there were the artists who had absolutely no idea about the real world. They thought that scientists were some kind of grand magicians who could make anything, and would say things like, "I want to make a picture in three dimensions where the figure is suspended in space and it glows and flickers." They made up the world they wanted, and had no idea what was reasonable or unreasonable to make.

Finally there was an exhibit, and I was asked to be on a panel which judged the works of art. Although there was some good stuff that was inspired by the artists' visiting the companies, I thought that most of the good works of art were things that were turned in at the last minute out of desperation, and didn't really have anything to do with technology. All of the other members of the panel disagreed, and I found myself in some difficulty. I'm no good at criticizing art, and I shouldn't have been on the panel in the first place.

There was a guy there at the Los Angeles County Art Museum named Maurice Tuchman who really knew what he was talking about when it came to art. He knew that I had had this one-man show at Caltech. He said, "You know, you're never going to draw again."

"What? That's ridiculous! Why should I never . . ."

"Because you've had a one-man show, and you're only an amateur."

Although I did draw after that, I never worked as hard, with the same energy and intensity, as I did before. I never sold a drawing after that, either. He was a smart fella, and I learned a lot from him. I could have learned a lot more, if I weren't so stubborn.

Judging Books
by Their Covers

After the war, physicists were often asked to go to Washington and give advice to various sections of the government, especially the military. What happened, I suppose, is that since the scientists had made these bombs that were so important, the military felt we were useful for something.

Once I was asked to serve on a committee which was to evaluate various weapons for the Army, and I wrote a letter back which explained that I was only a theoretical physicist, and I didn't know anything about weapons for the Army.

The Army responded that they had found in their experience that theoretical physicists were very useful to them in making decisions, so would I please reconsider?

I wrote back again and said I didn't really know anything, and doubted I could help them.

Finally I got a letter from the Secretary of the Army, which proposed a compromise: I would come to the first meeting, where I could listen and see whether I could make a contribution or not. Then I could decide whether I should continue.

I said I would, of course. What else could I do?

I went down to Washington and the first thing I went to was a cocktail party to meet everybody. There were generals and other important characters from the Army, and everybody talked. It was pleasant enough.

One guy in a uniform came to me and told me that the Army was glad that physicists were advising the military because it had a lot of problems. One of the problems was that tanks use up their fuel very quickly and thus can't go very far. So the question was how to refuel them as they're going along. Now this guy had the idea that, since the physicists can get energy out of uranium, could I work out a way in which we could use silicon dioxide—sand or dirt—as a fuel? If that were possible, then all this tank would have to do would be to have a little scoop underneath, and as it goes along, it would pick up the dirt and use it for fuel! He thought that was a great idea, and that all I had to do was to work out the details. That was the kind of problem I thought we would be talking about in the meeting the next day.

I went to the meeting and noticed that the guy who had introduced me to all the people at the cocktail party was sitting next to me. He was apparently some flunky assigned to be at my side at all times. On my other side was some super general I had heard of before.

At the first session of the meeting they talked about some technical matters, and I made a few comments. But later on, near the end of the meeting, they began to discuss some problem of logistics, about which I knew nothing. It had to do with figuring out how much stuff you should have at different places at different times. And although I tried to keep my trap shut, when you get into a situation like that, where you're sitting around a table with all these "important people" discussing these "important problems," you *can't* keep your mouth shut, even if you know nothing whatsoever! So I made some comments in that discussion, too.

During the next coffee break the guy who had been assigned to shepherd me around said, "I was very impressed by the things you said during the discussion. They certainly were an important contribution."

I stopped and thought about my "contribution" to the logistics problem, and realized that a man like the guy who orders the stuff for Christmas at Macy's would be better able to figure out how to handle problems like that than I. So I concluded: (a) if I had made an important contribution, it was sheer luck; (b) anybody else could have done as well, but *most* people could have done *better*; and (c) this flattery should wake me up to the fact that I am *not* capable of contributing much.

Right after that they decided, in the meeting, that they could do better discussing the *organization* of scientific research (such as, should scientific development be under the Corps of Engineers or the Quartermaster Division?) than specific technical matters. I knew that if there was to be *any* hope of my making a real contribution, it would be only on some specific technical matter, and surely not on how to organize research in the Army.

Until then I didn't let on any of my feelings about the situation to the chairman of the meeting—the big shot who had invited me in the first place. As we were packing our bags to leave, he said to me, all smiles, "You'll be joining us, then, for the next meeting . . ."

"No, I'm sorry, I won't." I could see his face change suddenly. He was very surprised that I would say no, after making those "contributions."

*   *   *

In the early Sixties, a lot of my friends were still giving advice to the government. Meanwhile, I was having no feeling of social responsibility and resisting, as much as possible, offers to go to Washington, which took a certain amount of courage in those times.

I was giving a series of freshman physics lectures at that time,* and after one of them, Tom Harvey, who assisted me in putting on the demonstrations, said, "You oughta see what's happening to mathematics in schoolbooks—my daughter comes home with a lot of crazy stuff!"

I didn't pay much attention to what he said.

But the next day I got a telephone call from a rather famous lawyer here in Pasadena, Mr. Norris, who was at that time on the State Board of Education. He asked me if I would serve on the State Curriculum Commission, which had to choose the new schoolbooks for the state of California. You see, the state had a law that all of the schoolbooks used by all of the kids in all of the public schools have to be chosen by the State Board of Education, so they have a committee to look over the books and to give them advice on which books to take.

It happened that a lot of the books were on a new method of teaching arithmetic that they called "new math," and since usually the only people to look at the books were schoolteachers or administrators in education, they thought it would be a good idea to have somebody who *uses* mathematics scientifically, who knows what the end product is and what we're trying to teach it for, to help in the evaluation of the schoolbooks.

I must have had, by this time, a guilty feeling about not cooperating with the government, because I agreed to get on this committee.

Immediately I began getting letters and telephone calls from book publishers. They said things like, "We're very glad to hear you're on the commission because we really wanted a scientific guy . . ." and "It's wonderful to have a scientist on the commission, because our books are scientifically oriented . . ." But they also said things like, "We'd like to explain to you what our book is about . . ." and "We'll be very glad to

*It was early 1963. The series later became known as *The Feynman Lectures on Physics.* —RL help you in any way we can to judge our books . . ." That seemed to me kind of crazy. I'm an objective scientist, and it seemed to me that since the only thing the kids in school are going to get is the books (and the teachers get the teacher's manual, which I would also get), any *extra* explanation from the company was a distortion. So I didn't want to speak to any of the publishers and always replied, "You don't have to explain; I'm sure the books will speak for themselves."

I represented a certain district, which comprised most of the Los Angeles area except for the city of Los Angeles, which was represented by a very nice lady from the L.A. school system named Mrs. Whitehouse. Mr. Norris suggested that I meet her and find out what the commission did and how it worked.

Mrs. Whitehouse started out telling me about the stuff they were going to talk about in the next meeting (they had already had one meeting; I was appointed late). "They're going to talk about the counting numbers"—I didn't know what that was, but it turned out they were what I used to call integers. They had different names for everything, so I had a lot of trouble right from the start.

Mrs. Whitehouse told me how the members of the commission normally rated the new schoolbooks. They would get a relatively large number of copies of each book and would give them to various teachers and administrators in their district. Then they would get reports back on what these people thought about the books. Since I didn't know a lot of teachers or administrators, and since I felt that I could, by reading the books myself, make up my mind as to how they looked to *me*, I chose to read all the books myself. (There were some people in my district who had expected to look at the books and wanted a chance to give their opinion. Mrs. Whitehouse offered to put their reports in with hers so they would feel better and I wouldn't have to worry about their complaints. They were satisfied, and I didn't get much trouble.)

A few days later a guy from the book depository called me up and said, "We're ready to send you the books, Mr. Feynman; there are three hundred pounds."

I was overwhelmed.

"It's all right, Mr. Feynman; we'll get someone to help you read them."

I couldn't figure out how you *do* that: You either read them or you don't read them. I had a special bookshelf put in my study downstairs (the books took up seventeen feet), and began reading all the books that were going to be discussed in the next meeting. We were going to start out with the elementary schoolbooks.

It was a pretty big job, and I worked all the time at it down in the basement. My wife says that during this period it was like living over a volcano: It would be quiet for a while, but then all of a sudden, "BLLLLLOOOOOOWWWWW!!!!"—there would be a big explosion from the "volcano" below.

The reason was that the books were so lousy. They were false. They were hurried. They would *try* to be rigorous, but they would use examples (like automobiles in the street for "sets") which were *almost* OK, but in which there were always some subtleties. The definitions weren't accurate. Everything was a little bit ambiguous—they weren't smart enough to understand what was meant by rigor. They were faking it. They were teaching something they didn't understand, and which was, in fact, *useless*, at that time, for the child.

I understood what they were trying to do. Many people thought we were behind the Russians after Sputnik, and some mathematicians were asked to give advice on how to teach math by using some of the rather interesting modern concepts of mathematics. The purpose was to enhance mathematics for the children who found it dull.

I'll give you an example: They would talk about different bases of numbers—base 5, base 6, and so on—to show the possibilities. That would be interesting for a kid who could understand base 10—something to entertain his mind. But what they had turned it into, in these books, was that *every* child had to learn another base! And then the usual horror would come: "Translate these numbers, which are written in base 7, to base 5." Translating from one base to another is an *utterly useless* thing: If you can do it, maybe it's entertaining; if you *can't* do it, forget it—there's no *point* to it!

Anyhow, I'm looking at all these books, all these books, and none of them has said anything about using arithmetic in science. If there are any examples on the use of arithmetic at all (most of the time it's this abstract new modern nonsense), they are about things like buying stamps.

Finally I come to a book that says, "Mathematics is used in science in many ways. We will give you an example from astronomy, which is the science of stars." I turn the page, and it says, "Red stars have a temperature of 4,000 degrees, yellow stars have a temperature of 5,000 degrees . . ."—so far, so good. It continues: "Green stars have a temperature of 7,000 degrees, blue stars have a temperature of 10,000 degrees, and violet stars have a temperature of . . . (some big number)." There are no green or violet stars, but the figures for the others are roughly correct. It's *vaguely* right—but already, trouble. That's the way everything was: Everything was written by somebody who didn't know what the hell he was talking about, so it was a little bit wrong, always—and how we are going to teach well by using books written by people who don't *quite* understand what they're talking about, I *cannot* understand. I don't know why, but the books are lousy: UNIVERSALLY LOUSY!

Anyway, I'm happy with this book, because it's the first example of applying arithmetic to science. I'm a *bit* unhappy when I read about the stars' temperatures, but I'm not *very* unhappy because it's more or less right—it's just an example of error.

Then comes the list of problems. It says, "John and his father go out to look at the stars. John sees two blue stars and a red star. His father sees a green star, a violet star, and two yellow stars. What is the total temperature of the stars seen by John and his father?"—and I would explode in horror.

My wife would talk about the volcano downstairs. That's only an example: it was *perpetually* like that. Perpetual absurdity! There's no purpose whatsoever in adding the temperature of two stars. Nobody *ever* does that except, maybe, to then take the *average* temperature of the stars, but *not* to find out the *total* temperature of all the stars! It was awful. It was only a game to get you to add, and they didn't understand what they were talking about. It was like reading sentences with a few typographical errors, and then suddenly a whole sentence is written backwards. The mathematics was like that—just hopeless!

* * *

Then I came to my first meeting. The other members had given some kind of ratings to some of the books, and they asked me what *my* ratings were. My rating was often different from theirs, and they would ask, "Why did you rate that book low?"

I would say the trouble with that book was this and this on page so-and-so—I had my notes.

They discovered that I was kind of a goldmine: I would tell them, in detail, what was good and bad in all the books; I had a reason for every rating.

I would ask them why they had rated this book so high, and they would say, "Let us hear what you thought about such-and-such a book." I would never find out why they rated anything the way they did. Instead, they kept asking me what *I* thought.

We came to a certain book, part of a set of three supplementary books published by the same company, and they asked me what I thought about it.

I said, "The book depository didn't send me that book, but the other two were OK."

Someone tried repeating the question: "What do you think about the *third* book?"

"I said they didn't send me that one, so I don't have any judgment on it."

The man from the book depository was there, and he said, "Excuse me; I can explain that. I didn't send it to you because that book hadn't been completed yet. There's a rule that you have to have every entry in by a certain time, and the publisher was a few days late with it. So it was sent to us with just the covers, and it's blank in between. The company sent a note excusing themselves and hoping they could have their set of three books considered, even though the third one would be late."

It turned out that the blank book had a rating by some of the other members! They couldn't believe it was blank, because they had a rating. In fact, the rating for the missing book was a little bit higher than for the two others. The fact that there was nothing inside the book had nothing to do with the rating.

I believe the reason for all this is that the system works this way: When you give books all over the place to people, they're busy; they're careless; they think, "Well, a lot of people are reading this book, so it doesn't make any difference." And they put in some kind of number— *some* of them, at least; not all of them, but *some* of them. Then when you receive your reports, you don't know *why* this particular book has fewer reports than the other books—that is, perhaps one book has ten, and this one only has six people reporting—so you average the rating of those who reported; you don't average the ones who didn't report, so you get a reasonable number. This process of averaging all the time misses the fact that there is absolutely nothing between the covers of the book.

I made that theory up because I saw what happened in the curriculum commission: For the blank book, only six out of the ten members were reporting, whereas with the other books, eight or nine out of the ten were reporting. And when they averaged the six, they got as good an average as when they averaged with eight or nine. They were very embarrassed to discover they were giving ratings to that book, and it gave me a little bit more confidence. It turned out the other members of the committee had done a lot of work in giving out the books and collecting reports, and had gone to sessions in which the book publishers would "explain" the books before they read them; I was the only guy on the commission who read all the books and didn't get any information from the book publishers except what was in the books themselves—the things that would ultimately go to the schools.

This question of trying to figure out whether a book is good or bad by looking at it carefully or by taking the reports of a lot of people who looked at it carelessly is like the famous old problem: Nobody was permitted to see the Emperor of China, and the question was, What is the length of the Emperor of China's nose? To find out, you go all over the country asking people what they think the length of the Emperor of China's nose is, and you *average* it. And that would be very "accurate" because you averaged so many people. But it's no way to find anything out: When you have a very wide range of people who contribute without looking carefully at it, you don't improve your knowledge of the situation by averaging.

· ■ ·

At first we weren't supposed to talk about the cost of the books. We were told how many books we could choose, so we designed a program which used a lot of supplementary books, because all the new textbooks had failures of one kind or another. The most serious failures were in the "new math" books: There were no applications; not enough word problems. There was no talk of selling stamps; instead there was too much talk about commutation and other abstract things, and not enough translation to situations in the world—no "What do you do: add, subtract, multiply, or divide?" So we suggested some books which *had* some of that as supplementary—one or two for each classroom—in addition to a textbook for each student. We had it all worked out to balance everything as best we could, after much discussion.

When we took our recommendations to the Board of Education, they told us they didn't have as much money as they had thought, so we'd have to go over the whole thing and cut out this and that, now taking the *cost* into consideration, and ruining what was a fairly balanced program, in which there was a *chance* for a teacher to find examples of the things (s)he needed.

Now that they changed the rules about how many books we could recommend and we had no more chance to balance the program, it was pretty lousy. When the Senate Budget Committee got to it, the program was emasculated still further—now it was *really* lousy! I was asked to appear before the state senators when the issue was being discussed, but I declined: By that time, having argued this stuff so much, I was tired. We had prepared our recommendations for the Board of Education, and I figured it was *their* job to present it to the senate—which was legally right, but not politically sound. I shouldn't have given up so soon, but to have worked so hard and discussed so much about all these books to make a fairly balanced program, and then to have the whole thing scrapped at the end—that was discouraging. The whole thing was an unnecessary effort that could have been turned around and done the opposite way: *Start* with the cost of the books, and buy what you can afford.

*   *   *

What finally clinched it, and made me ultimately resign, was that the following year we were going to discuss science books. I thought maybe the science would be different, so I looked at a few of them.

The same thing happened. Something would look good at first, and then turn out to be horrifying. For example, there was a book that started out with four pictures: first there was a wind-up toy; then there was an automobile; then there was a boy riding a bicycle; then there was something else. And underneath each picture it said, "What makes it go?"

I thought, "I know what it is: They're going to talk about mechanics, how the springs work inside the toy; about chemistry, how the engine of the automobile works; and biology, about how the muscles work."

It was the kind of thing my father would have talked about: "What makes it go? Everything goes because the sun is shining"—and then we would have fun discussing it:

"No, the toy goes because the spring is wound up," I would say.

"How did the spring get wound up?" he would ask.

"I wound it up."

"And how did you get moving?"

"From eating."

"And food grows only because the sun is shining. So it's because the sun is shining that all these things are moving." That would get the concept across that motion is simply the *transformation* of the sun's power.

I turned the page. The answer was, for the wind-up toy, "Energy makes it go." And for the boy on the bicycle, "Energy makes it go." For everything, "*Energy* makes it go."

Now that doesn't *mean* anything. Suppose it's "Wakalixes." That's the general principle: "Wakalixes makes it go." There's no knowledge coming in. The child doesn't learn anything; it's just a *word!*

What they should have done is to look at the wind-up toy, see that there are springs inside, learn about springs, learn about wheels, and never mind "energy." Later on, when the children know something about how the toy actually works, they can discuss the more general principles of energy.

It's also not even true that "energy makes it go," because if it stops, you could say, "energy makes it stop" just as well. What they're talking about is concentrated energy being transformed into more dilute forms, which is a very subtle aspect of energy. Energy is neither increased nor decreased in these examples; it's just changed from one form to another. And when the things stop, the energy is changed into heat, into general chaos.

But that's the way all the books were: They said things that were useless, mixed-up, ambiguous, confusing, and partially incorrect. How anybody can learn science from these books, I don't know, because it's not science.

So when I saw all these horrifying books with the same kind of trouble as the math books had, I saw my volcano process starting again. Since I was exhausted from reading all the math books, and discouraged from its all being a wasted effort, I couldn't face another year of that, and had to resign.

Sometime later I heard that the energy-makes-it-go book was going to be recommended by the curriculum commission to the State Board of Education, so I made one last effort. At each meeting of the commission the public was allowed to make comments, so I got up and said why I thought the book was bad.

The man who replaced me on the commission said, "That book was approved by sixty-five engineers at the Such-and-such Aircraft Company!"

I didn't doubt that the company had some pretty good engineers, but to take sixty-five engineers is to take a wide range of ability—and to necessarily include some pretty poor guys! It was once again the problem of *averaging* the length of the emperor's nose, or the ratings on a book with nothing between the covers. It would have been far better to have the company decide who their better engineers were, and to have *them* look at the book. I couldn't claim that I was smarter than sixty-five other guys—but the *average* of sixty-five other guys, certainly!

I couldn't get through to him, and the book was approved by the board.

▪   ▪   ▪

When I was still on the commission, I had to go to San Francisco a few times for some of the meetings, and when I returned to Los Angeles from the first trip, I stopped in the commission office to get reimbursed for my expenses.

"How much did it cost, Mr. Feynman?"

"Well, I flew to San Francisco, so it's the airfare, plus the parking at the airport while I was away."

"Do you have your ticket?"

I happened to have the ticket.

"Do you have a receipt for the parking?"

"No, but it cost $2.35 to park my car."

"But we have to have a receipt."

"I *told* you how much it cost. If you don't trust me, why do you let me tell you what I think is good and bad about the schoolbooks?"

There was a big stew about that. Unfortunately, I had been used to giving lectures for some company or university or for ordinary people, not for the government. I was used to, "What were your expenses?"—"So-and-so much."—"Here you are, Mr. Feynman."

I then decided I wasn't going to give them a receipt for *anything*.

After the second trip to San Francisco they again asked me for my ticket and receipts.

"I haven't *got* any."

"This can't go on, Mr. Feynman."

"When I accepted to serve on the commission, I was told you were going to pay my expenses."

"But we expected to have some receipts to *prove* the expenses."

"I have nothing to *prove* it, but you *know* I live in Los Angeles and I go to these other towns; how the hell do you think I *get* there?"

They didn't give in, and neither did I. I feel when you're in a position like that, where you choose not to buckle down to the System, you must pay the consequences if it doesn't work. So I'm perfectly satisfied, but I never did get compensation for the trips.

It's one of those games I play. They want a receipt? I'm not giving them a receipt. Then you're not going to get the money. OK, then I'm not taking the money. They don't trust me? The hell with it; they don't have to pay me. Of course it's absurd—I know that's the way government works; well, *screw* government! I feel that human beings should treat human beings like human beings—and unless I'm going to be treated like one, I'm not going to have anything to do with them! I know they're "protecting the taxpayer," but see how well you think the taxpayer was being protected in the following situation.

There were two books that we were unable to come to a decision about after much discussion; they were extremely close. So we left it open to the Board of Education to decide. Since the board was now taking the cost into consideration, and since the two books were so evenly matched, the board decided to open the bids and take the lower one.

Then the question came up, "Will the schools be getting the books at the regular time, or could they, perhaps, get them a little earlier, in time for the coming term?"

One publisher's representative got up and said, "We are happy that you accepted our bid; we can get it out in time for the next term."

A representative of the publisher that lost out was also there, and he got up and said, "Since our bids were submitted based on the later deadline, I think we should have a chance to bid again for the earlier deadline, because we too can meet the earlier deadline."

Mr. Norris, the Pasadena lawyer on the board, asked the guy from the other publisher, "And how much would it cost for us to get your books at the earlier date?"

And he gave a number: It was *less!*

The first guy got up: "If *he* changes his bid, I have the right to change *my* bid!"—and his bid is *still less!*

Norris asked, "Well how *is* that—we get the books earlier and it's *cheaper?*"

"Yes," one guy says. "We can use a special offset method we wouldn't normally use . . ."—some excuse why it came out cheaper.

The other guy agreed: "When you do it quicker, it costs less!"

That was really a shock. It ended up *two million dollars* less. Norris was really incensed by this sudden change.

What happened, of course, was that the uncertainty about the date had opened the possibility that these guys could bid against each other. Normally, when books were supposed to be chosen without taking the cost into consideration, there was no reason to lower the price; the book publishers could put the prices at any place they wanted to. There was no advantage in competing by lowering the price; the way you competed was to impress the members of the curriculum commission.

By the way, whenever we had a meeting, there were book publishers entertaining curriculum commission members by taking them to lunch and talking to them about their books. I never went.

It seems obvious now, but I didn't know what was happening the time I got a package of dried fruit and whatnot delivered by Western

Union with a message that read, "From our family to yours, Happy Thanksgiving—The Pamilios."

It was from a family I had never heard of in Long Beach, obviously someone wanting to send this to his friend's family who got the name and address wrong, so I thought I'd better straighten it out. I called up Western Union, got the telephone number of the people who sent the stuff, and I called them.

"Hello, my name is Mr. Feynman. I received a package . . ."

"Oh, hello, Mr. Feynman, this is Pete Pamilio," and he says it in such a friendly way that I think I'm supposed to know who he is. (I'm normally such a dunce that I can't remember who anyone is.)

"I'm sorry, Mr. Pamilio, but I don't quite remember who you are . . ."

It turned out he was a representative of one of the publishers whose books I had to judge on the curriculum commission.

"I see. But this could be misunderstood."

"It's only family to family."

"Yes, but I'm judging a book that you're publishing, and maybe someone might misinterpret your kindness!" I knew what was happening, but I made it sound like I was a complete idiot.

Another thing like this happened when one of the publishers sent me a leather briefcase with my name nicely written in gold on it. I gave them the same stuff: "I can't accept it; I'm judging some of the books you're publishing."

One commissioner, who had been there for the greatest length of time, said, "I never accept the stuff; it makes me very upset. But it just goes on."

But I *really* missed one opportunity. If I had only thought fast enough, I could have had a *very* good time on that commission. I got to the hotel in San Francisco in evening before my first meeting, and I decided to go out to wander in the town and eat something. I came out of the elevator, and sitting on a bench in the hotel lobby were two guys who jumped up and said, "Good evening, Mr. Feynman. Where are you going? Is there something we can show you in San Francisco?" They were from a publishing company, and I didn't want to have anything to do with them.

"I'm going out to eat."

"We can take you out to dinner."

"No, I want to be alone."

"Well, whatever you want, we can help you."

I couldn't resist. I said, "Well, I'm going out to do something a bit illicit . . ."

"I think we can help you in *that*, too . . ."

"No, I think I'll take care of that myself." Then I thought, "What an error! I should have let *all* of that stuff operate and keep a diary, so the people of the state of California could find out how far the publishers will go."—and when I found out about the two-million-dollar difference, god knows what the pressures are!

Who the Hell Is Herman?

One day I got a long-distance telephone call from an old friend in Los Alamos. She says in a very serious voice, "Richard, I have some sad news for you. Herman died."

I'm always feeling uncomfortable that I don't remember names and then I feel bad that I don't pay enough attention to people. So I said, "Oh?"—trying to be quiet and serious so I could get more information, but thinking to myself, "Who the hell is Herman?"

She says, "Herman and his mother were both killed in an automobile accident near Los Angeles. Since that is where his mother is from, the funeral will be held in Los Angeles at the Rose Hills Mortuary on May 3rd at three o'clock." Then she says, "Herman would have liked it very, very much to know that you would be one of his pallbearers."

I still can't remember him. I say, "Of course I'd be happy to do that." (At least this way I'll find out who Herman was.)

Then I get an idea: I call up the mortuary. "You're having a funeral on May 3rd at three o'clock . . ."

"Which funeral do you mean: the Goldschmidt funeral, or the Parnell funeral?"

"Well, uh, I don't know." It still doesn't click for me; I don't think it's either one of them. Finally, I say, "It might be a double funeral. His mother also died."

"Oh, yes. Then it's the Goldschmidt funeral."

"Herman Goldschmidt?"

"That's right; Herman Goldschmidt and Mrs. Goldschmidt."

Okay. It's Herman Goldschmidt. But I still can't remember a Herman Goldschmidt. I haven't any idea what it is I've forgotten; from the way she talked, my friend was sure that Herman and I knew each other well.

The last chance I have is to go to the funeral and look into the casket.

I go to the funeral, and the woman who had arranged everything comes over, dressed in black, and says in a sorrowful voice, "I'm *so* glad you're here. Herman would be so happy if he knew"—all this serious stuff. Everybody's got long faces about Herman, but I still don't know who Herman is—though I'm sure that if I knew, I'd feel very sorry that he was dead!

The funeral proceeded, and when it came time for everybody to file past the caskets, I went up. I looked into the first casket, and there was Herman's mother. I looked into the second casket, and there was Herman—and I swear to you, I'd never seen him before in my life!

It came time to carry the casket out, and I took my place among the pallbearers. I very carefully laid Herman to rest in his grave, because I knew he would have appreciated it. But I haven't any idea, to this day, who Herman was.

* * *

Many years later I finally got up enough courage to bring it up to my friend. "You know that funeral I went to, about ten years ago, for Howard . . ."

"You mean Herman."

"Oh yeah—Herman. You know, I didn't know who Herman was. I didn't even recognize him in the casket."

"But Richard, you knew each other in Los Alamos just after the war. You were both good friends of mine, and we had many conversations together."

"I still can't remember him."

A few days later she called and told me what might have happened: Maybe she had met Herman just after I had left Los Alamos—and therefore got the timing mixed up somehow—but because she was such good friends with each of us, she thought we must have known each other. So she was the one who had made the mistake, not me (which is usually the case). Or was she just being polite?

FEYNMAN
ſEXIſT PIG!

A few years after I gave some lectures for the freshmen at Caltech (which were published as *The Feynman Lectures on Physics)*, I received a long letter from a feminist group. I was accused of being anti-woman because of two stories: The first was a discussion of the subtleties of velocity, and involved a woman driver being stopped by a cop. There's a discussion about how fast she was going, and I had her raise valid objections to the cop's definitions of velocity. The letter said I was making the woman look stupid.

The other story they objected to was told by the great astronomer Arthur Eddington, who had just figured out that the stars get their power from burning hydrogen in a nuclear reaction producing helium. He recounted how, on the night after his discovery, he was sitting on a bench with his girlfriend. She said, "Look how pretty the stars shine!" To which he replied, "Yes, and right now, I'm the only man in the world who knows *how* they shine." He was describing a kind of wonderful loneliness you have when you make a discovery.

The letter claimed that I was saying a woman is incapable of understanding nuclear reactions.

I figured there was no point in trying to answer their accusations in detail, so I wrote a short letter back to them: "Don't bug me, man!"*

Needless to say, that didn't work too well. Another letter came: "Your response to our letter of September 29th is unsatisfactory . . ."— blah, blah, blah. This letter warned that if I didn't get the publisher to revise the things they objected to, there would be trouble.

I ignored the letter and forgot about it.

A year or so later, the American Association of Physics Teachers

---

*A confession is long overdue: the phrase was suggested by a young man Feynman often drummed with. —RL

awarded me a prize (the Oerstad Medal) for writing those books, and asked me to speak at their meeting in San Francisco. My sister, Joan, lived in Palo Alto—an hour's drive away—so I stayed with her the night before and we went to the meeting together.

As we approached the lecture hall, we found people standing there giving out handbills to everybody going in. We each took one, and glanced at it. At the top it said, "A PROTEST." Then it showed excerpts from the letters they sent me, and my response (in full). It concluded in large letters: "FEYNMAN SEXIST PIG!"

Joan stopped suddenly and rushed back: "These are interesting," she said to the protester. "I'd like some more of them!"

When she caught up with me, she said, "Gee whiz, Richard; what did you do?"

I told her what had happened as we walked into the hall.

At the front of the hall, near the stage, were two prominent women in the American Association of Physics Teachers. One was in charge of women's affairs for the organization, and the other was Fay Ajzenberg, a professor of physics I knew, from Pennsylvania. They saw me coming down towards the stage accompanied by this woman with a fistful of handbills, talking to me. Fay walked up to her and said, "Do you realize that Professor Feynman has a *sister* that he encouraged to go into physics, and that *she* has a Ph.D. in physics?"

"Of course I do," said Joan. "I'm that sister!"

Fay and her associate explained to me that the protesters were a group—led by a man, ironically—who were always disrupting meetings in Berkeley. "We'll sit on either side of you to show our solidarity, and just before you speak, I'll get up and say something to quiet the protesters," Fay said.

Because there was another talk before mine, I had time to think of something to say. I thanked Fay, but declined her offer.

As soon as I got up to speak, half a dozen protesters marched down to the front of the lecture hall and paraded right below the stage, holding their picket signs high, chanting, "Feynman sexist pig! Feynman sexist pig!"

I began my talk by telling the protesters, "I'm sorry that my short answer to your letter brought you here unnecessarily. There are more serious places to direct one's attention towards improving the status of women in physics than these relatively trivial mistakes—if that's what you want to call them—in a textbook. But perhaps, after all, it's good that you came. For women do indeed suffer from prejudice and discrimination in physics, and your presence here today serves to remind us of these difficulties and the need to remedy them."

The protesters looked at one another. Their picket signs began to come slowly down, like sails in a dying wind.

I continued: "Even though the American Association of Physics Teachers has given me an award for teaching, I must confess I don't know how to teach. Therefore, I have nothing to say about teaching. Instead, I would like to talk about something that will be especially interesting to the women in the audience: I would like to talk about the structure of the proton."

The protesters put their picket signs down and walked off. My hosts told me later that the man and his group of protesters had never been defeated so easily.

(Recently I discovered a transcript of my speech, and what I said at the beginning doesn't seem anywhere near as dramatic as the way I remember it. What I remember saying is much more wonderful than what I actually said!)

After my talk, some of the protesters came up to press me about the woman-driver story. "Why did it have to be a woman driver?" they said. "You are implying that all women are bad drivers."

"But the woman makes the cop look bad," I said. "Why aren't you concerned about the cop?"

"That's what you expect from cops!" one of the protesters said. "They're all pigs!"

"But you *should* be concerned," I said. "I forgot to say in the story that the cop was a woman!"

Thirteen
Times

One time a science teacher from the local city college came around and asked me if I'd give a talk there. He offered me fifty dollars, but I told him I wasn't worried about the money. "That's the *city* college, right?"

"Yes."

I thought about how much paperwork I usually had to get involved with when I deal with the government, so I laughed and said, "I'll be glad to give the talk. There's only one condition on the whole thing"—I pulled a number out of a hat and continued—"that I don't have to sign my name more than thirteen times, and that includes the check."

The guy laughs. "Thirteen times, ha, ha, ha! No problem."

So then it starts. First I have to sign something that says I'm loyal to the government, or else I can't talk at the city college—and I have to sign it double. Then I have to sign some kind of release to the city—I can't remember what. Pretty soon the numbers are beginning to climb up.

I had to sign that I was suitably employed as a professor—to ensure, of course, since it's a city thing, that no jerk at the other end was hiring his wife or a friend to come and not even give the lecture. There were all kinds of papers, and the signatures kept mounting.

Well, the guy who started out laughing got pretty nervous, but we just made it: I signed exactly twelve times. There was one more left for the check, so I went ahead and gave the talk.

A few days later the guy came around to give me the check, and he was really sweating. He couldn't give me the money unless I signed a form saying I really gave the talk.

I said, "If I sign the form, I can't sign the check. But *you* were there. You heard the talk; why don't *you* sign it?"

"Look," he said, "Isn't this whole thing rather silly?"

"No. It was an arrangement we made in the beginning. We didn't think it was really going to get to thirteen, but we agreed on it, and we should stick to it to the end."

He said, "I've been working very hard, calling all around. I've been trying *everything*, and they tell me it's impossible. You simply can't get your money unless you sign the form."

"It's OK," I said. "I've only signed twelve times, and I gave the talk. I don't need the money."

"But I hate to *do* this to you."

"It's all right. We made a deal; don't worry."

The next day he called me up. "They can't *not* give you the money: They've already earmarked the money and they've got it set aside, so they *have* to give it to you."

"OK, if they have to give me the money, let them give me the money!"

"But you have to sign the form."

"If I sign the form, I won't cash the check!"

They were stuck. There was no miscellaneous pot which was for money that this man deserves but won't sign for.

Finally, it got straightened out. It took a long time, and it was very complicated—but I used the thirteenth signature to cash my check.

ALFRED NOBEL'S
OTHER MISTAKE

In Canada they have a big association of physics students. They have meetings; they give papers, and so on. One time the Vancouver chapter wanted to have me come and talk to them. The girl in charge of it arranged with my secretary to fly all the way to Los Angeles without telling me. She just walked into my office. She was really cute, a beautiful blonde. (That helped; it's not supposed to, but it did.) And I was impressed that the students in Vancouver had financed the whole thing. They treated me so nicely in Vancouver that now I know the secret of how to really be entertained and give talks: Wait for the students to ask you.

One time, a few years after I had won the Nobel Prize, some kids from the Irvine students' physics club came around and wanted me to talk. I said, "I'd love to do it, but just to the physics club. I don't want to be immodest, but I've learned from experience that there'll be trouble."

I told them how I used to go over to a local high school every year to talk to the physics club about relativity, or whatever they asked about. Then, after I got the Prize, I went over there again, as usual, with no preparation, and they stuck me in front of an assembly of three hundred kids. It was a mess!

I got that shock about three or four times, being an idiot and not catching on right away. When I was invited to Berkeley to give a talk on something in physics, I prepared something rather technical, expecting to give it to the usual physics department group. But when I got there, this tremendous lecture hall is *full* of people. And I *know* there's not that many people in Berkeley who know the level at which I prepared my talk. My problem is, I like to please the people who come to hear me, and I can't do it if everybody and his brother wants to hear—I don't know my audience then.

After the Irvine students understood that I can't just easily go over somewhere and give a talk to the physics club, I said, "Let's cook up a dull-sounding title and a dull-sounding professor's name, and then only the kids who are really interested in physics will bother to come, and those are the ones we want, OK? You don't have to sell anything."

A few posters appeared on the Irvine campus: Professor Henry Warren from the University of Washington is going to talk about the structure of the proton on May 17th at 3:00 in Room D102.

Then I came and said, "Professor Warren had some personal difficulties and was unable to come and speak to you today, so he telephoned and asked me if I would talk to you about the subject, since I've been doing some work in the field. So here I am." It worked great.

But then, somehow or other, the faculty adviser of the club found out about the trick, and he got very angry at them. He said, "You know, if it were known that Professor Feynman was coming down here, a lot of people would like to have listened to him."

The students explained, "That's just *it!*" But the adviser was mad that he hadn't been allowed in on the joke.

Hearing that the students were in real trouble, I decided to write a letter to the adviser and explained that it was all my fault, that I wouldn't have given the talk unless this arrangement had been made; that I had told the students not to tell anyone; I'm very sorry; please excuse me, blah, blah, blah . . . That's the kind of stuff I have to go through on account of that damn prize.

Just last year I was invited by the students at the University of Alaska in Fairbanks to talk, and had a wonderful time, except for the interviews on local television. I don't need interviews; there's no point to it. I came to talk to the physics students, and that's it. If everybody in town wants to know that, let the school newspaper tell them. It's on account of the Nobel Prize that I've got to have an interview—I'm a big shot, right?

A friend of mine who's a rich man—he invented some kind of simple digital switch—tells me about these people who contribute money to make prizes or give lectures: "You always look at them carefully to find out what crookery they're trying to absolve their conscience of."

My friend Matt Sands was once going to write a book about the prize to be called *Alfred Nobel's Other Mistake.*

■ ■ ■

For many years I would look, when the time was coming around to give out the Prize, at who might get it. But after a while I wasn't even aware of when it was the right "season." I therefore had no idea why someone would be calling me at 3:30 or 4:00 in the morning in early October, 1965.

"Professor Feynman?"

"Hey! Why are you bothering me at this time in the morning?"

"I thought you'd like to know that you've won the Nobel Prize."

"Yeah, but I'm *sleeping!* It would have been better if you had called me in the morning!"—and I hung up.

My wife said, "Who was that?"

"They told me I won the Nobel Prize."

"Oh, Richard, who *was* it?" I often kid around and she is so smart that she never gets fooled, but this time I caught her.

The phone rings again: "Professor Feynman, have you heard . . ."

(In a disappointed voice) "Yeah."

Then I began to think, "How can I turn this all off? I don't want any of this!" So the first thing was to take the telephone off the hook, because calls were coming one right after the other. I tried to go back to sleep, but found it was impossible.

I went down to the study to think: What am I going to do? Maybe I won't *accept* the Prize. What would happen then? Maybe that's impossible.

I put the receiver back on the hook and the phone rang right away. It was a guy from *Time* magazine. I said to him, "Listen, I've got a problem, so I want this off the record. I don't know how to get out of this thing. Is there some way not to accept the Prize?"

He said, "I'm afraid, sir, that there isn't any way you can do it without making more of a fuss than if you leave it alone." It was obvious. We had quite a conversation, about fifteen or twenty minutes, and the *Time* guy never published anything about it.

I thanked the *Time* guy and hung up. The phone rang immediately: It was the newspaper.

"Yes, you can come up to the house. Yes, it's all right. Yes, Yes, Yes . . ."

One of the phone calls was a guy from the Swedish consulate. He was going to have a reception in Los Angeles.

I figured that since I decided to accept the Prize, I've got to go through with all this stuff.

The consul said, "Make a list of the people you would like to invite, and we'll make a list of the people we are inviting. Then I'll come to your office and we'll compare the lists for duplicates, and then we'll make up the invitations . . ."

So I made up my list. It had about eight people—my neighbor from across the street, my artist friend Zorthian, and so on.

The consul came over to my office with *his* list: the Governor of the State of California, the This, the That; Getty, the oilman; some actress—

it had three hundred people! And, needless to say, there was *no* duplication whatsoever.

Then I began to get a little bit nervous. The idea of meeting all these dignitaries frightened me.

The consul saw I was worried. "Oh, don't worry," he said. "Most of them don't come."

Well, I had never arranged a party that I invited people to, and knew to expect them *not* to come; I figured I don't have to kowtow to anybody and give them the delight of being honored with this invitation that they can refuse—it's stupid!

By the time I got home I was really upset with the whole thing. I called the consul back and said, "I've thought it over, and I realize that I just can't go through with the reception."

He was delighted. He said, "You're perfectly right." I think he was in the same position—having to set up a party for this jerk was just a pain in the neck. It turned out, in the end, everybody was happy. Nobody wanted to come, including the guest of honor! The host was much better off, too.

With son Carl on the day Richard won the Nobel Prize, 1965.

I had a certain psychological difficulty all the way through this period. You see, I had been brought up by my father against royalty and pomp: He was in the uniforms business, so he knew the difference between a man with a uniform on, and with the uniform off—it's the same man. I had actually learned to ridicule this stuff all my life, and it was so strong and deeply cut into me that I couldn't go up to a king without some strain. It was childish, I know, but I was brought up that way, so it was a problem.

People told me that there was a rule in Sweden that after you accept the Prize, you have to back away from the king without turning around. You come down some steps, accept the Prize, and then go back up the steps. So I said to myself, "All right, I'm gonna fix them"—and I practiced *jumping* up stairs, backwards, to show how ridiculous their custom was. I was in a terrible mood! (That was stupid and silly, of course.)

To my relief I found out this wasn't a rule any more; you could turn around when you left the king, and walk like a normal human being, in the direction you were intending to go, with your nose in front.

I was also pleased to find that not all the people in Sweden take the royal ceremonies as seriously as you might think. When you get there, you discover that they're on your side.

The students, for example, had a special ceremony in which they granted each Nobel Prize winner the special "Order of the Frog." When you get this little frog, you have to make a frog noise.

When I was younger I was anti-culture, but my father had some good books around. One was a book with the old Greek play *The Frogs* in it, and I glanced at it one time and I saw in there that a frog talks. It was written as "*brek, kek, kek.*" I thought, "No frog ever made a sound like that; that's a crazy way to describe it." But I tried it, and after practicing it awhile, I realized that it's pretty accurate.

My chance glance into that book by Aristophanes turned out to be useful later on: I could make a good frog noise at the students' ceremony for the Nobel Prize winners—and jumping backwards fit right in, too. So I *liked* that part of it; that ceremony went well.

While I had a lot of fun, I *did* still have this psychological difficulty all the way through. My greatest problem was the thank-you speech that you give at the King's Dinner. When they give you the Prize they give you some nicely bound books about the years before, and they have all the thank-you speeches written out as if they're some big deal. So you begin to think it's of some importance what you say in this thank-you speech, because it's going to be published. What I didn't realize was that hardly anyone was going to listen to it carefully, and nobody was going to read it! I had lost my sense of proportion: I couldn't just say thank you very much, blah-blah-blah-blah-blah; it would have been so easy to do that, but no, I have to make it honest. And the truth was, I didn't really want this Prize, so how do I say thank you when I don't want it?

My wife says I was a nervous wreck, worrying about what I was going to say in the speech, but I finally figured out a way to make a perfectly satisfactory-sounding speech that was nevertheless completely honest. I'm sure those who heard the speech had no idea what this guy had gone through in preparing it.

I started out by saying that I had already received my prize in the pleasure I got in discovering what I did, from the fact that others used my work, and so on. I tried to explain that I had already received everything I expected to get, and the rest was nothing compared to it. I had already received my prize.

But then I said I received, all at once, a big pile of letters—I said it much better in the speech—reminding me of all these people that I knew: letters from childhood friends who jumped up when they read the morning newspaper and cried out, "I know him! He's that kid we used to play with!" and so on; letters like that, which were very supportive and expressed what I interpreted as a kind of love. For *that* I thanked them.

▪ ▪ ▪

The speech went fine, but I was always getting into slight difficulties with royalty. During the King's Dinner I was sitting next to a princess who had gone to college in the United States. I assumed, incorrectly, that she had the same attitudes as I did—I figured she was just a kid like everybody else. I remarked on how the king and all the royalty had to stand for such a long time, shaking hands with all the guests at the reception before the dinner. "In America," I said, "we could make this more efficient. We would design a *machine* to shake hands."

"Yes, but there wouldn't be very much of a market for it here," she said, uneasily. "There's not that much royalty."

"On the contrary, there'd be a very big market. At first, only the king would have a machine, and we could give it to him free. Then, of course, other people would want a machine, too. The question now becomes, who will be *allowed* to have a machine? The prime minister is permitted to buy one; then the president of the senate is allowed to buy one, and then the most important senior deputies. So there's a very big, expanding market, and pretty soon, you wouldn't have to go through the reception line to shake hands with the machines; you'd send *your* machine!"

I also sat next to the lady who was in charge of organizing the dinner. A waitress came by to fill my wineglass, and I said, "No, thank you. I don't drink."

The lady said, "No, no. Let her pour the drink."

"But I *don't* drink."

She said, "It's all right. Just look. You see, she has two bottles. We know that number eighty-eight doesn't drink." (Number eighty-eight was on the back of my chair.) "They look exactly the same, but one has no alcohol."

"But how do you know?" I exclaimed.

She smiled. "Now watch the king," she said. "He doesn't drink either."

She told me some of the problems they had had this particular year. One of them was, where should the Russian ambassador sit? The problem always is, at dinners like this, who sits nearer to the king. The Prize winners normally sit closer to the king than the diplomatic corps does. And the order in which the diplomats sit is determined according to the length of time they have been in Sweden. Now at that time, the United States ambassador had been in Sweden longer than the Russian ambassador. But that year, the winner of the Nobel Prize for Literature was Mr. Sholokhov, a Russian, and the Russian ambassador wanted to be Mr. Sholokhov's translator—and therefore to sit next to him. So the problem was how to let the Russian ambassador sit closer to the king without offending the United States ambassador and the rest of the diplomatic corps.

She said, "You should have seen what a fuss they went through—letters back and forth, telephone calls, and so on—before I ever got *permission* to have the ambassador sit next to Mr. Sholokhov. It was finally agreed that the ambassador wouldn't officially represent the embassy of the Soviet Union that evening; rather, he was to be only the translator for Mr. Sholokhov."

After the dinner we went off into another room, where there were different conversations going on. There was a Princess Somebody of Denmark sitting at a table with a number of people around her, and I saw an empty chair at their table and sat down.

She turned to me and said, "Oh! You're one of the Nobel Prize winners. In what field did you do your work?"

"In physics," I said.

"Oh. Nobody knows anything about that, so I guess we can't talk about it."

"On the contrary," I answered. "It's because somebody knows *something* about it that we can't talk about physics. It's the things that nobody knows anything about that we *can* discuss: We can talk about the weather; we can talk about social problems; we can talk about psychology; we can talk about international finance—gold transfers we *can't* talk about, because those are understood—so it's the subject that nobody knows anything about that we can all talk about!"

I don't know how they do it: There's a way of forming *ice* on the surface of the face, and she *did* it. She turned to talk to somebody else.

After a while I could tell I was completely cut out of the conversation, so I got up and started away. The Japanese ambassador, who was also sitting at that table, jumped up and walked after me. "Professor Feynman," he said, "there is something I should like to tell you about diplomacy."

I thought he was going to scold me—diplomatically, of course: He went into a long story about how a young man in Japan goes to the university and studies international relations because he thinks he can make a contribution to his country. As a sophomore he begins to have slight twinges of doubt about what he is learning. After college he takes his first post in an embassy and has still more doubts about his understanding of diplomacy, until he finally realizes that *nobody* knows anything about international relations. Only at that point can he become an ambassador. "So Professor Feynman," he said, "next time you give examples of things that everybody talks about that nobody knows about, please include international relations!"

He was a very interesting man, and we got to talking. I had always been interested in how different countries and different peoples develop differently. I told the ambassador that there was one thing that always seemed to me to be a remarkable phenomenon: how Japan had developed itself so rapidly to become such a modern and important country in the world. "What is the aspect and character of the Japanese people that made it possible for the Japanese to do that?" I asked.

The ambassador answered in a way I like to hear: "I don't know," he said. "I might suppose something, but I don't know if it's true. The people of Japan believed they had only one way of moving up: to have their children educated more than they were; that it was very important for them to move out of their peasantry to become educated. So there has been a great energy in the family to encourage the children to do well in school, and to be pushed forward. Because of this tendency to learn things all the time, new ideas from the outside would spread through the educational system very easily. Perhaps that is one of the reasons why Japan has advanced so rapidly."

■ ■ ■

All in all, I must say I enjoyed the visit to Sweden, in the end. Instead of coming home immediately, I went to CERN, the European Center for Nuclear Research in Switzerland, to give a talk. I appeared before my colleagues in the suit that I had worn to the King's Dinner—I had never given a talk in a suit before—and I began by saying, "Funny thing, you know; in Sweden we were sitting around, talking about whether there are any changes as a result of our having won the Nobel Prize, and as a matter of fact, I think I already see a change: I rather like this suit."

Everybody says "Booooo!" and Weisskopf jumps up and tears off his coat and says, "We're not gonna wear suits at lectures!"

I took my coat and tie off and said, "By the time I had been through Sweden, I was beginning to *like* this stuff, but now that I'm back in the world, everything's all right again. Thanks for straightening me out!" They didn't want me to change. So it was very quick: At CERN they undid everything that had been done to me in Sweden.

It's nice that I got some money—I was able to buy a beach house—but altogether, I think it would have been much nicer not to have won the Prize—because you never, any longer, can be taken straightforwardly in any public situation.

In a way, the Nobel Prize has been something of a pain in the neck, though there was at least one time that I got some fun out of it. Shortly after I won the Prize, Gweneth and I received an invitation from the Brazilian government to be the guests of honor at the *Carnaval* celebrations in Rio. We gladly accepted and had a great time. We went from one dance to another and reviewed the big street parade that featured the famous samba schools playing their wonderful rhythms and music. Photographers from newspapers and magazines were taking pictures all the time—"Here, the Professor from America is dancing with Miss Brazil."

It was fun to be a "celebrity," but we were obviously the wrong celebrities. Nobody was very excited about the guests of honor that year. I found out later how our invitation had come about. Gina Lollobrigida was supposed to be the guest of honor, but just before *Carnaval*, she said no. The Minister of Tourism, who was in charge of organizing *Carnaval*, had some friends at the Center for Physical Research who knew I had played in a samba band, and since I had recently won the Nobel Prize, I was briefly in the news. In a moment of panic the Minister and his friends got this crazy idea to replace Gina Lollobrigida with a professor of physics!

Needless to say, the Minister did such a bad job on that *Carnaval* that he lost his position in the government.

BRINGING CULTURE

TO

THE PHYSICISTS

Nina Byers, a professor at UCLA, became in charge of the physics colloquium sometime in the early 1970s. The colloquia are normally a place where physicists from other universities come and talk pure technical stuff. But partly as a result of the atmosphere of that particular period, she got the idea that the physicists needed more culture, so she thought she would arrange something along those lines: Since Los Angeles is near Mexico, she would have a colloquium on the mathematics and astronomy of the Maya—the old civilization of Mexico.

(Remember my attitude to culture: This kind of thing would have driven me *crazy* if it were in *my* university!)

She started looking for a professor to lecture on the subject, and couldn't find anybody at UCLA who was quite an expert. She telephoned various places and still couldn't find anybody.

Then she remembered Professor Otto Neugebauer, of Brown University, the great expert on Babylonian mathematics.* She telephoned him in Rhode Island and asked if he knew someone on the West Coast who could lecture on Mayan mathematics and astronomy.

"Yes," he said. "I do. He's not a professional anthropologist or a

---

*When I was a young professor at Cornell, Professor Neugebauer had come one year to give a sequence of lectures, called the Messenger Lectures, on Babylonian mathematics. They were wonderful. Oppenheimer lectured the next year. I remember thinking to myself, "Wouldn't it be nice to come, someday, and be able to give lectures like that!" Some years later, when I was refusing invitations to lecture at various places, I was invited to give the Messenger Lectures at Cornell. Of course I couldn't refuse, because I had put that in my mind, so I accepted an invitation to go over to Bob Wilson's house for a weekend and we discussed various ideas. The result was a series of lectures called "The Character of Physical Law." —RPF

historian; he's an amateur. But he certainly knows a lot about it. His name is Richard Feynman."

She nearly died: She's trying to bring some culture to the physicists, and the only way to do it is to get a physicist!

The only reason I knew anything about Mayan mathematics was that I was getting exhausted on my honeymoon in Mexico and Guatemala with my second wife, Mary Lou. She was greatly interested in art history, particularly that of Mexico, so we went to Mexico for our honeymoon. We climbed up pyramids and down pyramids; she had me following her all over the place. She showed me many interesting things, such as certain relationships in the designs of various figures, but after a few days (and nights) of going up and down in hot and steamy jungles, I was exhausted.

In some little Guatemalan town in the middle of nowhere we went into a museum that had a case displaying a manuscript full of strange symbols, pictures, and bars and dots. It was a copy (made by a man named Villacorta) of the Dresden Codex, an original book made by the Maya that ended up in a museum in Dresden. I knew the bars and dots were numbers: My father had taken me to the New York World's Fair when I was a little kid, and there they had reconstructed a Mayan temple. I remembered him telling me how the Maya had invented the zero and had done many interesting things.

The museum had copies of the codex for sale, so I bought one. On each page at the left was the codex copy, and on the right a description and partial translation in Spanish.

I love puzzles and codes, so when I saw the bars and dots, I thought, "I'm gonna have some fun!" I covered up the Spanish with a piece of yellow paper and began playing this game of deciphering the Mayan bars and dots, sitting in the hotel room, while my wife climbed up and down the pyramids all day.

I quickly figured out that a bar was equal to five dots, what the symbol for zero was, and so on. It took me a little longer to figure out that the bars and dots always carried at twenty the first time, but they carried at eighteen the second time—making cycles of 360. I also worked out all kinds of things about various faces on the codex: they had surely meant certain days and weeks.

After we got back home I continued to work on it. Altogether, it's a lot of fun to try to decipher something like that, because when you start out you don't know anything—you have no clue to go by. But then you notice certain numbers that appear often, and add up to other numbers, and so on.

There was one place in the codex where the number 584 was very prominent. This 584 was divided into periods of 236, 90, 250, and 8. Another prominent number was 2920, or 584 × 5 (also 365 × 8). There was a table of multiples of 2920 up to 13 × 2920, then there were multiples of 13 × 2920 for a while, and then—*funny numbers!* They were errors, as far as I could tell. Only many years later did I figure out what they were.

Because figures denoting days were associated with this 584, which was divided up so peculiarly, I figured if it wasn't some mythical period of some sort, it might be something astronomical. Finally I went down to the astronomy library and looked it up, and found that 583.92 days is the period of Venus as it appears from the earth. Then the 236, 90, 250, 8 became apparent: it must be the phases that Venus goes through. It's a morning star, then it can't be seen (it's on the far side of the sun); then it's an evening star, and finally it disappears again (it's between the earth and the sun). The 90 and the 8 are different because Venus moves more slowly through the sky when it is on the far side of the sun compared to when it passes between the earth and the sun. It might also be related to the difference between the 236 and the 250, which might indicate a difference between the eastern and western horizons in Maya land.

I discovered another table nearby that had periods of 11,959 days. This turned out to be a table for predicting lunar eclipses. Still another table had multiples of 91 in descending order. I never did figure that one out (nor had anyone else).

When I had worked out as much as I could, I finally decided to look at the Spanish commentary to see how much I was able to figure out. The commentary was complete nonsense: This symbol was Saturn, this symbol was a god—it didn't make the slightest bit of sense. So it hadn't been necessary to cover the commentary; I wouldn't have learned anything from it anyway.

After that I began to read a lot about the Maya, and found that the great man in this business was Eric Thompson, some of whose books I now have.

When Nina Byers called me up I realized that I had lost my copy of the Dresden Codex. (I had lent it to Mrs. H. P. Robertson, who had found a Mayan codex in an old trunk of an antique dealer in Paris. She had brought it back to Pasadena for me to look at—I still remember driving home with it on the front seat of my car, thinking, "I've gotta be careful driving: I've got the new codex"—but as soon as I looked at it carefully, I could see immediately that it was a complete fake. After a little bit of work I could find where each picture in the new codex had come from in the Dresden Codex. So I lent her my book to show her, and I eventually forgot she had it.) So the librarians at UCLA worked very hard to find another copy of Villacorta's rendition of the Dresden Codex, and lent it to me.

I did the calculations all over again, and in fact I got a little bit further than I did before: I figured out that those "funny numbers" I thought were errors were really integer multiples of something closer to the correct period (583.923)—the Maya had realized that 584 wasn't exactly right!*

After the colloquium at UCLA, Professor Byers presented me with some beautiful color reproductions of the Dresden Codex. A few months later Caltech wanted me to give the same lecture to the public in Pasadena. Robert Rowan, a real estate man, lent me some valuable stone carvings of Mayan gods and ceramic figures for the Caltech lecture. It was probably highly illegal to take something like that out of Mexico, and they were so valuable that we hired security guards to protect them.

A few days before the Caltech lecture there was a big splurge in the *New York Times*, which reported that a new codex had been discovered. There were only three codices (two of which are hard to get anything out of) known to exist at the time—hundreds of thousands had been burned by Spanish priests as "works of the Devil." My cousin was working for the AP, so she got me a glossy picture copy of what the *New York Times* had published, and I made a slide of it to include in my talk.

This new codex was another fake. In my lecture I pointed out that the numbers were in the style of the Madrid Codex, but were 236, 90, 250, 8—rather a coincidence: Out of the hundred thousand books originally made we get another fragment, and it has the same thing on it as the other fragments! It was obviously, again, one of these put-together things which had nothing original in it.

---

*While I was studying this table of corrections for the period of Venus, I discovered a rare exaggeration by Mr. Thompson. He wrote that by looking at the table, you can deduce how the Maya calculated the correct period of Venus—use this number four times and that difference once and you get an accuracy of one day in 4000 years, which is really quite remarkable, especially since the Maya observed for only a few hundred years.

Thompson happened to pick a combination that fit what he thought was the right period for Venus, 583.92. But when you put in a more exact figure, something like 583.923, you find the Maya were off by more. Of course, by choosing a different combination, you can get the numbers in the table to give you 583.923 with the same remarkable accuracy. —RPF

(These people who copy things never have the courage to make up something really different. If you find something that is really new, it's *got* to have something different. A real hoax would be to take something like the period of Mars, invent a mythology to go with it, and then draw pictures associated with this mythology with numbers appropriate to Mars—not in an obvious fashion; rather, have tables of multiples of the period with some mysterious "errors," and so on. The numbers should have to be worked out a little bit. Then people would say, "Geez! This has to do with Mars!" In addition, there should be a number of things in it that are not understandable, and are not exactly like what has been seen before. That would make a *good* fake.)

I got a big kick out of giving my talk on "Deciphering Mayan Hieroglyphics." There I was, being something I'm not, again. People filed into the auditorium past these glass cases, admiring the color reproductions of the Dresden Codex and the authentic Mayan artifacts watched over by armed guards in uniform; they heard a two-hour lecture on Mayan mathematics and astronomy from an amateur expert in the field (who even told them how to spot a fake codex), and then they went out, admiring the cases again.

Murray Gell-Mann countered in the following weeks by giving a beautiful set of six lectures concerning the linguistic relations of all the languages of the world.

Altered

States

I used to give a lecture every Wednesday over at the Hughes Aircraft Company. One day I got there a little ahead of time, and was flirting around with the receptionist, as usual, when about half a dozen people came in—a man, a woman, and a few others. I had never seen them before. The man said, "Is this where Professor Feynman is giving some lectures?"

"This is the place," the receptionist replied.

The man asks if his group can come to the lectures.

"I don't think you'd like 'em much," I say. "They're kind of technical."

Pretty soon the woman, who was rather clever, figured it out: "I bet you're Professor Feynman!"

It turned out the man was John Lilly, who had earlier done some work with dolphins. He and his wife were doing some research into sense deprivation, and had built some tanks.

"Isn't it true that you're supposed to get hallucinations under those circumstances?" I asked.

"That is true indeed."

I had always had this fascination with the images from dreams and other images that come to the mind that haven't got a direct sensory source, and how it works in the head, and I wanted to see hallucinations. I had once thought to try hallucinogenic drugs, but I got kind of scared of that: I love to think, and I don't want to screw up the machine. But it seemed to me that just lying around in a sense-deprivation tank had no physiological danger, so I was very anxious to try it.

I quickly accepted the Lillys' invitation to use the tanks, a very kind invitation on their part, and they came to listen to the lecture with their group.

The following week I went to try the tanks. Mr. Lilly introduced me to the tanks as he must have done with other people. There were lots of bulbs, like neon lights, with different gases in them. He showed me the Periodic Table and made up a lot of mystic hokey-poke about different kinds of light that have different kinds of influences. He told me how you get ready to go into the tank by looking at yourself in the mirror with your nose up against it—all kinds of wicky-wack things, all kinds of gorp. I didn't pay any attention to the gorp, but I *did* everything because I wanted to get into the tanks, and I also thought that perhaps such preparations *might* make it easier to have hallucinations. So I went through everything according to the way he said. The only thing that proved difficult was choosing what color light I wanted, especially as the tank was supposed to be dark inside.

A sense-deprivation tank is like a big bathtub, but with a cover that comes down. It's completely dark inside, and because the cover is thick, there's no sound. There's a little pump that pumps air in, but it turns out you don't need to worry about air because the volume of air is rather large, and you're only in there for two or three hours, and you don't really consume a lot of air when you breathe normally. Mr. Lilly said that the pumps were there to put people at ease, so I figured it's just psychological, and asked him to turn the pump off, because it made a little bit of noise.

The water in the tank has Epsom salts in it to make it denser than normal water, so you float in it rather easily. The temperature is kept at body temperature, or 94, or something—he had it all figured out. There wasn't supposed to be any light, any sound, any temperature sensation, no nothing! Once in a while you might drift over to the side and bump slightly, or because of condensation on the ceiling of the tank a drop of water might fall, but these slight disturbances were very rare.

I must have gone about a dozen times, each time spending about two and a half hours in the tank. The first time I didn't get any hallucinations, but after I had been in the tank, the Lillys introduced me to a man billed as a medical doctor, who told me about a drug called ketamine, which was used as an anesthetic. I've always been interested in questions related to what happens when you go to sleep, or what happens when you get conked out, so they showed me the papers that came with the medicine and gave me one tenth of the normal dose.

I got this strange kind of feeling which I've never been able to figure out whenever I tried to characterize what the effect *was*. For instance, the drug had quite an effect on my vision; I felt I couldn't see clearly. But when I'd look *hard* at something, it would be OK. It was sort of as if you didn't *care* to look at things; you're sloppily doing this and that, feeling kind of woozy, but as soon as you look, and concentrate, everything is, for a moment at least, all right. I took a book they had on organic chemistry and looked at a table full of complicated substances, and to my surprise was able to read them.

I did all kinds of other things, like moving my hands toward each other from a distance to see if my fingers would touch each other, and although I had a feeling of complete disorientation, a feeling of an inability to do practically anything, I never found a specific thing I couldn't do.

As I said before, the first time in the tank I didn't get any hallucinations, and the second time I also didn't get any hallucinations. But the Lillys were interesting people; I enjoyed them very, very much. They often gave me lunch, and after a while we discussed things on a different level than the early stuff with the lights. I realized that other people had found the sense-deprivation tank somewhat frightening, but to me it was a pretty interesting invention. I wasn't afraid because I knew what it was: It was just a tank of Epsom salts.

. . .

The third time there was a man visiting—I met many interesting people there—who went by the name Baba Ram Das. He was a fella from Harvard who had gone to India and had written a popular book called *Be Here Now*. He related how his guru in India told him how to have an "out-of-body experience" (words I had often seen written on the bulletin board): Concentrate on your breath, on how it goes in and out of your nose as you breathe.

I figured I'd try anything to get a hallucination, and went into the tank. At some stage of the game I suddenly realized that—it's hard to explain—I'm an inch to one side. In other words, where my breath is going, in and out, in and out, is not centered: My ego is off to one side a little bit, by about an inch.

I thought: "Now where *is* the ego located? I know everybody thinks the seat of thinking is in the brain, but how do they *know* that?" I knew already from reading things that it wasn't so obvious to people before a lot of psychological studies were made. The Greeks thought the seat of thinking was in the liver, for instance. I wondered, "Is it possible that where the ego is located is learned by children looking at people putting their hand to their head when they say, 'Let me think'? Therefore the idea that the ego is located up there, behind the eyes, might be conventional!" I figured that if I could move my ego an inch to one side, I could move it further. This was the beginning of my hallucinations.

I tried and after a while I got my ego to go down through my neck into the middle of my chest. When a drop of water came down and hit me on the shoulder, I felt it "up there," above where "I" was. Every time a drop came I was startled a little bit, and my ego would jump back up through the neck to the usual place. Then I would have to work my way down again. At first it took a lot of work to go down each time, but gradually it got easier. I was able to get myself all the way down to the loins, to one side, but that was about as far as I could go for quite a while.

It was another time I was in the tank when I decided that if I could move myself to my loins, I should be able to get completely outside of my body. So I was able to "sit to one side." It's hard to explain—I'd move my hands and shake the water, and although I couldn't *see* them, I knew where they were. But unlike in real life, where the hands are to *each* side, part way *down*, they were both to *one* side! The feeling in my fingers and everything else was exactly the same as normal, only my ego was sitting outside, "observing" all this.

From then on I had hallucinations almost every time, and was able to move further and further outside of my body. It developed that when I would move my hands I would see them as sort of mechanical things that were going up and down—they weren't flesh; they were mechanical. But I was still able to feel everything. The feelings would be exactly consistent with the motion, but I also had this feeling of "he is that." "I" even got out of the room, ultimately, and wandered about, going some distance to locations where things happened that I had seen earlier another day.

I had many types of out-of-body experiences. One time, for example, I could "see" the back of my head, with my hands resting against it. When I moved my fingers, I saw them move, but between the fingers and the thumb I saw the blue sky. Of course that wasn't right; it was a hallucination. But the point is that as I moved my fingers, their movement was exactly consistent with the motion that I was imagining I was seeing. The entire imagery would appear, and be consistent with what you feel and are doing, much like when you slowly wake up in the morning and are touching something (and you don't know what it is), and suddenly it becomes clear what it is. So the entire imagery would suddenly appear, except it's *unusual*, in the sense that you usually would imagine the ego to be located in *front* of the back of the head, but instead you have it *behind* the back of the head.

One of the things that perpetually bothered me, psychologically, while I was having a hallucination, was that I might have fallen asleep and would therefore be only dreaming. I had already had some experience with dreams, and I wanted a new experience. It was kind of dopey, because when you're having hallucinations, you're not very sharp, so you do these dumb things that you set your mind to do, such as checking that you're not dreaming. So I *perpetually* was checking that I wasn't dreaming by—since my hands were often behind my head—rubbing my thumbs together, back and forth, feeling them. Of course I could have been dreaming that, but I wasn't: I knew it was real.

After the very beginning, when the excitement of having a hallucination made them "jump out," or stop happening, I was able to relax and have long hallucinations.

■ ■ ■

A week or two after, I was thinking a great deal about how the brain works compared to how a computing machine works—especially how information is stored. One of the interesting problems in this area is how memories are stored in the brain: You can get at them from so many directions compared to a machine—you don't have to come directly with the correct address to the memory. If I want to get at the word "rent," for example, I can be filling in a crossword puzzle, looking for a four-letter word that begins with r and ends in t; I can be thinking of types of income, or activities such as borrowing and lending; this in turn can lead to all sorts of other related memories or information. I was thinking about how to make an "imitating machine," which would learn language as a child does—you would talk to the machine. But I couldn't figure out how to store the stuff in an organized way so the machine could get it out for its own purposes.

When I went into the tank that week and had my hallucination, I tried to think of very early memories. I kept saying to myself, "It's gotta be earlier; it's gotta be earlier"—I was never satisfied that the memories were early enough. When I got a very early memory—let's say from my home town of Far Rockaway—then immediately would come a whole sequence of memories, all from the town of Far Rockaway. If I then would think of something from another city—Cedarhurst, or something—then a whole lot of stuff that was associated with Cedarhurst would come. And so I realized that things are stored according to the *location* where you had the experience.

I felt pretty good about this discovery, and came out of the tank, had a shower, got dressed, and so forth, and started driving to Hughes

Aircraft to give my weekly lecture. It was therefore about forty-five minutes after I came out of the tank that I suddenly realized for the first time that I hadn't the slightest idea of how memories are stored in the brain; all I had was a *hallucination* as to how memories are stored in the brain! What I had "discovered" had nothing to do with the way memories are stored in the brain; it had to do with the way I was playing games with myself.

In our numerous discussions about hallucinations on my earlier visits, I had been trying to explain to Lilly and others that the feeling that things are real does not represent true *reality*. If you see golden globes, for example, several times, and they talk to you during your hallucination and tell you they are another intelligence, it doesn't *mean* they're another intelligence; it just means that you have had this particular hallucination. So here I had this tremendous feeling of discovering how memories are stored, and it's surprising that it took forty-five minutes before I realized the error that I had been trying to explain to everyone else.

One of the questions I thought about was whether hallucinations, like dreams, are influenced by what you already have in your mind—from other experiences during the day or before, or from things you are expecting to see. The reason, I believe, that I had an out-of-body experience was that we were discussing out-of-body experiences just before I went into the tank. And the reason I had a hallucination about how memories are stored in the brain was, I think, that I had been thinking about that problem all week.

I had considerable discussion with the various people there about the reality of experiences. They argued that something is considered real, in experimental science, if the experience can be reproduced. Thus when many people see golden globes that talk to them, time after time, the globes must be real. My claim was that in such situations there was a bit of discussion previous to going into the tank *about* the golden globes, so when the person hallucinating, with his mind already thinking about golden globes when he went into the tank, sees some approximation of the globes—maybe they're blue, or something—he thinks he's reproducing the experience. I felt that I could understand the difference between the type of agreement among people whose minds are set to agree, and the kind of agreement that you get in experimental work. It's rather amusing that it's so easy tell the difference—but so hard to define it.

I believe there's *nothing* in hallucinations that has anything to do with anything external to the internal psychological state of the person who's got the hallucination. But there are nevertheless a lot of experiences by a lot of people who believe there's reality in hallucinations. The same general idea may account for a certain amount of success that interpreters of dreams have. For example, some psychoanalysts interpret dreams by talking about the meanings of various symbols. And then, it's not completely impossible that these symbols *do* appear in dreams that follow. So I think that, perhaps, the interpretation of hallucinations and dreams is a self-propagating process: You'll have a more or less general success at it, especially if you discuss it carefully ahead of time.

Ordinarily it would take me about fifteen minutes to get a hallucination going, but on a few occasions, when I smoked some marijuana beforehand, it came very quickly. But fifteen minutes was fast enough for me.

One thing that often happened was that as the hallucination was coming on, what you might describe as "garbage" would come: There were simply chaotic images—complete, random junk. I tried to remember some of the items of the junk in order to be able to characterize it again, but it was particularly difficult to remember. I think I was getting close to the kind of thing that happens when you begin to fall asleep: There are apparent logical connections, but when you try to remember what made you think of what you're thinking about, you can't remember. As a matter of fact, you soon forget what it *is* that you're trying to remember. I can only remember things like a white sign with a pimple on it, in Chicago, and then it disappears—that kind of stuff all the time.

Mr. Lilly had a number of different tanks, and we tried a number of different experiments. It didn't seem to make much difference as far as hallucinations were concerned, and I became convinced that the tank was unnecessary. Now that I saw what to do, I realized that all you have to do is sit quietly—why was it necessary that you had to have everything absolutely super duper?

So when I'd come home I'd turn out the lights and sit in the living room in a comfortable chair, and try and try—but it never worked. I've never been able to have a hallucination outside of the tanks. Of course I would *like* to have done it at home, and I don't doubt that you could meditate and *do* it if you practiced, but I didn't practice.

Found Out
in Paris

I gave a series of lectures in physics that the Addison-Wesley Company made into a set of three books (*The Feynman Lectures on Physics*), and one time at lunch we were discussing what the cover of the book should look like. I thought that since the lectures were a combination of the real world and mathematics, it would be a good idea to have a picture of a drum, and on top of it some mathematical diagrams—circles and lines for the nodes of the oscillating drumheads, which were discussed in the book.

The book came out with a plain, red cover, but for some reason, in the preface, there's a picture of me playing a drum. I think they put it in there to satisfy this idea they got that "the author wants a drum somewhere." Anyway, everybody wonders why that picture of me playing a drum is in the preface of *The Feynman Lectures*, because it doesn't have any diagrams on it, or any other things which would make it clear. (It's true that I like drumming, but that's another story.)

At Los Alamos things were pretty tense from all the work, and there wasn't any way to amuse yourself—there weren't any movies, or anything like that. But I discovered some drums that the boys' school, which had been there previously, had collected: Los Alamos was in the middle of New Mexico, where there are lots of Indian villages around. So I amused myself—sometimes alone, sometimes with another guy—just making noise, playing on these drums. I didn't know any particular rhythm, but the rhythms of the Indians were rather simple, the drums were good, and I had fun.

Sometimes I would take a drum with me into the woods at some distance, so I wouldn't disturb anybody, and would beat it with a stick, and sing. I remember one night walking around a tree, looking at the moon, and beating the drum, making believe I was an Indian.

One day a guy came up to me and said, "Around Thanksgiving you weren't out in the woods beating a drum, were you?"

"Yes, I was," I said.

"Oh! Then my wife was right!" Then he told me this story:

One night he heard some drums beating in the distance, and went upstairs to the other guy in the duplex house that they lived in, and the other guy heard it too. Remember, all these guys were from the East. They didn't know anything about Indians, and they were very interested: The Indians must have been having some kind of ceremony, or something exciting, and the two men decided to go out to see what it was.

As they walked along, the rhythms got louder as they came nearer, and they began to get nervous. They realized that the Indians probably had scouts out watching so that nobody would disturb their ceremony. So they got down on their bellies and crawled along the trail until the sound was just over the next hill, apparently. They crawled up over the hill and discovered to their surprise that it was only one Indian, doing the ceremony all by himself—dancing around a tree, beating a drum with a stick, chanting. The two guys backed away from him slowly, because they didn't want to disturb him: He was probably setting up some kind of spell, or something.

They told their wives what they saw, and the wives said, "Oh, it must have been Dick Feynman—he likes to beat drums."

"Don't be ridiculous!" the men said. "Even *Feynman* wouldn't be *that* crazy!"

So the next week they set about trying to figure out who the Indian was. There were Indians from the nearby reservation working at Los Alamos, so they asked one Indian, who was a technician in the technical area, who it could be. The Indian asked around, but none of the other Indians knew who it might be, except there was one Indian whom nobody could talk to. *He* was an Indian who knew his heritage: He had two big braids down his back and held his head high; whenever he walked anywhere he walked with dignity, alone. Nobody could talk to him: You would be *afraid* to go up to him and ask him anything—he had too much dignity. He was a furnace man. So nobody ever had the nerve to ask *this* Indian, and they decided it must have been *him*. (I was pleased to find that they had discovered such a typical Indian, such a wonderful Indian, that I might have been. It was quite an honor to be mistaken for this man.)

So the fella who'd been talking to me was just checking at the last minute—husbands always like to prove their wives wrong—and he found out, as husbands often do, that his wife was quite right.

I got pretty good at playing drums, and would play them when we had parties. I didn't know what I was doing—I just made rhythms—but I got a reputation: everybody at Los Alamos knew I liked to play drums.

When the war was over, and we were going back to "civilization," the people there at Los Alamos teased me that I wouldn't be able to play drums any more because they made too much noise. And since I was trying to become a dignified professor in Ithaca, I sold the drum that I had bought sometime during my stay at Los Alamos.

The following summer I went back out to New Mexico to work on some report, and when I saw the drums again, I couldn't stand it. I bought myself another drum, and thought, "I'll just bring it back with me this time so I can *look* at it."

That year at Cornell I had a small apartment inside a bigger house. I had the drum in there, just to look at, but one day I couldn't quite resist: I said, "Well, I'll just be very quiet . . ."

I sat on a chair and put the drum between my legs and played it with my fingers a little bit: *bup, bup, bup, buddle bup*. Then a little bit louder—after all, it was tempting me. I got a little bit louder and *brrrring!*—the telephone rang.

"Hello?"

"This is your landlady. Are you beating drums down there?"

"Yes; I'm sor—"

"It sounds so good! I wonder if I could come down and listen to it more directly . . ."

So from that time on the landlady would always come down when I'd start to drum. I had a very good time from then on, beating drums.

* * *

Around that time I met a lady from the Belgian Congo who gave me some ethnological records. In those days, records like that were rare, with drum music from the Watusi and other tribes of Africa. I admired the Watusi drummers very, very much, and I used to try to imitate them—not very accurately, but just to sound something like them—and I developed a larger number of rhythms as a result of that.

One time I was in the recreation hall, late at night, when there weren't many people, and I picked up a wastebasket and started to beat the back end of it. Some guy from way downstairs came running all the way up and said, "Hey! You play drums!" It turned out he *really* knew how to play drums, and he taught me how to play bongos.

There was some guy in the music department who had a collection of African music, and I'd come to his house and play drums. He'd make recordings of me, and then at his parties, he had a game that he called "Africa or Ithaca?" in which he'd play some recordings of drum music, and the idea was to guess whether what you were hearing was manufactured in the continent of Africa, or locally. So I must have been fairly good at imitating African drumming by that time.

When I came to Caltech, I used to go down to the Sunset Strip a lot. One time there was a group of drummers led by a big fella from Nigeria called Ukonu, playing this wonderful drum music—just percussion—at one of the nightclubs. The second-in-command, who was especially nice to me, invited me to come up on the stage with them and play a little. So I got up there with the other guys and played along with them. It was great!

I asked the second guy if Ukonu ever gave lessons, and he said yes. So I used to go down to Ukonu's place, near Century Boulevard in Watts, to get lessons in drumming. The lessons weren't very efficient: He would stall around, talk to other people, and be interrupted by all kinds of things. But when they worked they were very exciting, and I learned a lot from him.

At dances near Ukonu's place, there would be only a few whites, but it was much more relaxed than it is today. One time they had a drumming contest, and I didn't do very well: They said my drumming was "too intellectual"; theirs was much more pulsing.

One day when I was at Caltech I got a very serious telephone call. "Hello?"

"This is Mr. Trowbridge, Mahster of the Polytechnic School." The Polytechnic School was a small, private school which was across the street diagonally from Caltech. Mr. Trowbridge continued in a very formal voice: "I have a friend of yours here, who would like to speak to you."

"OK."

"Hello, Dick!" It was Ukonu! It turned out the Master of the Polytechnic School was not as formal as he was making himself out to be, and had a great sense of humor. Ukonu was visiting the school to play for the kids, so he invited me to come over and be on the stage with him, and play along. So we played for the kids together: I played bongos (which I had in my office) against his big tumba drum.

Ukonu had a regular gig: He went to various schools and talked about the African drums and what they meant, and told about the music. He had a terrific personality and a grand smile; he was a very,

very nice man. He was just sensational on the drums—he had records out—and was here studying medicine. He went back to Nigeria at the beginning of the war there—or before the war—and I don't know what happened to him.

■ ■ ■

After Ukonu left I didn't do very much drumming, except at parties once in a while, entertaining a little bit. One time I was at a dinner party at the Leightons' house, and Bob's son Ralph and his friend Tom asked me if I wanted to drum. Thinking that they were asking me to do a solo, I said no. But then they started drumming on some little wooden tables, and I couldn't resist: I grabbed a table too, and the three of us played on these little wooden tables, which made lots of interesting sounds.

Ralph and Tom liked playing drums, and we began meeting every week to just ad lib, develop rhythms, and work stuff out. These two guys were real musicians: Ralph played piano, and Tom played the cello. All I had done was rhythms, and I didn't know anything about music, which, as far as I could tell, was just drumming with notes. But we worked out a lot of good rhythms and played a few times at some local schools to entertain the kids. We also played rhythms for a dance class at the city college—something I learned was fun to do when I was working at Brookhaven for a while—and called ourselves The Three Quarks (Up, Down, and Strange), so you can figure out when *that* was.

One time I went to Vancouver to talk to the students there, and they had a party with a real hot rock-type band playing down in the basement. The band was great: They had an extra cowbell lying around, and they encouraged me to play it. So I started to play a little bit, and since their music was very rhythmic, I really got hot.

After the party was over, the guy who organized it told me that the bandleader said, "Geez! Who was that guy who came down and played on the cowbell? He can really knock out a rhythm on that thing! And by the way, that big shot this party was supposed to be *for*? You know, he never came down here; I never *did* see who it was."

At Caltech there's a group that puts on plays. Some of the actors are Caltech students; others are from outside. When there's a small part, such as a policeman who's supposed to arrest somebody, they get one of the professors to do it. It's always a big joke—the professor comes on and arrests somebody, and goes off again.

A few years ago the group was doing *Guys and Dolls*, and there was a scene where the main guy takes the girl to Havana, and they're in a nightclub. The director thought it would be a good idea to have the bongo player on the stage in the nightclub be me.

I went to the first rehearsal, and the lady directing the show pointed to the orchestra conductor and said, "Jack will show you the music."

Well, that petrified me. I don't know how to read music; I thought all I had to do was get up there on the stage and make some noise.

Jack was sitting by the piano, and he pointed to the music and said, "OK, you start here, you see, and you do this. Then I play *plonk, plonk, plonk*"—he played a few notes on the piano. He turned the page. "Then you play this, and now we both pause for a speech, you see, here"—and he turned some more pages and said, "Finally, you play this."

He showed me this "music" that was written in some kind of crazy pattern of little x's in the bars and lines. He kept telling me all this stuff, thinking I was a musician, and it was completely impossible for me to remember any of it.

Fortunately, I got ill the next day, and couldn't go to the next rehearsal. I asked my friend Ralph to go for me, and since he's a musician, he should know what it's all about. Ralph came back and said, "It's not so bad. First, at the very beginning, you have to do something exactly right because you're starting the rhythm out for the rest of the orchestra, which will mesh in with it. But after the orchestra comes in, it's a matter of ad-libbing, and there will be times when we have to pause for speeches, but I think we'll be able to figure that out from the cues the orchestra conductor gives."

In the meantime I had gotten the director to accept Ralph too, so the two of us would be on the stage. He'd play the tumba and I'd play the bongos —so that made it a helluva lot easier for me.

So Ralph showed me what the rhythm was. It must have been only about twenty or thirty beats, but it had to be just so. I'd never had to play anything just so, and it was very hard for me to get it right. Ralph would patiently explain, "Left hand, and right hand, and two left hands, then right . . ." I worked very hard, and finally, very slowly, I began to get the rhythm just right. It took me a helluva long time—many days— to get it.

A week later we went to the rehearsal and found there was a new drummer there—the regular drummer had quit the band to do something else—and we introduced ourselves to him:

"Hi. We're the guys who are going to be on stage for the Havana scene."

"Oh, hi. Let me find the scene here . . ." and he turned to the page where our scene was, took out his drumming stick, and said, "Oh, you start off the scene with . . ." and with his stick against the side of his drum he goes *bing, bong, bang-a-bang, bing-a-bing, bang, bang* at full speed, while he was looking at the music! What a shock that was to me. I had worked for *four days* to try to get that damn rhythm, and he could just patter it right out!

Anyway, after practicing again and again I finally got it straight and played it in the show. It was pretty successful: Everybody was amused to see the professor on stage playing the bongos, and the music wasn't so bad; the ad-libbing part was different in every show, and was easy, but that part at the beginning, that had to be the same— that was always hard.

*   *   *

In the Havana nightclub scene some of the students had to do some sort of dance that had to be choreographed. So the director had gotten the wife of one of the guys at Caltech, who was a choreographer working at that time for Universal Studios, to teach the boys how to dance. She liked our drumming, and when the shows were over, she asked us if we would like to drum in San Francisco for a ballet.

"What?"

Yes. She was moving to San Francisco, and was choreographing a ballet for a small ballet school there. She had the idea of creating a ballet in which the music was nothing but percussion. She wanted Ralph and me to come over to her house before she moved and play the different rhythms that we knew, and from those she would make up a story that went with the rhythms.

Ralph had some misgivings, but I encouraged him to go along with this adventure. I did insist, however, that she not tell anybody there that I was a professor of physics, Nobel Prize winner, or any other baloney. As Samuel Johnson said, If you see a dog walking on his hind legs, it's not so much that he does it well, as that he does it at all. I didn't want to do it if I was a physics professor doing it at all; we were just some musicians she had found in Los Angeles, who were going to come up and play this drum music that they had composed.

So we went over to her house and played various rhythms we had worked out. She took some notes, and soon after, that same night, she got this story cooked up in her mind and said, "OK, I want fifty-two repetitions of this; forty bars of that; whatever of this, that, this, that . . ."

We went home, and the next night we made a tape at Ralph's house. We played all the rhythms for a few minutes, and then Ralph made some cuts and splices with his tape recorder to get the various lengths right. She took a copy of our tape with her when she moved, and began training the dancers with it in San Francisco.

Meanwhile we had to practice what was on that tape: fifty-two cycles of this, forty cycles of that, and so on. What we had done spontaneously (and spliced) earlier, we now had to learn exactly. We had to imitate our own damn tape!

The big problem was counting. I thought Ralph would know how to do that because he's a musician, but we both discovered something: The "playing department" in our minds was also the "talking department" for counting—we couldn't play and count at the same time! So we invented a way of counting that involved *looking* at different corners of the room in a sequential pattern.

When we got to our first rehearsal in San Francisco, we discovered that by watching the dancers we didn't have to count anything, because the dancers went through certain motions that we could see.

There were a number of things that happened to us because we were supposed to be professional musicians and I wasn't. For example, one of the scenes was about a beggar woman who sifts through the sand on a Caribbean beach where the society ladies, who had come out at the beginning of the ballet, had been. The music that the choerographer had used to create this scene was made on a special tuneable drum that Ralph and his father had made some years before, and out of which we had never had much luck in getting a good tone. But we discovered that if we sat opposite each other on chairs and put this "crazy drum" between us on our knees, with one guy beating *bidda-bidda-bidda-bidda-bidda* rapidly with his two fingers, constantly, the other fella could push on the drum in different places with his two hands and change the pitch. Now it would go *booda-booda-booda-bidda-beeda-beeda-beeda-bidda-booda-booda-booda-badda-bidda-bidda-bidda-badda*, creating a lot of interesting sounds.

Well, the dancer who played the beggar woman wanted the rises and falls to coincide with her dance (our tape had been made arbitrarily for this scene), so she proceeded to explain to us what she was going to do: "First, I do four of these movements this way; then I bend down and sift through the sand this way for eight counts; then I stand and turn this way." I knew damn well I couldn't keep track of this, so I interrupted her:

"Just go ahead and do the dance, and I'll play along."

"But don't you want to know how the dance goes? You see, after I've finished the second sifting part, I go for eight counts over this way." It was no use; I couldn't remember anything, and I wanted to interrupt her again, but then there was this problem: I would look like I was not a real musician!

Well, Ralph covered for me very smoothly by explaining, "Mr. Feynman has a special technique for this type of situation: He prefers to develop the dynamics directly and intuitively, as he sees you dance. Let's try it once that way, and if you're not satisfied, we can correct it."

Well, she was a first-rate dancer, and you could anticipate what she was going to do. If she was going to dig into the sand, she would get *ready* to go down into the sand; every motion was smooth and expected, so it was rather easy to make the *bzzzz*s and *bshsh*s and *booda*s and *bidda*s with my hands quite appropriate to what she was doing, and she was very satisfied with it. So we got past that moment where we might have had our cover blown.

The ballet was a modest success. Although there weren't many people in the audience, the people who came to see the performances (including my mother and Ralph's mother) liked it very much.

Before we went to San Francisco for the rehearsals and the performances, we weren't sure of the whole idea. I mean, we thought the choreographer was insane: First, the ballet has only percussion; second, that we're good enough to make music for a ballet and get *paid* for it was *surely* crazy! For me, who had never had any "culture," to end up as a professional musician for a ballet was the height of achievement, as it were.

We didn't think that she'd be able to find ballet dancers who would be willing to *dance* to our drum music. (As a matter of fact, there was one prima donna from Brazil, the wife of the Portuguese consul, who decided it was beneath *her* to dance to it.) But the other dancers seemed to like it very much, and my heart felt good when we played for them for the first time in rehearsal. The delight they felt when they heard how our rhythms *really* sounded (they had until then been using our tape played on a small cassette machine) was genuine, and I had much more confidence when I saw how they reacted to our actual playing. And from the comments of the people who had come to the performances, we realized that we were a modest success.

The choreographer wanted to do another ballet to our drumming the following spring, so we went through the same procedure. We made a tape of some more rhythms,* and she made up another story, this time set in Africa. I talked to Professor Munger at Caltech and got some real African phrases to sing at the beginning *(GAwa baNYUma GAwa wo,* or something like that), and I practiced them until I had them just so.

Later, we went up to San Francisco for a few rehearsals. When we first got there, we found they had a problem. They couldn't figure out how to make elephant tusks that looked good on stage. The ones they had made out of papier mâché were so bad that some of the dancers were embarrassed to dance in front of them.

We didn't offer any solution, but rather waited to see what would happen when the performances came the following weekend. Meanwhile, I arranged to visit Werner Erhard, whom I had known from participating in some conferences he had organized. I was sitting in his beautiful home, listening to some philosophy or idea he was trying to explain to me, when all of a sudden I was hypnotized.

"What's the matter?" he said.

My eyes popped out as I exclaimed, *"Tusks!"* Behind him, on the floor, were these *enormous, massive, beautiful* ivory tusks!

He lent us the tusks. They looked very good on stage (to the great relief of the dancers): *real* elephant tusks, *super* size, courtesy of Werner Erhard.

The choreographer went to the East Coast, and put on her Caribbean ballet there. We heard later that she entered that ballet in a contest for choreographers from all over the United States, and she finished first or second. Encouraged by this success, she entered another competition, this time in Paris, for choreographers from all over the world. She brought a high-quality tape we had made in San Francisco and trained some dancers there in France to do a small section of the ballet—that's how she entered the contest.

She did very well. She got into the final round, where there were only two left—a Latvian group that was doing a standard ballet with their regular dancers to beautiful classical music, and a maverick from America, with only the two dancers that she had trained in France, dancing to a ballet which had nothing but our drum music.

*Some of these rhythms ended up on two Warner Bros. CDs: *Back TUVA Future* and *Tuva Groove.* —RL

She was the favorite of the audience, but it wasn't a popularity contest, and the judges decided that the Latvians had won. She went to the judges afterwards to find out the weakness in her ballet.

"Well, Madame, the music was not really satisfactory. It was not subtle enough. Controlled crescendoes were missing . . ."

And so we were at last found out: When we came to some really cultured people in Paris, who knew music from drums, we flunked out.

Modulating sounds of the "crazy drum" with Ralph Leighton, 1984.

I Just Shook
His Hand,
Can You
Believe It?

For some years Kyoto University had been inviting me to visit Japan. But every time I accepted their invitation, I would happen to get sick and not be able to go.

In the summer of 1986 there was going to be a conference in Kyoto and the university again invited me to come. Although I love Japan and wanted very much to visit, I felt uncomfortable at the invitation because I had no paper to give. The university said it would be all right for me to give a summary paper, but I said I don't like to do that. But then they said they would be honored if I would be the chairman of one session of the conference—that's all I would have to do. So I finally said okay.

I was lucky this time and didn't get sick.* So Gweneth and I went to Kyoto, and I was chairman of one session.

The chairman is supposed to make sure that the speakers only talk for a certain length of time, in order to leave enough time for the next speaker. The chairman occupies a position of such high honor that there are two co-chairmen to assist him. My co-chairmen said they would take care of introducing the speakers, as well as telling them when it's time to stop.

Things went smoothly for most of the session until one speaker—a Japanese man—didn't stop talking when his time was up. I look at the clock and figure it's time he should stop. I look over at the co-chairmen and gesture a little bit.

---

*Feynman was suffering from abdominal cancer. He had surgery in 1978 and 1981. After he returned from Japan, he had more surgery, in October 1986 and October 1987. —RL

370

They come up to me and say, "Don't do anything; we'll take care of it. He's talking about Yukawa.* It's all right."

So I was the honorary chairman of one session, and I felt I didn't even do my job right. And for that, the university paid my way to Japan.

. . .

One afternoon we were talking to the host who was arranging our trip. He shows us a railroad map, and Gweneth sees a curved line with lots of stops in the middle of the Ise Peninsula—it's not near the water; it's not near anywhere. She puts her finger on the end of the line and says, "We want to go here."

He looks at it, and says, "Oh! You want to go to . . . Iseokitsu?"

She says, "Yes."

"But there's *nothing* in Iseokitsu," he says, looking at me as if my wife is crazy, and hoping I'll bring her back to her senses.

So I say, "Yes, that's right; we want to go to Iseokitsu."

Gweneth hadn't talked to me about it, but I knew what she was thinking: We enjoy traveling to places in the middle of nowhere, places we've never heard of, places which have nothing.

Our host becomes a little bit upset: he's never made a hotel reservation for Iseokitsu; he doesn't even know if there's an inn there.

He gets on the telephone and calls up Iseokitsu for us. In Iseokitsu, it turns out, there are no accommodations. But there's another town—about seven kilometers beyond the end of the line—that has a Japanese-style inn.

We say, "Fine! That's just what we want—a Japanese-style inn." They give him the number and he calls.

The man at the inn is very reluctant: "Ours is a very small inn. It's a family-run place."

"That's what they want," our host reassures him.

"Did he say yes?" I ask.

After more discussion, our host says, "He agrees."

But the next morning, our host gets a telephone call from this same inn: Last night they had a family conference, and they decided they can't handle the situation. They can't take care of foreigners.

I say, "What's the trouble?"

Our host telephones the inn and asks what the problem is. He turns to us and says, "It's the toilet—they don't have a Western-style toilet."

*Hideki Yukawa, an eminent Japanese physicist, won the Nobel Prize in 1949. —RL

I say, "Tell them that the last time my wife and I went on a trip, we carried a small shovel and toilet paper, and dug holes for ourselves in the dirt. Ask him, 'Shall we bring our shovel?' "

Our host explains something over the telephone, and after some discussion, they relent. He says to us, "It's okay. You can go for one night. You don't need to take your shovel."

*   *   *

The innkeeper picked us up at the railroad station in Iseokitsu and took us to his inn. There was a beautiful garden outside our room. We noticed a brilliant, emerald-green tree frog climbing a metal frame with horizontal bars (used for hanging out the wet clothes), and a tiny yellow snake in a shrub in front of our *engawa* (veranda). Yes, there was "nothing" in Iseokitsu—but everything was beautiful and interesting to us.

It turned out there was a shrine about a mile away—that's why this little inn was there—so we walked to it. On our way back, it began to rain. A guy passed us in his car, then turned around and came back. "Where are you going?" he asked in Japanese. "To the inn," I said. So he took us there.

When we got back to our room, we discovered that Gweneth had lost a roll of film—perhaps in the man's car. So I got the dictionary out and looked up "film" and "lost," and tried to explain it to the innkeeper. I don't know how he did it, but he found the man who had given us the ride, and in his car we found the film.

The bath was interesting; we had to go through another room to get to it. The bathtub was wooden, and around it were all kinds of little toys—little boats and so on. There was also a towel with Mickey Mouse on it.

The innkeeper and his wife had a little daughter who was two, and a small baby. They dressed their daughter in a kimono and brought her up to our room. Her mother made origami things for her; I made some drawings for her, and we played with her.

A lady across the street gave us a beautiful silk ball that she had made. Everyone was friendly; everything was very good.

The next morning we were supposed to leave. We had a reservation at one of the more famous resorts, at a spa somewhere. I looked in the dictionary again; then I came down and showed the innkeeper the receipt for our reservation at the big resort hotel—it was called the Grand View, or something like that. I said, "We don't want stay big hotel tomorrow night; we want stay *here* tomorrow night. We happy here. Please you call them; change this."

He says, "Certainly! Certainly!" I could tell he was pleased by the idea that these foreigners were canceling their reservation in this big, fancy hotel in order to stay in his little inn another night.

. . .

After we returned to Tokyo, we went to the University of Kanazawa. Some professors arranged to drive us along the coast of nearby Noto Peninsula. We passed through several delightful fishing villages, and went to visit a pagoda in the middle of the countryside.

Then we visited a shrine with an enclave behind it, where one could go only by special invitation. The Shinto priest there was very gracious and invited us into his private rooms for tea, and he did some calligraphy for us.

After our hosts had taken us a little farther along the coast, they had to return to Kanazawa. Gweneth and I decided to stay in Togi for two or three days. We stayed in a Japanese-style hotel, and the lady innkeeper there was very, very nice to us. She arranged for her brother to take us by car down the coast to several villages, and then we came back by bus.

The next morning the innkeeper told us there was something important happening in town. A new shrine, replacing an old one, was being dedicated.

When we arrived at the grounds we were invited to sit on a bench, and were served tea. There were many people milling around, and eventually a procession came out from behind the shrine. We were delighted to see the leading figure was the head priest from the shrine we had visited a few days before. He was dressed in a big, ceremonial outfit, and was obviously in charge of everything.

After a little while the ceremony began. We didn't want to intrude into a religious place, so we stayed back from the shrine itself. But there were kids running up and down the steps, playing and making noise, so we figured it wasn't so formal. We came a little closer and stood on the steps so we could see inside.

The ceremony was wonderful. There was a ceremonial cup with branches and leaves on it; there was a group of girls in special uniforms; there were dancers, and so on. It was quite elaborate.

We're watching all these performances when all of a sudden we feel a tap on the shoulder. It's the head priest! He gestures to us to follow him.

We go around the shrine and enter from the side. The head priest introduces us to the mayor and other dignitaries, and invites us to sit down. A *noh* actor does a dance, and all kinds of other wonderful things go on.

Then there are speeches. First, the mayor gives a speech. Then the head priest gets up to speak. He says something that sounds to me like, "Unano, utsini kuntana kanao. Untanao uni kanao. Uniyo zoimasu doi zinti Fain-man-san-to unakano kane gozaimas . . ."—and he points to "Fain-man-san" and tells me to say something!

My Japanese is very poor, so I say something in English: "I love Japan," I say. "I am particularly impressed by your tremendous rate of technological change, while at the same time your traditions still mean so much, as you are showing with this shrine dedication." I tried to express the mixture I saw in Japan: change, but without losing respect for traditions.

The head priest says something in Japanese which I do not believe is what I said (although I couldn't really tell), because he had never understood anything I had said to him previously. But he *acted* as if he understood *exactly* what I said, and he "translated" it with complete confidence for everyone. He was much like I am, in this respect.

Anyway, the people politely listened to whatever it was that I said, and then another priest gave a speech. He was a young man, a student of the head priest, dressed in a wonderful outfit with big, wide pant legs and a big, wide hat. He looked so gorgeous, so wonderful.

Then we went to lunch with all the dignitaries, and felt very honored to be included.

After the shrine dedication ceremony was over, Gweneth and I thanked the head priest and left the dining hall to walk around the village for a while. After a bit we found some people pulling a big wagon, with a shrine in it, through the streets. They're all dressed up in outfits with symbols on the back, singing, "Eyo! Eyo!"

We follow the procession, enjoying the festivities, when a policeman with a walkie-talkie comes up to us. He takes off his white glove and puts out his hand. I shake hands with him.

As we leave the policeman and begin to follow the procession again, we hear a loud, high-pitched voice behind us, speaking very rapidly. We turn around and see the policeman clutching his walkie-talkie, speaking into it with great excitement: "O gano fana miyo ganu Fain-man-san iyo kano muri tono muroto kala . . ."—and I could just imagine him telling the person at the other end: "Do you remember that Mr. Fain-man who spoke at the shrine dedication? I just shook his hand, can you believe it?"

The priest must have "translated" something very impressive!

With Michelle, 3, and Carl, 10, in Yorkshire, England.

The chief from Bali Hai in South Pacific, *1982.*

In the Caltech production of Fiorello, *1978.*

Gesturing at a Caltech Alumni Day lecture, 1978.

Describing Feynman diagrams, 1984.

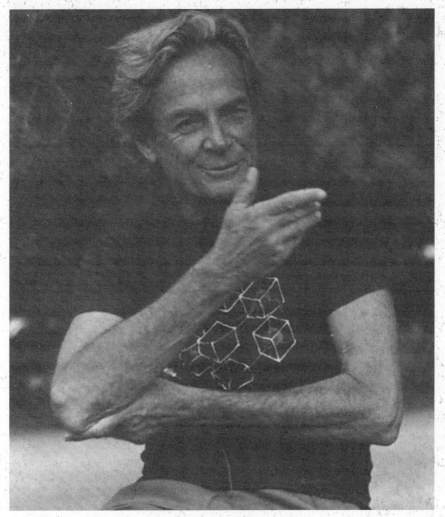

At the Esalen Institute, 1984.

Richard and Gweneth on their silver wedding anniversary, 1985.

Mr. Feynman Goes to Washington: Investigating the Space Shuttle Challenger Disaster

The space shuttle Challenger. *The fuel tank, flanked by two solid-fuel rocket boosters, is attached to the orbiter, whose main engines burn liquid hydrogen and liquid oxygen.*

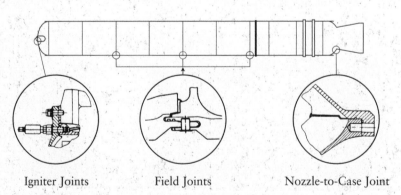

Igniter Joints   Field Joints   Nozzle-to-Case Joint

Locations and close-up views of booster-rocket field joints.

PRELIMINARIES

In this story I'm going to talk a lot about the National Aeronautics and Space Administration (NASA), but when I say "NASA did this" and "NASA did that," I don't mean all of NASA; I just mean that part of NASA associated with the shuttle.

To remind you about the shuttle, the large central part is the tank, which holds the fuel: Liquid oxygen is at the top, and liquid hydrogen is in the main part. The engines that burn this fuel are at the back end of the orbiter, which goes into space. The crew sits in the front of the orbiter; behind them is the cargo bay.

During the launch, two solid-fuel rockets boost the shuttle for a few minutes before they separate and fall back into the sea. The tank separates from the orbiter a few minutes later—much higher in the atmosphere—and breaks up as it falls back to earth.

The solid rocket boosters are made in sections. There are two types of joints to hold the sections together: the permanent "factory joints" are sealed at the Morton Thiokol factory in Utah; the temporary "field joints" are sealed before each flight—"in the field"—at the Kennedy Space Center in Florida.

COMMITTING *J*UICIDE

As you probably know, the space shuttle *Challenger* had an accident on Tuesday, January 28, 1986. I saw the explosion on the TV news, but apart from the tragedy of losing seven people, I didn't think much about it.

In the newspaper I used to read about shuttles going up and down all the time, but it bothered me a little bit that I never saw in any scientific journal any results of the experiments on the shuttle that were supposed to be so important. So I wasn't paying very much attention to it.

Well, a few days after the accident, I got a telephone call from the head of NASA, William Graham, asking me to be on the commission investigating what went wrong with the shuttle. Dr. Graham said he had been a student of mine at Caltech, and later had worked at the Hughes Aircraft Company, where I gave lectures every Wednesday afternoon.

I still wasn't exactly sure who he was.

When I heard the investigation would be in Washington, my immediate reaction was not to do it: I have a principle of not going anywhere near Washington or having anything to do with government, so my immediate reaction was, how am I gonna get out of this?

I called various friends like Al Hibbs and Dick Davies, but they explained to me that investigating the *Challenger* accident was very important for the nation, and that I should do it.

My last chance was to convince my wife. "Look," I said. "Anybody could do it. They can get somebody else."

"No," said Gweneth. "If you don't do it, there will be twelve people, all in a group, going around from place to place together. But if you join the commission, there will be eleven people—all in a group, going around from place to place together—while the twelfth one runs around all over the place, checking all kinds of unusual things. There probably won't be anything, but if there is, you'll find it." She said, "There isn't anyone else who can do that like you can."

Being very immodest, I believed her.

Well, it's one thing to figure out what went wrong with the shuttle. But the next thing would be to find out what was the matter with the organization of NASA. Then there are questions like, Should we continue with the shuttle system, or is it better to use expendable rockets? And then come even bigger questions: Where do we go from here? What should be our future goals in space? I could see a commission that started out trying to find out what happened to the shuttle ending up as a commission trying to decide national policy, and go on forever!

That made me quite nervous. I decided to get out at the end of six months, no matter what.

But I also resolved that while I was investigating the accident, I shouldn't do anything else. There were some physics problems I was playing with. There was a computer class at Caltech I was teaching with another professor. (He offered to take over the course.) There was the Thinking Machines Company in Boston I was going to consult for. (They said they would wait.) My physics would have to wait, too.

By this time it was Sunday. I said to Gweneth, "I'm gonna commit suicide for six months," and picked up the telephone.

THE COLD FACTS

When I called Graham and accepted, he didn't know exactly what the commission was going to do, who it was going to be under, or even if I would be accepted onto it. (There was still hope!)

But the next day, Monday, I got a telephone call at 4 P.M.: "Mr. Feynman, you have been accepted onto the commission"—which by that time was a "Presidential Commission" headed by William P. Rogers.

I remembered Mr. Rogers. I felt sorry for him when he was secretary of state, because it seemed to me that President Nixon was using the national security adviser (Henry Kissinger) more and more, to the point where the secretary of state was not really functioning.

At any rate, the first meeting would be on Wednesday. I figured there's nothing to do on Tuesday—I could fly to Washington Tuesday night—so I called up Al Hibbs and asked him to get some people at JPL* who knew something about the shuttle project to brief me.

On Tuesday morning I rush over to JPL, full of steam, ready to roll. Al sits me down, and different engineers come in, one after the other, and explain the various parts of the shuttle. I don't know *how* they knew, but they knew all about the shuttle. I got a very thorough, high-speed, intense briefing. The guys at JPL had the same enthusiasm that I did. It was really quite exciting.

When I look at my notes now, I see how quickly they gave me hints about where to look for the shuttle's problems. The first line of my notes says "Inhibit burning. Liner." (To inhibit propellant from burning through the metal wall of each booster rocket, there's a liner, which was not working right.) The second line of my notes says "O-rings show scorching in clevis check." It was noticed that hot gas occasionally burned past the O-rings in booster-rocket field joints.

*NASA's Jet Propulsion Laboratory, located in Pasadena; it is administered by Caltech. —RL

The beginning of Feynman's notes from his informal JPL briefing.

On the same line it says "Zn CrO$_4$ makes bubbles." (The zinc chromate putty, packed as an insulator behind the O-rings, makes bubbles that can become enlarged very fast when hot gas leaks through, eroding the O-rings.)

Photograph of bubbles in zinc chromate putty, which can lead to erosion of the O-rings.

Segment Tang

Propellant

Insulation

Primary O-Ring

Secondary O-Ring

Leak Test Port
Plug and Packing

Grease Bead

Propellant
Relief Flap

AFT Facing
Inhibitor

Pin Retainer Clip

Zinc Chromate
Putty

Pin Retainer Band

Insulation

Clevis Pin

Pin Retainer Band
Cork Insulation

Forward Facing
Inhibitor

Insulation

Segment Clevis

Propellant

Detailed diagram of a field joint.

The engineers told me how much the pressures change inside the solid rocket boosters during flight, what the propellant is made of, how the propellant is cast and then baked at different temperatures, the percentages of asbestos, polymers, and whatnot in the liner, and all kinds of other stuff. I learned about the thrusts and forces in the engines, which are the most powerful engines for their weight ever built. The engines had many difficulties, especially cracked turbine blades. The engineers told me that some of the people who worked on the engines always had their fingers crossed on each flight, and the moment they saw the shuttle explode, they were sure it was the engines.

If the engineers didn't know something, they'd say something like, "Oh, Lifer knows about that; let's get *him* in." Al would call up Lifer, who would come right away. I couldn't have had a better briefing.

It's called a briefing, but it wasn't brief: It was *very* intense, very fast, and very complete. It's the only way I know to get technical information quickly: You don't just sit there while they go through what *they* think would be interesting; instead, you ask a lot of questions, you get quick answers, and soon you begin to understand the circumstances and learn just what to ask to get the next piece of information you need. I got one hell of a good education that day, and I sucked up the information like a sponge.

* * *

That night I took the red-eye* to Washington, and got there early Wednesday morning. (I never took the red-eye again—I learned!)

I checked into the Holiday Inn in downtown Washington, and got a cab to take me to the first meeting of the Commission.

"Where to?" the driver says.

All I have is a little piece of paper. "1415 8th Street."

We start off. I'm new in Washington. The Capitol is over here, the Washington Monument is over there; everything seems very close. But the taxi goes on and on, farther and farther into worse and worse territory. Buildings get smaller, and they begin to look run down a little bit. Finally, we get onto 8th Street, and as we go along, the buildings begin to disappear altogether. Finally we find the address—by interpolation: it's an empty lot between two buildings!

By this time I realize something is completely cockeyed. I don't know what to do, because I've only got this slip of paper, and I don't know where to go.

I say to the taxi driver, "The meeting I'm going to has something to do with NASA. Can you take me to NASA?"

"Sure," he says. "You know where it is, don't you? It's right where I picked you up!"

It was true. I could have walked to NASA from the Holiday Inn—it was right across the street! I go in, past the guard at the gate, and start wandering around.

I find my way to Graham's office, and ask if there's a meeting about the shuttle.

"Yes, I know where it is," somebody says. "I'll take you down there."

They take me to a room and, sure enough, there's a big meeting going on: There are bright lights and television cameras down in front; the room is completely full, bursting with people, and all I can do is barely squash

---

*A flight that leaves the West Coast around 11 P.M. and arrives on the East Coast around 7 A.M., five hours and three time zones later. —RL

my way into the back. I'm thinking, "There's only one door to this place. How the hell am I gonna get down to the front from here?"

Then I overhear something a little bit—it's so far down there that I can't make out exactly what it is—but it's evidently a different subject!

So I go back to Graham's office and find his secretary. She calls around and finds out where the Commission is meeting. "I don't know, either," she says to the person on the other end. "He simply wandered in here!"

The meeting was in Mr. Rogers' law offices, at 1415 *H* Street. My slip of paper said 1415 *8th* Street. (The address had been given over the telephone.)

■   ■   ■

I finally got to Mr. Rogers' office—I was the only one late—and Mr. Rogers introduced me to the other commissioners. The only one I had ever heard of besides Mr. Rogers was Neil Armstrong, the moon man, who was serving as vice-chairman. (Sally Ride was on the Commission, but I didn't realize who she was until later.*) There was a very handsome-looking guy in a uniform, a General Kutyna (pronounced Koo-*tee*-na). He looked formidable in his outfit, while the other people had on ordinary suits.

This first meeting was really just an informal get-together. That bothered me, because I was still wound up like a spring from my JPL briefing the day before.

Mr. Rogers did announce a few things. He read from the executive order that defined our work:

The Commission shall:

1. Review the circumstances surrounding the accident and establish the probable cause or causes of the accident; and
2. Develop recommendations for corrective or other action based upon the Commission's findings and determinations.

Mr. Rogers also said we would complete our investigation within 120 days.

That was a relief: the scope of our commission would be limited to investigating the accident, and our work might be finished before I was done committing suicide!

*Sally Ride was the first American woman in space. —RL

. . .

Mr. Rogers asked each of us how much of our time we could spend on the Commission. Some of the commissioners were retired, and almost everybody said they had rearranged their schedules. I said, "I'm ready to work 100 percent, starting right now!"

Mr. Rogers asked, "Who will be in charge of writing the report?"

A Mr. Hotz, who had been the editor of *Aviation Week* magazine, volunteered to do that.

Then Mr. Rogers brought up another matter. "I've been in Washington a long time," he said, "and there's one thing you all must know: No matter what we do, there will always be leaks to the press. The best we can do is just try to minimize them. The proper way to deal with leaks is to have public meetings. We will have closed meetings, of course, but if we find anything important, we will have an open meeting right away, so the public will always know what is going on."

Mr. Rogers continued, "To start things off right with the press, our first official meeting will be a public meeting. We'll meet tomorrow at 10 A.M."

As we were leaving the get-together, I heard General Kutyna say, "Could someone tell me, where's the nearest Metro station?"

I thought, "This guy, I'm gonna get along with fine: He's dressed so fancy, but inside, he's honest. He's not the kind of general who's looking for his driver and his special car; he goes back to the Pentagon by the Metro." Right away I liked him, and over the course of the Commission I found my judgment in this case was excellent.

. . .

The next morning, a limousine called for me—someone had arranged for us to arrive at our first official meeting in limousines. I sat in the front seat, next to the driver.

On the way to the meeting, the driver says to me, "I understand a lot of important people are on this commission . . ."

"Yeah, I s'pose . . ."

"Well, I collect autographs," he says. "Could you do me a favor?"

"Sure," I say.

I'm reaching for my pen when he says, "When we get there, could you point out to me which one Neil Armstrong is, so I can get his autograph?"

Before the meeting started, we were sworn in. People were milling around; a secretary handed us each a badge with our picture on it so we could go anywhere in NASA. There were also some forms to sign, saying you agree to this and that so you can get your expenses paid, and so on.

After we were sworn in, I met Bill Graham. I did recognize him, and remembered him as a nice guy.

This first public meeting was going to be a general briefing and presentation by the big cheeses of NASA—Mr. Moore, Mr. Aldrich, Mr. Lovingood, and others. We were seated in big leather chairs on a dais, and there were bright lights and TV cameras pointing at us every time we scratched our noses.

I happened to sit next to General Kutyna. Just before the meeting started, he leans over and says, "Co-pilot to pilot: Comb your hair."

I say, "Pilot to co-pilot: Can I borrow your comb?"

■   ■   ■

The first thing we had to learn was the crazy acronyms that NASA uses all over the place: "SRMs" are the solid rocket motors, which make up most of the "SRBs," the solid rocket boosters. The "SSMEs" are the space shuttle main engines; they burn "LH" (liquid hydrogen) and "LOX" (liquid oxygen), which are stored in the "ET," the external tank. Everything's got letters.

And not just the big things: Practically every valve has an acronym, so they said, "We'll give you a dictionary for the acronyms—it's really very simple." Simple, sure, but the dictionary is a great, big, fat book that you've gotta keep looking through for things like "HPFTP" (high-pressure fuel turbopump) and "HPOTP" (high-pressure oxygen turbopump).

Then we learned about "bullets"—little black circles in front of phrases that were supposed to summarize things. There was one after another of these little goddamn bullets in our briefing books and on the slides.

It turned out that apart from Mr. Rogers and Mr. Acheson, who were lawyers, and Mr. Hotz, who was an editor, we all had degrees in science: General Kutyna had a degree from MIT; Mr. Armstrong, Mr. Covert, Mr. Rummel, and Mr. Sutter were all aeronautical engineers, while Ms. Ride, Mr. Walker, Mr. Wheelon, and I were all physicists. Most of us seemed to have done some preliminary work on our own. We kept asking questions that were much more technical than some of the big cheeses were prepared for.

When one of them couldn't answer a question, Mr. Rogers would reassure him that we understood he wasn't expecting such detailed questions, and that we were satisfied, for the time being at least, by the perpetual answer, "We'll get that information to you later."

STS 51–L CARGO ELEMENTS

- TRACKING AND DATA RELAY SATELLITE-B/INERTIAL UPPER STAGE
- SPARTAN–HALLEY/MISSION PECULIAR SUPPORT STRUCTURE
- CREW COMPARTMENT
  - TISP—TEACHER IN SPACE PROGRAM
  - CHAMP—COMET HALLEY ACTIVE MONITORING PROGRAM
  - FDE—FLUID DYNAMICS EXPERIMENT
  - STUDENT EXPERIMENTS
  - RME—RADIATION MONITORING EXPERIMENT
  - PPE—PHASE PARTITIONING EXPERIMENT

An example of "bullets."

The main thing I learned at that meeting was how inefficient a public inquiry is: Most of the time, other people are asking questions you already know the answer to—or are not interested in—and you get so fogged out that you're hardly listening when important points are being passed over.

What a contrast to JPL, where I had been filled with all sorts of information very fast. On Wednesday we have a "get-together" in Mr. Rogers' office—that takes two hours—and then we've got the rest of the day to do what? Nothing. And that night? Nothing. The next day, we have the public meeting—"We'll get back to you on that"—which equals nothing! Although it *looked* like we were doing something every day in Washington, we were, in reality, sitting around doing nothing most of the time.

That night I gave myself something to do: I wrote out the kinds of questions I thought we should ask during our investigation, and what topics we should study. My plan was to find out what the rest of the Commission wanted to do, so we could divide up the work and get going.

■　■　■

The next day, Friday, we had our first real meeting. By this time we had an office—we met in the Old Executive Office Building—and there was even a guy there to transcribe every word we said.

Mr. Rogers was delayed for some reason, so while we waited for him, General Kutyna offered to tell us what an accident investigation is like. We thought that was a good idea, so he got up and explained to us how the Air Force had proceeded with its investigation of an unmanned Titan rocket that had failed.

I was pleased to see that the system he described—what the questions were, and the way they went about finding the answers—was very much like what I had laid out the night before, except that it was much more methodical than I had envisioned. General Kutyna warned us that sometimes it looks like the cause is obvious, but when you investigate more carefully you have to change your mind. They had very few clues, and changed their minds three times in the case of the Titan.

I'm all excited. I want to do this kind of investigation, and figure we can get started right away—all we have to do is decide who will do what.

But Mr. Rogers, who came in partway through General Kutyna's presentation, says, "Yes, your investigation was a great success, General, but we won't be able to use your methods here because we can't get as much information as you had."

Perhaps Mr. Rogers, who is not a technical man, did not realize how patently false that was. The Titan, being an unmanned rocket, didn't have anywhere near the number of check gadgets the shuttle did. We had television pictures showing a flame coming out the side of a booster rocket a few seconds before the explosion; all we could see in General Kutyna's pictures of the Titan was a lousy dot in the sky—just a little, tiny flash—and he was able to figure stuff out from that.

Mr. Rogers says, "I have arranged for us to go to Florida next Thursday. We'll get a briefing there from NASA officials, and they'll take us on a tour of the Kennedy Space Center."

I get this picture of the czarina coming to a Potemkin village: Everything is all arranged; they show us how the rocket looks and how they put it together. It's not the way to find out how things *really* are.

Then Mr. Armstrong says, "We can't expect to do a technical investigation like General Kutyna did." This bothered me a lot, because the only things I pictured myself doing were technical! I didn't know exactly what he meant: Perhaps he was saying that all the technical lab work would be done by NASA.

I began suggesting things I could do.

While I'm in the middle of my list, a secretary comes in with a letter for Mr. Rogers to sign. In the interim, when I've just been shut up and I'm waiting to come back, various other Commission members offer to work with me. Then Mr. Rogers looks up again to continue the meeting, but he calls on somebody else—as if he's absentminded and forgot I'd been interrupted. So I have to get the floor again, but when I start my stuff again, another "accident" happens.

In fact, Mr. Rogers brought the meeting to a close while I was in midstream! He repeated his worry that we'll never really figure out what happened to the shuttle.

This was extremely discouraging. It's hard to understand now, because NASA has been taking at least two years to put the shuttle back on track. But at the time, I thought it would be a matter of days.

I went over to Mr. Rogers and said, "We're going to Florida next Thursday. That means we've got nothing to do for *five days:* What'll I do for five days?"

"Well, what would you have done if you hadn't been on the commission?"

"I was going to go to Boston to consult, but I canceled it in order to work 100 percent."

"Well, why don't you go to Boston for the five days?"

I couldn't take that. I thought, "I'm dead already—the goddamn thing isn't working right!" I went back to my hotel, devastated.

Then I thought of Bill Graham, and called him up. "Listen, Bill," I said. "You got me into this; now you've gotta save me: I'm completely depressed; I can't stand it."

He says, "What's the matter?"

"I want to *do* something: I want to go around and talk to some engineers."

He says, "I'll arrange a trip for you. You can go wherever you want: You could go to Johnson, you could go to Marshall, or you could go to Kennedy . . ."

I thought I wouldn't go to Kennedy, because it would look like I'm rushing to find out everything ahead of the others. Sally Ride worked at Johnson, and had offered to work with me, so I said, "I'll go to Johnson."

"Fine," he says. "I'll tell David Acheson. He's a personal friend of Rogers, and he's a friend of mine. I'm sure everything will be okay."

Half an hour later, Acheson calls me: "I think it's a great idea," he says, "and I told Mr. Rogers so, but he says no. I just don't know why I can't convince him."

Meanwhile, Graham thought of a compromise: I would stay in Washington, and he would get people to come to his office at NASA, right across the street from my hotel. I would get the kind of briefing I wanted, but I wouldn't be running around.

Then Mr. Rogers calls me: He's against Graham's compromise. "We're all going to Florida next Thursday," he says.

I say, "If the idea is that we sit and listen to briefings, it won't work with me. I can work much more efficiently if I talk to engineers directly."

"We have to proceed in an orderly manner."

"We've had several meetings by now, but we still haven't been assigned anything to do!"

Rogers says, "Well, do you want me to bother all the other commissioners and call a special meeting for Monday, so we can make such assignments?"

"Well, yes!" I figured our job was to work, and we *should* be bothered.

So he changes the subject, naturally. He says, "I understand you don't like the hotel you're in. Let me put you in a good hotel."

"No, thank you; everything is fine with my hotel."

Pretty soon he tries again, so I say, "Mr. Rogers, my personal comfort is not what I'm concerned with. I'm trying to get to work. I want to *do* something!"

Finally, Rogers says it's okay to go across the street to talk to people at NASA.

I was obviously quite a pain in the neck for Mr. Rogers. Later, Graham tried to explain it to me. "Suppose you, as a technical person, were given the job as chairman of a committee to look into some legal question. Your commission is mostly lawyers, and one of them keeps saying, 'I can work more effectively if I talk directly to other lawyers.' I assume you'd want to get your bearings first, before letting anybody rush off investigating on his own."

Much later, I appreciated that there were lots of problems which Mr. Rogers had to address. For example, any piece of information any of us received had to be entered into the record and made available to the other commissioners, so a central library had to be set up. Things like that took time.

* * *

On Saturday morning I went to NASA. Graham brought in guys to tell me all about the shuttle. Although they were pretty high up in NASA, the guys were technical.

The first guy told me all about the solid rocket boosters—the propellant, the motor, the whole thing except the seals. He said, "The seals expert will be here this afternoon."

The next guy told me all about the engine. The basic operation was more or less straightforward, but then there were all kinds of controls, with backing and hauling from pipes, heating from this and that, with high-pressure hydrogen pushing a little propeller which turns something else, which pumps oxygen through a vent valve—that kind of stuff.

It was interesting, and I did my best to understand it, but after a while I told the fella, "That's as much as I'm going to take, now, on the engine."

"But there are many problems with the engines that you should hear about," he says.

I was hot on the trail of the booster rocket, so I said, "I'll have to put off the main engines till later, when I have more time."

Then a guy came in to tell me about the orbiter. I felt terrible, because he had come in on a Saturday to see me, and it didn't look like the orbiter had anything to do with the accident. I was having enough trouble understanding the rest of the shuttle—there's only a certain amount of information per cubic inch a brain can hold—so I let him tell me some of the stuff, but soon I had to tell him that it was getting too detailed, so we just had a pleasant conversation.

. . .

In the afternoon, the seals expert came in—his name was Mr. Weeks—and gave me what amounted to a continuation of my JPL briefing, with still more details.

There's putty and other things, but the ultimate seal is supposed to be two rubber rings, called O-rings, which are approximately a quarter of an inch thick and lie on a circle 12 feet in diameter—that's something like 37 feet long.

When the seals were originally designed by the Morton Thiokol Company, it was expected that pressure from the burning propellant would squash the O-rings. But because the joint is stronger than the wall (it's three times thicker), the wall bows outward, causing the joint to bend a little—enough to lift the rubber O-rings off the seal area. Mr. Weeks told me this phenomenon is called "joint rotation," and it was discovered very early, before they ever flew the shuttle.

The pieces of rubber in the joints are called O-rings, but they're not used like normal O-rings are. In ordinary circumstances, such as sealing oil in the motor of an automobile, there are sliding parts and rotating shafts, but the gaps are always the same. An O-ring just sits there, in a fixed position.

But in the case of the shuttle, the gap *expands* as the pressure builds up in the rocket. And to maintain the seal, the rubber has to expand fast enough to close the gap—and during a launch, the gap opens in a *fraction of a second*. Thus the resilience of the rubber became a very essential part of the design.

Solid Rocket Booster

O-Rings

Pin

Pin

Pin

Joint rotation is caused by pressure from inside the rocket pushing the walls out farther than the joints. A gap opens, and hot gas flows past one or both of the O-rings.

When the Thiokol engineers were discovering these problems, they went to the Parker Seal Company, which manufactures the rubber, to ask for advice. The Parker Seal Company told Thiokol that O-rings are not meant to be used that way, so they could give no advice.

Although it was known from nearly the beginning that the joint was not working as it was designed to, Thiokol kept struggling with the device. They made a number of makeshift improvements. One was to put shims in to keep the joint tight, but the joint still leaked. Mr. Weeks showed me pictures of leaks on previous flights—what the engineers called "blowby," a blackening behind an O-ring where hot gas leaked through, and what they called "erosion," where an O-ring had burned a little bit. There was a chart showing all the fights, and how serious the

Thiokol attempted to cure the joint-rotation problem with shims.

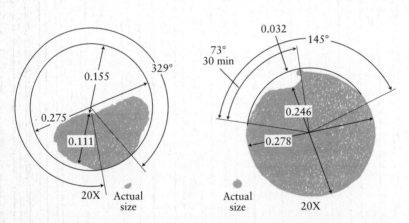

Two examples of O-ring erosion. Such erosion would occur unpredictably along 2 or 3 inches of the 37-foot-long O-ring. ("Actual size" is about $\frac{1}{4}$ inch in diameter.)

blowby and erosion were on each one. We went through the whole history up to *the* flight, 51-L.

I said, "Where does it say they were ever discussing the problem—how it's going along, or whether there's some progress?"

The correlation between temperature and O-ring incidents.

Recommendations

- The lack of a good secondary seal in the field <u>joint is most critical and ways to</u> reduce joint rotation should be incorporated as soon as possible to reduce criticality
- The flow conditions in the joint areas during ignition and motor operation need to be established through cold flow modeling to eliminate O-ring erosion
- QM-5 static test should be used to qualify a second source of the only flight certified joint filler material (asbestos-filled vacuum putty) to protect the flight program schedule
- VLS-1 should use the only flight certified joint filler material (Randolph asbestos-filled vacuum putty) in all joints
- Additional hot and cold subscale tests need to be conducted to improve analytical modeling of O-ring erosion problem and for establishing margins of safety for eroded O-rings
- <u>Analysis of existing data indicates that it is safe to continue flying existing design as long as all joints are leak checked with a 200 psig stabilization pressure, are free of contamination in the seal areas and meet O-ring squeeze requirements</u>
- Efforts needs to continue at an accelerated pace to eliminate SRM seal erosion

Self-contradictory recommendations of the seals report were underlined.

The only place was in the "flight readiness reviews"—between flights there was no discussion of the seals problem!

We looked at the summary of the report. Everything was behind little bullets, as usual. The top line says:

- The lack of a good secondary seal in the field joint is most critical and ways to reduce joint rotation should be incorporated as soon as possible to reduce criticality.

And then, near the bottom, it says:

- Analysis of existing data indicates that it is safe to continue flying existing design as long as all joints are leak checked* with a 200 psig stabilization pressure . . .

I was struck by the contradiction: "If it's 'most critical,' how could it be 'safe to continue flying'? What's the *logic* of this?"

Mr. Weeks says, "Yes, I see what you mean. Well, let's see: It says here, 'Analysis of existing data . . .' "

We went back through the report and found the analysis. It was some kind of computer model with various assumptions that were not necessarily right. You know the danger of computers: it's called GIGO— garbage in, garbage out. The analysis concluded that a little unpredictable leakage here and there could be tolerated, even though it wasn't part of the original design.

If *all* the seals had leaked, it would have been obvious even to NASA that the problem was serious. But only a few of the seals leaked on only some of the flights. So NASA had developed a peculiar kind of attitude: If one of the seals leaks a little and the flight is successful, the problem isn't so serious. Try playing Russian roulette that way: You pull the trigger and the gun doesn't go off, so it must be safe to pull the trigger again . . .

Mr. Weeks said there was a rumor that the history of the seals problem was being leaked to the newspapers. That bothered him a little bit, because it made NASA look like it was trying to keep things secret.

I told him I was entirely satisfied with the people Graham had

---

*Later in our investigation we discovered it was this leak check that was a likely cause of the dangerous bubbles in the zinc chromate putty that I had heard about at JPL. —RPF

brought in to talk to me, and that since I had already heard about the seals problem at JPL, it wasn't any big deal.

·   ·   ·

The next day, Sunday, Bill Graham took me with his family to the National Air and Space Museum. We had an early breakfast together, and then we went across the street to the museum.

I was expecting to see big crowds there, but I had forgotten that Graham was such a big shot. The museum wasn't open yet, so we had the whole place to ourselves for a while.

We did see Sally Ride there. She was in a display case, in an astronaut's suit, holding a helmet and everything. The wax model looked exactly like her.

At the museum there was a special theater with a movie about NASA and its achievements. The movie was wonderful. I had not fully appreciated the enormous number of people who were working on the shuttle, and all the effort that had gone into making it. And you know how a movie is; they can make it dramatic. It was so dramatic that I almost began to cry. I could see that the accident was a terrible blow. To think that so many people were working so hard to make it go—and then it busts—made me even more determined to help straighten out the problems of the shuttle as quickly as possible, to get all those people back on track. After seeing this movie I was very changed, from my semi anti-NASA attitude to a strong pro-NASA attitude.

·   ·   ·

That afternoon I got a telephone call from General Kutyna.

"Professor Feynman?" he says. "I have some urgent news for you. Uh, just a minute."

I hear some military-type band music in the background.

The music stops, and General Kutyna says, "Excuse me, Professor; I'm at an Air Force Band concert, and they just played the national anthem."

I could picture him in his uniform, standing at attention while the band is playing the "Star Spangled Banner," saluting with one hand and holding the telephone with the other. "What's the news, General?"

"Well, the first thing is, Rogers told me to tell you not to go over to NASA."

I didn't pay any attention to that, because I had already gone over to NASA the day before.

He continued, "The other thing is, we're going to have a special meeting tomorrow afternoon to hear from a guy whose story came out in the *New York Times* today."

I laughed inside: So now we're going to have a special meeting on Monday, anyway!

Then he says, "I was working on my carburetor this morning, and I was thinking: The shuttle took off when the temperature was 28 or 29 degrees. The coldest temperature previous to that was 53 degrees. You're a professor; what, sir, is the effect of cold on the O-rings?"

"Oh!" I said. "It makes them stiff. Yes, of course!"

That's all he had to tell me. It was a clue for which I got a lot of credit later, but it was his observation. A professor of theoretical physics always has to be told what to look for: He just uses his knowledge to explain the observations of the experimenters!

. . .

On Monday morning General Kutyna and I went over to Dr. Graham's office and asked him if he had any information on the effects of temperature on the O-rings. He didn't have it on hand, but said he would get it to us as soon as possible.

Graham did, however, have some interesting photographs to show us. They showed a flame growing from the right-hand solid rocket booster a few seconds before the explosion. It was hard to tell exactly where the flame was coming out, but there was a model of the shuttle right there in the office. I put the model on the floor and walked around it until it looked exactly like the picture—in size, and in orientation.

I noticed that on each booster rocket there's a little hole—called the leak test port—where you can put pressure in to test the seals. It's *between* the two O-rings, so if it's not closed right and if the first O-ring fails, the gas would go out through the hole, and it would be a catastrophe. It was just about where the flame was. Of course, it was still a question whether the flame was coming out of the leak test port or a larger flame was coming out farther around, and we were seeing only the tip of it.

. . .

That afternoon we had our emergency closed meeting to hear from the guy whose story was in the *New York Times*. His name was Mr. Cook.

Progression of a flame, possibly from the leak test port area.

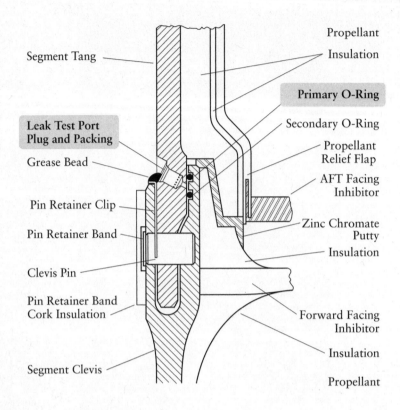

Segment Tang

Propellant

Insulation

Primary O-Ring

Leak Test Port Plug and Packing

Secondary O-Ring

Grease Bead

Propellant Relief Flap

AFT Facing Inhibitor

Pin Retainer Clip

Zinc Chromate Putty

Pin Retainer Band

Insulation

Clevis Pin

Pin Retainer Band Cork Insulation

Forward Facing Inhibitor

Insulation

Segment Clevis

Propellant

An incorrectly sealed leak test port could provide an escape route for a flame that burns past the primary O-ring.

He was in the budget department of NASA when he was asked to look into a possible seals problem and to estimate the costs needed to rectify it.

By talking to the engineers, he found out that the seals had been a big problem for a long time. So he reported that it would cost so-and-so much to fix it—a lot of money. From the point of view of the press and some of the commissioners, Mr. Cook's story sounded like a big exposé, as if NASA was hiding the seals problem from us.

I had to sit through this big, unnecessary excitement, wondering if every time there was an article in the newspaper, would we have to have a special meeting. We would never get anywhere that way.

But later, during that same meeting, some very interesting things happened. First, we saw some pictures which showed puffs of smoke coming out of a field joint just after ignition, before the shuttle even got off the pad. The smoke was coming out of the same place—possibly the

Puffs of black "smoke" (fine, unburned particles) were seen escaping from the same place where the flame was observed.

leak test port—where the flame appeared later. There wasn't much question, now. It was all fitting together.

Then something happened that was completely unexpected. An engineer from the Morton Thiokol Company, a Mr. McDonald, wanted to tell us something. He had come to our meeting on his own, uninvited. Mr. McDonald reported that the Thiokol engineers had come to the conclusion that low temperatures had something to do with the seals problem, and they were very, very worried about it. On the night before the launch, during the flight readiness review, they told NASA the shuttle shouldn't fly if the temperature was below 53 degrees—the previous lowest temperature—and on that morning it was 29.

Mr. McDonald said NASA was "appalled" by that statement. The man in charge of the meeting, a Mr. Mulloy, argued that the evidence was "incomplete"—some flights with erosion and blowby had occurred at *higher* than 53 degrees—so Thiokol should reconsider its opposition to flying.

Thiokol reversed itself, but McDonald refused to go along, saying, "If something goes wrong with this flight, I wouldn't want to stand up in front of a board of inquiry and say that I went ahead and told them to go ahead and fly this thing outside what it was qualified to."

That was so astonishing that Mr. Rogers had to ask, "Did I understand you correctly, that you said . . . ," and he repeated the story. And McDonald said, "Yes, sir."

The whole Commission was shocked, because this was the first time any of us had heard *this* story: Not only was there a failure in the seals, but there may have been a failure in management, too.

Mr. Rogers decided that we should look carefully into Mr. McDonald's story, and get more details before we made it public. But to keep the public informed, we would have an open meeting the following day, Tuesday, in which Mr. Cook would testify.

I thought, "This is going to be like an act: We're going to say the same things tomorrow as we did today, and we won't learn anything new."

■   ■   ■

As we were leaving, Bill Graham came over with a stack of papers for me.

"Geez! That's fast!" I said. "I only asked you for the information this morning!" Graham was always very cooperative.

The paper on top says, "Professor Feynman of the Presidential Commission wants to know about the effects over time of temperature on the resiliency of the O-rings . . ."—it's a memorandum addressed to a subordinate.

Under that memo is another memo: "Professor Feynman of the Presidential Commission wants to know . . ."— from that subordinate to *his* subordinate, and so on down the line.

There's a paper with some numbers on it from the poor bastard at the bottom, and then there's a series of submission papers which explain that the answer is being sent up to the next level.

So here's this stack of papers, just like a sandwich, and in the middle is the answer—to the wrong question! The answer was: "You squeeze the rubber for two hours at a certain temperature and pressure, and then see how long it takes to creep back"—over *hours*. I wanted to know how fast the rubber responds in *milliseconds* during a launch. So the information was of no use.

I went back to my hotel. I'm feeling lousy and I'm eating dinner; I look at the table, and there's the customary glass of ice water. I look at the ice water and say to myself, "Damn it, *I* can find out about that rubber *without* having NASA send notes back and forth; I just have to try it *myself!*"

I think, "I could do this tomorrow while we're all sittin' around, listening to this Cook crap we heard today. We always get ice water in those meetings; that's something I can do to save time."

Then I think, "No, that would be gauche."

But then I think of Luis Alvarez, the physicist. He's a guy I admire for his gutsiness and sense of humor, and I think, "If Alvarez was on this commission, he would do it, and that's good enough for me."

There are stories of physicists—great heroes—who have gotten information one, two, three—just like that—where everybody else is trying to do it in a complicated way. For example, after ultraviolet rays and X-rays had been discovered, there was a new type, called N-rays, discovered by André Blondel, in France. It was hard to detect the N-rays: Other scientists had difficulty repeating Blondel's experiments, so someone asked the great American physicist R. W. Wood to go to Blondel's laboratory.

Blondel gave a public lecture and demonstration. N-rays were bent by aluminum, so he had all kinds of lenses lined up, followed by a big disk with an aluminum prism in the middle. As the aluminum prism slowly turned, the N-rays came up this way and bent that way, and Blondel's assistant reported their intensity—different numbers for different angles.

N-rays were affected by light, so Blondel turned out the lights to make his readings more sensitive. His assistant continued to report their intensity.

When the lights came back on, there's R. W. Wood in the front row, holding the prism high in the air, balanced on the tips of his fingers, for all to see! So that was the end of the N-ray.

I think, "Exactly! I've got to get a sample of the rubber." I call Bill Graham.

It's impossible to get: it's kept somewhere down at Kennedy. But then Graham remembers that the model of the field joint we're going to use in our meeting tomorrow has two samples of the rubber in it. He says, "We could meet in my office before the meeting and see if we can get the rubber out."

*   *   *

The next morning I get up early and go out in front of my hotel. It's eight in the morning and it's snowing. I find a taxi and say to the driver, "I'd like to go to a hardware store."

"A hardware store, sir?"

"Yeah. I gotta get some tools."

"Sir, there's no hardware stores around here; the Capitol is over there, the White House is over there—wait a minute: I think I remember passing one the other day."

He found the hardware store, and it turned out it didn't open till 8:30—it was about 8:15—so I waited outside, in my suitcoat and tie, a costume I had assumed since I came to Washington in order to move among the natives without being too conspicuous.

The suitcoats that the natives wear inside their buildings (which are well heated) are sufficient for walking from one building to another—or from a building to a taxi if the buildings are too far apart. (All the taxis are heated.) But the natives seem to have a strange fear of the cold: They put overcoats on top of their suitcoats if they wish to step outside. I hadn't bought an overcoat yet, so I was still rather conspicuous standing outside the hardware store in the snow.

At 8:30 I went in and bought a couple of screwdrivers, some pliers, and the smallest C-clamp I could find. Then I went to NASA.

On the way to Graham's office, I thought maybe the clamp was too big. I didn't have much time, so I ran down to the medical department of NASA. (I knew where it was, because I had been going there for blood tests ordered by my cardiologist, who was trying to treat me by telephone.) I asked for a medical clamp like they put on tubes.

They didn't have any. But the guy says, "Well, let's see if your C-clamp fits inside a glass!" It fitted easily.

The field-joint model from which Feynman got the O-ring sample.

I went up to Graham's office.

The rubber came out of the model easily with just a pair of pliers. So there I was with the rubber sample in my hand. Although I knew it would be more dramatic and honest to do the experiment for the first time in the public meeting, I did something that I'm a little bit ashamed of. I cheated. I couldn't resist. I tried it. So, following the example of having a closed meeting before an open meeting, I discovered it worked before I did it in the open meeting. Then I put the rubber back into the model so Graham could take it to the meeting.

■ ■ ■

I go to the meeting, all ready, with pliers in one pocket and a C-clamp in the other. I sit down next to General Kutyna.

At the previous meeting, there was ice water for everybody. This time, there's no ice water. I get up and go over to somebody who looks like he's in charge, and I say, "I'd like a glass of ice water, please."

He says, "Certainly! Certainly!"

Five minutes later, the guards close the doors, the meeting starts, and I haven't got my ice water.

I gesture over to the guy I just talked to. He comes over and says, "Don't worry, it's coming."

The meeting is going along, and now Mr. Mulloy begins to tell us about the seals. (Apparently, NASA wants to tell us about the seals before Mr. Cook does.) The model starts to go around, and each commissioner looks at it a little bit.

Meanwhile, no ice water.

Mr. Mulloy explains how the seals are supposed to work—in the usual NASA way: He uses funny words and acronyms, and it's hard for anybody else to understand.

Richard Feynman listens to testimony.

In order to set things up while I'm waiting for the ice water, I start out: "During a launch, there are vibrations which cause the rocket joints to move a little bit—is that correct?"

"That is correct, sir."

"And inside the joints, these so-called O-rings are supposed to expand to make a seal—is that right?"

"Yes, sir. In static conditions they should be in direct contact with the tang and clevis* and squeezed twenty-thousandths of an inch."

"Why don't we take the O-rings out?"

"Because then you would have hot gas expanding through the joint . . ."

---

*The tang is the male part of the joint; the clevis is the female part. —RL

The O-ring ice-water demonstration.

"Now, in order for the seal to work correctly, the O-rings must be made of rubber—not something like lead, which, when you squash it, it stays."

"Yes, sir."

"Now, if the O-ring weren't resilient for a second or two, would that be enough to be a very dangerous situation?"

"Yes, sir."

That led us right up to the question of cold temperature and the resilience of the rubber. I wanted to prove that Mr. Mulloy must have known that temperature had an effect, although—according to Mr. McDonald—he claimed that the evidence was "incomplete." But still, no ice water! So I had to stop, and somebody else started asking questions.

The model comes around to General Kutyna, and then to me. The clamp and pliers come out of my pocket, I take the model apart, I've got the O-ring pieces in my hand, but I still haven't got any ice water! I turn around again and signal the guy I've been bothering about it, and he signals back, "Don't worry, you'll get it!"

Pretty soon I see a young woman, way down in front, bringing in a tray with glasses on it. She gives a glass of ice water to Mr. Rogers, she gives a glass of ice water to Mr. Armstrong, she works her way back and forth along the rows of the dais, giving ice water to everybody! The poor woman had gotten everything together—jug, glasses, ice, tray, the whole thing—so that everybody could have ice water.

So finally, when I get my ice water, I don't drink it; I squeeze the pieces of rubber in the C-clamp, and put them in the glass of ice water.

After a few minutes, I'm ready to show the results of my little experiment. I reach for the little button that activates my microphone.

General Kutyna, who's caught on to what I'm doing, quickly leans over to me and says, "Co-pilot to pilot: not now."

Pretty soon, I'm reaching for my microphone again.

"Not now!" He points in our briefing book—with all the charts and slides Mr. Mulloy is going through—and says, "When he comes to this slide, here, that's the right time to do it."

Finally Mr. Mulloy comes to the place, I press the button for my microphone, and I say, "I took this rubber from the model and put it in a clamp in ice water for a while . . ."

I take the clamp out, hold it up in the air, and loosen it as I talk: "I discovered that when you undo the clamp, the rubber doesn't spring back. In other words, for more than a few seconds, there is no resilience in this particular material when it is at a temperature of 32 degrees. I believe that has some significance for our problem."

Before Mr. Mulloy could say anything, Mr. Rogers says, "That is a matter we will consider, of course, at length in the session that we will hold on the weather, and I think it is an important point which I'm sure Mr. Mulloy acknowledges and will comment on in a further session."

During the lunch break, reporters came up to me and asked questions like, "Were you talking about the O-ring, or the putty?" and "Would you explain to us what an O-ring is, exactly?" So I was rather depressed that I wasn't able to make my point. But that night, all the news shows caught on to the significance of the experiment, and the next day, the newspaper articles explained everything perfectly.

CHECK ſIX!

My cousin Frances educated me about the press. She had been the AP White House correspondent during the Nixon and Ford administrations, and was now working for CNN. Frances would tell me stories of guys running out back doors because they're afraid of the press. From her I got the idea that the press isn't doing anything evil; the reporters are simply trying to help people know what's going on, and it doesn't do any harm to be courteous to them.

I found out that they're really quite friendly, if you give them a chance. So I wasn't afraid of the press, and I would always answer their questions.

Reporters would explain to me that I could say, "Not for attribution." But I didn't want any hocus-pocus. I didn't want it to sound like I'm leaking something. So whenever I talked to the press, I was straight. As a result of this, my name was in the newspaper every day, all over the place.

It seemed like I was always the one answering the reporters' questions. Often the rest of the commissioners would be anxious to go off to lunch, and I'd still be there, answering questions. But I figured, "What's the point of having a public meeting if you run away when they ask you what a word meant?"

When we'd finally get to our lunch, Mr. Rogers would remind us to be careful not to talk to the press. I would say something like, "Well, I was just telling them about the O-rings."

He would say, "That's okay. You've been doing all right, Dr. Feynman; I have no problem with that." So I never did figure out, exactly, what he meant by "not talking to the press."

Being on the Commission was rather tense work, so I enjoyed having dinner once in a while with Frances and Chuck, my sister's son, who was working for the *Washington Post*. Because Mr. Rogers kept talking about leaks, we made sure we never said a *word* about anything I was doing. If CNN needed to find out something from me, they'd have to send a different reporter. The same went for the *Post*.

I told Mr. Rogers about my relatives working for the press: "We've agreed not to talk about my work. Do you think there's any problem?"

He smiled and said, "It's perfectly all right. I have a cousin in the press, too. There's no problem at all."

■   ■   ■

On Wednesday the commission had nothing to do, so General Kutyna invited me over to the Pentagon to educate me on the relationship between the Air Force and NASA.

It was the first time I had ever been in the Pentagon. There were all these guys in uniform who would take orders—not like in civilian life. He says to one of them, "I'd like to use the briefing room . . ."

"Yes, sir!"

". . . and we'll need to see slides number such-and-such and so-and-so."

"Yes, sir! Yes, sir!"

We've got all these guys working for us while General Kutyna gives me a big presentation in this special briefing room. The slides are shown from the back on a transparent wall. It was really fancy.

General Kutyna would say things like, "Senator So-and-so is in NASA's pocket," and I would say, half-joking, "Don't give me these side remarks, General; you're filling my head! But don't worry, I'll forget it all." I wanted to be naïve: I'd find out what happened to the shuttle first; I'd worry about the big political pressures later.

Somewhere in his presentation, General Kutyna observed that everybody on the commission has some weakness because of their connections: He, having worked very closely with NASA personnel in his former position as Air Force Space Shuttle Program manager, finds it difficult, if not impossible, to drive home some of the tougher questions on NASA management. Sally Ride still has a job with NASA, so she can't just say everything she wants. Mr. Covert had worked on the engines, and had been a consultant to NASA, and so on.

I said, "I'm associated with Caltech, but I don't consider that a weakness."

"Well," he says, "that's right. You're invincible—as far as we can see. But in the Air Force we have a rule: check six."

He explained, "A guy is flying along, looking in all directions, and feeling very safe. Another guy flies up behind him (at 'six o'clock'—

'twelve o'clock' is directly in front), and shoots. Most airplanes are shot down that way. Thinking that you're safe is very dangerous! Somewhere, there's a weakness you've got to find. You must always check six o'clock."

An underling comes in. There's some mumbling about somebody else needing the briefing room now. General Kutyna says, "Tell them I'll be finished in ten minutes."

"Yes, sir!"

Finally, we go out. There, in the hall, are TEN GENERALS waiting to use the room—and I had been sitting in there, getting this personal briefing. I felt great.

* * *

For the rest of the day, I wrote a letter home. I began to worry about "check six" when I described Mr. Rogers' reaction to my visiting Frances and Chuck. I wrote,

> . . . I was pleased by Rogers' reaction, but now as I write this I have second thoughts. It was too easy—after he explicitly talked about the importance of no leaks etc. at earlier meetings. Am I being set up? (SEE, DARLING, WASHINGTON PARANOIA IS SETTING IN.) . . . I think it is possible that there are things in this somebody might be trying to keep me from finding out, and might try to discredit me if I get too close. . . . So, reluctantly, I will have to not visit Frances and Chuck any more. Well, I'll ask Fran first if that is *too* paranoid. Rogers seemed so agreeable and reassuring. It was so easy, yet I am probably a thorn in his side. . . .
>
> Tomorrow at 6:15 am we go by special airplane (two planes) to Kennedy Space Center to be "briefed." No doubt we shall wander about, being shown everything—gee whiz—but no time to get into technical details with anybody. Well, it won't work. If I am not satisfied by Friday, I will stay over Sat & Sun, or if they don't work then, Monday & Tuesday. I am determined to do the job of finding out what happened—let the chips fall!
>
> My guess is that I will be allowed to do this, overwhelmed with data and details . . . , so they have time to soften up dangerous witnesses etc. But it won't work because (1) I do technical information exchange and understanding much faster than they imagine, and (2) I already smell certain rats that I will not forget, because I just love the smell of rats, for it is the spoor of exciting adventure.
>
> I feel like a bull in a china shop. The best thing is to put the bull

out to work on the plow. A better metaphor will be an ox in a china shop, because the china is the bull, of course.*

So, much as I would rather be home and doing something else, I am having a wonderful time.

Love,
Richard

The press was reporting rumors that NASA was under great political pressure to launch the shuttle, and there were various theories as to where the pressure was coming from. It was a great big world of mystery to me, with tremendous forces. I would investigate it, all right, and if I protected myself, nothing would happen. But I had to watch out.

---

*The thing Feynman was going to break up was the baloney (the "bull—") about how good everything was at NASA. —RL

Gumshoes

Finally, early on Thursday morning, we get to Florida. The original idea was that we would go around the Kennedy Space Center at Cape Canaveral and see everything on a guided tour. But because information was coming out in the newspapers so fast, we had a public meeting first.

First, we saw some detailed pictures of the smoke coming out of the shuttle while it was still on the launch pad. There are cameras all over the place watching the launch—something like a hundred of them. Where the smoke came out, there were two cameras looking straight at it—but both failed, curiously. Nevertheless, from other cameras we could see four or five puffs of black smoke coming out from a field joint. This "smoke" was not burning material; it was simply carbon and mucky stuff that was pushed out because of pressure inside the rocket.

The puffs stopped after a few seconds: the seal got plugged up somehow, temporarily, only to break open again a minute later.

There was some discussion about how much matter came out in the smoke. The puffs of smoke were about six feet long, and a few feet thick. The amount of matter depends on how fine the particles are, and there could always be a big piece of glop inside the smoke cloud, so it's hard to judge. And because the pictures were taken from the side, it was possible there was more smoke farther around the rocket.

To establish a minimum, I assumed a particle size that would produce as much smoke as possible out of a given amount of material. It came out surprisingly small—approximately one cubic inch: if you have a cubic inch of stuff, you can get that much smoke.

We asked for pictures from other launches. We found out later that there had never been any puffs of smoke on any previous flights.

We also heard about the low temperatures before the launch from a man named Charlie Stevenson, who was in charge of the ice crew. He said the temperature had gone down to 22 degrees during the night, but

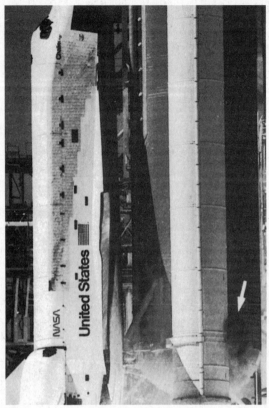

Detailed picture, taken from the launch pad, of the "smoke."

his crew got readings as low as 8 degrees at some places on the launch pad, and they couldn't understand why.

During the lunch break, a reporter from a local TV station asked me what I thought about the low temperature readings. I said it seemed to me that the liquid hydrogen and oxygen had chilled the 22-degree air even further as it flowed down the big fuel tank onto the rocket booster. For some reason, the reporter thought I had just told him some important, secret information, so he didn't use my name in his report that evening. Instead, he said, "This explanation comes from a Nobel Prize winner, so it must be right."

In the afternoon, the telemetry people gave us all kinds of information on the last moments of the shuttle. Hundreds of things had been measured, all of which indicated that everything was working as well as it could under the circumstances: The pressure in the hydrogen tank suddenly fell a few seconds after the flame had been observed; the gyros that steer the shuttle were working perfectly until one had to work harder than the other because there were side forces from the flame shooting out of the side of the booster rocket; the main engines even shut themselves down when the hydrogen tank exploded, because there was a pressure drop in the fuel lines.

That meeting lasted until 7:30 in the evening, so we postponed the tour until Friday and went straight to a dinner set up by Mr. Rogers.

■   ■   ■

At the dinner I happened to be seated next to Al Keel, who had joined the commission on Monday as its executive officer to help Mr. Rogers organize and run our work. He came to us from the White House—from something called the Office of Management and Budget—and had a good reputation for doing a fine job. Mr. Rogers kept saying how lucky we were to get somebody with such high qualifications.

One thing that impressed me, though, was that Dr. Keel had a Ph.D. in aerospace, and had done some post-doc work at Berkeley. When he introduced himself on Monday, he joked that the last "honest work" he had done for a living was some aerodynamics work for the shuttle program ten or twelve years ago. So I felt very comfortable with him.

Well, I haven't been talking to Dr. Keel for more than five minutes, when he tells me he's never been so insulted in his life, that he didn't take this job to be so insulted, and that he doesn't want to talk to me anymore!

Now, I have a way of not remembering things when I do something dumb or annoying to people, so I forget what I said that put him out. Whatever it was, I thought I was joking, so I was very surprised by his reaction. I had undoubtedly said some boorish, brash, damn-fool thing, which I therefore can't remember!

Then there was a rather tense period of five or ten minutes, with me apologizing and trying to get a conversation going again. We finally got to talking again, somewhat. We were not big friends, but at least there was peace.

■   ■   ■

On Friday morning, we had another public meeting, this time to hear people from Morton Thiokol and NASA talk about the night before the launch. Everything came out so slowly: The witness doesn't really want to tell you everything, so you have to get the answers out by asking exactly the right questions.

Other guys on the Commission were completely awake—Mr. Sutter, for instance. "Exactly what were your quality criteria for acceptance under such-and-such and so-and-so?"—he'd ask specific questions like that, and it would turn out they didn't have any such criteria. Mr. Covert and Mr. Walker were the same way. Everybody was asking good questions, but I was fogged out most of the time, feeling a little bit behind.

Then this business of Thiokol changing its position came up. Mr. Rogers and Dr. Ride were asking two Thiokol managers, Mr. Mason and Mr. Lund, how many people were against the launch, even at the last moment.

"We didn't poll everyone," says Mr. Mason.

"Was there a substantial number against the launch, or just one or two?"

"There were, I would say, probably five or six in engineering who at that point would have said it is not as conservative to go with that temperature, and we don't know. The issue was we didn't know for sure that it would work."

"So it was evenly divided?"

"That's a very estimated number."

It struck me that the Thiokol managers were waffling. But I only knew how to ask simpleminded questions. So I said, "Could you tell me, sirs, the names of your four best seals experts, in order of ability?"

"Roger Boisjoly and Arnie Thompson are one and two. Then there's Jack Kapp and, uh . . . Jerry Burns."

I turned to Mr. Boisjoly, who was right there, at the meeting. "Mr. Boisjoly, were you in agreement that it was okay to fly?"

He says, "No, I was not."

I ask Mr. Thompson, who was also there.

"No, I was not."

I say, "Mr. Kapp?"

Mr. Lund says, "He is not here. I talked to him after the meeting, and he said, 'I would have made that decision, given the information we had.' "

"And the fourth man?"

"Jerry Burns. I don't know what his position was."

"So," I said, "of the four, we have one 'don't know,' one 'very likely yes,' and the first two, who were mentioned right away as being the *best* seal experts, *both said no.*" So this "evenly split" stuff was a lot of crap. The guys who knew the *most* about the seals—what were *they* saying?

= = =

Late in the afternoon, we were shown around the Kennedy Space Center. It was interesting; it wasn't as bad as I had predicted. The other commissioners asked a lot of important questions. We didn't have time to see the booster-rocket assembly, but near the end we were going to see the wreckage that had been recovered so far. I was pretty tired of this group stuff, so I excused myself from the rest of the tour.

I ran down to Charlie Stevenson's place to see more pictures of the launch. I also found out more about the unusually low temperature readings. The guys were very cooperative, and wanted me to work with them. I had been waiting for *ten days* to run around in one of these places, and here I was, *at last!*

At dinner that night, I said to Mr. Rogers, "I was thinking of staying here over the weekend."

"Well, Dr. Feynman," he said, "I'd prefer you come back to Washington with us tonight. But of course, you're free to do whatever you want."

"Well, then," I said, "I'll stay."

= = =

On Saturday I talked to the guy who had actually taken the temperature readings the morning of the launch—a nice fella named B. K. Davis. Next to each temperature he had written the exact time he had measured it, and then took a picture of it. You could see large gaps between the times as he climbed up and down the big launch tower. He measured the temperature of the air, the rocket, the ground, the ice, and even a puddle of slush with antifreeze in it. He did a very complete job.

NASA had a theoretical calculation of how the temperatures should vary around the launch pad: They should have been more uniform, and higher. Somebody thought that heat radiating to the clear sky had something to do with it. But then someone else noticed that BK's reading for the slush was much lower than the photograph indicated: at 8 degrees, the slush—even with antifreeze in it—should have been frozen solid.

Then we looked at the device the ice crew used for measuring the temperatures. I got the instruction manual out, and found that you're supposed to put the instrument out in the environment for at least 20 minutes before using it. Mr. Davis said he had taken it out of the box— at 70 degrees—and began making measurements right away. Therefore we had to find out whether the errors were reproducible. In other words, could the circumstances be duplicated?

On Monday I called up the company that made the device, and talked to one of their technical guys: "Hi, my name is Dick Feynman," I said. "I'm on the Commission investigating the *Challenger* accident, and I have some questions about your infrared scanning gun . . ."

"May I call you right back?" he says.

"Sure."

After a little while he calls me back: "I'm sorry, but it's proprietary information. I can't discuss it with you."

By this time I realized what the real difficulty was: The company was *scared green* that we were going to blame the accident on their instrument. I said, "Sir, your scanning gun has nothing to do with the accident. It was used by the people here in a way that's contrary to the procedures in your instruction manual, and I'm trying to figure out if we can reproduce the errors and determine what the temperatures really were that morning. To do this, I need to know more about your instrument."

The guy finally came around, and became quite cooperative. With his help, I advised the ice-crew guys on an experiment. They cooled a room down to about 40 degrees, and put a big block of ice in it—with ice, you can be sure the surface temperature is 32 degrees. Then they brought in the scanning gun from a room which was 70 degrees inside, and made measurements of the ice block every 30 seconds. They were able to measure how far off the instrument was as a function of time.

Mr. Davis had written his measurements so carefully that it was very easy to fix all the numbers. And then, remarkably, the recalculated temperatures were close to what was expected according to the theoretical model. It looked very sensible.

The next time I talked to a reporter, I straightened everything out about the temperatures, and informed him that the earlier theory expounded by the Nobel Prize winner was wrong.

I wrote a report for the other commissioners on the temperature problem, and sent it to Dr. Keel.

. . .

Then I investigated something we were looking into as a possible contributing cause of the accident: When the booster rockets hit the ocean, they became out of round a little bit from the impact. At Kennedy they're taken apart, and the sections—four for each rocket—are sent by rail to Thiokol in Utah, where they are packed with new propellant. Then they're put back on a train to Florida. During transport, the sections (which are hauled on their side) get squashed a little bit—the softish propellant is very heavy. The total amount of squashing is only a fraction of an inch, but when you put the rocket sections back together, a small gap is enough to let hot gases through: the O-rings are only a quarter of an inch thick, and compressed only two-hundredths of an inch!

I thought I'd do some calculations. NASA gave me all the numbers on how far out of round the sections can get, so I tried to figure out how much the resulting squeeze was, and where it was located—maybe the minimum squeeze was where the leak occurred. The numbers were measurements taken along three diameters, every 60 degrees. But three matching diameters won't guarantee that things will fit; six diameters, or any other number of diameters, won't do, either.

For example, you can make a figure something like a triangle with rounded corners, in which three diameters, 60 degrees apart, have the same length.

I remembered seeing such a trick at a museum when I was a kid. There was a gear rack that moved back and forth perfectly smoothly, while underneath it were some noncircular, funny-looking, crazy-shaped gears turning on shafts that wobbled. It looked impossible, but the reason it worked was that the gears were shapes whose diameters were always the same.

So the numbers NASA gave me were useless.

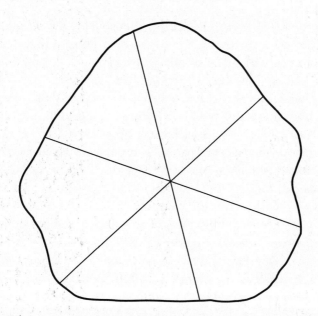

This figure has three diameters the same length—yet it is obviously not round.

* * *

During that weekend, just as I had predicted in my letter home, I kept getting notes from the Commission headquarters in Washington: "Check the temperature readings, check the pictures, check this, check that . . ."— there was quite a list. But as the instructions came in, I had done most of them already.

One note had to do with a mysterious piece of paper. Someone at Kennedy had reportedly written "Let's go for it" while assembling one of the solid booster rockets. Such language appeared to show a certain recklessness. My mission: Find that piece of paper.

Well, by this time I understood how much paper there was in NASA. I was sure it was a trick to make me get lost, so I did nothing about it.

Instead, I pursued something surreptitiously.

It was rumored that the reason NASA tried to make the shuttle fly on January 28th, in spite of the cold, was that the President was going to give his State of the Union address that night. According to the theory, the White House had it all cooked up so that during the State of the Union address, the teacher, Mrs. McAuliffe, would talk to the President and Congress from space. It was gonna be great: The President would say, "Hello! How are you doing?" And she would say, "Fine"—something very dramatic.

Since it sounded logical, I began by supposing it was very likely possible. But was there any evidence? This kind of thing I didn't know how to investigate. I could only think of this: It's very hard to get through to the President; I also can't just call up an astronaut and talk to her—if she's in space. Therefore, switching the signals down from the shuttle over to the President while he's talking to Congress must be a complicated business.

To find out whether anybody had set up to do that, I went down to the lowest levels and asked guys at the bottom some technical questions.

They showed me the antennas, they told me about the frequencies, they showed me the big radio system and the computer system; they showed me all the ways they did things.

I said, "If you had to send a transmission somewhere else—to Marshall, say—how would you do it?"

They said, "Oh, we're just a relay station. Everything is automatically sent over to Houston, and they switch everything out from there. We don't do any switching here."

So I didn't find any evidence—at least at Kennedy. But the guys there were so nice to me, and everything was so pleasant, that I feel bad. I don't like to cheat people. It was a little sneaky, what I was doing. Nevertheless, I thought I'd better do the same thing when I got to Houston.

*   *   *

On Monday, Mr. Hotz came down to Florida to work with me. (He told me later that he had been sent down with specific instructions to see what I was doing, and to keep me from "going wild.") Mr. Hotz brought a list of things to look into: "There are a lot of things on this list," he said, "so I'd be happy to split the work with you." Some things he said he could do more easily, and the rest of the things I had already done—except for that piece of paper which said "Let's go for it." Mr. Hotz hinted around that it might have come from the diary of someone in the booster-rocket assembly. That wasn't enough of a clue for me; I just wasn't gonna do it. Instead, I went to see a Mr. Lamberth, who had said he wanted to talk to me.

Mr. Lamberth was way up in the works, a big cheese in charge of assembling the solid-rocket boosters. He wanted to tell me about some problems he had. "The workers used to have much better discipline," he explained, "but nowadays they're not like they used to be." He gave me a couple of examples.

The first incident had to do with taking the booster rockets apart after they had been recovered from the sea. The rocket sections are held together by 180 pins—each about an inch and a half in diameter and two inches long—all the way around.

There was some kind of procedure for taking sections apart, in which the workers were supposed to pull the rocket up a certain distance. They had gotten to paying attention only to the amount of *force* they were applying—about 11,000 pounds. That was a better method, from a physical standpoint, because the idea is to take the load off the pins.

One time the force gauge wasn't working right. The workers kept putting more force on, wondering why they weren't reaching 11,000 pounds, when all of a sudden one of the pins broke.

Mr. Lamberth reprimanded the workers for not following procedures. It reminded me of when I tried to make things work better at my aunt's hotel: Your method is better than the regular way, but then you have a little accident . . .

The second story Mr. Lamberth told me had to do with putting the rocket sections together. The regular procedure was to stack one section on top of the other and match the upper section to the lower one.

If a section needed to be reshaped a little bit, the procedure was to first pick up the section with a crane and let it hang sideways a few days. It's rather simpleminded.

If they couldn't make a section round enough by the hanging method, there was another procedure: Use the "rounding machine"—a rod with a hydraulic press on one end and a nut on the other—and increase the pressure.

Mr. Lamberth told me the pressure shouldn't exceed 1200 pounds per square inch (psi). One time, a section wasn't round enough at 1200 psi, so the workers took a wrench and began turning the nut on the other end. When they finally got the section round enough, the pressure was up to 1350. "This is another example of the lack of discipline among the workers," Mr. Lamberth said.

I had wanted to talk with the assembly workers anyway (I love that kind of thing), so I arranged to see them the next day at 2:30 in the afternoon.

* * *

At 2:30 I walk into this room, and there's a long table with thirty or forty people—they're all sitting there with morose faces, very serious, ready to talk to The Commissioner.

I was terrified. I hadn't realized my terrible power. I could see they were worried: They must have been told I was investigating the errors they had made!

So right away I said, "I had nothin' to do, so I thought I'd come over and talk to the guys who put the rockets together. I didn't want everybody to stop working just 'cause I wanna find out something for my own curiosity; I only wanted to talk with the workers . . ."

Most of the people got up and left. Six or seven guys stayed—the crew who actually put the rocket sections together, their foreman, and some boss who was higher up in the system.

Well, these guys were still a bit scared. They didn't really want to open up. The first thing I think to say is, "I have a question: when you measure the three diameters and all the diameters match, do the sections really fit together? It seems to me that you could have some bumps on one side and some flat areas directly across, so the three diameters would match, but the sections wouldn't fit."

"Yes, yes!" they say. "We get bumps like that. We call them nipples."

The only woman there said, "It's got nothing to do with me!"—and everybody laughed.

"We get nipples all the time," they continued. "We've been tryin' to tell the supervisor about it, but we never get anywhere!"

We were talking details, and that works wonders. I would ask questions based on what could happen theoretically, but to them it looked like I was a regular guy who knew about their technical problems. They loosened up very rapidly, and told me all kinds of ideas they had to improve things.

For example, when they use the rounding machine, they have to put a rod through holes exactly opposite each other. There are 180 holes, so they have to make sure the other end of the rod goes through the hole 90 holes away. Now, it turns out you have to climb up into an awkward place to count the holes. It's very slow and very difficult.

They thought it would be very helpful if there were four paint marks, 90 degrees apart, put on at the factory. That way, they would never have to count more than 22 holes to the nearest mark. For example, if they put the rod through a hole which is 9 holes clockwise from a paint mark, then the other end of the rod would go through the hole which is 9 holes clockwise from the opposite mark.

The foreman, Mr. Fichtel, said he wrote a memo with this suggestion to his superiors two years ago, but nothing had happened yet. When he asked why, he was told the suggestion was too expensive.

"Too expensive to paint *four little lines?*" I said in disbelief.

They all laughed. "It's not the paint; it's the paperwork," Mr. Fichtel said. "They would have to revise all the manuals."

The assembly workers had other observations and suggestions. They were concerned that if two rocket sections scrape as they're being put together, metal filings could get into the rubber seals and damage them. They even had some suggestions for redesigning the seal. Those suggestions weren't very good, but the point is, the workers were *thinking!* I got the impression that they were *not* lacking discipline; they were very interested in what they were doing, but they weren't being given much encouragement—nobody was paying much attention to them. It was remarkable that their morale was as high as it was under the circumstances.

Then the workers began to talk to the boss who had stayed. "We're disappointed by something," one of them said. "When the Commission was going to see the booster-rocket assembly, the demonstration was going to be done by the managers. Why wouldn't you let *us* do it?"

"We were afraid you'd be frightened by the commissioners and you wouldn't want to do it."

"No, no," said the workmen. "We think we do a good job, and we wanted to show what we do."

After that meeting, the boss took me to the cafeteria. As we were eating—the workmen weren't with us anymore—he said, "I was surprised they were so concerned about that."

■   ■   ■

Later, I talked to Mr. Fichtel about this incident of increasing the pressure past 1200. He showed me the notes he made as he went along: They weren't the formal papers that are stamped; they were part of an informal but carefully written diary.

I said, "I hear the pressure got up to 1350."

"Yes," he said, "we had tightened the nut at the other end."

"Was that the regular procedure?"

"Oh, yes," he said, "it's in the book."

He opens up the manual and shows me the procedure. It says, "Build up the pressure on the hydraulic jack. If this is insufficient to obtain desired roundness, then very carefully tighten nut on other end to get to the desired roundness"—it said so in black and white! It didn't say that tightening the nut would increase the pressure past 1200 psi; the people who wrote the manual probably weren't quite aware of that.

Mr. Fichtel had written in his diary, "We very carefully tightened the nut"—exactly the same language as the instructions.

I said, "Mr. Lamberth told me he admonished you about going above 1200."

"He never admonished me about that—why should he?"

We figured out what probably happened. Mr. Lamberth's admonishment went down through the levels until somebody in middle management realized that Mr. Fichtel had gone by the book, and that the error was in the manual. But instead of telling Mr. Lamberth about the error, they simply threw away the admonishment, and just kept quiet.

■   ■   ■

Over lunch, Mr. Fichtel told me about the inspection procedures. "There's a sheet for each procedure, like this one for the rounding procedure," he said. "On it there are boxes for stamps—one from the supervisor, one from quality control, one from the manufacturer—and for the bigger jobs, one from NASA."

He continued, "We make the measurements, go through one course of rounding, and then make the measurements again. If they don't match well enough, we repeat the steps. Finally, when the diameter differences are small enough, we go for it."

I woke up. "What do you mean, 'go for it'?" I said. "It sounds sort of cavalier . . ."

"No, no," he says. "That's just the lingo we use when we mean that all the conditions are satisfied, and we're ready to move to the next phase of the operation."

"Do you ever write that down—that 'go for it'?"

"Yes, sometimes."

"Let's see if we can find a place where you wrote it."

Mr. Fichtel looked through his diary, and found an example. The expression was completely natural to him—it wasn't reckless or cavalier; it was just his way of speaking.

■   ■   ■

On Monday and Tuesday, while I was running around down at Kennedy, Mr. Rogers was in Washington appearing before a Senate committee. Congress was considering whether it should have its own investigation.

Senator Hollings, from South Carolina, was giving Mr. Rogers a hard time: "Secretary Rogers," he says, "I'm anxious that you have an adequate staff thayah. How many *investigators* does yo' commission have?"

Mr. Rogers says, "We don't have investigators in the police sense. We're reading documents, understanding what they mean, organizing hearings, talking to witnesses—that sort of thing. We'll have an adequate staff, I assure you."

"Well, that's the point," Senator Hollings says. "From my experience in investigating cases, I'd want four or five investigators steeped in science and space technology going around down there at Canaveral talking to everybody, eating lunch with them. You'd be amazed, if you eat in the restaurants around there for two or three weeks, what you'll find out. You can't just sit and read what's given to you."

"We're not just going to sit and read," Mr. Rogers says defensively. "We've gotten a lot of people in a room and asked them questions all at the same time, rather than have a gumshoe walking around, talking to people one at a time."

"I understand," says Senator Hollings. "Yet I'm concerned about yo' product if you don't have some gumshoes. That's the trouble with Presidential Commissions; I've been on 'em: they go on what's *fed* to 'em, and they don't look behind it. Then we end up with investigative reporters, people writing books, and everything else. People are *still* second-guessing the Warren Commission Report around this town." *

Mr. Rogers calmly says, "I appreciate your comments, Senator. You'll be interested to know that one of our commission members—he's a Nobel laureate—is down there in Florida today, investigating in the way you'd like him to investigate."

(Mr. Rogers didn't know it, but I was actually eating lunch with some engineers when he said that.)

Senator Hollings says, "I'm not questioning the competence of the Nobel laureate; I've been reading with great interest what he said. There's no question about the competence of the Commission itself. It's just that when you investigate a case, you need investigators. You have already brought to the public's attention a lot of very interesting facts, so I think you haven't been negligent in any fashion."

So I saved Mr. Rogers a little bit. He saw that he had an answer for Senator Hollings by the *good luck* that I had stayed in Florida anyway—against his wishes.

---

*The Warren Commission, headed by retired Supreme Court Chief Justice Earl Warren, investigated the assassination of President John F. Kennedy. —RL

FANTAƒTIC
FIGUREƒ

On Tuesday afternoon I flew back to Washington, and went to the
next meeting of the Commission, on Wednesday. It was another public
meeting. A manager of the Morton Thiokol Company named Mr. Lund
was testifying. On the night before the launch, Mr. Mulloy had told him
to put on his "management hat" instead of his "engineering hat," so he
changed his opposition to launch and overruled his own engineers. I was
asking him some harsh questions when suddenly I had this feeling of the
Inquisition.

Mr. Rogers had pointed out to us that we ought to be careful with
these people, whose careers depend on us. He said, "We have all the
advantages: we're sitting up here; they're sitting down there. They have
to answer our questions; we don't have to answer their questions."
Suddenly, all this came back to me and I felt terrible, and I couldn't do it
the next day. I went back to California for a few days, to recover.

While I was in Pasadena, I went over to JPL and met with Jerry
Solomon and Meemong Lee. They were studying the flame that appeared
a few seconds before the main fuel tank exploded, and were able to
bring out all kinds of details. (JPL has good enhancers of TV pictures
from all their experience with planetary missions.) Later, I took the
enhancements over to Charlie Stevenson and his crew at Kennedy to
expedite things.

■　■　■

Somewhere along the line, somebody from the staff brought me
something to sign: It said that my expenses were so-and-so much, but
they weren't—they were more. I said, "This is not the amount I actually spent."

The guy said, "I know that, sir; you're only allowed a maximum of
$75 a day for the hotel and food."

"Then why did you guys set me up in a hotel which costs $80 or $90 a night, and then you give me only $75 a day?"

"Yes, I agree; it's too bad, but that's the way it goes!"

I thought of Mr. Rogers' offer to put me in a "good hotel." What did he mean by that—that it would cost me *more*?

If you're asked to contribute months of time and effort to the government (and you lose money you would have made consulting for a company), the government ought to appreciate it a little more than to be cheap about paying you back. I'm not trying to make money off the government, but I'm not wanting to *lose* money, either. I said, "I'm not going to sign this."

Mr. Rogers came over and promised he would straighten it out, so I signed the paper.

I really think Mr. Rogers tried to fix it, but he was unable to. I thought of fighting this one to the end, but then I realized it's impossible: If I had been paid for my actual expenses, then of course all the other commissioners would have to be paid, too. That would be all right, but it would also mean that this commission was the only commission to be paid its actual expenses—and pretty soon, word would get out.

They have a saying in New York: "You can't fight City Hall," meaning "It's impossible." But this time, it was a hell of a lot bigger than City Hall: the $75 a day rule is a law of the U.S. government! It might have been fun to fight it to the end, but I guess I was tired—I'm not as young as I used to be—so I just gave up.

Somebody told me they heard commissioners make $1,000 a day, but the truth is, our government doesn't even pay back their costs.

．　．　．

At the beginning of March, about a month after the Commission started, we finally split up into working groups: the Pre-Launch Activities group was headed by Mr. Acheson; Mr. Sutter was in charge of the Design, Development, and Production panel; General Kutyna was leader of the Accident Analysis group; and Dr. Ride was in charge of the Mission Planning and Operations group.

I spent most of my time in Kutyna's group. I was in Ride's group, too, but I ended up not doing very much for her.

General Kutyna's group went to Marshall Space Flight Center in Huntsville, Alabama, to do its work. The first thing that happened there was, a man named Ullian came in to tell us something. As range safety officer at Kennedy, Mr. Ullian had to decide whether to put destruct charges on the shuttle. (If a rocket goes out of control, the destruct charges enable it to be blown up into small bits. That's much less perilous than a rocket flying around loose, ready to explode when it hits the ground.)

Every unmanned rocket has these charges. Mr. Ullian told us that 5 out of 127 rockets he looked at had failed—a rate of about 4 percent. He took that 4 percent and divided it by 4, because he assumed a manned flight would be safer than an unmanned one. He came out with about a 1 percent chance of failure, and that was enough to warrant the destruct charges.

But NASA told Mr. Ullian that the probability of failure was more like 1 in 10^5.

I tried to make sense out of that number. "Did you say 1 in 10^5?"

"That's right; 1 in 100,000."

I did some quick figuring. "That means you could fly the shuttle *every day* for an average of *300 years* between accidents—every day, one flight, for 300 years—which is obviously crazy!"

"Yes, I know," said Mr. Ullian. "I moved my number up to 1 in 1,000 to answer all of NASA's claims—that they were much more careful with manned flights, that the typical rocket isn't a valid comparison, et cetera—and put the destruct charges on anyway."

But then a new problem came up: the Jupiter probe, *Galileo*, was going to use a power supply that runs on heat generated by radioactivity. If the shuttle carrying *Galileo* failed, radioactivity could be spread over a large area. So the argument continued: NASA kept saying 1 in 100,000 and Mr. Ullian kept saying 1 in 1,000—at best.

Mr. Ullian also told us about the problems he had in trying to talk to the man in charge, Mr. Kingsbury: He could get appointments with underlings, but he never could get through to Kingsbury and find out how NASA got its figure of 1 in 100,000. The details of the story I can't remember exactly, but I thought Mr. Ullian was doing everything sensibly.

■ ■ ■

Our panel supervised the tests that NASA was doing to discover the properties of the seals—how much pressure the putty could take, and so on—in order to find out exactly what had happened. General Kutyna didn't want to jump to conclusions, so we went over and over things, checking all the evidence and seeing how well everything fitted together.

There was an awful lot of detailed discussion about exactly what happened in the last few seconds of the flight, but I didn't pay much attention to any of it. It was as though a train had crashed because the track had a gap in it, and we were analyzing which cars broke apart first, which cars broke apart second, and why some car turned over on its side. I figured once the train goes off the track, it doesn't make any difference—it's done. I became bored.

So I made up a game for myself: "Imagine that something else had failed—the main engines, for instance—and we were making the same kind of intensive investigation as we are now: Would we discover the same slipping safety criteria and lack of communication?"

I thought I would do my standard thing—find out from the engineers how the engine works, what all the dangers are, what problems they've had, and everything else—and then, when I'm all loaded up so I know what I'm talking about, I'd confront whoever was claiming the probability of failure was 1 in 100,000.

I asked to talk to a couple of engineers about the engines. The guy says, "Okay, I'll fix it up. Is 9:00 tomorrow morning okay?"

This time there were three engineers, their boss, Mr. Lovingood, and a few assistants—about eight or nine people.

Everybody had big, thick notebooks, full of papers, all nicely organized. On the front they said:

REPORT ON MATERIAL GIVEN TO COMMISSIONER
RICHARD P. FEYNMAN ON MARCH WA-WA,* 1986.

I said, "Geez! You guys must have worked hard all night!"

"No, it's not so much work; we just put in the regular papers that we use all the time."

I said, "I just wanted to talk to a few engineers. There are so many problems to work on, I can't expect you all to stay here and talk to me."

But this time, everybody stayed.

Mr. Lovingood got up and began to explain everything to me in the usual NASA way, with charts and graphs that matched the information in my big book—all with bullets, of course.

I won't bother you with all the details, but I wanted to understand everything about the engine. So I kept asking my usual dumb-sounding questions.

After a while, Mr. Lovingood says, "Dr. Feynman, we've been going for two hours, now. There are 123 pages, and we've only covered 20 so far."

My first reaction was to say, "Well, it isn't really going to take such

*Feynman's way of saying "something-or-other." —RL

a long time. I'm always a little slow at the beginning; it takes me a while to catch on. We'll be able to go much faster near the end."

But then I had a second thought. I said, "In order to speed things up, I'll tell you what I'm doing, so you'll know where I'm aiming. I want to know whether there's the same lack of communication between the engineers and the management who are working on the engine as we found in the case of the booster rockets."

Mr. Lovingood says, "I don't think so. As a matter of fact, although I'm now a manager, I was trained as an engineer."

"All right," I said. "Here's a piece of paper each. Please write on your paper the answer to this question: What do you think is the probability that a flight would be uncompleted due to a failure in this engine?"

They write down their answers and hand in their papers. One guy wrote "$99\frac{44}{100}$% pure" (copying the Ivory soap slogan), meaning about 1 in 200. Another guy wrote something very technical and highly quantitative in the standard statistical way, carefully defining everything, that I had to translate—which also meant about 1 in 200. The third guy wrote, simply, "1 in 300."

Mr. Lovingood's paper, however, said,

Cannot quantify. Reliability is judged from:
- past experience
- quality control in manufacturing
- engineering judgment

"Well," I said, "I've got four answers, and one of them weaseled." I turned to Mr. Lovingood: "I think you weaseled."

"I don't think I weaseled."

"You didn't tell me *what* your confidence was, sir; you told me *how* you determined it. What I want to know is: after you determined it, what *was* it?"

He says, "100 percent"—the engineers' jaws drop, my jaw drops; I look at him, everybody looks at him—"uh, uh, minus epsilon . . ."

So I say, "Well, yes; that's fine. Now, the only problem is, WHAT IS EPSILON?"

He says, "10^{-5}." It was the same number that Mr. Ullian had told us about: 1 in 100,000.

I showed Mr. Lovingood the other answers and said, "You'll be interested to know that there *is* a difference between engineers and management here—a factor of more than 300."

He says, "Sir, I'll be glad to send you the document that contains this estimate, so you can understand it."*

I said, "Thank you very much. Now, let's get back to the engine." So we continued and, just like I guessed, we went faster near the end. I had to understand how the engine worked—the precise shape of the turbine blades, exactly how they turned, and so on—so I could understand its problems.

■   ■   ■

After lunch, the engineers told me all the problems of the engines: blades cracking in the oxygen pump, blades cracking in the hydrogen pump, casings getting blisters and cracks, and so on. They looked for these things with periscopes and special instruments when the shuttle came down after each flight.

There was a problem called "subsynchronous whirl," in which the shaft gets bent into a slightly parabolic shape at high speed. The wear on the bearings was so terrible—all the noise and the vibration—that it seemed hopeless. But they had found a way to get rid of it. There were about a dozen very serious problems; about half of them were fixed.

Most airplanes are designed "from the bottom up," with parts that have already been extensively tested. The shuttle, however, was designed "from the top down"—to save time. But whenever a problem was discovered, a lot of redesigning was required in order to fix it.

Mr. Lovingood isn't saying much now, but different engineers, depending on which problem it is, are telling me all this stuff, just like I could have found out if I went down to the engineers at Morton Thiokol. I gained a great deal of respect for them. They were all very straight, and everything was great. We went all the way down to the end of the book. We made it.

---

*Later, Mr. Lovingood sent me that report. It said things like "The probability of mission success is necessarily very close to 1.0"—does that mean it *is* close to 1.0, or it *ought to be* close to 1.0?—and "Historically, this high degree of mission success has given rise to a difference in philosophy between un-manned and manned space flight programs; i.e., numerical probability versus engineering judgment." As far as I can tell, "engineering judgment" means they're just going to make up numbers! The probability of an engine-blade failure was given as a universal constant, as if all the blades were exactly the same, under the same conditions. The whole paper was quantifying everything. Just about every nut and bolt was in there: "The chance that a HPHTP pipe will burst is 10^{-7}." You can't estimate things like that; a probability of 1 in 10,000,000 is almost impossible to estimate. It was clear that the numbers for each part of the engine were chosen so that when you put everything together you get 1 in 100,000. —RPF

Then I said, "What about this high-frequency vibration where some engines get it and others don't?"*

There's a quick motion, and a little stack of papers appears. It's all put together nicely; it fits nicely into my book. It's all about the 4,000-cycle vibration!

Maybe I'm a little dull, but I tried my best not to accuse anybody of anything. I just let them show me what they showed me, and acted like I didn't see their trick. I'm not the kind of investigator you see on TV, who jumps up and accuses the corrupt organization of withholding information. But I was fully aware that they hadn't told me about the problem until I asked about it. I usually acted quite naïve—which I was, for the most part.

At any rate, the engineers all leaped forward. They got all excited and began to describe the problem to me. I'm sure they were delighted, because technical people love to discuss technical problems with technical people who might have an opinion or a suggestion that could be useful. And of course, they were very anxious to cure it.

They kept referring to the problem by some complicated name—a "pressure-induced vorticity oscillatory wa-wa," or something.

I said, "Oh, you mean a whistle!"

"Yes," they said; "it exhibits the characteristics of a whistle."

They thought the whistle could be coming from a place where the gas rushed through a pipe at high speed and split into three smaller pipes—where there were two partitions. They explained how far they had gotten in figuring out the problem.

When I left the meeting, I had the definite impression that I had found the same game as with the seals: management reducing criteria and accepting more and more errors that weren't designed into the device, while the engineers are screaming from below, "HELP!" and "THIS IS A RED ALERT!"

(The next evening, on my way home in the airplane, I was having dinner. After I finished buttering my roll, I took the little piece of thin cardboard that the butter pat comes on, and bent it around in a U shape

---

*I had heard about this from Bill Graham. He said that when he was first on the job as head of NASA, he was looking through some reports and noticed a little bullet: "•4,000 cycle vibration is within our data base." He thought it was a funny-looking phrase, so he began asking questions. When he got all the way through, he discovered it was a rather serious matter: Some of the engines would vibrate so much that they couldn't be used. He used it as an example of how difficult it is to get information unless you go down and check on it yourself. —RPF

so there were two edges facing me. I held it up and started blowing on it, and pretty soon I got it to make a noise like a whistle. I don't know if I got any funny looks from other passengers.)

*   *   *

Back in California, I got some more information on the shuttle engine and its probability of failure. I went to Rocketdyne and talked to engineers who were building the engines. I also talked to consultants for the engine. In fact one of them, Mr. Covert, was on the Commission. I also found out that a Caltech professor had been a consultant for Rocketdyne. He was very friendly and informative, and told me about all the problems the engine had, and what he thought the probability of failure was.

I went to JPL and met a fellow who had just written a report for NASA on the methods used by the Federal Aviation Administration (FAA) and the military to certify their gas turbine and rocket engines. We spent the whole day going back and forth over how to determine the probability of failure in a machine. I learned a lot of new names—like "Weibull," a particular mathematical distribution that makes a certain shape on a graph. He said that the original safety rules for the shuttle were very similar to those of the FAA, but that NASA had modified them as they began to get problems.

It turned out that NASA's Marshall Space Center in Huntsville designed the engine, Rocketdyne built them, Lockheed wrote the instructions, and NASA's Kennedy Space Center installed them. It may be a genius system of organization, but it was a complete fuzdazzle, as far as I was concerned. It got me terribly confused: I didn't know whether I was talking to the Marshall man, the Rocketdyne man, the Lockheed man, or the Kennedy man! So in the middle of all this, I got lost. In fact, all during this time—in March and April—I was running back and forth so much between California, Alabama, Houston, Florida, and Washington, D.C., that I often didn't know what day it was, or where I was.

*   *   *

After all this investigating on my own, I thought I'd write up a little report on the engine for the other commissioners. But when I looked at my notes on the testing schedules, there was some confusion: There would be talk about "engine #12" and how long "the engine" flew. But no engine ever was like that—it would be repaired all the time. After each flight, technicians would inspect the engines and see how many cracked blades there were on the rotor, how many splits there were in the casing, and so on. Then they'd repair "the engine" by putting on a new casing, a new rotor, or new bearings—they would replace lots of parts. So I would read that a particular engine had rotor #2009, which had run for 27 minutes in flight such-and-such, and casing #4091, which had run for 53 minutes in flights such-and-such and so-and-so. It was all mixed up.

When I finished my report, I wanted to check it. So the next time I was at Marshall, I said I wanted to talk to the engineers about a few very technical problems, just to check the details—I didn't need any management there.

This time, to my surprise, nobody came but the three engineers I had talked to before, and we straightened everything out.

When I was about to leave, one of them said, "You know that question you asked us last time—with the papers? We felt that was a loaded question. It wasn't fair."

I said, "Yes, you're quite right. It *was* a loaded question. I had an idea of what would happen."

The guy says, "I would like to revise my answer. I want to say that I cannot quantify it." (This guy was the one who had the most detailed answer before.)

I said, "That's fine. But do you agree that the chance of failure is 1 in 100,000?"

"Well, uh, no, I don't. I just don't want to answer."

Then one of the other guys says, "I said it was 1 in 300, and I still say it's 1 in 300, but I don't want to tell you how I got my number."

I said, "It's okay. You don't have to."

An Inflamed
Appendix

All during this time, I had the impression that somewhere along the line the whole commission would come together again so we could talk to each other about what we had found out.

In order to aid such a discussion, I thought I'd write little reports along the way: I wrote about my work with the ice crew (analyzing the pictures and the faulty temperature readings); I wrote about my conversations with Mr. Lamberth and the assembly workers; and I even wrote about the piece of paper that said "Let's go for it." All these little reports I sent to Al Keel, the executive officer, to give to the other commissioners.

Now, this particular adventure—investigating the lack of communication between the managers and the engineers who were working on the engine—I also wrote about, on my little IBM PC at home. I was kind of tired, so I didn't have the control I wanted—it wasn't written with the same care as my other reports. But since I was writing it only as a report to the other commissioners, I didn't change the language before I sent it on to Dr. Keel. I simply attached a note that said "I think the other commissioners would be interested in this, but you can do with it what you want—it's a little strong at the end."

He thanked me, and said he sent my report to everybody.

Then I went to the Johnson Space Center, in Houston, to look into the avionics. Sally Ride's group was there, investigating safety matters in connection with the astronauts' experiences. Sally introduced me to the software engineers, and they gave me a tour of the training facilities for the astronauts.

It's really quite wonderful. There are different kinds of simulators with varying degrees of sophistication that the astronauts practice on. One of them is just like the real thing: You climb up, you get in; at the windows, computers are producing pictures. When the pilot moves the controls, the view out of the windows changes.

This particular simulator had the double purpose of teaching the astronauts and checking the computers. In the back of the crew area there were trays full of cables running down through the cargo bay to somewhere in the back, where instruments simulated signals from the engines—pressures, fuel flow rates, and so on. (The cables were accessible because the technicians were checking for "cross talk"—interferences in the signals going back and forth.)

The shuttle itself is operated essentially by computer. Once it's lit up and starts to go, nobody inside does anything because there's tremendous acceleration. When the shuttle reaches a certain altitude, the computers adjust the engine thrust down for a little while, and as the air thins out the computers adjust the thrust up again. About a minute later the two solid rocket boosters fall away, and a few minutes after that the main fuel tank falls away; each operation is controlled by the computers. The shuttle gets into orbit automatically—the astronauts just sit in their seats.

The shuttle's computers don't have enough memory to hold all the programs for the whole flight. After the shuttle gets into orbit, the astronauts take out some tapes and load in the program for the next phase of the flight—there are as many as six in all. Near the end of the flight, the astronauts load in the program for coming down.

The shuttle has four computers on board, all running the same programs. All four are normally in agreement. If one computer is out of agreement, the flight can still continue. If only two computers agree, the flight has to be curtailed and the shuttle brought back immediately.

For even more safety, there's a fifth computer—located away from the other four computers, with its wires going on different paths—which has only the program for going up and the program for coming down. (Both programs can barely fit into its memory.) If something happens to the other computers, this fifth computer can bring the shuttle back down. It's never been needed.

The most dramatic thing is the landing. Once the astronauts know where they're supposed to land, they push one of three buttons—marked Edwards, White Sands, and Kennedy—which tells the computer where the shuttle's going to land. Then some small rockets slow the shuttle down a little, and get it into the atmosphere at just the right angle. That's the dangerous part, where all the tiles heat up.

During this time, the astronauts can't see anything, and everything's changing so fast that the descent has to be done automatically. At around 35,000 feet the shuttle slows down to less than the speed of sound, and the steering can be done manually, if necessary. But at 4,000 feet something happens that is not done by the computer: the pilot pushes a button to lower the landing wheels.

I found that very odd—a kind of silliness having to do with the psychology of the pilots: They're heroes in the eyes of the public; everybody has the idea that they're steering the shuttle around, whereas the truth is they don't have to do anything until they push that button to lower the landing gear. They can't stand the idea that they really have nothing to do.

I thought it would be safer if the computer would lower the landing wheels, in case the astronauts were unconscious for some reason. The software engineers agreed, and added that putting down the landing wheels at the wrong time is very dangerous.

The engineers told me that ground control can send up the signal to lower the landing wheels, but this backup gave them some pause: What happens if the pilot is half-conscious, and thinks the wheels should go down at a certain time, and the controller on the ground knows it's the wrong time? It's much better to have the whole thing done by computer.

The pilots also used to control the brakes, but there was lots of trouble: if you braked too much at the beginning, you'd have no more brake-pad material left when you reached the end of the runway—and you're still moving! So the software engineers were asked to design a computer program to control the braking. At first the astronauts objected to the change, but now they're very delighted because the automatic braking works so well.

.   .   .

Although there's a lot of good software being written at Johnson, the computers on the shuttle are so obsolete that the manufacturers don't make them anymore. The memories in them are the old kind, made with little ferrite cores that have wires going through them. In the meantime we've developed much better hardware: The memory chips of today are much, much smaller; they have much greater capacity; and they're much more reliable. They have internal error-correcting codes that automatically keep the memory good. With today's computers we can design separate program modules so that changing the payload doesn't require so much program rewriting.

Because of the huge investment in the flight simulators and all the other hardware, to start all over again and replace the millions of lines of code that they've already built up would be very costly.

I learned how the software engineers developed the avionics for the shuttle. One group would design the software programs, in pieces. After that, the parts would be put together into huge programs, and tested by an independent group.

After both groups thought all the bugs had been worked out, they would have a simulation of an entire flight, in which every part of the shuttle system is tested. In such cases, they had a principle: This simulation is not just an exercise to check if the programs are all right; it is a *real flight*—if anything fails now, it's extremely serious, as if the astronauts were really on board and in trouble. Your reputation is on the line.

In the many years they had been doing this, they had had only six failures at the level of flight simulation, and not one in an actual flight.

So the computer people looked like they knew what they were doing: They knew the computer business was vital to the shuttle but potentially dangerous, and they were being extremely careful. They were writing programs that operate a very complex machine in an environment where conditions are changing drastically—programs that measure those changes, are flexible in their responses, and maintain high safety and accuracy. I would say that in some ways they were once in the forefront of how to ensure quality in robotic or interactive computer systems, but because of the obsolete hardware, it's no longer true today.

I didn't investigate the avionics as extensively as I did the engines, so I might have been getting a little bit of a sales talk, but I don't think so. The engineers and the managers communicated well with each other, and they were all very careful not to change their criteria for safety.

I told the software engineers I thought their system and their attitude were very good.

One guy muttered something about higher-ups in NASA wanting to cut back on testing to save money: "They keep saying we always pass the tests, so what's the use of having so many?"

. . .

Before I left Houston, I continued my surreptitious investigation of the rumor that the White House had put pressure on NASA to launch the shuttle. Houston is the center of communication, so I went over to the telemetry people and asked about their switching system. I went through the same stuff as I did in Florida—and they were just as nice to me—but this time I found out that if they wanted to tie in the shuttle to the Congress, the White House, or to anywhere, they need a three-minute warning—not three months, not three days, not three hours—three minutes. Therefore they can do it whenever they want, and nothing has to be written down in advance. So that was a blind alley.

I talked to a *New York Times* reporter about this rumor one time. I asked him, "How do you find out if things like this are true?"

He says, "One of the things I thought to do was to go down and talk to the people who run the switching system. I tried that, but I wasn't able to come up with anything."

■   ■   ■

During the first half of April, General Kutyna's group received the final results of the tests NASA was making at Marshall. NASA included its own interpretations of the results, but we thought we should write everything over again in our own way. (The only exceptions were when a test didn't show anything.)

General Kutyna set up a whole system at Marshall for writing our group's report. It lasted about two days. Before we could get anywhere, we got a message from Mr. Rogers: "Come back to Washington. You shouldn't do the writing down there."

So we went back to Washington, and General Kutyna gave me an office in the Pentagon. It was fine, but there was no secretary, so I couldn't work fast.

Bill Graham had always been very cooperative, so I called him up. He arranged for me to use a guy's office—the guy was out of town—and his secretary. She was very, very helpful: She could write up something as fast as I could say it, and then she'd revamp it, correcting my mistakes. We worked very hard for about two or three days, and got large pieces of the report written that way. It worked very well.

Neil Armstrong, who was in our group, is extremely good at writing. He would look at my work and immediately find every weak spot, just like that—he was right every time—and I was very impressed.

Each group was writing a chapter or two of the main report. Our group wrote some of the stuff in "Chapter 3: The Accident," but our main work was "Chapter 4: The Cause of the Accident." One result of this system, however, was that we never had a meeting to discuss what each of our groups found out—to comment on each other's findings from our different perspectives. Instead, we did what they call "wordsmithing"—or what Mr. Hotz later called "tombstone engraving"—correcting punctuation, refining phrases, and so on. We never had a *real* discussion of ideas, except incidentally in the course of this wordsmithing.

For example, a question would come up: "Should this sentence about the engines be worded this way or that way?"

I would try to get a little discussion started. "From my own experiences, I got the impression that the engines aren't as good as you're say-ing here . . ."

So they'd say, "Then we'll use the more conservative wording here," and they'd go on to the next sentence. Perhaps that's a very efficient way to get a report out quickly, but we spent meeting after meeting doing this wordsmithing.

Every once in a while we'd interrupt that to discuss the typography and the color of the cover. And after each discussion, we were asked to vote. I thought it would be most efficient to vote for the same color we had decided on in the meeting before, but it turned out I was always in the minority. We finally chose red. (It came out blue.)

* * *

One time I was talking to Sally Ride about something I mentioned in my report on the engines, and she didn't seem to know about it. I said, "Didn't you see my report?"

She says, "No, I didn't get a copy."

I go over to Keel's office and say, "Sally tells me she didn't get a copy of my report."

He looks surprised, and turns to his secretary. "Please make a copy of Dr. Feynman's report for Dr. Ride."

Then I discover Mr. Acheson hasn't seen it.

"Make a copy and give it to Mr. Acheson."

I finally caught on, so I said, "Dr. Keel, I don't think anybody has seen my report."

So he says to his secretary, "Please make a copy for all the commis-sioners and give it to them."

Then I said to him, "I appreciate how much work you're doing, and that it's difficult to keep everything in mind. But I thought you told me that you showed my report to everybody."

He says, "Yes, well, I meant all of the staff."

I later discovered, by talking to people on the staff, that they hadn't seen it either.

* * *

When the other commissioners finally got to see my report, most of them thought it was very good, and it ought to be in the Commission Report somewhere.

Encouraged by that, I kept bringing up my report. "I'd like to have a meeting to discuss what to do with it," I kept saying.

"We'll have a meeting about it next week" was the standard answer. (We were too busy wordsmithing and voting on the color of the cover.)

Gradually I realized that the way my report was written, it would require a lot of wordsmithing—and we were running out of time. Then somebody suggested that my report could go in as an appendix. That way, it wouldn't have to be wordsmithed to fit in with anything else.

But some of the commissioners felt strongly that my report should go in the main report somehow: "The appendices won't come out until months later, so nobody will read your report if it's an appendix," they said.

I thought I'd compromise, however, and let it go in as an appendix.

But now there was a new problem: my report, which I had written on my word processor at home, would have to be converted from the IBM format to the big document system the commission was using. They had a way of doing that with an optical scanning device.

I had to go to a little bit of trouble to find the right guy to do it. Then, it didn't get done right away. When I asked what happened, the guy said he couldn't find the copy I had given him. So I had to give him another copy.

A few days later, I finished writing my report about the avionics, and I wanted to combine it with my report on the engines. So I took the avionics report to the guy and I said, "I'd like to put this in with my other report."

Then I needed to see a copy of my new report for some reason, but the guy gave me an old copy, before the avionics was added. "Where's the new one with the avionics?" I said.

"I can't find it"—and so on. I don't remember all the details, but it seemed my report was always missing or half-cooked. It could easily have been mistakes, but there were too many of them. It was quite a struggle, nursing my report along.

Then, in the last couple of days, when the main report is ready to be sent to the printer, Dr. Keel wants my report to be wordsmithed too, even though it's going in as an appendix. So I took it to the regular editor there, a capable man named Hansen, and he fixed it up without changing the sense of it. Then it was put back into the machine as "Version #23"—there were revisions and revisions.

(By the way: *everything* had twenty-three versions. It has been noted that computers, which are supposed to increase the speed at which we do things, have not increased the speed at which we write reports: We used to make only three versions—because they're so hard to type—and now we make *twenty*-three versions!)

The next day I noticed Keel working on my report: He had put all kinds of big circles around whole sections, with X's through them; there were all kinds of thoughts left out. He explained, "This part doesn't have to go in because it says more or less what we said in the main report."

I tried to explain that it's much easier to get the logic if all the ideas are together, instead of everything being distributed in little pieces all over the main report. "After all," I said, "it's only gonna be an appendix. It won't make any difference if there's a little repetition."

Dr. Keel put back something here and there when I asked him to, but there was still so much missing that my report wasn't anything like it was before.

The Tenth
Recommendation

Sometime in May, at one of our last meetings, we got around to making a list of possible recommendations. Somebody would say, "Maybe one of the things we should discuss is the establishment of a safety board."

"Okay, we'll put that down."

I'm thinking, "At last! We're going to have a discussion!"

But it turns out that this tentative list of topics *becomes* the recommendations—that there be a safety board, that there be a this, that there be a that. The only discussion was about which recommendation we should write first, which one should come second, and so forth.

There were many things I wanted to discuss further. For example, in regard to a safety board, one could ask: "Wouldn't such a committee just add another layer to an already overgrown bureaucracy?"

There had been safety boards before. In 1967, after the Apollo accident, the investigating committee at the time invented a special panel for safety. It worked for a while, but it didn't last.

We didn't discuss why the earlier safety boards were no longer effective; instead, we just made up more safety boards: We called them the "Independent Solid Rocket Motor Design Oversight Committee," the "Shuttle Transportation System Safety Advisory Panel," and the "Office of Safety, Reliability, and Quality Assurance." We decided who would oversee each safety board, but we didn't discuss whether the safety boards created by our commission had any better chance of working, whether we could fix the existing boards so they *would* work, or whether we should have them at all.

I'm generally not as sure about a lot of things as everybody else. Things need to be thought out a little bit, and we weren't doing enough *thinking* together. Quick decisions on important matters are not very good—and at the speed we were going, we were bound to make some impractical recommendations.

We ended up rearranging the list of possible recommendations and wordsmithing them a little, and then we voted yes or no. It was an odd way of doing things, and I wasn't used to it. In fact, I got the feeling we were being railroaded: Things were being decided, somehow, a little out of our control.

At any rate, in our last meeting, we agreed to nine recommendations. Many of the commissioners went home after that meeting, but I was going to New York a few days later, so I stayed in Washington.

The next day, I happened to be standing around in Mr. Rogers's office with Neil Armstrong and another commissioner when Rogers says, "I thought we should have a tenth recommendation. Everything in our report is so negative; I think we need something positive at the end to balance it."

He shows me a piece of paper. It says,

> The Commission strongly recommends that NASA continue to receive the support of the Administration and the nation. The agency constitutes a national resource and plays a critical role in space exploration and development. It also provides a symbol of national pride and technological leadership. The Commission applauds NASA's spectacular achievements of the past and anticipates impressive achievements to come. The findings and recommendations presented in this report are intended to contribute to the future NASA successes that the nation both expects and requires as the 21st Century approaches.

In our four months of work as a commission, we had never discussed a policy question like that, so I felt there was no reason to put it in. And although I'm not saying I disagreed with it, it wasn't obvious that it was true, either. I said, "I think this tenth recommendation is inappropriate."

I think I heard Armstrong say, "Well, if somebody's not in favor of it, I think we shouldn't put it in."

But Rogers kept working on me. We argued back and forth a little bit, but then I had to catch my flight to New York.

While I was in the airplane, I thought about this tenth recommendation some more. I wanted to lay out my arguments carefully on paper, so when I got to my hotel in New York, I wrote Rogers a letter. At the end I wrote, "This recommendation reminds me of the NASA flight reviews: 'There are critical problems, but never mind—keep on flying!'"

It was Saturday, and I wanted Mr. Rogers to read my letter before Monday. So I called up his secretary—everybody was working seven days a week to get the report out in time—and I said, "I'd like to dictate a letter to you; is that all right?"

She says, "Sure! To save you some money, let me call you right back." She calls me back, I dictate the letter, and she hands it directly to Rogers.

■　■　■

When I came back on Monday, Mr. Rogers said, "Dr. Feynman, I've read your letter, and I agree with everything it says. But you've been out-voted."

"Out-voted? How was I out-voted, when there was no meeting?"

Keel was there, too. He says, "We called everybody, and they all agree with the recommendation. They all voted for it."

"I don't think that's fair!" I protested. "If I could have presented my arguments to the other commissioners, I don't think I'd have been out-voted." I didn't know what to do, so I said, "I'd like to make a copy of it."

When I came back, Keel says, "We just remembered that we didn't talk to Hotz about it, because he was in a meeting. We forgot to get his vote."

I didn't know what to make of that, but I found out later that Mr. Hotz was in the building, not far from the copy machine.

Later, I talked to David Acheson about the tenth recommendation. He explained, "It doesn't really mean anything; it's only motherhood and apple pie."

I said, "Well, if it doesn't mean anything, it's not necessary, then."

"If this were a commission for the National Academy of Sciences, your objections would be proper. But don't forget," he says, "this is a Presidential Commission. We should say something for the President."

"I don't understand the difference," I said. *"Why can't I be careful and scientific when I'm writing a report to the President?"*

Being naïve doesn't always work—my argument had no effect. Acheson kept telling me I was making a big thing out of nothing, and I kept saying it weakened our report and it shouldn't go in.

So that's where it ended up: "The Commission strongly recommends that NASA continue to receive the support of the Administration and the nation . . ."—all this "motherhood and apple pie" stuff to "balance" the report.

While I was flying home, I thought to myself, "It's funny that the only part of the report that was *genuinely* balanced was my own report: I said negative things about the engine, and positive things about the avionics. And I had to struggle with them to get it in, even as a lousy appendix!"

I thought about the tenth recommendation. All the other recommendations were based on evidence we had found, but this one had no evidence whatsoever. I could see the whitewash dripping down. It was *obviously* a mistake: It would make our report look bad; I was very disturbed.

When I got home, I talked to Joan, my sister. I told her about the tenth recommendation, and how I had been "out-voted."

"Did you call any of the other commissioners and talk to them yourself?" she said.

"Well, I talked to Acheson, but he was for it."

"Any others?"

"Uh, no." So I called up three other commissioners—I'll call them A, B, and C.

I call A, who says, "*What* tenth recommendation?"

I call B, who says, "Tenth recommendation? What are you talking about?"

I call C, who says, "Don't you remember, you dope? I was in the office when Rogers first told us, and I don't see anything wrong with it."

It appeared that the only people who knew about the tenth recommendation were the people who were in the office when Rogers told us. I didn't bother to make any more telephone calls. After all, it's enough—I didn't feel that I had to open all the safes to check that the combination is the same.

Then I told Joan about my report—how it was so emasculated, even though it was going in as an appendix.

She says, "Well, if they do that to your report, what have you accomplished, being on the Commission? What's the result of all your work?"

"Aha!"

I sent a telegram to Mr. Rogers:

PLEASE TAKE MY SIGNATURE OFF THE REPORT UNLESS TWO THINGS OCCUR: 1) THERE IS NO TENTH RECOMMENDATION, AND 2) MY REPORT APPEARS WITHOUT MODIFICATION FROM VERSION #23.

(I knew by this time I had to define everything carefully.)

In order to get the number of the version I wanted, I had called Mr. Hotz, who was in charge of the documentation system and publishing the report. He sent me Version #23, so I had something definite to publish on my own, if worse came to worst.

■   ■   ■

The result of this telegram was that Rogers and Keel tried to negotiate with me. They asked General Kutyna to be the intermediary, because they knew he was a friend of mine. What a *good* friend of mine he was, they didn't know.

Kutyna says, "Hello, Professor, I just wanted to tell you that I think you're doing very well. But I've been given the job of trying to talk you out of it, so I'm going to give you the arguments."

"Fear not!" I said. "I'm not gonna change my mind. Just give me the arguments, and fear not."

The first argument was that if I don't accept the tenth recommendation, they won't accept my report, even as an appendix.

I didn't worry about that one, because I could always put out my report myself.

All the arguments were like that: None of them was very good, and none of them had any effect. I had thought through carefully what I was doing, so I just stuck to my guns.

Then Kutyna suggested a compromise: They were willing to go along with my report as I wrote it, except for one sentence near the end.

I looked at the sentence and I realized that I had already made my point in the previous paragraph. Repeating the point amounted to polemics; removing the phrase made my report much better. I accepted the compromise.

Then I offered a compromise on the tenth recommendation: "If they want to say something nice about NASA at the end, just don't call it a recommendation. That way, people will know that it's not in the same class as the other recommendations—call it a 'concluding thought' if you want. And to avoid confusion, don't use the words 'strongly recommends.' Just say 'urges'—'The Commission urges that NASA continue to receive the support of the Administration and the nation.' All the other stuff can stay the same."

A little bit later, Keel calls me up: "Can we say '*strongly* urges'?"

"No. Just 'urges'."

"Okay," he said. And that was the final decision.

Meet the Press

I put my name on the main report, my own report got in as an appendix, and everything was all right. In early June we went back to Washington and gave our report to the President in a ceremony held in the Rose Garden of the White House. That was on a Thursday. The report was not to be released to the public until the following Monday, so the President could study it.

Meanwhile, the newspaper reporters were working like demons: They knew our report was finished and they were trying to scoop each other to find out what was in it. I knew they would be calling me up day

The Commission Report was presented to the President in the Rose Garden at the White House. Visible, from left to right, are General Kutyna, William Rogers, Eugene Covert, President Reagan, Neil Armstrong, and Richard Feynman.

At the White House reception.

and night, and I was afraid I would say something about a technical matter that would give them a hint.

Reporters are very clever and persistent. They'll say, "We heard such-and-such—is it true?" And pretty soon, what you're thinking you didn't tell them shows up in the newspaper!

I was determined not to say a word about the report until it was made public, on Monday. A friend of mine convinced me to go on the *MacNeil/Lehrer NewsHour*, so I said yes for Monday evening's show.

I also had my secretary set up a press conference for Tuesday at Caltech. I said, "Tell the reporters who want to talk to me that I haven't any comment on anything: Any questions they have, I'll be glad to answer on Tuesday at my press conference."

Over the weekend, while I was still in Washington, it leaked somehow that I had threatened to take my name off the report. Some paper in Miami started it, and soon the story was running all over about this argument between me and Rogers. When the reporters who were used to covering Washington heard "Mr. Feynman has nothing to say; he'll answer all your questions at his press conference on Tuesday," it sounded suspicious—as though the argument was still on, and I was going to have this press conference on Tuesday to explain why I took my name off the report.

But I didn't know anything about it. I isolated myself from the press so much that I wasn't even reading the newspapers.

*   *   *

On Sunday night, the Commission had a goodbye dinner arranged by Mr. Rogers at some club. After we finished eating, I said to General Kutyna, "I can't stay around anymore. I have to leave a little early."

He says, "What can be so important?"

I didn't want to say.

He comes outside with me, to see what this "important" something is. It's a bright red sports car with two beautiful blondes inside, waiting to whisk me away.

I get in the car. We're about to speed off, leaving General Kutyna standing there scratching his head, when one of the blondes says, "Oh! General Kutyna! I'm Ms. So-and-so. I interviewed you on the phone a few weeks ago."

So he caught on. They were reporters from the *MacNeil/Lehrer NewsHour*.

They were very nice, and we talked about this and that for the show Monday night. Somewhere along the line I told them I was going to have my own press conference on Tuesday, and I was going to give out my report—even though it was going to appear as an appendix three months later. They said my report sounded interesting, and they'd like to see it. By this time we're all very friendly, so I gave them a copy.

*   *   *

They dropped me off at my cousin's house, where I was staying. I told Frances about the show, and how I gave the reporters a copy of my report. Frances puts her hands to her head, horrified.

I said, "Yes, that was a dumb mistake, wasn't it! I'd better call 'em up and tell 'em not to use it."

I could tell by the way Frances shook her head that it wasn't gonna be so easy . . .

I call one of them up: "I'm sorry, but I made a mistake—I shouldn't have given my report to you, so I'd prefer you didn't use it."

"We're in the news business, Dr. Feynman. The goal of the news business is to get news, and your report is newsworthy. It would be completely against our instincts and practice not to use it."

"I know, but I'm naïve about these things. I simply made a mistake. It's not fair to the other reporters who will be at the press conference on Tuesday. After all, would you like it if you came to a press conference and the guy had mistakenly given his report to somebody else? I think you can understand that."

"I'll talk to my colleague and call you back."

Two hours later, they call back—they're both on the line—and they try to explain to me why they should use it: "In the news business, it's customary that whenever we get a document from somebody the way we did from you, it means we can use it."

"I appreciate that there are conventions in the news business, but I don't know anything about these things, so as a courtesy to me, please don't use it."

It went back and forth a little more like that. Then another "We'll call you back," and another long delay. I could tell from the long delays that they were having a lot of trouble with this problem.

I was in a very good fettle, for some reason. I had already lost, and I knew what I needed, so I could focus easily. I had no difficulty admitting complete idiocy—which is usually the case when I deal with the world—and I didn't think there was any law of nature which said I had to give in. I just kept going, and didn't waver at all.

It went late into the night: one o'clock, two o'clock, we're still working on it. "Dr. Feynman, it's very unprofessional to give someone a story and then retract it. This is not the way people behave in Washington."

"It's obvious I don't know anything about Washington. But this is the way *I* behave—like a fool. I'm sorry, but it was simply an error, so as a courtesy, please don't use it."

Then, somewhere along the line, one of them says, "If we go ahead and use your report, does that mean you won't go on the show?"

"*You* said it; *I* didn't."

"We'll call you back."

Another delay.

Actually, I hadn't decided whether I'd refuse to go on the show, because I kept thinking it was possible I could undo my mistake. When I thought about it, I didn't think I could legitimately play that card. But when one of them made the mistake of proposing the possibility, I said, "*You* said it; *I* didn't"—very cold—as if to say, "I'm not threatening you, but you can figure it out for yourself, honey!"

They called me back, and said they wouldn't use my report.

When I went on the show, I never got the impression that any of the questions were based on my report. Mr. Lehrer did ask me whether there had been any problems between me and Mr. Rogers, but I weaseled: I said there had been no problems.

After the show was over, the two reporters told me they thought the show went fine without my report. We left good friends.

I flew back to California that night, and had my press conference on Tuesday at Caltech. A large number of reporters came. A few asked questions about my report, but most of them were interested in the rumor that I had threatened to take my name off the Commission Report. I found myself telling them over and over that I had no problem with Mr. Rogers.

AFTERTHOUGHTS

Now that I've had more time to think about it, I still like Mr. Rogers, and I still feel that everything's okay. It's my judgment that he's a fine man. Over the course of the Commission I got to appreciate his talents and his abilities, and I have great respect for him. Mr. Rogers has a very good, smooth way about him, so I reserve in my head the possibility—not as a suspicion, but as an unknown—that I like him because he knew how to make me like him. I prefer to assume he's a genuinely fine fellow, and that he is the way he appears. But I was in Washington long enough to know that I can't tell.

I'm not exactly sure what Mr. Rogers thinks of me. He gives me the impression that, in spite of my being such a pain in the ass to him in the beginning, he likes me very much. I may be wrong, but if he feels the way I feel toward him, it's good.

＊　＊　＊

Mr. Rogers, being a lawyer, had a difficult job to run a commission investigating what was essentially a technical question. With Dr. Keel's help, I think the technical part of it was handled well. But it struck me that there were several fishinesses associated with the big cheeses at NASA.

Every time we talked to higher level managers, they kept saying they didn't know anything about the problems below them. We're getting this kind of thing again in the Iran-Contra hearings,* but at that time, this kind of situation was new to me: Either the guys at the top didn't know,

---

*The 1987 Senate hearings exposed how the Reagan administration circumvented Congress by waging a covert war in Central America, illegally supporting the "Contras" in Nicaragua with profits from the secret sale of U.S. arms to Iran, which was under embargo after seizing Americans as hostages in 1979. —RL

in which case they should have known, or they did know, in which case they're lying to us.

When we learned that Mr. Mulloy had put pressure on Morton Thiokol to launch, we heard time after time that the next level up at NASA knew nothing about it. You'd think Mr. Mulloy would have notified a higher-up during this big discussion, saying something like, "There's a question as to whether we should fly tomorrow morning, and there's been some objection by the Thiokol engineers, but we've decided to fly anyway—what do you think?" But instead, Mulloy said something like, "All the questions have been resolved." There seemed to be some reason why guys at the lower level didn't bring problems up to the next level.

I invented a theory which I have discussed with a considerable number of people, and many people have explained to me why it's wrong. But I don't remember their explanations, so I cannot resist telling you what I think led to this lack of communication in NASA.

When NASA was trying to go to the moon, there was a great deal of enthusiasm: It was a goal everyone was anxious to achieve. They didn't know if they could do it, but they were all working together.

I have this idea because I worked at Los Alamos, and I experienced the tension and the pressure of everybody working together to make the atomic bomb. When somebody's having a problem—say, with the detonator—everybody knows that it's a big problem, they're thinking of ways to beat it, they're making suggestions, and when they hear about the solution they're excited, because that means their work is now useful: if the detonator didn't work, the bomb wouldn't work.

I figured the same thing had gone on at NASA in the early days: If the space suit didn't work, they couldn't go to the moon. So everybody's interested in everybody else's problems.

But then, when the moon project was over, NASA had all these people together: There's a big organization in Houston and a big organization in Huntsville, not to mention at Kennedy, in Florida. You don't want to fire people and send them out in the street when you're done with a big project, so the problem is, what to do?

You have to convince Congress that there exists a project that only NASA can do. In order to do so, it is necessary—at least it was *apparently* necessary in this case—to exaggerate: to exaggerate how economical the shuttle would be, to exaggerate how often it could fly, to exaggerate how safe it would be, to exaggerate the big scientific facts that would be discovered. "The shuttle can make so-and-so many flights and it'll cost such-and-such; we went to the moon, so we can *do* it!"

Meanwhile, I would guess, the engineers at the bottom are saying, "No, no! We can't make that many flights. If we had to make that many flights, it would mean such-and-such." And, "No, we can't do it for that amount of money, because that would mean we'd have to do thus-and-so."

Well, the guys who are trying to get Congress to okay their projects don't want to hear such talk. It's better if they don't hear, so they can be more "honest"—they don't want to be in the position of lying to Congress. So pretty soon the attitudes begin to change: Information from the bottom which is disagreeable—"We're having a problem with the seals; we should fix it before we fly again"—is suppressed by big cheeses and middle managers who say, "If you tell me about the seals problems, we'll have to ground the shuttle and fix it." Or, "No, no, keep on flying, because otherwise, it'll look bad." Or "Don't tell me; I don't want to hear about it."

Maybe they don't say explicitly "Don't tell me," but they discourage communication, which amounts to the same thing. It's not a question of what has been written down, or who should tell what to whom; it's a question of whether, when you *do* tell somebody about some problem, they're *delighted* to hear about it and they say "Tell me more" and "Have you tried such-and-such?"—or whether they say "Well, see what you can do about it," which is a completely different atmosphere. If you try once or twice to communicate, and you get pushed back, pretty soon you decide "To hell with it."

So that's my theory: Because of the exaggeration at the top being inconsistent with the reality at the bottom, communication got slowed up and ultimately jammed—that's how it's possible that the higher-ups didn't know.

■　■　■

The other possibility is that the higher-ups did know, and they just *said* they didn't know.

I looked up a former director of NASA—I don't remember his name now—who is the head of some company in California. I thought I'd go and talk to him when I was on one of my breaks at home, and say, "They all *say* they haven't heard. Does that make any sense? How does someone go about investigating them?"

He never returned my calls. Perhaps he didn't want to talk to the commissioner investigating higher-ups; maybe he had had enough of

NASA, and didn't want to get involved. And because I was busy with so many other things, I didn't push it.

There were all kinds of questions we didn't investigate. One was this mystery of Mr. Beggs, the former director of NASA who was removed from his job pending an investigation that had nothing to do with the shuttle; he was replaced by Graham shortly before the accident. Nevertheless, it turned out that, every day, Beggs came to his old office. People came in to see him, although he never talked to Graham. What was he doing? Was there some activity still being directed by Beggs?

From time to time I would try to get Mr. Rogers interested in investigating such fishiness. I said, "We have lawyers on the commission, we have company managers, we have very fine people with a large range of experiences. We have people who know how to get an answer out of a guy when he doesn't want to say something; I don't know how to do that. If a guy tells me the probability of failure is 1 in 10^5, I know he's full of crap—but I don't know what's natural in a bureaucratic system. We oughta get some of the big shots together and ask them questions: Just like we asked the second-level managers like Mr. Mulloy, we should ask the first level."

He would say, "Yes, well, I think so."

Mr. Rogers told me later that he wrote a letter to each of the big shots, but they replied that they didn't have anything they wanted to say to us.

. . .

There was also the question of pressure from the White House.

It was the President's idea to put a teacher in space as a symbol of the nation's commitment to education. He had proposed the idea a year before, in his State of the Union address. Now, one year later, the State of the Union speech was coming up again. It would be perfect to have the teacher in space, talking to the President and the Congress. All the circumstantial evidence was very strong.

I talked to a number of people about it, and heard various opinions, but I finally concluded that there was no pressure from the White House.

First of all, the man who pressured Thiokol to change its position, Mr. Mulloy, was a second-level manager. Ahead of time, nobody could predict what might get in the way of a launch. If you imagine Mulloy was told "Make sure the shuttle flies tomorrow, because the President wants it," you'd have to imagine that *everybody else* at his level had to be told—and there are a lot of people at his level. To tell that many people would make it sure to leak out. So that way of putting on pressure was very unlikely.

By the time the Commission was over, I understood much better the character of operations in Washington and in NASA. I learned, by seeing how they worked, that the people in a big system like NASA *know* what has to be done—*without* being told.

There was *already* a big pressure to keep the shuttle flying. NASA had a flight schedule they were trying to meet, just to show the capabilities of NASA—never mind whether the President was going to give a speech that night or not. So I don't believe there was any direct activity or any special effort from the White House: There was no need to do it, so I don't believe it was done.

I can give you an analog of that. You know those signs that appear in the back windows of automobiles—those little yellow diamonds that say BABY ON BOARD, and things like that? You don't have to *tell* me there's a baby on board; I'm gonna drive carefully *anyway*. What am I supposed to do when I see there's a baby on board—act differently? As if I'm suddenly gonna drive more carefully and not hit the car because there's a baby on board, when all I'm trying to do is not hit it anyway!

So NASA was trying to get the shuttle up anyway: You don't have to say there's a baby on board, or there's a teacher on board, or it's important to get this one up for the President.

• • •

Now that I've talked to some people about my experiences on the commission, I think I understand a few things that I didn't understand so well earlier. One of them has to do with what I said to Dr. Keel that upset him so much. Recently I was talking to a man who spent a lot of time in Washington, and I asked him a particular question which, if he didn't take it right, could be considered a grave insult. I would like to explain the question, because it seems to me to be a real possibility of what I said to Dr. Keel.

The only way to have real success in science, the field I'm familiar with, is to describe the evidence very carefully without regard to the way you feel it *should* be. If you have a theory, you must try to explain what's good and what's bad about it equally. In science, you learn a kind of standard integrity and honesty.

In other fields, such as business, it's different. For example, almost every advertisement you see is obviously designed, in some way or another, to fool the customer: The print that they don't want you to read is small; the statements are written in an obscure way. It is obvious to anybody that the product is not being presented in a scientific and balanced way. Therefore, in the selling business, there's a lack of integrity.

My father had the spirit and integrity of a scientist, but he was a salesman. I remember asking him the question "How can a man of integrity be a salesman?"

He said to me, "Frankly, many salesmen in the business are not straightforward—they think it's a better way to sell. But I've tried being straightforward, and I find it has its advantages. In fact, I wouldn't do it any other way. If the customer thinks at all, he'll realize he has had some bad experience with another salesman, but hasn't had that kind of experience with you. So in the end, several customers will stay with you for a long time and appreciate it."

My father was not a big, successful, famous salesman; he was the sales manager for a medium-sized uniform company. He was successful, but not enormously so.

When I see a congressman giving his opinion on something, I always wonder if it represents his *real* opinion or if it represents an opinion that he's designed in order to be elected. It seems to be a central problem for politicians. So I often wonder: what is the relation of integrity to working in the government?

Now, Dr. Keel started out by telling me that he had a degree in physics. I always assume that everybody in physics has integrity—perhaps I'm naïve about that—so I must have asked him a question I often think about: "How can a man of integrity get along in Washington?"

It's very easy to read that question another way: "Since you're getting along in Washington, you can't be a man of integrity!"

■   ■   ■

Another thing I understand better now has to do with where the idea came from that cold affects the O-rings. It was General Kutyna who called me up and said, "I was working on my carburetor, and I was thinking: What is the effect of cold on the O-rings?"

Well, it turns out that one of NASA's own astronauts told him there was information, somewhere in the works of NASA, that the O-rings had no resilience whatever at low temperatures—and NASA wasn't saying anything about it.

But General Kutyna had the career of that astronaut to worry about, so the *real* question the general was thinking about while he was working on his carburetor was, "How can I get this information out without jeopardizing my astronaut friend?" His solution was to get the professor excited about it, and his plan worked perfectly.*

*General Kutyna has his own version of many of the events recounted here that offer even more intrigue. Perhaps he will be able to put them into print one day. —RL

4 6 4

Appendix F
Personal Observations
on the Reliability
of the Shuttle

Introduction*

It appears that there are enormous differences of opinion as to the probability of a failure with loss of vehicle and of human life. The estimates range from roughly 1 in 100 to 1 in 100,000. The higher figures come from the working engineers, and the very low figures from management. What are the causes and consequences of this lack of agreement? Since 1 part in 100,000 would imply that one could put a Shuttle up each day for 300 years expecting to lose only one, we could properly ask "What is the cause of management's fantastic faith in the machinery?"

We have also found that certification criteria used in Flight Readiness Reviews often develop a gradually decreasing strictness. The argument that the same risk was flown before without failure is often accepted as an argument for the safety of accepting it again. Because of this, obvious weaknesses are accepted again and again—sometimes without a sufficiently serious attempt to remedy them, or to delay a flight because of their continued presence.

There are several sources of information. There are published criteria for certification, including a history of modifications in the form of

---

*In *"What Do You Care What Other People Think?"*, I made several minor grammatical changes to Feynman's report to "smooth it out a little bit." As useful as those changes might have been, they detracted from the historical value of presenting Feynman's report as it appeared officially. On this occassion I have gone back to the original, correcting only spelling and punctuation errors (mainly misplaced commas), and allowing the font styles to be modified to conform to the design of this book. Any other changes are in brackets. —RL waivers and deviations. In addition, the records of the Flight Readiness Reviews for each flight document the arguments used to accept the risks of the flight. Information was obtained from the direct testimony and the reports of the range safety officer, Louis J. Ullian, with respect to the history of success of solid fuel rockets. There was a further study by him (as chairman of the launch abort safety panel [LASP]) in an attempt to determine the risks involved in possible accidents leading to radioactive contamination from attempting to fly a plutonium power supply (RTG [radioactive thermal generator]) for future planetary missions. The NASA study of the same question is also available. For the History of the Space Shuttle Main Engines, interviews with management and engineers at Marshall, and informal interviews with engineers at Rocketdyne, were made. An independent (Caltech) mechanical engineer who consulted for NASA about engines was also interviewed informally. A visit to Johnson was made to gather information on the reliability of the avionics (computers, sensors, and effectors). Finally there is a report "A Review of Certification Practices, Potentially Applicable to Man-rated Reusable Rocket Engines," prepared at the Jet Propulsion Laboratory by N. Moore, et al., in February, 1986, for NASA Headquarters, Office of Space Flight. It deals with the methods used by the FAA and the military to certify their gas turbine and rocket engines. These authors were also interviewed informally.

Solid Fuel Rockets (SRB)

An estimate of the reliability of solid rockets was made by the range safety officer by studying the experience of all previous rocket flights. Out of a total of nearly 2,900 flights, 121 failed (1 in 25). This includes, however, what may be called early errors—rockets flown for the first few times in which design errors are discovered and fixed. A more reasonable figure for the mature rockets might be 1 in 50. With special care in the selection of parts and in inspection, a figure of below 1 in 100 might be achieved, but 1 in 1,000 is probably not attainable with today's technology. (Since there are two rockets on the Shuttle, these rocket failure rates must be doubled to get Shuttle failure rates from Solid Rocket Booster failure.)

NASA officials argue that the figure is much lower. They point out that these figures are for unmanned rockets but since the Shuttle is a manned vehicle "the probability of mission success is necessarily very close to 1.0." It is not very clear what this phrase means. Does it mean it *is* close to 1 or that it *ought to be* close to 1? They go on to explain, "Historically this extremely high degree of mission success has given rise to a difference in philosophy between manned space flight programs and unmanned programs; i.e., numerical probability usage versus engineering judgment." (These quotations are from "Space Shuttle Data for Planetary Mission RTG Safety Analysis," Pages 3-1, 3-2, February 15, 1985, NASA, JSC.) It is true that if the probability of failure was as low as 1 in 100,000 it would take an inordinate number of tests to determine it (you would get nothing but a string of perfect flights from which no precise figure, other than that the probability is likely less than the number of such flights in the string so far). But if the real probability is not so small, flights would show troubles, near failures, and possible actual failures with a reasonable number of trials, and standard statistical methods could give a reasonable estimate. In fact, previous NASA experience had shown, on occasion, just such difficulties, near accidents, and [even] accidents, all giving warning that the probability of flight failure was not so very small. The inconsistency of the argument not to determine reliability through historical experience, as the range safety officer did, is that NASA also appeals to history, beginning [with] "Historically this high degree of mission success . . ."

Finally, if we are to replace standard numerical probability usage with engineering judgment, why do we find such an enormous disparity between the management estimate and the judgment of the engineers? It would appear that, for whatever purpose, be it for internal or external consumption, the management of NASA exaggerates the reliability of its product, to the point of fantasy.

The history of the certification and Flight Readiness Reviews will not be repeated here. (See other part of Commission reports.) The phenomenon of accepting for flight, seals that had shown erosion and blow-by in previous flights, is very clear. The Challenger flight is an excellent example. There are several references to flights that had gone before. The acceptance and success of these flights are taken as evidence of safety. But erosion and blow-by are not what the design expected. They are warnings that something is wrong. The equipment is not operating as expected, and therefore there is a danger that it can operate with even wider deviations in this unexpected and not thoroughly understood way. The fact that this danger did not lead to a catastrophe before is no guarantee that it will not the next time, unless it is completely understood. When playing Russian roulette the fact that the first shot got off safely is little comfort for the next. The origin and consequences of the erosion and blow-by were not understood. They did not occur equally on all flights and all joints; sometimes more, and sometimes less. Why not sometime, when whatever conditions determined it were right, [wouldn't there be] still more [erosion and blow-by], leading to catastrophe?

In spite of these variations from case to case, officials behaved as if they understood them, giving apparently logical arguments to each other, often depending on the "success" of previous flights. For example, in determining if flight 51-L [the *Challenger*] was safe to fly in the face of ring erosion in flight 51-C, it was noted that the erosion depth was only one-third of the radius. It had been noted in an experiment cutting the ring that cutting it as deep as one radius was necessary before the ring failed. Instead of being very concerned that variations of poorly understood conditions might reasonably create a deeper erosion this time, it was asserted [that] there was "a safety factor of three." This is a strange use of the engineer's term, "safety factor." If a bridge is built to withstand a certain load without the beams permanently deforming, cracking, or breaking, it may be designed for the materials used to actually stand up under three times the load. This "safety factor" is to allow for uncertain excesses of load, or unknown extra loads, or weaknesses in the material that might have unexpected flaws, etc. If now the expected load comes on to the new bridge and a crack appears in a beam, this is a failure of the design. There was no safety factor at all, even though the bridge did not actually collapse because the crack went only one-third of the way through the beam. The O-rings of the Solid Rocket Boosters were not designed to erode. Erosion was a clue that something was wrong. Erosion was not something from which safety can be inferred.

There was no way, without full understanding, that one could have confidence that conditions the next time might not produce erosion three times more severe than the time before. Nevertheless, officials fooled themselves into thinking they had such understanding and confidence, in spite of the peculiar variations from case to case. A mathematical model was made to calculate erosion. This was a model based not on physical understanding but on empirical curve fitting. To be more detailed, it was supposed a stream of hot gas impinged on the O-ring material, and the heat was determined at the point of stagnation (so far, with reasonable physical, thermodynamic laws). But to determine how much rubber eroded it was assumed this depended only on this heat by a formula suggested by data on a similar material. A logarithmic plot suggested a straight line, so it was supposed that the erosion varied as the .58 power of the heat, the .58 being determined by a nearest fit. At any rate, adjusting some other numbers, it was determined that the model agreed with the erosion (to depth of one-third the radius of the ring). There is nothing much so wrong with this as believing the answer! Uncertainties appear everywhere [in the model]. How strong the gas stream might be was unpredictable, it depended on holes formed in the putty. Blow-by showed that the ring might fail even though not, or only partially, eroded through. The empirical formula was known to be uncertain, for it did not go directly through the very data points by which it was determined. There was a cloud of points, some twice above, and some twice below the fitted curve, so erosions twice [those] predicted were reasonable from that cause alone. Similar uncertainties surrounded the other constants in the formula, etc., etc. When using a mathematical model, careful attention must be given to uncertainties in the model.

LIQUID FUEL ENGINE (SSME)

During the flight of 51-L the three Space Shuttle Main Engines all worked perfectly, even, at the last moment, beginning to shut down the engines as the fuel supply began to fail. The question arises, however, as to whether—had it failed, and we were to investigate it in as much detail as we did the Solid Rocket Booster—we would find a similar lack of attention to faults and a deteriorating reliability. In other words, were the organization weaknesses that contributed to the accident confined to the Solid Rocket Booster sector, or were they a more general characteristic of NASA? To that end the Space Shuttle Main Engines and the avionics were both investigated. No similar study of the Orbiter, or the External Tank, was made.

The engine is a much more complicated structure than the Solid Rocket Booster, and a great deal more detailed engineering goes into it. Generally, the engineering seems to be of high quality, and apparently considerable attention is paid to deficiencies and faults found in operation.

The usual way that such engines are designed (for military or civilian aircraft) may be called the component system, or bottom-up design. First it is necessary to thoroughly understand the properties and limitations of the materials to be used (for turbine blades, for example), and tests are begun in experimental rigs to determine those. With this knowledge larger component parts (such as bearings) are designed and tested individually. As deficiencies and design errors are noted they are corrected and verified with further testing. Since one tests only parts at a time, these tests and modifications are not overly expensive. Finally one works up to the final design of the entire engine, to the necessary specifications. There is a good chance, by this time, that the engine will generally succeed, or that any failures are easily isolated and analyzed because the failure modes, limitations of materials, etc., are so well understood. There is a very good chance that the modifications to the engine to get around the final difficulties are not very hard to make, for most of the serious problems have already been discovered and dealt with in the earlier, less expensive, stages of the process.

The Space Shuttle Main Engine was handled in a different manner—top down, we might say. The engine was designed and put together all at once with relatively little detailed preliminary study of the material and components. Then when troubles are found in the bearings, turbine blades, coolant pipes, etc., it is more expensive and difficult to discover the causes and make changes. For example, cracks have been found in the turbine blades of the high pressure oxygen turbopump. Are they caused by flaws in the material, the effect of the oxygen atmosphere on the properties of the material, the thermal stresses of startup or shutdown, the vibration and stresses of steady running, or mainly at some resonance at certain speeds, etc.? How long can we run from crack initiation to crack failure, and how does this depend on power level? Using the completed engine as a test bed to resolve such questions is extremely expensive. One does not wish to lose an entire engine in order to find out where and how failure occurs. Yet, an accurate knowledge of this information is essential to acquire a confidence in the engine reliability in use. Without detailed understanding, confidence cannot be attained.

A further disadvantage of the top-down method is that, if an understanding of a fault is obtained, a simple fix—such as a new shape for the turbine housing—may be impossible to implement without a redesign of the entire engine.

The Space Shuttle Main Engine is a very remarkable machine. It has a greater ratio of thrust to weight than any previous engine. It is built at the edge of, or outside of, previous engineering experience. Therefore, as expected, many different kinds of flaws and difficulties have turned up. Because, unfortunately, it was built in the top-down manner, they are difficult to find and fix. The design aim of a lifetime of 55 missions equivalent firings (27,000 seconds of operation, either in a mission of 500 seconds, or on a test stand) has not been obtained. The engine now requires very frequent maintenance and replacement of important parts, such as turbopumps, bearings, sheet metal housings, etc. The high-pressure fuel turbopump had to be replaced every three or four mission equivalents (although that may have been fixed, now) and the high pressure oxygen turbopump every five or six. This is at most ten percent of the original specification. But our main concern here is the determination of reliability.

In a total of about 250,000 seconds of operation, the engines have failed seriously perhaps 16 times. Engineering pays close attention to these failings and tries to remedy them as quickly as possible. This it does by test studies on special rigs experimentally designed for the flaws in question, by careful inspection of the engine for suggestive clues (like cracks), and by considerable study and analysis. In this way, in spite of the difficulties of top-down design, through hard work, many of the problems have apparently been solved.

A list of some of the problems follows. Those followed by an asterisk (*) are probably solved:

■ Turbine blade cracks in high pressure fuel turbopumps (HPFTP). (May have been solved.)

■ Turbine blade cracks in high pressure oxygen turbopumps (HPOTP).

■ Augmented Spark Igniter (ASI) line rupture.*

■ Purge check valve failure.*

■ ASI chamber erosion.*

■ HPFTP turbine sheet metal cracking.

■ HPFTP coolant liner failure.*

■ Main combustion chamber outlet elbow failure.*

■ Main combustion chamber inlet elbow weld offset.*

■ HPOTP subsynchronous whirl.*

■ Flight acceleration safety cutoff system (partial failure in a redundant system).*

■ Bearing spalling (partially solved).

■ A vibration at 4,000 Hertz making some engines inoperable, etc.

Many of these solved problems are the early difficulties of a new design, for 13 of them occurred in the first 125,000 seconds and only three in the second 125,000 seconds. Naturally, one can never be sure that all the bugs are out, and, for some, the fix may not have addressed the true cause. Thus, it is not unreasonable to guess there may be at least one surprise in the next 250,000 seconds, a probability of 1/500 per engine per mission. On a mission there are three engines, but some accidents would possibly be contained, and only affect one engine. The system can abort with only two engines. Therefore let us say that the unknown surprises do not, in and of themselves, permit us to guess that the probability of mission failure due to the Space Shuttle Main Engine is less than 1/500. To this we must add the chance of failure from known, but as yet unsolved, problems (those without the asterisk in the list above). These we discuss below. (Engineers at Rocketdyne, the manufacturer, estimate the total probability as 1/10,000. Engineers at Marshall estimate it as 1/300, while NASA management, to whom these engineers report, claims it is 1/100,000. An independent engineer consulting for NASA thought 1 or 2 per 100 a reasonable estimate.)

The history of the certification principles for these engines is confusing and difficult to explain. Initially the rule seems to have been that two sample engines must each have had twice the time operating without failure as the operating time of the engine to be certified (rule of 2x). At least that is the FAA practice, and NASA seems to have adopted it, originally expecting the certified time to be 10 missions (hence 20 missions for each sample). Obviously the best engines to use for comparison would be those of greatest total (flight plus test) operating time—the so-called "fleet leaders." But what if a third sample and several others fail in a short time? Surely we will not be safe because two were unusual in lasting longer. The short time might be more representative of the real possibilities, and in the spirit of the safety factor of 2, we should only operate at half the time of the short-lived samples.

The slow shift toward decreasing safety factor can be seen in many examples. We take that of the HPFTP turbine blades. First of all the idea of testing an entire engine was abandoned. Each engine number has had many important parts (like the turbopumps themselves) replaced at frequent intervals, so that the rule must be shifted from engines to components. We accept an HPFTP for a certification time if two samples have each run successfully for twice that time (and of course, as a practical matter, no longer insisting that this time be as large as 10 missions). But what is "successfully?" The FAA calls a turbine blade crack a failure, in order, in practice, to really provide a safety factor greater than 2. There is some time that an engine can run between the time a crack originally starts until the time it has grown large enough to fracture. (The FAA is contemplating new rules that take this extra safety time into account, but only if it is very carefully analyzed through known models within a known range of experience and with materials thoroughly tested. None of these conditions apply to the Space Shuttle Main Engine.)

Cracks were found in many second stage HPFTP turbine blades. In one case three were found after 1,900 seconds, while in another they were not found after 4,200 seconds, although usually these longer runs showed cracks. To follow this story further we shall have to realize that the stress depends a great deal on the power level. The Challenger flight was to be at, and previous flights had been at, a power level called 104% of rated power level during most of the time the engines were operating. Judging from some material data it is supposed that at the level 104% of rated power level, the time to crack is about twice that at 109% or full power level (FPL). Future flights were to be at this level because of heavier payloads, and many tests were made at this level. Therefore dividing time at 104% by 2, we obtain units called equivalent full power level (EFPL). (Obviously, some uncertainty is introduced by that, but it has not been studied.) The earliest cracks mentioned above occurred at 1,375 EFPL.

Now the certification rule becomes "limit all second stage blades to a maximum of 1,375 seconds EFPL." If one objects that the safety factor of 2 is lost it is pointed out that the one turbine ran for 3,800 seconds EFPL without cracks, and half of this is 1,900 so we are being more conservative. We have fooled ourselves in three ways. First, we have only one sample, and it is not the fleet leader, for the other two samples of 3,800 or more seconds had 17 cracked blades between them. (There are 59 blades in the engine.) Next, we have abandoned the 2x rule and substituted equal time. And finally, 1,375 is where we did see a crack. We can say that no crack had been found below 1,375, but the last time we looked and saw no cracks was 1,100 seconds EFPL. We do not know when the crack formed between these times, for example cracks may have formed at 1,150 seconds EFPL. (Approximately 2/3 of the blade sets tested in excess of 1,375 seconds EFPL had cracks. Some recent experiments have, indeed, shown cracks as early as 1,150 seconds.) It was important to keep the number high, for the Challenger was to fly an engine very close to the limit by the time the flight was over.

Finally it is claimed that the criteria are not abandoned, and the system is safe, by giving up the FAA convention that there should be no cracks, and considering only a completely fractured blade a failure. With this definition no engine has yet failed. The idea is that since there is sufficient time for a crack to grow to a fracture we can ensure that all is safe by inspecting all blades for cracks. If they are found, replace them, and if none are found we have enough time for a safe mission. This makes the crack problem not a flight safety problem, but merely a maintenance problem.

This may in fact be true. But how well do we know that cracks always grow slowly enough that no fracture can occur in a mission? Three engines have run for long times with a few cracked blades (about 3,000 seconds EFPL) with no blades broken off.

But a fix for this cracking may have been found. By changing the blade shape, shot-peening the surface, and covering with insulation to exclude thermal shock, the blades have not cracked so far.

A very similar story appears in the history of certification of the HPOTP, but we shall not give the details here.

It is evident, in summary, that the Flight Readiness Reviews and certification rules show a deterioration for some of the problems of the Space Shuttle Main Engine that is closely analogous to the deterioration seen in the rules for the Solid Rocket Booster.

AVIONICS

By "avionics" is meant the computer system on the Orbiter as well as its input sensors and output actuators. At first we will restrict ourselves to the computers proper and not be concerned with the reliability of the input information from the sensors of temperature, pressure, etc., nor with whether the computer output is faithfully followed by the actuators of rocket firings, mechanical controls, displays to astronauts, etc.

The computer system is very elaborate, having over 250,000 lines of code. It is responsible, among many other things, for the automatic control of the entire ascent to orbit, and for the descent until well into the atmosphere (below Mach 1) once one button is pushed deciding the landing site desired. It would be possible to make the entire landing automatic (except that the landing gear lowering signal is expressly left out of computer control, and must be provided by the pilot, ostensibly for safety reasons) but such an entirely automatic landing is probably not as safe as a pilot controlled landing.* During orbital flight it is used in the control of payloads, in displaying information to the astronauts, and the exchange of information to the ground. It is evident that the safety of flight requires guaranteed accuracy of this elaborate system of computer hardware and software.

In brief, the hardware reliability is ensured by having four essentially independent identical computer systems. Where possible each sensor also has multiple copies, usually four, and each copy feeds all four of the computer lines. If the inputs from the sensors disagree, depending on circumstances, certain averages, or a majority selection is used as the effective input. The algorithm used by each of the four computers is exactly the same, so their inputs (since each sees all copies of the sensors) are the same. Therefore at each step the results in each computer should be identical. From time to time they are compared, but because they might operate at slightly different speeds a system of stopping and waiting at specific times is instituted before each comparison is made. If one of the computers disagrees, or is too late in having its answer ready, the three which do agree are assumed to be correct and the errant computer is taken completely out of the system. If, now, another computer fails, as judged by the agreement of the other two, it is taken out of the system, and the rest of the flight canceled, and descent to the landing site is instituted, controlled by the two remaining computers. It is seen that this is a redundant system since the failure of only one computer does not affect the mission. Finally, as an extra feature of safety, there is a fifth independent computer, whose memory is loaded with only the programs of ascent and descent, and which is capable of controlling the descent if there is a failure of more than two of the computers of the main line of four.

There is not enough room in the memory of the main line computers for all the programs of ascent, descent, and payload programs in flight, so the memory is loaded about four times from tapes, by the astronauts.

Because of the enormous effort required to replace the software for such an elaborate system, and for checking a new system out, no change has been made to the hardware since the system began about fifteen years ago. The actual hardware is obsolete; for example, the memories are of the old ferrite core type. It is becoming more difficult to find manufacturers to supply such old-fashioned computers reliably and of high quality. Modern computers are very much more reliable, can run much

---

* This statement is surprising, given Feynman's thoughts expressed on page 442.

faster, simplifying circuits, and allowing more to be done, and would not require so much loading of memory, for the memories are much larger.

The software is checked very carefully in a bottom-up fashion. First, each new line of code is checked, then sections of code or modules with special functions are verified. The scope is increased step by step until the new changes are incorporated into a complete system and checked. This complete output is considered the final product, newly released. But completely independently there is an independent verification group that takes an adversary attitude to the software development group, and tests and verifies the software as if it were a customer of the delivered product. There is additional verification in using the new programs in simulators, etc. A discovery of an error during verification testing is considered very serious, and its origin studied very carefully to avoid such mistakes in the future. Such unexpected errors have been found only about six times in all the programming and program changing (for new or altered payloads) that has been done. The principle that is followed is that all the verification is not an aspect of program safety, it is merely a test of that safety in a non-catastrophic verification. Flight safety is to be judged solely on how well the programs do in the verification tests. A failure here generates considerable concern.

To summarize then, the computer software checking system and attitude is of the highest quality. There appears to be no process of gradually fooling oneself while degrading standards so characteristic of the Solid Rocket Booster or Space Shuttle Main Engine safety systems. To be sure, there have been recent suggestions by management to curtail such elaborate and expensive tests as being unnecessary at this late date in Shuttle history. This must be resisted for it does not appreciate the mutual subtle influences, and sources of error generated by even small changes of one part of a program on another. There are perpetual requests for changes as new payloads and new demands and modifications are suggested by the users. Changes are expensive because they require extensive testing. The proper way to save money is to curtail the number of requested changes, not the quality of testing for each.

One might add that the elaborate system could be very much improved by more modern hardware and programming techniques. Any outside competition would have all the advantages of starting over, and whether that is a good idea for NASA now should be carefully considered.

Finally, returning to the sensors and actuators of the avionics system, we find that the attitude to system failure and reliability is not nearly as good as for the computer system. For example, a difficulty was found with certain temperature sensors sometimes failing. Yet 18 months later the same sensors were still being used, still sometimes failing, until a launch had to be scrubbed because two of them failed at the same time. Even on a succeeding flight this unreliable sensor was used again. Again, reaction control systems, the rocket jets used for reorienting and control in flight, still are somewhat unreliable. There is considerable redundancy, but a long history of failures, none of which has yet been extensive enough to seriously affect flight. The action of the jets is checked by sensors, and, if they fail to fire, the computers choose another jet to fire. But they are not designed to fail, and the problem should be solved.

CONCLUSIONS

If a reasonable launch schedule is to be maintained, engineering often cannot be done fast enough to keep up with the expectations of originally conservative certification criteria designed to guarantee a very safe vehicle. In these situations, subtly, and often with apparently logical arguments, the criteria are altered so that flights may still be certified in time. They therefore fly in a relatively unsafe condition, with a chance of failure of the order of a percent (it is difficult to be more accurate).

Official management, on the other hand, claims to believe the probability of failure is a thousand times less. One reason for this may be an attempt to assure the government of NASA perfection and success in order to ensure the supply of funds. The other may be that they sincerely believed it to be true, demonstrating an almost incredible lack of communication between themselves and their working engineers.

In any event, this has had very unfortunate consequences, the most serious of which is to encourage ordinary citizens to fly in such a dangerous machine as if it had attained the safety of an ordinary airliner. The astronauts, like test pilots, should know their risks, and we honor them for their courage. Who can doubt that [schoolteacher Christa] McAuliffe was equally a person of great courage, who was closer to an awareness of the true risk than NASA management would have us believe?

Let us make recommendations to ensure that NASA officials deal in a world of reality in understanding technological weaknesses and imperfections well enough to be actively trying to eliminate them. They must live in reality in comparing the costs and utility of the Shuttle to other methods of entering space. And they must be realistic in making contracts, in estimating costs and the difficulty of the projects. Only realistic flight schedules should be proposed, schedules that have a reasonable chance of being met. If in this way the government would not support them, then so be it. NASA owes it to the citizens from whom it asks support to be frank, honest, and informative, so that these citizens can make the wisest decisions for the use of their limited resources.

For a successful technology, reality must take precedence over public relations, for nature cannot be fooled.

POSTSCRIPT: Although Feynman's report was relegated as an appendix to the Commission Report (and thus perhaps not widely read at NASA), it has been cited in the field of failure analysis—most recently at the award session of the Risk Management and Dependability Conference held in Bourges, France, in October 2004. —RL

EPILOGUES

Reflections

When I was younger, I thought science would make good things for everybody. It was obviously useful; it was good. During the war I worked on the atomic bomb. This result of science was obviously a very serious matter: It represented the destruction of people.

After the war I was very worried about the bomb. I didn't know what the future was going to look like, and I certainly wasn't anywhere near sure that we would last until now. Therefore one question was: is there some evil involved in science?

Put another way, what is the value of the science I had dedicated myself to—the thing I loved—when I saw what terrible things it could do? It was a question I had to answer.

"The Value of Science" was a kind of report,* if you will, on many of the thoughts that came to me when I tried to answer that question.

Richard Feynman
January 1988

*Feynman gave that "report" as a public address to a 1955 meeting of the National Academy of Sciences. —RL

THE VALUE
OF SCIENCE

From time to time people suggest to me that scientists ought to give more consideration to social problems—especially that they should be more responsible in considering the impact of science on society. It seems to be generally believed that if the scientists would only look at these very difficult social problems and not spend so much time fooling with less vital scientific ones, great success would come of it.

It seems to me that we *do* think about these problems from time to time, but we don't put a full-time effort into them—the reasons being that we know we don't have any magic formula for solving social problems, that social problems are very much harder than scientific ones, and that we usually don't get anywhere when we do think about them.

I believe that a scientist looking at nonscientific problems is just as dumb as the next guy—and when he talks about a nonscientific matter, he sounds as naïve as anyone untrained in the matter. Since the question of the value of science is *not* a scientific subject, this talk is dedicated to proving my point—by example.

The first way in which science is of value is familiar to everyone. It is that scientific knowledge enables us to do all kinds of things and to make all kinds of things. Of course if we make *good* things, it is not only to the credit of science; it is also to the credit of the moral choice which led us to good work. Scientific knowledge is an enabling power to do either good or bad—but it does not carry instructions on how to use it. Such power has evident value, even though the power may be negated by what one does with it.

I learned a way of expressing this common human problem on a trip to Honolulu. In a Buddhist temple there, the man in charge explained a little bit about the Buddhist religion for tourists, and then ended his talk by telling them he had something to say to them that they would *never* forget—and I have never forgotten it. It was a proverb of the Buddhist religion:

To every man is given the key to the gates of heaven;
The same key opens the gates of hell.

What then, is the value of the key to heaven? It is true that if we lack clear instructions that enable us to determine which is the gate to heaven and which the gate to hell, the key may be a dangerous object to use.

But the key obviously has value: How can we enter heaven without it?

Instructions would be of no value without the key. So it is evident that, in spite of the fact that it could produce enormous horror in the world, science is of value because it *can* produce *something*.

Another value of science is the fun called intellectual enjoyment, which some people get from reading and learning and thinking about it, and which others get from working in it. This is an important point, one which is not considered enough by those who tell us it is our social responsibility to reflect on the impact of science on society.

Is this mere personal enjoyment of value to society as a whole? No. But it is also a responsibility to consider the aim of society itself. Is it to arrange matters so that people can enjoy things? If so, then the enjoyment of science is as important as anything else.

But I would like *not* to underestimate the value of the world view which is the result of scientific effort. We have been led to imagine all sorts of things infinitely more marvelous than the imaginings of poets and dreamers of the past. It shows that the imagination of nature is far, far greater than the imagination of man. For instance, how much more remarkable it is for us all to be stuck—half of us upside down—by a mysterious attraction to a spinning ball that has been swinging in space for billions of years than to be carried on the back of an elephant supported on a tortoise swimming in a bottomless sea.

I have thought about these things so many times alone that I hope you will excuse me if I remind you of this type of thought that I am sure many of you have had, which no one could ever have had in the past because people then didn't have the information we have about the world today.

For instance, I stand at the seashore, alone, and start to think:

There are the rushing waves
mountains of molecules
each stupidly minding its own business
trillions apart
yet forming white surf in unison.

Ages on ages
before any eyes could see
year after year
thunderously pounding the shore as now.
For whom, for what?
On a dead planet
with no life to entertain.

Never at rest
tortured by energy
wasted prodigiously by the sun
poured into space.
A mite makes the sea roar.

Deep in the sea
all molecules repeat
the patterns of one another
till complex new ones are formed.
They make others like themselves
and a new dance starts.

Growing in size and complexity
living things
masses of atoms
DNA, protein
dancing a pattern ever more intricate.

Out of the cradle
onto dry land
here it is
standing:
atoms with consciousness;
matter with curiosity.

Stands at the sea,
wonders at wondering: I
a universe of atoms
an atom in the universe.

The same thrill, the same awe and mystery, comes again and again when we look at any question deeply enough. With more knowledge comes a deeper, more wonderful mystery, luring one on to penetrate deeper still. Never concerned that the answer may prove disappointing, with pleasure and confidence we turn over each new stone to find unimagined strangeness leading on to more wonderful questions and mysteries—certainly a grand adventure!

It is true that few unscientific people have this particular type of religious experience. Our poets do not write about it; our artists do not try to portray this remarkable thing. I don't know why. Is no one inspired by our present picture of the universe? This value of science remains unsung by singers: You are reduced to hearing not a song or poem, but an evening lecture about it. This is not yet a scientific age.

Perhaps one of the reasons for this silence is that you have to know how to read the music. For instance, the scientific article may say, "The radioactive phosphorus content of the cerebrum of the rat decreases to one-half in a period of two weeks." Now what does that mean?

It means that phosphorus that is in the brain of a rat—and also in mine, and yours—is not the same phosphorus as it was two weeks ago. It means the atoms that are in the brain are being replaced; the ones that were there before have gone away.

So what is this mind of ours, what are these atoms with consciousness? Last week's potatoes! They now can *remember* what was going on in my mind a year ago—a mind that has long ago been replaced.

To note that the thing I call my individuality is only a pattern or dance, *that* is what it means when one discovers how long it takes for the atoms of the brain to be replaced by other atoms. The atoms come into my brain, dance a dance, and then go out—there are always new atoms, but always doing the same dance, remembering what the dance was yesterday.

When we read about this in the newspaper, it says "Scientists say this discovery may have importance in the search for a cure for cancer." The paper is only interested in the use of the idea, not the idea itself. Hardly anyone can understand the importance of an idea, it is so remarkable. Except that, possibly, some children catch on. And when a child catches on to an idea like that, we have a scientist. It is too late* for them to get the spirit when they are in our universities, so we must attempt to explain these ideas to children.

*I would now say, "It is late—although not too late—for them to get the spirit . . ." —RPF

I would now like to turn to a third value that science has. It is a little less direct, but not much. The scientist has a lot of experience with ignorance and doubt and uncertainty, and this experience is of very great importance, I think. When a scientist doesn't know the answer to a problem, he is ignorant. When he has a hunch as to what the result is, he is uncertain. And when he is pretty darn sure of what the result is going to be, he is still in some doubt. We have found it of paramount importance that in order to progress we must recognize our ignorance and leave room for doubt. Scientific knowledge is a body of statements of varying degrees of certainty—some most unsure, some nearly sure, but none *absolutely* certain.

Now, we scientists are used to this, and we take it for granted that it is perfectly consistent to be unsure, that it is possible to live and *not* know. But I don't know whether everyone realizes this is true. Our freedom to doubt was born out of a struggle against authority in the early days of science. It was a very deep and strong struggle: Permit us to question—to doubt—to not be sure. I think that it is important that we do not forget this struggle and thus perhaps lose what we have gained. Herein lies a responsibility to society.

We are all sad when we think of the wondrous potentialities human beings seem to have, as contrasted with their small accomplishments. Again and again people have thought that we could do much better. Those of the past saw in the nightmare of their times a dream for the future. We, of *their* future, see that their dreams, in certain ways surpassed, have in many ways remained dreams. The hopes for the future today are, in good share, those of yesterday.

It was once thought that the possibilities people had were not developed because most of the people were ignorant. With universal education, could all men be Voltaires? Bad can be taught at least as efficiently as good. Education is a strong force, but for either good or evil.

Communications between nations must promote understanding—so went another dream. But the machines of communication can be manipulated. What is communicated can be truth or lie. Communication is a strong force, but also for either good or evil.

The applied sciences should free men of material problems at least. Medicine controls diseases. And the record here seems all to the good. Yet there are some patiently working today to create great plagues and poisons for use in warfare tomorrow.

Nearly everyone dislikes war. Our dream today is peace. In peace, man can develop best the enormous possibilities he seems to have. But maybe future men will find that peace, too, can be good and bad. Perhaps peaceful men will drink out of boredom. Then perhaps drink will become the great problem which seems to keep man from getting all he thinks he should out of his abilities.

Clearly, peace is a great force—as are sobriety, material power, communication, education, honesty, and the ideals of many dreamers. We have more of these forces to control than did the ancients. And maybe we are doing a little better than most of them could do. But what we ought to be able to do seems gigantic compared with our confused accomplishments.

Why is this? Why can't we conquer ourselves?

Because we find that even great forces and abilities do not seem to carry with them clear instructions on how to use them. As an example, the great accumulation of understanding as to how the physical world behaves only convinces one that this behavior seems to have a kind of meaninglessness. The sciences do not directly teach good and bad.

Through all ages of our past, people have tried to fathom the meaning of life. They have realized that if some direction or meaning could be given to our actions, great human forces would be unleashed. So, very many answers have been given to the question of the meaning of it all. But the answers have been of all different sorts, and the proponents of one answer have looked with horror at the actions of the believers in another—horror, because from a disagreeing point of view all the great potentialities of the human race are channeled into a false and confining blind alley. In fact, it is from the history of the enormous monstrosities created by false belief that philosophers have realized the apparently infinite and wondrous capacities of human beings. The dream is to find the open channel.

What, then, is the meaning of it all? What can we say to dispel the mystery of existence?

If we take everything into account—not only what the ancients knew, but all of what we know today that they didn't know—then I think we must frankly admit that *we do not know.*

But, in admitting this, we have probably found the open channel.

This is not a new idea; this is the idea of the age of reason. This is the philosophy that guided the men who made the democracy that we live under. The idea that no one really knew how to run a government led to the idea that we should arrange a system by which new ideas could be developed, tried out, and tossed out if necessary, with more new ideas brought in—a trial-and-error system. This method was a result of the fact that science was already showing itself to be a successful venture at the end of the eighteenth century. Even then it was clear to socially minded people that the openness of possibilities was an opportunity, and that doubt and discussion were essential to progress into the unknown. If we want to solve a problem that we have never solved before, we must leave the door to the unknown ajar.

We are at the very beginning of time for the human race. It is not unreasonable that we grapple with problems. But there are tens of thousands of years in the future. Our responsibility is to do what we can, learn what we can, improve the solutions, and pass them on. It is our responsibility to leave the people of the future a free hand. In the impetuous youth of humanity, we can make grave errors that can stunt our growth for a long time. This we will do if we say we have the answers now, so young and ignorant as we are. If we suppress all discussion, all criticism, proclaiming "This is the answer, my friends; man is saved!" we will doom humanity for a long time to the chains of authority, confined to the limits of our present imagination. It has been done so many times before.

It is our responsibility as scientists, knowing the great progress which comes from a satisfactory philosophy of ignorance, the great progress which is the fruit of freedom of thought, to proclaim the value of this freedom; to teach how doubt is not to be feared but welcomed and discussed; and to demand this freedom as our duty to all coming generations.

CARGO CULT
ƒCIENCE

During the Middle Ages there were all kinds of crazy ideas, such as that a piece of rhinoceros horn would increase potency. (Another crazy idea of the Middle Ages is these hats we have on today—which is too loose, in my case.)* Then a method was discovered for separating the ideas—which was to try one to see if it worked, and if it didn't work, to eliminate it. This method became organized, of course, into science. And it developed very well, so that we are now in the scientific age. It is such a scientific age, in fact, that we have difficulty in understanding how witch doctors could ever have existed, when nothing that they proposed ever really worked—or very little of it did.

But even today I meet lots of people who sooner or later get me into a conversation about UFOs, or astrology, or some form of mysticism, expanded consciousness, new types of awareness, ESP, and so forth. And I've concluded that it's *not* a scientific world.

Most people believe so many wonderful things that I decided to investigate why they did. And what has been referred to as my curiosity for investigation has landed me in a difficulty where I found so much junk that I'm overwhelmed. First I started out by investigating various ideas of mysticism, and mystic experiences. I went into isolation tanks and got many hours of hallucinations, so I know something about that. Then I went to Esalen, which is a hotbed of this kind of thought (it's a wonderful place; you should go visit there). Then I became overwhelmed—I didn't realize how *much* there was.

At Esalen there are some large baths fed by hot springs situated on a ledge about thirty feet above the ocean. One of my most pleasurable experiences has been to sit in one of those baths and watch the waves crashing onto the rocky shore below, to gaze into the clear blue sky

*Feynman wore a cap and gown at his Caltech commencement address, given in 1974. —RL

above, and to study a beautiful nude as she quietly appears and settles into the bath with me.

One time I sat down in a bath where there was a beautiful girl sitting with a guy who didn't seem to know her. Right away I began thinking, "Gee! How am I gonna get started talking to this beautiful nude babe?"

I'm trying to figure out what to say, when the guy says to her, "I'm, uh, studying massage. Could I practice on you?"

"Sure," she says. They get out of the bath and she lies down on a massage table nearby.

I think to myself, "What a nifty line! I can never think of anything like that." He starts to rub her big toe. "I think I feel it," he says. "I feel a kind of dent—is that the pituitary?"

I blurt out, "You're a helluva long way from the pituitary, man!"

They looked at me, horrified—I had blown my cover—and said, "It's reflexology!"

I quickly closed my eyes and appeared to be meditating.

That's just an example of the kind of things that overwhelm me. I also looked into extrasensory perception and "psi" phenomena, and the latest craze there was Uri Geller, a man who is supposed to be able to bend keys by rubbing them with his finger. So I went to his hotel room, on his invitation, to see a demonstration of both mind reading and bending keys. He didn't do any mind reading that succeeded; nobody can read my mind, I guess. And my boy held a key and Geller rubbed it, and nothing happened. Then he told us it works better under water, and so you can picture all of us standing in the bathroom with the water turned on and the key under it, and him rubbing the key with his finger. Nothing happened. So I was unable to investigate that phenomenon.

But then I began to think, what else is there that we believe? (And I thought then about the witch doctors, and how easy it would have been to check on them by noticing that nothing really worked.) So I found things that even *more* people believe, such as that we have some knowledge of how to educate. There are big schools of reading methods and mathematics methods, and so forth, but if you notice, you'll see the reading scores keep going down—or hardly going up—in spite of the fact that we continually use these same people to improve the methods. *There's* a witch doctor remedy that doesn't work. It ought to be looked into: How do they know that their method should work? Another example is how to treat criminals. We obviously have made no progress—lots of theory, but no progress—in decreasing the amount of crime by the method that we use to handle criminals.

Yet these things are said to be scientific. We study them. And I think ordinary people with commonsense ideas are intimidated by this pseudo-science. A teacher who has some good idea of how to teach her children to read is forced by the school system to do it some other way—or is even fooled by the school system into thinking that her method is not necessarily a good one. Or a parent of bad boys, after disciplining them in one way or another, feels guilty for the rest of her life because she didn't do "the right thing," according to the experts.

So we really ought to look into theories that don't work, and science that isn't science.

I think the educational and psychological studies I mentioned are examples of what I would like to call cargo cult science. In the South Seas there is a cargo cult of people. During the war they saw airplanes land with lots of good materials, and they want the same thing to happen now. So they've arranged to make things like runways, to put fires along the sides of the runways, to make a wooden hut for a man to sit in, with two wooden pieces on his head like headphones and bars of bamboo sticking out like antennas—he's the controller—and they wait for the airplanes to land. They're doing everything right—the form is perfect; it looks exactly the way it looked before—but it doesn't work. No airplanes land. So I call these things cargo cult science, because they follow all the apparent precepts and forms of scientific investigation, but they're missing something essential, because the planes don't land.

Now it behooves me, of course, to tell you what they're missing. But it would be just about as difficult to explain to the South Sea Islanders how they have to arrange things so that they get some wealth in their system. It is not something simple like telling them how to improve the shapes of the earphones. But there is *one* feature I notice that is generally missing in cargo cult science. That is the idea that we all hope you have learned in studying science in school—we never explicitly say what this *is*, but just hope that you catch on by all the examples of scientific investigation. It is interesting, therefore, to bring it out now and speak of it explicitly. It's a kind of scientific integrity, a principle of scientific thought that corresponds to a kind of utter honesty—a kind of leaning over backwards. For example, if you're doing an experiment, you should report everything that you think might make it *invalid*—not only what you think is right about it, but other causes that could possibly explain your results, things you thought of that you've eliminated by some other experiment, and how they worked—to make sure the other fellow can tell they have been eliminated.

Details that could throw doubt on your interpretation must be given, if you know them. You must do the best you can—if you know anything at all wrong, or possibly wrong—to explain it. If you make a theory, for example, and advertise it, or put it out, then you must also put down all the facts that *disagree* with it, as well as those that agree with it. There is also a more subtle problem. When you have put a lot of ideas together to make an elaborate theory, you want to make sure, when explaining what it fits, that those things it fits are not just the things that gave you the idea for the theory, but that the finished theory makes something *else* come out right, in addition.

In summary, the idea is to try to give *all* of the information to help others to judge the value of your contribution; not just the information that leads to judgment in one particular direction or another.

The easiest way to explain this idea is to contrast it, for example, with advertising. Last night I heard that Wesson oil doesn't soak through food. Well, that's true. It's not dishonest—but the thing I'm talking about is not just a matter of not being dishonest, it's a matter of scientific integrity, which is another level. The fact which should be added to this advertising statement is that *no* oils soak through food, if operated at a certain temperature. If operated at another temperature, they *all* will—including Wesson oil. So it's the implication which has been conveyed, not the fact, and the difference is what we have to deal with.

We've learned from experience that the truth will out. Other experimenters will repeat your experiment and find out whether you were wrong or right. Nature's phenomena will agree or they'll disagree with your theory. And, although you may gain some temporary fame and excitement, you will not gain a good reputation as a scientist if you haven't tried to be very careful in this kind of work. And it's this type of integrity, this kind of care not to fool yourself, that is missing to a large extent in much of the research in cargo cult science.

A great deal of their difficulty is, of course, the difficulty of the subject and the inapplicability of the scientific method to the subject. Nevertheless, it should be remarked that this is not the only difficulty. That's *why* the planes don't land—but they still don't land.

We have learned a lot from experience about how to handle some of the ways we fool ourselves. One example: Millikan measured the charge on an electron by an experiment with falling oil drops, and got an answer that we now know not to be quite right. It's a little bit off, because he had the incorrect value for the viscosity of air. It's interesting to look at the history of measurements of the charge of the electron, after Millikan. If you plot them as a function of time, you find that one is a little bigger than Millikan's, and the next one's a little bit bigger than that, and the next one's a little bit bigger than that, until finally they settle down to a number which is higher.

Why didn't they discover that the new number was higher right away? It's a thing that scientists are ashamed of—this history—because it's apparent that people did things like this: When they got a number that was too high above Millikan's, they thought something must be wrong—and they would look for and find a reason why something might be wrong. When they got a number closer to Millikan's value they didn't look so hard. And so they eliminated the numbers that were too far off, and did other things like that. We've learned those tricks nowadays, and now we don't have that kind of a disease.

But this long history of learning how to not fool ourselves—of having utter scientific integrity—is, I'm sorry to say, something that we haven't specifically included in any particular course that I know of. We just hope you've caught on by osmosis.

The first principle is that you must not fool yourself—and you are the easiest person to fool. So you have to be very careful about that. After you've not fooled yourself, it's easy not to fool other scientists. You just have to be honest in a conventional way after that.

I would like to add something that's not essential to the science itself, but something I believe: You should not fool the layman when you're talking as a scientist. I am not trying to tell you what to do about cheating on your wife, or fooling your girlfriend, or something like that, when you're not trying to be a scientist, when you're just trying to be an ordinary human being—we'll leave those problems up to you and your rabbi. I'm talking about a specific, extra type of integrity that is not lying, but bending over backwards to show how you're maybe wrong, that you ought to have when acting as a scientist. And this is our responsibility as scientists, certainly to other scientists, and I think to laymen.

For example, I was a little surprised when I was talking to a friend who was going to go on the radio. He does work on cosmology and astronomy, and he wondered how he would explain what the applications of this work were. "Well," I said, "there aren't any." He said, "Yes, but then we won't get support for more research of this kind." *I* think that's kind of dishonest. If you're representing yourself as a scientist, then you should explain to the layman what you're doing—and if they don't want to support you under those circumstances, then that's their decision.

One example of the principle is this: If you've made up your mind to test a theory, or you want to explain some idea, you should always decide to publish it whichever way it comes out. If we only publish results of a certain kind, we can make the argument look good. We must publish *both* kinds of results.

I say that's also important in giving certain types of government advice. Supposing a senator asked you for advice about whether drilling a hole should be done in his state, and you decide it would be better in some other state. If you don't publish such a result, it seems to me you're not giving scientific advice. You're being used. If your answer happens to come out in the direction the government or the politicians like, they can use it as an argument in their favor; if it comes out the other way, they don't publish it at all. That's not giving scientific advice.

Other kinds of errors are more characteristic of poor science. When I was at Cornell, I often talked to the people in the psychology department. One of the students told me she wanted to do an experiment that went something like this: It had been found by others that under certain circumstances, X, rats did something, A. She was curious as to whether, if she changed the circumstances to Y, they would still do A. So her proposal was to do the experiment under circumstances Y and see if they still did A.

I explained to her that it was necessary first to repeat in her laboratory the experiment of the other person—to do it under condition X to see if she could also get result A, and *then* change to Y and see if A changed. Then she would know that the real difference was the thing she thought she had under control.

She was very delighted with this new idea, and went to her professor. And his reply was, no, you cannot do that, because the experiment has already been done and you would be wasting time. This was in about 1947 or so, and it seems to have been the general policy then to not try to repeat psychological experiments, but only to change the conditions and see what happens.

Nowadays there's a certain danger of the same thing happening, even in the famous field of physics. I was shocked to hear of an experiment done at the big accelerator at the National Accelerator Laboratory, where a person used deuterium. In order to compare his heavy hydrogen results to what might happen with light hydrogen, he had to use data from someone else's experiment on light hydrogen, which was done on different apparatus. When asked why, he said it was because there's so little time and it's such an expensive apparatus, and to do the experiment with light hydrogen on this apparatus wouldn't give any new result. And so the men in charge of programs at NAL are so anxious for new results—in order to get more money to keep the thing going for public relations purposes—they are destroying, possibly, the value of the experiments themselves, which is the whole purpose of the thing. It is often hard for the experimenters there to complete their work as their scientific integrity demands.

All experiments in psychology are not of this type, however. For example, there have been many experiments running rats through all kinds of mazes, and so on—with little clear result. But in 1937 a man named Young did a very interesting one. He had a long corridor with doors all along one side where the rats came in, and doors along the other side where the food was. He wanted to see if he could train the rats to go in at the third door down from wherever he started them off. No. The rats went immediately to the door where the food had been the time before.

The question was, how did the rats know, because the corridor was so beautifully built and so uniform, that this was the same door as before? Obviously there was something about the door that was different from the other doors. So he painted the doors very carefully, arranging the textures on the faces of the doors exactly the same. Still the rats could tell. Then he thought maybe the rats were smelling the food, so he used chemicals to change the smell after each run. Still the rats could tell. Then he realized the rats might be able to tell by seeing the lights and the arrangement in the laboratory like any commonsense person. So he covered the corridor, and still the rats could tell.

He finally found that they could tell by the way the floor sounded when they ran over it. And he could only fix that by putting his corridor in sand. So he covered one after another of all possible clues and finally was able to fool the rats so that they had to learn to go in the third door. If he relaxed any of his conditions, the rats could tell.

Now, from a scientific standpoint, that is an A-number-one experiment. That is the experiment that makes rat-running experiments sensible, because it uncovers the clues that the rat is really using—not what you think it's using. And that is the experiment that tells exactly what conditions you have to use in order to be careful and control everything in an experiment with rat-running.

I looked into the subsequent history of this research. The next experiment, and the one after that, never referred to Mr. Young. They never used any of his criteria of putting the corridor on sand, or being very careful. They just went right on running rats in the same old way, and paid no attention to the great discoveries of Mr. Young, and his papers are not referred to, because he didn't discover anything about the rats. In fact, he discovered *all* the things you have to do to discover something about rats. But not paying attention to experiments like that is a characteristic of cargo cult science.

Another example is the ESP experiments of Mr. Rhine, and other people. As various people have made criticisms—and they themselves have made criticisms of their own experiments—they improve the techniques so that the effects are smaller, and smaller, and smaller until they gradually disappear. All the parapsychologists are looking for some experiment that can be repeated, that you can do again and get the same effect—statistically, at least. They run a million rats—no, it's people this time—they do a lot of things and get a certain statistical effect. Next time they try it they don't get it any more. And now you find a man saying that it is an irrelevant demand to expect a repeatable experiment. This is *science?*

This man also speaks about a new institution, in a talk in which he was resigning as Director of the Institute of Parapsychology. And, in telling people what to do next, he says that one of the things they have to do is be sure they only train students who have shown their ability to get PSI results to an acceptable extent—not to waste their time on those ambitious and interested students who get only chance results. It is very dangerous to have such a policy in teaching—to teach students only how to get certain results, rather than how to do an experiment with scientific integrity.

I have no more time, so I have just one wish for you: the good luck to be somewhere where you are free to maintain the kind of integrity I have described, and where you do not feel forced by a need to maintain your position in the organization, or financial support, or so on, to lose your integrity. May you have that freedom.

May I also give you one last bit of advice: Never say you'll give a talk unless you know clearly what you're gonna talk about, and more or less what you're gonna say!

FINDING FEYNMAN

BY ALAN ALDA

Twenty-five or thirty years ago, on my days off from the Korean War—which was at that time being waged at Twentieth Century Fox in Beverly Hills—I would often drive out to Pasadena to visit the Rembrandts at the Norton Simon Gallery, or I'd take a walk in the Huntington Gardens. And sometimes I would drive by Caltech and give it a glance and wonder what kind of interesting stuff was going on in there. I had been reading about science avidly for many years, and I was immensely curious about the way scientists went about what they did.*
But it didn't occur to me, each time I passed by, that there might have been one particular man in one of these buildings who at that moment was drawing gluon tubes on a blackboard, or playing the bongos, or just looking out the window as a young woman passed by—a man in whom, in a few years, I would become intensely interested.

And as you know, one day, exactly twenty-eight years ago, he was standing right here, giving the commencement address. This is the way the universe operates: first, Richard Feynman gives the talk; then, twenty-eight years later, an actor who played him on the stage gives the talk. This is what's called entropy; this is what happens just before the cosmos reaches a temperature of absolute zero . . .

Let me tell you a little about the path that led me here. After I had read several books about Richard Feynman, I brought one of them, a touching and insightful book by Ralph Leighton called *Tuva or Bust!*, to Gordon Davidson at the Mark Taper Forum in Los Angeles. I wondered if we might be able to make a play about Feynman. Davidson suggested Peter Parnell to write the script, and the three of us started off on a jour-

---

*Alan Alda gave this commencement speech to the graduating class at Caltech in June 2002. Alda has shared his love for science by hosting the award-winning PBS series *Scientific American Frontiers* for many years. —RL ney to find out who Richard Feynman really was. We thought we'd open the play a year or so later. Instead, it took us over six years.

We had no idea how hard it would be. For one thing, he was an extremely unusual person. Toward the end of his life he knew he was dying, he knew exactly what the most important questions were in physics, and he knew he had a shot at answering them—and yet he kept to his habit of doing only what interested him. He spent a good part of his time trying to get to this little place in the middle of Asia called Tuva, whose capital was spelled with no vowels, and for some reason he found that *extremely* interesting!

But, just as getting to Tuva was tantalizingly difficult for Feynman, getting to Feynman became maddeningly hard for us.

What part of him do you focus on? He helped create the atomic bomb. He helped figure out why the *Challenger* blew up. He understood the most puzzling questions in physics so deeply that they gave him the Nobel Prize. Which facet of him do you let catch the most light—the one who was a revered teacher, a bongo player, an artist, a hilarious raconteur, or a safecracker? We wanted to make a play about Feynman, but *which* Feynman?

A mathematician friend of mine suggested that a central image for a play about him could be Feynman's own idea of a sum over histories: just as Feynman saw a photon taking every possible path on its way to your eye, Feynman himself took every possible path on his way through life—he was the sum of all his histories.

Well, nature may be smart enough to know how to average all the paths of a photon, but we three theater people couldn't figure out how to add up all the histories that made up Feynman. At one point I said, "You know what we ought to do? We ought to write a play about three guys sitting around in a hotel room, trying to figure out a play about Feynman: they never figure it out; they just drive themselves crazy!"

We researched him like mad, of course. The people who knew him and worked with him and loved him here at Caltech opened their doors and their hearts to us. They were extremely generous and helpful, and we got a tremendous amount of insight into Richard Feynman. But I always felt that we'd get a hold of him for a while, and then he'd slip through our fingers. It was hard: we were trying to reduce this irreducible person to an evening in the theater.

I think one of the things I most hoped would come through was his honesty. He never wanted to deceive anyone, especially himself. He questioned his every assumption. And when he talked about physics to ordinary people with no training in physics, he never fell back on his authority as a great thinker. He felt that if he couldn't say it in everyday words, he probably didn't really understand it himself.

I was fascinated by this in him. He knew more than most of us will ever know, and yet he insisted on speaking our language.

Like Dante in his time, he could say the most exquisitely subtle things in the language of the common people. He was an American genius, and like many American artists, he was direct and colloquial—not afraid to take a look at the ordinary, and not afraid to go deeply into it to reveal the extraordinary roots of ordinary things.

And yet he recoiled from oversimplification. He wasn't interested in dumbing down science; he was interested in clarity. If he left something out, he told you about it, so you wouldn't get a false picture of a simplicity that wasn't there. And later, when things got more complex, you were prepared for that. In other words, he treated you with respect.

But there was something else about him that fascinates me. I was reading a book by Freeman Dyson the other day, and a paragraph about Feynman jumped off the page at me: "Dick was . . . a profoundly original scientist," Dyson wrote. "He refused to take anybody's word for anything. This meant that he was forced to rediscover or reinvent for himself almost the whole of physics. . . . He said that he couldn't understand the official version of quantum mechanics that was taught in textbooks, and so he began afresh from the beginning. . . . At the end he had a version of quantum mechanics that he could understand."

I saw something in this paragraph that clicked into place for me. The fact that Feynman wouldn't take anybody's word for anything wasn't new to me, or that he needed to go through every step for himself in order to understand it—that wasn't new to me either. A phrase of his has been on the blackboard behind me every night as I've played Feynman: "What I cannot create, I do not understand." (People have asked why that phrase has so much prominence in the play. It's because the blackboard on our set contains pretty much everything that was on the final blackboard that Feynman left in his office when he died. And "What I cannot create, I do not understand" was right up there at the top.)

But what *did* jump out at me the other day was the phrase "he couldn't understand the official version of quantum mechanics that was taught in textbooks." Now, this is *Feynman* we're talking about. I suddenly had this picture in my head of Feynman going through the same experience the rest of us do, meeting that same blank wall halfway up the mountain. I wondered: Did that give him the ability to remember what it was like to start that climb?

So, maybe it wasn't just that he could visualize these little particles and their interactions that made him able to communicate it to the rest of us; maybe it was also that he could remember what it was like to feel dumb.

Now, here's why I'm going on about this. It may not seem important how Feynman did it. Maybe we should just be glad he could do it and let it go at that. But I think it *is* important: I think we have to figure out how *we* can do it, too.

For one thing, we live in a time when massive means of destruction are right here in our hands. We're probably the first species capable of doing this much damage to our planet. We can make the birds stop singing; we can still the fish and make the insects fall from the trees like black rain. And, ironically, we've been brought here by reason, by rationality.

We cannot afford to live in a culture that doesn't use the power in its hands with the kind of rationality that produced it in the first place.

But right now, instead of reason, a lot of people are making use of wishes, dreams, mantras, and incantations. They're trying to heal themselves with crystals, magnets, and herbs with unknown properties. People will offer you a pill made from the leaf of an obscure plant and say, "Take it—it can't hurt you; it's natural . . ."

So is deadly nightshade.

Interestingly, they expect the plant to have active properties that will cure them, but they're certain it has no active properties that can harm them. How do they *know* this?

I mention this not to denigrate anyone's beliefs—we're all entitled to our beliefs, just as we're all entitled to our feelings—but I bring it up to point out that we're in a culture that increasingly holds that science is just another belief. I guess it's easier to believe something—anything—rather than not know. We don't like uncertainty, so we gravitate back to the last comfortable solution we had—no matter how cockeyed it is.

But Feynman was comfortable with not knowing. He enjoyed it. He would proceed for a while with an idea as if he believed it was the answer—but that was only a temporary belief in order to allow himself to follow it wherever it led. Then, a little while later, he would vigorously attack the idea, to see if it could stand up to every test he could think of—and if it couldn't stand up, then he said he simply didn't know. "Not knowing," he said, "is much more interesting than believing an answer which might be wrong."

You're graduating today partly as Feynman's heirs. You're Feynman's heirs in this gloriously courageous willingness to be unsure. And just as Feynman was heir to Newton, who was in turn heir to Galileo, I hope you'll think about devoting some time to helping the rest of us become *your* heirs.

I'm assuming you're here at Caltech because you love science, and I'm assuming you've learned a great deal here about how to do science. I'm asking you today to devote some significant part of your life to figuring out how to share your love of science with the rest of us. Not just because explaining to us what you do will get you more funding for what you do (although it surely will), but just because you *love* what you do. And while you're explaining it, remember that dazzling us with jargon might make us sit in awe of your work, but it won't make us love it.

Tell us frankly how you got there. If you got there by many twists and turns and blind alleys, don't leave that out—we love a detective story. If you enjoyed the adventure of getting there, then so will we.

Most scientists *do* leave that out. By the time we hear about their great discoveries, a lot of the doubt is gone—the mistakes and wrong turns are left out—and it doesn't sound like a human experience they've gone through. It separates us from the process.

Whatever you do, help us love science the way you do.

Like the young man so head-over-heels about his sweetheart he can't stop talking about her, like the young woman so in love with her young man she wants everyone to know how wonderful he is—show us pictures, tell us stories, make us crave to meet your beloved.

Don't just tell us science is good for us and therefore we ought to fund you for it; don't tell us to trust you that your fancy words actually mean something; don't keep the tricks of your trade up an elite sleeve. Don't be merchants, or mandarins, or magicians; be *lovers*.

We're accustomed in our culture to know when a commercial is coming—we know how to turn it off. But love, we can't resist.

You may be swayed by people who insist they're only interested in hearing about the practical applications of science. You may be tempted to bend over backwards and tell them what they want to hear. When Feynman stood here twenty-eight years ago, he cautioned scientists against going too far in telling laypeople about the wonderful everyday applications of their work, especially if there aren't any. He felt it wasn't honest to pretend there was such a benefit just to get funding for your work. It's a powerful urge, but it's possible to resist it.

Robert R. Wilson resisted it beautifully, some years ago. Bob Wilson was a physicist Feynman had known very well. He had helped recruit Feynman for the Los Alamos project. Wilson was also an accomplished sculptor—he had a foot in each of C. P. Snow's "Two Cultures."

Wilson built Fermilab, the giant atom smasher in Illinois. But before that, at a congressional hearing in 1969, he was grilled by Senator John Pastore, who wanted to know what an atom smasher was good for: "Does it in any way contribute to the security of the country?"

Wilson said, "No, sir, I don't believe so."

"It has no value in that respect?" the senator asked.

Wilson looked at him and said, "It has only to do with the respect with which we regard one another, the dignity of people, our love of culture. It has to do with are we good painters, good sculptors, great poets? I mean all the things we really venerate in our country and are patriotic about. It has nothing to do directly with defending our country except to make it worth defending."

Like Wilson, I don't think Feynman needed to justify his curiosity about nature—pure science was pure pleasure. It was fun.

It's like the story of the plate.

The one thing I was certain of from the beginning was that we had to have the story of the plate in the play. It was central, I thought. The author, Peter Parnell, would do draft after draft, and I'd look at it and say, "Where's the plate?" I practically drove him crazy.

Here's the story of the plate, for those of you who don't know it: After the war, Feynman became very depressed. His first wife had just died of tuberculosis, and the terrible, destructive power of the bomb he had helped create was sinking in on him. He had a job teaching at Cornell, but he couldn't concentrate. He couldn't get down to work.

One day, he was in the school cafeteria and he saw some guy fooling around—this guy was tossing a plate up in the air. Feynman saw the plate was spinning—he could see the little medallion on it going around—and he could also see a wobble. He got fascinated with this. He thought, "There seems to be a relationship between the spin and the wobble: what *is* that relationship?" He started to do calculations on it, and discovered that out of complicated equations come surprisingly simple results. He showed Hans Bethe, and Bethe said, "That's pretty interesting, Feynman, but what's the importance of it?" And Feynman said, "It *has* no importance, it's just fun!"

But here's the thing: that playful inquiry not only brought him out of his slump, but according to Feynman, it led to the work that won him the Nobel Prize.

But no matter where it was going to lead him, Feynman made up his mind that day in the cafeteria that he would never work on anything again that didn't interest him, that wasn't fun. Of course, what Feynman was looking for was *serious* fun: it was the awe he felt when he looked at nature—not just the official great wonders of nature, but any little part of nature, because any little part of it is as amazing and beautiful and complicated as the whole thing is.

So, this is interesting: I'm urging you to be like someone who I admit I have found to be pretty elusive. Here I am, seven years later—and just as Feynman never got to see Tuva, I never really found Feynman. I came very close, but he was too many things—he was too many histories.

We came up with a play, in *QED*, that was immensely satisfying. It was beautifully written and beautifully directed. It gave the audience a Feynman that was as close an approximation as we could come up with. But I have to tell you, I still feel—part of me still knows—that a large chunk of the man is still beyond our reach—probably beyond anybody's reach. He's always just out of sight, smiling at us, laughing at how he put one over on us, letting us think he was just an ordinary guy, a guy we could "get." It turns out, though, that the old saying about the destination not being as valuable as the journey really is true. Because when we began, *finding* Feynman seemed important—and I guess it was—but as it turned out, *looking* for Feynman has been the fun.

Every once in a while, though, I can feel Feynman looking over my shoulder, and he's *not* smiling—like right now. I'm at the end of my talk, and I feel the pressure of Feynman's final words at the end of *his* talk twenty-eight years ago: "One last bit of advice," he said; "Never say you'll give a talk unless you know clearly what you're gonna talk about, and more or less what you're gonna say!"

In other words, where are the brass tacks?

Okay, let me be more or less practical. I'm going to propose something to you today. I realize it's a childish idea; it's something only an unschooled layperson would come up with, but it's specific enough that it might get you thinking.

What if each one of you decided to take just one thing you love about science and, no matter how complicated it is, figure out how to make it understood by a million people? There are about five hundred of you taking part in this ceremony today. If just a few of you were successful, several million people would be a lot smarter.

How you do it is up to you. You're very smart people; you're very clever and I'm sure you'll come up with some ingenious solutions. On the other hand, you may be thinking, "*Why?* Why should I do this impossible thing?"

Well, I don't know; maybe for the same reason that the birds sing— if it does for you what it does for birds, there's a lot to recommend it:

1. It's a good way to improve your chances of having sex.
2. It feels *good* to sing.
3. Singing is the music nature makes when it dances the dance of life. You're the universe announcing itself to itself: you open your mouth, and a little muscle in the back of your throat makes a corner of nature vibrate. You're one part of the forest saying, "This is what I think I know," while another part of the forest says, "Yeah? Well this is what I think *I* know!" Your chirpings are the harmony of knowledge.

You've learned *so much* in this place about how nature works. Is there anything more *beautiful* than that? Is there anything greater to sing about?

So, sing. Sing *out*. Sing! Out!

Thank you, and good luck.

THE COMMEMORATIVE CD

About the CD

Los Alamos from Below

Most of the stories in this book were recorded on a substandard, shoe-box-sized cassette tape recorder under intimate, informal circumstances. But one story, *Los Alamos from Below,* was recorded on proper equipment at a public lecture. Richard Feynman was one of nine speakers for a lecture series at the University of California at Santa Barbara in 1975, marking thirty years after the making of the atomic bomb.

The original tape, preserved by the Department of Special Collections at UCSB, was over 100 minutes long (too long for an audio CD), and contained thousands of little clicks plus some intermittent hiss and 60-cycle hum—all apparently produced by the otherwise excellent recording equipment at the time. Nevertheless, despite its imperfections, this remarkable tape revealed Feynman the raconteur at the top of his game, clearly enjoying himself in front of an enthusiastic audience.

I decided to see what I could do to cut and polish this diamond in the rough. Armed with digital editing software, I carefully made several hundred tiny cuts and a few pastes (which affected only misspoken or inconsequential words), allowing the recording to fit onto a single audio CD without losing any essential content. Then I turned the audio files over to John Polito at Audio Mechanics to eliminate the clicks, hiss, and hum to the maximum extent practicable. The result, I hope, is a shining performance to be treasured for many years to come by fans of Richard Feynman.

Here is a track list for the commemorative CD:

Track	Title	Time
1	Intro by J. O. Hirschfelder	1:45
2	Feynman begins	1:25
3	Princeton, part 1	4:08
4	Princeton, part 2	3:55

5	Arrival at Los Alamos	2:34
6	Luck with Hans Bethe	3:09
7	Dormitory politics	5:24
8	Censorship, part 1	5:57
9	Censorship, part 2	4:01
10	Trying to trick Teller	2:46
11	Oak Ridge, part 1	5:40
12	Oak Ridge, part 2	5:56
13	Calculations, part 1	6:10
14	Calculations, part 2	5:14
15	Nicholas Baker et al.	4:34
16	Trinity, part 1	3:10
17	Trinity, part 2	3:13
18	Safecracking, part 1	4:18
19	Safecracking, part 2	4:33

Total time: 77:52

OTHER FEYNMAN CDs

Over the past fifteen years I have produced four CDs from my informal recordings of Richard Feynman. Those CDs (whose titles are in parentheses) include several stories from this book, including: "He Fixes Radios by Thinking!" (*The Feynman Tapes, Volume 0*); "The Chief Research Chemist of the Metaplast Corporation," "I Want My Dollar!," "Thirteen Times," and "Judging Books by Their Covers" (*The Feynman Tapes, Volume 1*); "The Dignified Professor" and "Uncle Sam Doesn't Need *You*!" (*The Feynman Tapes, Volume 2*); and "Safecracker Meets Safecracker" (*Safecracker Suite,* which also includes drumming described in "Found Out in Paris"). I also produced a CD (*Tuva Talk*) that features Feynman recounting his quest to reach the lost land of Tannu Tuva, accompanied by drumming and Tuvan throat-singing, from a recording made by the University of Southern California.

These CDs, as well as other Feynman memorabilia, are presently available from www.TuvaTrader.com and from www.bookstore.caltech.edu.

Downloadable audio files of these CDs can be found at www.lulu.com/TuvaMuch, or by searching the Internet for "downloads" and "Feynman."

—Ralph Leighton